Israeli Counter-Insurgency and the *Intifadas*

This book analyses the conduct of the Israel Defence Forces' (IDF) counter-insurgency operations during the two major Palestinian uprisings (1987–93 and 2000–5) in the territories of the West Bank and Gaza Strip.

Divided into two parts, the book explores, first, the function and historical background of the IDF, and, second, how the IDF has coped with and adapted to the two *Intifadas*. Drawing on a variety of sources, it analyses the degree of success experienced by the IDF in adapting its conventional conduct of warfare to the realities of the Israeli–Palestinian low-intensity conflict. By examining the way in which the IDF and the Israeli security doctrine were formed and developed over time, the book also explores how far Israeli strategic assumptions, civil–military relations, the organisational culture, command and control structure, and conduct of the IDF have affected its adaptation to the contemporary Israeli–Palestinian conflict. It also provides new insights into how conventional armies struggle with contemporary insurgency.

This book will be of much interest to students of low-intensity conflict and counter-insurgency, the Israeli army, the Middle Eastern conflict and strategic studies in general.

Sergio Catignani is a Max Weber Fellow at the European University Institute, Florence. He has a PhD in War Studies from King's College London.

Middle Eastern military studies
Series Editor: Barry Rubin, Interdisciplinary Center, Herzliya, Israel

The Israeli Military and the Origins of the 1967 War
Army command vs. political leadership, 1963–1967
Ami Gluska

Israeli Counter-Insurgency and the *Intifadas*
Dilemmas of a conventional army
Sergio Catignani

Israeli Counter-Insurgency and the *Intifadas*
Dilemmas of a conventional army

Sergio Catignani

LONDON AND NEW YORK

First published 2008
by Routledge
2 Park Square, Milton Park, Abingdon, Oxon OX14 4RN

Simultaneously published in the USA and Canada
by Routledge
270 Madison Ave, New York, NY 10016

Routledge is an imprint of the Taylor & Francis Group, an informa business

Transferred to Digital Printing 2009

© 2008 Sergio Catignani

Typeset in Sabon by Wearset Ltd, Boldon, Tyne and Wear

All rights reserved. No part of this book may be reprinted or
reproduced or utilised in any form or by any electronic, mechanical,
or other means, now known or hereafter invented, including
photocopying and recording, or in any information storage or
retrieval system, without permission in writing from the publishers.

Scripture quotations marked NLT are taken from the Holy Bible,
New Living Translation, copyright 1996, 2004. Used by permission
of Tyndale House Publishers, Inc., Wheaton, Illinois 60189.
All rights reserved.

British Library Cataloguing in Publication Data
A catalogue record for this book is available from the British Library

Library of Congress Cataloging in Publication Data
A catalog record for this book has been requested

ISBN10: 0-415-43388-6 (hbk)
ISBN10: 0-415-57012-3 (pbk)
ISBN10: 0-203-93069-X (ebk)

ISBN13: 978-0-415-43388-4 (hbk)
ISBN13: 978-0-415-57012-1 (pbk)
ISBN13: 978-0-203-93069-4 (ebk)

In that day of peace, battle gear will no longer be issued. Never again will uniforms be bloodstained by war. All such equipment will be burned.

Isaiah 9:5 (NLT)

Contents

List of figures viii
List of tables ix
Acknowledgements x

1 Introduction 1

2 Combat motivation 17

3 Political–military relations 28

4 National security doctrine 44

5 Land and the rise of the LIC struggle 61

6 The *Intifada* 72

7 The *Al-Aqsa Intifada* 102

8 Strategic impasse 142

9 Unilateral disengagement 170

10 Conclusion 180

11 Postscript: the Lebanon Summer War 187

Notes 195
Bibliography 231
Index 241

Figures

5.1	*Hizbullah* attacks against Israeli targets, 1990–95	69
7.1	Palestinian suicide attacks perpetrated versus thwarted, 2001–04	121
7.2	*Qassam* attacks on Israeli targets, 2000–04	130
7.3	Mortar shell attacks on Israeli targets, 2000–04	130
7.4	IDF house demolitions of Palestinian homes in the Occupied Territories for punitive purposes, 2001–05	134
7.5	IDF house demolitions of Palestinian homes for alleged military purposes, 2004	135
8.1	Israeli GDP per capita growth, 2000–04	143
8.2	Israeli unemployment rate, 2000–04	143
8.3	Percentage of Israeli population under the poverty line, 1999–2004	163

Tables

5.1	IDF personnel killed by *Hizbullah* attacks, 1992–98	67
6.1	Jewish settlers in the West Bank, 1976–86	76
6.2	Demolition of homes, 9 December 1987–91	83
6.3	Sealing of homes, 1988–90	83
7.1	Israeli casualties, 29 September 2000–9 August 2005	105
7.2	Palestinian casualties, 29 September 2000–9 August 2005	106
7.3	Israeli public opinion on IDF military options	108
7.4	Weapons seized during operation 'Defensive Shield'	112
7.5	Total hours of IDF curfews on major Palestinian population centres, 18 June 2002–25 January 2004	122

Acknowledgements

I would like to thank Professor Sir Lawrence Freedman for the supervision, mentorship and the timely encouragement given that enabled me to complete my PhD, which forms the basis of this book. I would like to thank the Department of War Studies and, in particular, the School of Social Science and Public Policy, which provided me with the funding necessary to conduct research at King's College London and carry out various research trips to Israel between 2003 and 2004. Special thanks go also to my two *viva voce* examiners, Professor Clive Jones (Leeds University) and Professor Caroline Kennedy-Pipe (Sheffield University) for their valuable input and suggestions on how to improve my manuscript.

I would also like to express my appreciation towards Capt. Henrietta Levi and Sal'it Braginsky of the IDF Spokesperson's Office who, after a lot of negotiating and cajoling, were able to help me interview serving members of the IDF. I must express my deep gratitude to friends, colleagues and family, who at one time or another provided moral support, wise counsel and a shoulder to sulk on: Professor Theo Farrell, Menisha Gor, Dr David Betz, Dr Rachel Kerr, Anne-Lucie Norton, Professor Christopher Dandeker, Dr Joe Maiolo, Eitan Shamir, Wrenford Hylton, my family, Antonio, Carmen, Gianluca and Rosy Catignani and, most importantly my wife, Sabina (*Spasibo, dorogaya moya*).

Finally I would like to thank the editors of *Parameters*, *Terrorism and Political Violence*, *Journal of Strategic Studies* and *The Royal United Services Institute Journal*, the director of the Global Strategy Forum, Jonathan Lehrle, the president of the Society for Military and Strategic Studies at the University of Calgary, Colin Gainer, and the director of the Canadian Forces Leadership Institute, Col. Bernd Horn, for having granted me permission to reprint excerpts of articles already published by their organisations.[1]

1 Introduction

The literature on Israel's security dilemmas and its armed forces is extensive both in terms of depth as well as breadth. There is, however, a major gap in the literature relating to the Israel Defence Forces (IDF), or *Tsahal*.[1] The gap concerns the way in which it has been able to adapt to and cope with the low-intensity conflict (LIC) in the Occupied/Disputed Territories of the West Bank and Gaza Strip over the last two decades.[2]

This book analyses the tactical and operational conduct of the Israel Defence Forces' counter-insurgency operations during the two major Palestinian uprisings (1987–93 and 2000–05) in the Territories. It sets out to see whether or not the IDF has been able to adapt its conventional order of battle and conduct of warfare to the realities of the Israeli–Palestinian LIC and achieve some sort of victory over the Palestinian insurgency.

Whilst examining the IDF's attempts at adapting to Palestinian insurgency over the last two decades, this book will also look at what effects both *Intifadas* have had on the combat morale of the IDF. IDF combat morale surveys are security-sensitive and, thus, not available for public scrutiny. By bringing together evidence from academic and professional studies, media reports and data gathered through interviews conducted in Israel, I have been able to provide an analysis of the combat morale trends affecting IDF ground forces combat personnel during the two *Intifadas*.

In examining the core literature on combat motivation, this book has been able to draw out the most salient factors affecting, either negatively or positively, the combat motivation of armed forces (see Chapter 2). Having done so, the book has looked at the strategic, operational, tactical and organisational changes and adaptation that the IDF has undergone in response to Palestinian insurgency. By relating such changes (or lack thereof) to the factors affecting combat motivation the book has shed greater light on the combat motivation trends of the IDF during the two *Intifadas*.

Furthermore, by providing a historical examination of the way in which the IDF and the Israeli security doctrine were formed and developed over time, the book explores the extent to which Israeli security assumptions, civil–military relations, and the organisational culture, structure and conduct of the IDF have affected its ability to adapt, successfully, to the contemporary Israeli–Palestinian LIC. As it begins to consider the evolution of Israel's national security strategy and the nature of its civil–military relations, it will explore, particularly in the chapters covering the two *Intifadas*, the extent to which Israel's security policy-making establishment has been able to adopt a strategy relevant to the nature and magnitude of the current conflict, between the Israeli state and the Palestinian community.

The book will delve into the various dilemmas that the IDF as a 'conservative organisation', and IDF personnel involved in the two *Intifadas*, have endured. These include, upholding the purity of arms principle (use of weapons for solely defensive purposes), despite the risk of causing significant collateral damage, instances of excessive force and abuse during military operations carried out in Palestinian urban centres, and of using a war-fighting organisation to conduct constabulary duties in densely populated areas. In particular, the growing phenomenon of IDF conscientious objectors caused by the politically and ethically controversial nature of maintaining (and providing security within) the Territories, will be highlighted. Yoram Peri defined the phenomenon of conscientious objection as one of those 'challenges of an unprecedented nature and difficulty for Israeli society'.[3] Although this book looks at the justifications that conscientious objectors voiced in regards to their radical protest, it does not provide lengthy personal accounts of selected individuals' experiences, as do the works of Ronit Chacham or Peretz Kidron.[4] Rather, it discusses how the tactics adopted by the IDF against Palestinian insurgency as well as general Israeli national security strategy vis-à-vis the Territories affected motivations to serve.

The growing discontent of many reservists, with conditions in terms of compensation, training and the unsatisfactory equipment with which they serve during their periodic reserve duty, will be addressed. Such discontent has lowered their will to serve in regular training and routine security duties on a yearly basis in the IDF. It has especially affected combat reservists who, in effect, have been disproportionately used during the two *Intifadas*.

The majority of non-combat reservists have not been called up, due to the relatively low, albeit unrelenting, level of violence during the two *Intifadas*. The lack of an imminent conventional threat on any of Israel's borders over almost the last two decades means a smaller number of reservists have carried the growing burden of maintaining Israel's national security. This situation has occurred in spite of the continued rhetoric that the IDF is a 'people's army' and that the burden of security should rest on all of its (male, Jewish and non-Ultra Orthodox) citizens. It has, consequently, created resentment on the part of quite a few combat reservists, creating the eventual reluctance to serve, not on the basis of conscientious objection, but because of not wanting to carry the security burden without greater financial remuneration and/or greater social appreciation.

Introduction 3

Lastly, this book will address the question of whether or not the use of the IDF to 'solve' militarily the Israeli–Palestinian conflict has been a successful strategy given the politically complex nature of the conflict.

Why study the IDF during the two *Intifadas*?

One reason for studying the IDF's LIC experiences in the Territories is the fact that, as suggested by recent experience, as well as by contemporary military experts, future warfare is likely to involve comparable operations within urban arenas. LICs have been the most common conflicts in international relations since the Second World War. Around 80 per cent of the conflicts during the Cold War were LICs, as were 95 per cent of the conflicts occurring between 1989 and 1996.[5] This trend has only increased over the last decade.[6]

Not only are such operations likely to become more common, but also more challenging. These operations, in fact, already entail huge economic expenditure, high domestic and international political costs, problematical moral dilemmas, and public-image blunders that are not exclusively relevant to the IDF. The IDF is a unique organisation in that it is a 'people's army'. In addition, Israel and its precursor *Yishuv* ('settlement' – term used by the Zionist movement to indicate the group of Jewish residents in Palestine) community in Palestine have been in a constant state of conflict, in one form or the other, with its Arab neighbours over the last 80 years or so. Nonetheless, the ethical and operational dilemmas and issues of political legitimacy that the IDF has experienced over the last 20 years whilst carrying out low-intensity operations, whether counter-terrorist, counter-guerrilla or constabulary, are similar to those that have affected armed forces involved in peace-keeping and peace-enforcement operations since the end of the Cold War, as well as in the 'global war on terror' (GWOT) since 9/11.

IDF COIN (Counter-Insurgency) operations are also relevant to comparable operations, such as those in Afghanistan and Iraq, which increasingly involve populated civilian areas. The problematic nature of such operations often affects ground forces, not only because of the close contact they have with the hostile civilian population, but also due to the fact that given the decentralised nature of urban conflict operations, low-ranking officers and even non-commissioned officers (NCOs) sometimes take tactical decisions, which may have dramatic strategic consequences. Consequently, the responsibility and pressures on low-ranking officers and soldiers have increased considerably.

The stresses and challenges that officers and soldiers undergo in LIC scenarios and during periods of transformation/adaptation make it necessary to study the effects they have on their combat motivation. This is crucial for understanding combat motivation factors that influence immediate operational performance, and essential in attempting to understand the combat motivation outcomes that armed forces might experience in the medium to long-term.

Despite the worldwide increase of low-intensity warfare most armed forces have continued to focus their training and materiel acquisition efforts on large-scale intensity conflicts.[7] This has been the case for Israel. Notwithstanding the IDF's involvement since the early 1950s in *bitachon shotef* (*batash*) – that is, 'current security operations' – such as the interception of guerrilla and terrorist combatants during border patrols, retaliatory operations and cross-border punitive strikes,[8] the IDF's main preoccupation until very recently has been the threat of high-intensity warfare from the states bordering Israel. Its focus, in terms of order of battle and training of military staff, has been geared towards conventional, high-intensity conflict (HIC). The IDF's last Gaza Brigade Commander, Brig. Gen. Aviv Kohavi, stated in early 2003 that in the IDF's case, at the start of the *Al-Aqsa Intifada* in September 2000 'there was no relevant doctrine and techniques for LIC combat in urban populated areas'.[9] This was the case in spite of the fact that Israel had been involved extensively since the mid-1980s in guerrilla warfare in South Lebanon and in COIN operations within the Territories since the late 1980s.

In fact, with the rise of LICs as the main form of warfare that conventional armies, such as the IDF face, 'the distinction between "front" and "rear" and "war" and "peace" have become more blurred'.[10] Consequently, the conventional differences between 'combatant' and 'noncombatant' and between 'battleground' and 'civilian quarters' have also become confused. These distinctions have been particularly problematic in Israel's case, because of the very narrow distance between Israel and its zone of conflict/operations and the consequential narrow margin of error allowed in these operations.

Moreover, given the generally equivocal nature of low-intensity threats to the core national interests of a specific state, the legitimacy of the use or threat of military force in order to stabilise and impose order over a particular theatre of operations has become paramount from a legal point of view,[11] and also from an ethical standpoint.[12] More than ever before, military leaders have to deal with the moral misgivings that may arise amongst both their soldiers and themselves. Thus, military leaders have found themselves continually trying 'to build an internal credibility for their operations' and 'to constantly respond to a sensitive civilian environment ... in order to construct an external legitimacy for their actions'.[13] This credibility and legitimacy have become even more poignant issues in Israel's LIC strategy vis-à-vis the Palestinians, given the rise of domestic dissent within a society that relies predominantly on conscript and reservist armed personnel.

The question of legitimacy when using military force in LICs is especially crucial even if fought out on the basis of self-defence, as in the Israeli case. The issue of the legitimacy of the use of force has become, in fact, very relevant as the media can easily weaken such legitimacy by exposing operational blunders or even abuses carried out by armed forces and, thus, influence heavily international and domestic public opinion. The exposition of such operational errors and abuses has also become easier to monitor as local civilians have increasingly been able to acquire relatively inexpensive video and digital recorders and disseminate them through various media outlets to their advantage.

Tactical mistakes by forces on the ground may have extraordinary strategic consequences due to pervasive media coverage and due to the overall greater political and diplomatic stakes involved in LICs. This may result in greater political interference from the government sanctioning the use of the military in a particular mission, from aborting the actual operation to modifying it. This would mostly be due to the fear of operational failure being highlighted on the media almost immediately, whether or not that would come in the guise of suffering one's own casualties, inflicting civilian casualties, causing collateral damage, demonstrating 'excessive force' and so on. In fact, 'the presence of the news media is a primary reason for the increasing link between tactics and strategy'.[14] Such a linkage has become so strong that it has recently led armed forces like the IDF to factor in the media when planning missions at the operational and tactical levels.

Whereas during the first *Intifada* such legitimacy proved very hard to defend both at the international, but more importantly, at the domestic level, given the vast asymmetry of violence used between the Israelis and Palestinians, the more violent *Al-Aqsa Intifada* strengthened Israel's resolve to fight and its self-perception of fighting a legitimate conflict. Yet, even at the higher end of the spectrum of such low-intensity violence (i.e. terrorism and guerrilla warfare), the IDF Head of Doctrine for the Ground Forces Command, Col. Roi Elcabets, plainly stated that 'we know that the legitimacy of our struggle is a major thing and every act of any soldier might on occasion harm the *battle of the narrative*' [emphasis mine].[15] One would think that the principle of self-defence would be adequate enough to justify the use of force in Israel's specific case. For clashes such as LICs, which are objectively not perceived as being existential threats (despite former Prime Minister Ariel Sharon's and other top IDF officers' remarks to the contrary), the issue of the narrative of the conflict has become an important aspect for legitimising and creating a consensus on the use of force and in defining the strategic intent of any force used.[16] Consequently, it seems that even in the Israeli case, where the level of violence during the current *Al-Aqsa Intifada* has been significantly high and the targets of such violence are clearly Israeli civilians and military units, 'this lack of consensus [has led] … to an inherent controversy on the question of defining strategic objectives' and that 'the lack of clarity regarding the greater objectives [has made] it harder to clarify the means for achieving them'.[17]

This suggests that military operations, which may be brilliant from a tactical point of view, against insurgents who are seeking self-determination (whether religious – that is, Islamic – political or ethnic) within the Middle East, may not achieve the intended strategic outcomes. Some have argued that the political nature of LICs precludes the ability to impose unilaterally a strategic solution through the sole use of military means or through the imposition of peace terms. This book will consider whether or not this has been the case with the two *Intifadas*.

Moreover, by studying the Israeli case, one can learn that interpreting guerrilla insurgency as terror and actual terror as an existential threat reduces the threshold by which 'conventional' states and their armed forces are willing to use (excessive) military force. The current US government has interpreted *Al Qaeda* terror as an existential threat.[18] The USA's closest ally, the United Kingdom, has also followed suit and has come to interpret terrorism as an existential threat.[19] As a result, both states have spearheaded two major campaigns in Afghanistan and Iraq since 9/11 as part of the 'global war on terrorism' and both are still intent on defeating global Islamist terrorism wherever it crops up in the world.

Interpretations of the Palestinian terror (and guerrilla) threat as existential during various periods of the Israeli–Palestinian conflict led to Israel's use of force as a panacea for the political echelon's inability to find a political solution to the Palestinian question (most notably during Menachem Begin's and Ariel Sharon's governments). Given the relatively ambiguous strategic guidance given by the political establishment, the IDF has often achieved short-term and, arguably, successful tactical goals such as the pre-emptive elimination of 'ticking bomb' suicide bombers. The attainment of such short-term tactical aims has often worsened Israel's chances of realising the ultimate strategic goal of peace, or at least a state of 'non-war', with the Palestinians due to the escalatory nature that such reprisal operations have had on the Israeli–Palestinian conflict.

Literature review

When analysing the Israeli case study, the uniqueness of the Israeli state of military affairs precludes the possibility of using any over-arching theory that might be applicable to other countries. According to Dan Horowitz, who has researched extensively on Israeli security matters, 'in spite of the many references to Israel and the IDF ... none of the existing conceptual frameworks ... appear to be fully applicable to the case of Israel'.[20]

The fact that the Israeli case study cannot be boxed into a particular strict theoretical framework does not preclude the fact that policy-relevant lessons can be learned from its particular COIN experiences in its fight against the Palestinian insurgency in the Territories of the West Bank and Gaza Strip. Militaries currently involved in the global war on terror in Afghanistan and Iraq have faced, in fact, similar operational and tactical dilemmas to those that Israel has been facing in the Territories over roughly the last 15 years. For example, the difficulty in distinguishing combatant from non-combatant, the strategic effect of actions carried out by soldiers or lower-ranking officers on the ground, cases of disproportionate force or outright abuse against civilians,[21] the role of the media in framing the nature of the conflict fought,[22] and the burnout of personnel constantly involved in COIN operations are but a few of the problems that the IDF and other Western militaries have been facing in their particular COIN campaign.[23] As Israel's atypical case can barely be restricted within a rigid theoretical structure, this book has utilised a historical framework of analysis. Rather than providing an exhaustive historical examination of the IDF or a blow-by-blow account of its more recent operations and actions during the two *Intifadas*, it focuses on the most salient events, issues and dilemmas that shed light on the IDF's ability or inability to adapt its armed forces to the Israeli–Palestinian conflict.

A multidisciplinary approach has been adopted by looking at the sociological, psychological and political aspects that have influenced the Israeli security doctrine and the IDF. As such, the literature here reviewed that relates to Israeli security doctrine, the IDF and combat motivation is quite broad and multidisciplinary. It does no justice to the extensive research already carried out on Israeli security issues; it only attempts to situate this book within the subject matter.

A starting point for analysing Israeli security issues is the country's national security doctrine. Although, as Yoram Peri states, there is no formal Israeli security doctrine in the sense of 'a close-knit, well-formulated aggregate of security principles',[24] many Israeli security analysts, both from the IDF and from the academic community, have written substantially on the main security assumptions and strategies that the IDF and the rest of the security establishment have developed and acted upon since the establishment of the IDF in 1948. Most of these studies have tended to adopt the historical approach in order to examine the IDF's success in adapting its doctrine and tactics to the security environment it was facing at the time. Edward Luttwak and Dan Horowitz's text, *The Israeli Army*, is a classic, yet slightly outdated, study on the IDF's origins, evolution, organisation, command ethos as well as its overall strategic doctrine.[25] Nonetheless, it still stands the test of time as a general reader of the IDF.

Dan Horowitz manages to overview succinctly the main tenets and security assumptions of Israeli security thinking and provides also a very clear examination of the demise of the national security consensus regarding the occupation and maintenance of the Territories since 1967, particularly following the improved strategic situation Israel found itself in after the 1979 Israeli–Egyptian peace agreement.

Horowitz, in fact, points to the main consequence of this demise in the national security consensus as the intrusion of ideological and political considerations into Israeli security thinking. As a result, 'the defence establishment, including the high command of the IDF, could no longer maintain the autonomy traditionally accorded those in the field of professional security considerations'.[26] This reduction in the national security consensus, as we shall see in this study, was particularly problematic for the IDF during the *Intifadas* given the political and ethical controversy surrounding the use of force and maintenance of IDF troops within the Territories.

Ariel Levite also provides an exhaustive analytical and historical review of Israel's offensive military doctrine and its development over time in order to criticise Israel's inability to reappraise its operational (and tactical) offensive posture in the light of the radically altered strategic environment it found itself in during the late 1980s.[27] He comes to charge the IDF of 'profound military conservatism' and of suffering an 'offensive bias' based on the 'cult of the offensive', that is, on the need to attack at all times.[28] Although his conclusions are correct, his works as well as those of many others, tend to focus almost solely on the conventional threats to Israeli security and the ways the IDF has been able to tackle them.

Israel Tal's *National Security* also gives an overview of the factors that make up the Israeli security doctrine, of the IDF's organisation and the relationship between the IDF and Ministry of Defence (MOD).[29] It, however, glosses over in a perfunctory manner the conflicts and wars that the IDF confronted following the 1973 *Yom Kippur* War in spite of its relatively recent publication. When tackling Israel's future security challenges Tal concentrates on the non-conventional weapons of mass destruction and ballistic missile threat. He also predicts, in hindsight erroneously, that 'a future war is liable to be a total war'.[30] Even though Tal raises the possibility of 'warfare involving low-level, chronic military activity and violations of internal security', he does not examine those threats or overview in any way how the IDF has, or even will, address them in spite of the long track record of such violations and violence during the Oslo Peace Process and the track record of Israeli–Palestinian violence during the first *Intifada*.[31]

Mark Heller's *Adelphi Paper* study, on the other hand, concentrates on testing whether or not the 'Ben-Gurionist assumptions' underlying Israel's national security doctrine are still applicable today 'in light of the diminishing conventional threat' and the materialisation of novel and more challenges, amongst which he mentions terrorism and COIN.[32] Heller provides a thorough overview of the IDF's traditional security concept, the evolution of the various threats facing Israel since 1967, the societal and political challenges to the Israeli national security consensus. He also looks at recent organisational changes (e.g. the establishment of the Ground Forces Command), which have attempted to strengthen the IDF's efforts at improving Israel's security and to address more effectively Israel's new security – both non-conventional and sub-conventional – threats. Heller deems IDF attempts in recent years to adapt its 'organizational, operational and combat concepts' to the changing security environment in which it functions as falling 'short of a comprehensive national-security concept formulated at the highest level of national decision-making'.[33]

Heller argues that Israel's inability to re-conceptualise its national security concept results from the political and domestic internal impasse over how it should conceive its relationship with other states and the Palestinian people within the Middle East.[34] Similar arguments are advocated in this book. However, I go as far as to argue that this impasse in turn leads the political echelon to constantly use the IDF in order to maintain the status quo as political–diplomatic alternatives are brushed aside in the name of achieving (elusive) security conditions before any serious negotiations with the Palestinians can occur.

Moreover, besides pointing to the political echelon's inability to review Israel's national security doctrine as a source of the IDF's difficulty in updating its 'organizational, operational and combat concepts', this book argues that the IDF's *bitsuist* ('doer' performance-oriented) ethos has created in the IDF an inclination for the 'institutionalisation of temporary solutions', which precludes long-term strategic thinking.[35] Given that the IDF has significant influence on strategic planning this ethos also affects the civilian leadership echelons.

This has also been the case in relation to the issue of maintaining a 'people's army' (based for the most part on conscript and reservist personnel) – or at least in semblance of it – in the face of such a transformed strategic environment and the increased strategic burden that reservists have faced whilst conducting ongoing duties in the Territories (and Lebanon until 2000) over the last 20 years.[36]

The IDF has developed over the years an organisational culture that leads its command echelons to pay constant attention to finding short-term solutions to pressing tactical problems in current security operations (i.e. patrols, retaliatory operations, etc.) at the expense of developing detailed planning, training and education for the next war to come. This culture, and the Ben-Gurion assumptions underlying it, developed because of the IDF's necessity to find solutions to constant and looming LIC and HIC attacks from its neighbours.[37] I argue that this *bitsuist* ethos also affects the way in which general upper echelon commanders lead as Emmanuel Wald states that 'improvisationalism also provides fertile ground for the growth of antiprofessional orientations among General Staff officers' as well as a 'pronounced aversion to abstract thinking'.[38]

Although the term 'culture' was first defined over 125 years ago, today there are over 250 accepted definitions. Moreover, many researchers recognise that there is no universally accepted definition for the term 'organisational culture'.[39] Yet, authors such as Terry Terriff, Theo Farrell and Peter Katzenstein have shown in their studies how specific military cultures have affected the way military organisations have conducted war in the past.[40]

Robert Cassidy defines organisational, or more specifically, military culture 'as the embedded beliefs and attitudes within a military organization that shape that organization's preference on when and how the military instrument should be used'.[41] According to Kier, militaries vary in how they perceive their surroundings and the appropriate ways in which they carry out their mission. A military's organisational culture, thus, influences how it reacts to constraints laid down by civilian decision-makers, whereas a military's beliefs determine 'how the organisation reacts to changes in its external environment'.[42]

However, as Clive Jones points out when drawing lessons from Peter Katzenstein's book on how norms influence organisational behaviour, militaries are not just influenced by the external environment in which they operate. The behaviour of a military organisation can also be influenced by how its members maintain that they should reproduce the indoctrination of the organisation's values. In Israel's case,

> The behaviour of military officers is not only determined by a particular perception of their immediate external environment – the constitutive norm – but also by received wisdom born from military tradition of how an Israeli officer, for example, is supposed to act in a given situation. Regulatory norms give meaning to constitutive norms in that they may proscribe or advocate a particular course of action.[43]

Culture affects how militaries behave and organise themselves for warfare. Culture, however, does not influence the specific outcome of a certain military action. Rather, culture influences the means by which a military organisation attempts to achieve its strategic, operational and tactical objectives. Consequently, '[c]ulture influences action not by providing the ultimate values toward which action is orientated, but by shaping a repertoire or "tool kit" of habits, skills and styles from which people construct "strategies of action"'.[44]

Moreover, according to Terry Terriff, 'organizational culture ... can provide a compelling explanation for why specific military organisations may continue to pursue ways of warfare that are incompatible with emerging or prevailing strategic and operational realities, or why they resist change'.[45] Throughout this book, the reader will be able to appreciate the way in which the IDF's organisational culture of *bitsuism* has influenced the way it has been able or has failed to adapt, under the constraints and leadership (or lack thereof during certain crises) of the upper political echelons, to the threats facing the state of Israel. This book will also show how the organisational culture of *bitsuism* has been perpetuated throughout the IDF's history since the 1950s, given the great emphasis that commanders at all levels, especially within the ground forces units, have traditionally put on perpetuating the values of tactical hyperactivism, anti-intellectualism and the achievement of 'the mission' at all costs within the IDF.

Very few authors have used, in fact, the IDF's *bitsuist* ethos as a major explanatory factor for its incapability to adapt its armed forces to the new strategic realities Israel has faced over the years. Yaacov Hasdai lucidly defines *bitsuism* and explains the IDF's weakness in long-term strategic planning, which he also sees as a symptom of Israeli society in general.[46] Eliot Cohen *et al.* also found that in spite of the IDF's ability to innovate its armed forces at the tactical and operational levels, it was less capable of undergoing a 'more thorough-going reconsideration of its first-order [strategic] assumptions'.[47] In Chapter 7 I go on to show that the IDF has been unable to reconsider its first-order strategic assumptions even in the case of the IDF's recent re-organisation plans, dubbed *'Kela 2008'* (Katapult 2008), which almost entirely centres on the HIC scenario to the extent that even the former head of the IDF's Ground Forces Command, Maj. Gen. Yiftah Ron-Tal, admitted that the IDF was still preparing for a major conflict over territory.

Whereas Cohen *et al.* conclude that part of the conservatism of 'Israeli military thinking and practice' resides in the IDF's understanding that what it can achieve strategically through military means is quite limited and that losing a war is impermissible.[48] This book maintains that such conservatism is also caused by the IDF's organisational culture of *bitsuism*.

This book will argue that performance-oriented, anti-intellectual, *bitsuist* attitudes within the IDF, although good at encouraging initiative and aggressiveness in commanders, is counterproductive in the complex LIC environment. Within the LIC environment the initiative of lower-level commanders often leads to escalation or blunders that result in strategically detrimental outcomes, which go against overall mission objectives. As Ze'ev Drory has pointed out when analysing Israel's reprisal policy during the early 1950s, 'during periods of continuous reprisal actions, the power of the tactical unit is great'. This is because, for the military 'creating and maintaining a record of operational success [that is, of achieving the mission's objectives] stands above any other consideration, for without such a record, the political echelon will not risk deploying this capability'.[49] This was also the case during the *Al-Aqsa Intifada*, which during the first four years was characterised by continuous IDF reprisal operations triggered in response to Palestinian terror and guerrilla operations both within and beyond the 1967 Green Line. The military often conducted reprisal or even pre-emptive missions, which although successful from a tactical point of view, often had negative strategic and political implications (usually further Palestinian escalation or international condemnation). Its anti-intellectual proclivity in turn stopped higher echelons from drawing major strategic lessons until very late into the conflict.

Consequently, the military may often overlook political and strategic considerations because of its undue focus on 'performing' well on the tactical battlefield. This emphasis on performing and tactical hyper-activism has serious implications in states such as Israel where the nature of

12 *Introduction*

civil–military relationships is not clearly outlined. The success or failure of any COIN campaign is the attainment of national objectives. As John Nagl argues, even though the attainment of national objectives 'may not be determined entirely by the [armed forces'] counterinsurgency doctrine and practice, [the military] as a powerful bureaucratic actor inevitably affects the definition of national objectives for the conflict'.[50] This is even more the case in Israel where strategic planning and intelligence estimates are overwhelmingly focused on the hands of the military echelons.

The way in which Israeli civil–military and, in particular political–military, relations were set up by David Ben-Gurion has had significant implications for the way in which Israeli security policy and decision-making processes as well as outcomes have developed. Almost all researchers of the IDF agree that the IDF has had a central, if not dominant, role in moulding Israel's security policy. Amos Perlmutter, for instance, stated in 1985 that, 'aside from the [now-defunct] Soviet military', the IDF can be regarded as the only armed forces in the world that 'wields almost complete power over strategic and tactical questions'.[51]

When looking at civil–military relations, this book does not attempt to examine such relations for the purpose of creating some new theoretical or analytical model that would be able to classify the structure and nature of civil–military relations in Israel. In fact, when examining Israeli civil–military relations, it does not try to test whether or not Israel is a garrison state,[52] whether the boundaries between the military and civilian sectors of society are 'integral',[53] 'permeable',[54] 'fragmented'.[55] Instead, in Chapter 3, it examines the extent to which the imprint of Ben-Gurion's conceptualisation of civil–military relations has left such relations open to abuse from either the political or military echelons because of the unclear demarcation of roles and processes affecting security decision-making in Israel.[56] Such an examination is important, because as the national security consensus becomes subject to greater public dispute, the possibility of there being tensions between the civil (and political) and military echelons over what course to take vis-à-vis a security threat may become more likely.

This was the case during the first and *Al-Aqsa Intifadas* when civil–military tensions became quite high, because of the political controversy involving the use or non-use of forces against the Palestinians in the Territories. Political disputes over the use of force, the maintenance or restitution of the Territories of the West Bank and Gaza Strip, constant scrutiny over the IDF's capabilities as well as questions on the appropriateness of its use as a constabulary force became commonplace.

A lot has been written on the IDF's involvement in the first *Intifada*, less so on the *Al-Aqsa Intifada*. Zeev Schiff and Ehud Ya'ari's *Intifada* gives an in-depth account of the first *Intifada* by providing a very thorough examination of what actually occurred during the first two years of the uprising. Unlike Schiff's and Ya'ari's study, this book focuses specifically on the way

Introduction 13

the IDF dealt with both *Intifadas*: what tactics it used, whether or not it made significant changes to its strategic, operational and tactical posture in order to deal with low-intensity type scenarios within the urban arena.[57] Aryeh Shalev's *The Intifada* and Efraim Inbar's 'Israel's Small War' article are two good examples of studies that look at the tactical methods used by the IDF to quell the uprising, the difficulties experienced by its personnel during the conflict, as well as the *Intifada*'s repercussions on Israeli society.[58] Stuart Cohen and Martin Van Creveld's studies scrutinise to what extent the *Intifada* had a deleterious effect on the IDF's fighting capabilities as well as its overall standing in society.[59]

As for the *Al-Aqsa Intifada*, Yaacov Bar-Siman-Tov's study not only provides a meticulous analysis of the IDF's conduct during the current conflict, but also shows to what degree Israel's security assumptions and perceptions of the current conflict, which are explained in detail in Chapter 4, affected the IDF's strategy and general conduct vis-à-vis the Palestinians. Regarding whether or not the IDF was able to achieve a battlefield decision/victory over the Palestinians during both *Intifadas*, this book corroborates Bar-Siman-Tov's conclusion that during the *Al-Aqsa Intifada* 'the political and military–strategic basic assumptions about the possibility of achieving a conclusive military or political decision were unrealistic [and that] Israel's hard-handed policy and heavy pressure against the Palestinian population and the security units' resulted in strategically counter-productive results, if not escalation.[60] Again, I point to the IDF's organisational ethos of *bitsuism* as one of the main sources of such a failure.

Methodology

There are major difficulties in studying the IDF and Israeli security in general. Yoram Peri indicated the crux of such difficulties when writing that: 'The all-encompassing nature of war in Israel and the centrality of security to national existence have created a situation whereby numerous spheres ... fall within the security ambit and are enveloped in secrecy.'[61] So ingrained is the secretive mind-set of the Israeli security establishment that native researchers with ties to the IDF have stated that even data on the Israeli reserve army is hard to access or find. This is even more the case for the regular and professional branches of the IDF. Despite this remarkable obstacle, this book has tried to examine both the IDF's adaptation to the two *Intifadas* and the effects that both conflicts have had on it and, to a certain degree, on Israeli society.

Given the impossibility of accessing official IDF documentation, over 50 personal in-depth interviews were conducted with military personnel, key security decision-makers and Israeli academics that have worked closely with or researched extensively on the IDF in various capacities. These interviewees have been in a position to shed fuller light on the events and

14 *Introduction*

their effects under examination. Interviews with both professional and conscript members of the IDF were carried out with the supervision and assistance of the IDF Spokesperson's Unit. However, such assistance was not especially forthcoming during my initial contacts with the IDF. It took me, in fact, almost three years to convince the IDF to allow me to interview serving IDF personnel. Furthermore, when in Israel, many interviews were either cancelled or had to be rescheduled because of the ongoing hostilities with the Palestinians. Nonetheless, the sample provided in this book together with the interviews conducted with reservist and retired combat personnel and other security-related interviewees were sufficient for the purposes of my analysis.

Because of the need for an in-depth comprehension and thorough description of the IDF's experiences during the *Intifadas*, exploring how both individuals and group members within Israeli society as a whole have perceived and expressed their understanding of such experiences and of the Israeli–Palestinian conflict in general, reliance has been placed mostly on qualitative data in the form of in-depth semi-structured interviews.[62] This method was found to be a crucial source of information given that access to other primary sources was somewhat restricted. All interviews, apart from two, were taped and have been preserved. Interviews lasted between one and two hours (most lasted around one and one-half hours) and were conducted in English.[63] All were transcribed verbatim. Not all of the interviews or interviewees' details were cited in this study given the highly security-sensitive nature of some of the information disclosed. The interviews that were not quoted directly in this study played, nonetheless, an important part in corroborating facts and viewpoints shared by other interviewees or material used in this study. Hence, they played a part in the triangulation of evidence and information provided throughout the book's analysis. Other evidence was collected from documentation, memoirs, research papers that contain relevant primary data from official governmental and non-governmental literature and statistics and, most importantly, from foreign and Israeli press.[64]

The structure of the study

This study is divided into two main parts. The first part looks at the functional and historical background of the IDF by charting the foundation and development of the Israeli national security doctrine and of the IDF as well as of civil–military relations in Israel. The second part looks at how the IDF has coped with and adapted to the two *Intifadas*.

Chapter 2 overviews the theory and literature of combat motivation. The chapter gives a working definition of combat motivation and then outlines the various factors that affect the combat motivation of troops involved in warfare. It does so with particular reference to the Israeli case study. This chapter forms the basis on which I am able to determine throughout the latter part of this study whether or not the two *Intifadas* have affected negatively the combat motivation of IDF troops.

Chapter 3 looks at the establishment and development of civil–military relations in Israel. It shows, furthermore, how Ben-Gurion's inability, or unwillingness, to clearly define the relationship between the upper political and military echelons involved in security policy and decision-making have left security decision-making issues subject to periodical manipulation by the defence and military establishments.

Chapter 4 looks at the Israeli national strategic doctrine and at how it has evolved over time. It examines the security assumptions underlying the national security doctrine and shows how such assumptions and their application have endured. It shows how the Israeli strategic doctrine has not been able to move beyond the conventional warfare paradigm, despite the fact that the Arab–Israeli conflict has evolved into a more circumscribed, yet more problematic Israeli–Palestinian conflict due to the intercommunal nature of the conflict since the 1982 Lebanon War.[65]

Chapter 5 examines how the perception of the Arab–Israeli conflict and of the Palestinian threat by the Israeli political and military leadership echelons changed radically once the *Likud* came to power in 1977. It explores, in particular, how the Israeli military and political leaders came to perceive Palestinian terror as an existential threat and how they came to interpret the Arab–Israeli inter-state conflict as an Israeli–Palestinian intercommunal one. These perceptions dramatically reduced Israel's threshold for the use of violence and led eventually to the Lebanon invasion. It also analyses the IDF's counter-guerrilla strategy in Lebanon and points to the difficulties it faced in frustrating *Hizbullah*'s very effective guerrilla campaign.

Chapter 6 looks at how the first *Intifada* began, what methods the Palestinians used to voice their opposition to the occupation and, in more detail, the tactics the IDF used to try to quell such opposition. The chapter also looks at what effect the *Intifada* had on the combat motivation of IDF troops and at how such troops dealt with the ethical and political controversy surrounding their actions in the Territories. It highlights especially the rising phenomenon of conscientious objection, which until the 1982 Lebanon War was almost non-existent.

Chapter 7 examines the *Al-Aqsa Intifada*, pointing to how much more violent both the Palestinian insurgency and Israeli COIN actions have become. This chapter examines in detail Israeli efforts at fighting both terror and guerrilla attacks perpetrated by Palestinian terror/guerrilla groups and the IDF's unsuccessful efforts at obtaining its overall strategic goal of imposing victory on the Palestinians. The chapter also explores the heavy costs that Israel has had to bear in order to keep on fighting a costly war of attrition against the Palestinians: economic (worsening economic conditions), morale (increase in conscientious objection and absenteeism), and military (budgetary cuts, training and weapons development programme cancellations and the increasing reservist burden). Although the IDF and other security apparatuses' efforts have been relatively successful, this study will show that it has not been able to achieve the objective set out at the start of the conflict by the upper political and military echelons of winning the war.

Chapter 8 will demonstrate, despite extensive structural reforms as well as tactical and technical innovations, that the IDF has not been able to overcome the strategic impasse with the Palestinians through military means. This study will argue that this has been due to the fact that the IDF cannot provide unilaterally a military solution, particularly when its ground forces have caused collateral damage and civilian casualties. It also argues that this has been the case due to the hyper-activism of the forces involved in the fight against the Palestinian terror and guerrilla threat and civil disobedience.

Chapter 9 looks at Ariel Sharon's political decision to create and execute the 'Unilateral Disengagement Plan' as a way of breaking the strategic deadlock in the Israeli–Palestinian conflict. Although surprisingly successful, the disengagement plan did raise the spectre of further cases of conscientious objection, albeit this time from the right-wing nationalist and (mostly) national-religious constituencies. The chapter raises the issue that without an adequate revision of the Israeli national security doctrine, which takes into account the political complexity of LICs, the continuous use of force to address the effects of Palestinian violence rather than its symptoms will continue to perpetuate the conflict, rather than reduce it. Moreover, the use of the IDF in the ever-decreasing national security consensus regarding the Territories will not make things any easier for the IDF to carry out its future missions in the Territories, particularly further disengagement.

Whilst *Chapter 10* provides the overall conclusions of this study, I have added *Chapter 11* as a postface that analyses briefly the events of the Second Lebanon War during the summer of 2006, because many of the problems that the IDF faced during the last Lebanon campaign can be traced back to some of the doctrinal, organisational and cultural weaknesses that I have highlighted through this book.

2 Combat motivation

The centrality of combat motivation to a successful outcome in military operations, from regular patrolling to full-scale wars, cannot be overstated. Combat motivation, in fact, is a key factor in enabling standing armies to win conflicts; in Israel's case, it has been 'referred to as the "secret weapon" of the IDF'.[1] On numerous occasions quantitatively inferior armies have been able to have the upper hand because of their fighting spirit, aggressiveness and relatively buoyant high morale. Indeed, research has consistently demonstrated that there is a 'strong relationship between cohesion, soldiers' level of morale and combat efficiency'.[2]

In spite of the fact that combat motivation is such a key ingredient to winning battles, most military and academic establishments have found some difficulty in measuring and regarding combat motivation when analysing an army's overall power capabilities or when giving a threat assessment of such an army's enemies. Their problem has often been in labelling the intangibles – such as combat motivation – correctly, because 'an idea that is not observable and measurable (strength of will) is hard to compare against one that is (physical strength)'.[3] Yet, if according to Carl von Clausewitz, 'war is ... an act of force to compel our enemy to do our will',[4] then it is important to take account of an army's combat morale, because 'will' in the context of a battlefield can be equated to combat motivation.

The importance of looking at combat motivation when analysing militaries lies in the fact that despite all the technological advances in warfare and the continuous debate on the extent to which there has been a revolution in military affairs, the nature of man has not changed.[5] Regardless of the vast technological advances that warfare will undergo, its conduct for the foreseeable future will be in the hands of human beings. 'This means that individual actions, human imperfections, performance thresholds and varying personalities will still influence and determine a conflict's outcome.'[6]

Thus, it is important to look at the human element of the battlefield, particularly combat motivation and morale. Indeed, taking account of the human element is even more compelling in the future battlefield, which I believe, will be for the most part the urban arena. This is due to the fact that 'a battlefield filled with buildings, tight streets, underground tunnels, and the other obstacles of a built-up area takes away the range of many of today's most highly developed weapons systems' and emphasises the individual soldier's tactical initiative.[7]

Defining combat motivation

However, what is meant by motivation in the military context? Despite the many definitions of motivation/morale, the one provided by John Baynes offers a good starting point. He defines motivation as ' "the enthusiasm and persistence with which a member of a group engages in the prescribed activities of that group" '.[8] Within the military setting, ' "morale" and "motivation" are frequently used interchangeably.... Although morale delineates more the condition of the group (or the unit) whereas motivation delineates primarily the attribute of an individual.'[9]

Manning, furthermore, defines morale as 'a function of cohesion and *esprit de corps*'.[10] Unit cohesion, as a matter of a fact, has always been necessary in combat, because each member of the unit relies on the other in order to survive and to carry out successful combat operations. Cohesion has been defined as 'the bonding together of members of an organisation/unit in such a way as to sustain their will and commitment to each other, their unit and the mission'.[11] The IDF has had the reputation of high combat motivation and effectiveness. This was due to various other factors besides cohesion and *esprit de corps*. Nevertheless, these have been decisive factors in its case. Together with the leadership example of small unit commanders, they have been considered 'the most important source of combat motivation'.[12]

As will be seen later in this book, the concept of *milkhemet ein breira* (war of no choice) has also been a strong motivational and morale-boosting factor in the IDF. This is the belief that war is thrust on Israel by its Arab enemies, that the Holocaust must never happen again to the Jewish people and that only the IDF stands in the way of the Arab states' attempts at eliminating Israel. This has also been a factor in providing the moral justification for all of Israel's wars and military operations and which have, thus, enabled Israel to uphold its belief in *tohar haneshek*, i.e. the 'purity of arms' concept. The purity of arms concept is, in fact, the most important moral rule for conduct in the IDF. It stresses the soldiers' duty of self-control, compassion and of the preservation of human life and plays a strong part in legitimising the IDF's use of force given the general perception that force will always be used by the IDF for defensive purposes.

A crucial *esprit de corps* factor affecting combat motivation is the institutional value system a particular army embodies, values which are most relevant to the unit member combatant are especially important. In the IDF's case these are: '1) Tenacity of purpose in performing missions and drive to victory; 2) Responsibility; 3) Credibility; 4) Personal Example; 5) Human Life; 6) Purity of Arms; 7) Professionalism; 8) Discipline; 9) Comradeship; and 10) Sense of Mission.'[13]

One of the most important institutional values of the IDF has been encapsulated in the concept of ' "*achavat lochameem*" (combatant's brotherhood)',[14] which fulfils the IDF's tenet of comradeship. Indeed, 'if the soldier trusts his comrades, he will probably perceive more safety in continuing to fight alongside them'.[15] Such trust can only be formed through shared experience of mutual support found in a typical family. Likewise, such comradeship is crucial, because it satisfies another factor impinging on combat motivation, which is the soldier's need to belong (affiliative need) and to feel that he is part of something significant and to which he can personally contribute.[16]

In the IDF, such a family is found in the form of the battalion, described by the IDF as 'an "organic unit" (*yechida organit*). Organizationally this implies (1) a framework characterized by a permanent membership and structure of roles, and (2) that upon mobilisation the whole battalion (as one complete organizational unit) is recruited' for up to 25 years after regular military service.[17] Such cohesion, thus, has not only developed in times of peace, but even more so during wars. Many IDF battalions have reservists that have fought in at least one previous conflict. For example, there were plenty of battalions with veterans who had fought in the *Yom Kippur* War, the Lebanon War and grappled with the first *Intifada*.

Furthermore, according to Kellett, 'Israelis regard fighting as very much a social act based on collective activity, cooperation, and mutual support',[18] whereby every member relies on the other and especially on the professionalism and leadership of the unit commander. According to the IDF, for example, the company commander should possess several attributes and values such as 'face-to-face leadership quality, personal integrity and the ability to create mutual trust between the sub-commanders and the soldier and to [instil] trust in the weapon and fighting systems'.[19] Indeed, the Combat Readiness Questionnaire survey of over 1,200 Israeli combat soldiers conducted by the IDF Department of Behavioural Sciences in May 1981 showed that the soldier's trust in his immediate leaders contributed positively in boosting his combat motivation and his unit's combat morale. Such trust in their commanders was shown to depend 'upon the commander's professional capability, his credibility as a source of information and the amount of care and attention that he pays to his men'.[20] According to one reserve company commander of the IDF Paratroopers Brigade:

> A good commander is very proficient in what he does; from small arms to tactics, he has to know his stuff [i.e. professional capability]. He is able to analyse a situation very quickly. He is not afraid to take control and responsibility in situations where the higher level commanders are fucking up [i.e. credibility]. A good commander has to

walk a really fine line between getting the job done and getting his men home alive [i.e. care of subordinates].[21]

A leader's professional competency

In fact, 'a leader's professional competency is the primary leadership factor that soldiers say decreases their stress'.[22] Stress generally lowers combat motivation and can eventually lead to psychiatric disabilities. Military command is also made easier when the actual commander is considered to be professional by his subordinates as his professionalism arouses authority. Subordinates 'appreciate professionals, acknowledge their supremacy and accept their command without hesitation'.[23] This is even more the case in the IDF reserves where military know-how and experience, rather than rank, play a much greater part in instilling discipline and the duty to obey orders amongst subordinates.

The leader as source of information

Another important role that the leader must take on is that of information provider for his subordinates. Communication and trust between the provider and recipient are crucial, because informing soldiers during combat of the real state of affairs will help lessen the fear caused by the unknown. Reuven Gal's 'Golan Heights' study showed, in effect, that the assessment and awareness of the expected combat zone and of the adversary's power and ability not only improve the soldier's self-confidence as a fighter, but also further develop his combat motivation, because such knowledge reduces the uncertainty factor, which often plays on the imaginary fears of a combat soldier in action.[24]

Furthermore, for deployed armed forces LIC missions necessitate an improved stress on 'meaning management' in terms of internalising the purposes and mission of a particular operation due to the mission's inherent ambiguities.[25] It is the task of the leader to provide such 'meaning' to his subordinates. According to 'attribution theory',[26] in fact, when confronted with ambiguous situations, individuals ascribe to leaders the understanding of what needs to be achieved, the course of action to take, of how and what to prioritise; 'briefly, the ability to "make sense of things" in chaotic environments'.[27]

Other circumstances of uncertainty, which negatively impinge on the soldier's combat motivation or the unit's combat morale, are related to his time of service both at the operational level and at the professional level. At the operational level, soldiers will often deploy and serve willingly, 'but when their redeployment date is uncertain, trust with the institution is strained'.[28] At the professional level, uncertainty often comes in the guise of personnel downsizing. Research has shown that 'downsizing severely damages the psychological contract between an organisation and its downsizing survivors'.²⁹ Downsizing raises the soldier's levels of uncertainty in terms of 'if or when' the downsizing will affect him at all, both in regard to his tenure and in regard to the increased workload he will be taking on. As shall be seen in Chapter 8, extensive budgetary cutbacks and personnel downsizing in the IDF over the last few years may have had a deleterious effect on motivation to serve of the professional corps.

The leader as protector

The leader is also the crucial link between the higher echelons that are geographically removed from the frontline of the battlefield and his subordinates who must accomplish the tasks assigned to them. The unit leader must make sure that such tasks do not recklessly endanger his men, but at the same time are accomplished anyhow.³⁰ In order to do so, a field commander needs to gain his subordinates' trust before he can exert any influence, which is best achieved when his soldiers are able to identify with their commander, the organisational values, which he must embody and with the missions that he is ordering them to accomplish. Frequently, the identification with the unit leader and with the military's values and missions that the unit leader must promote occurs when the leader is involved with, if not leading, his subordinates during actual combat and training, because status differences become blurred when such officers live with their men and share their discomfort and fears.³¹

The unit leader quite often must also demonstrate to his subordinates that he genuinely cares about them by taking care of their physical – and quite often emotional – needs. Indeed, leaders should make sure that they care about their soldiers, because if soldiers appreciate this, then they will more diligently carry out their duties, and typically, without the need for any supervision. This is particularly the case when the unit leader is able to provide the best equipment for his unit, because it demonstrates that the leader is making sure that his subordinates have the best chances of surviving combat due to their – real or perceived – technological superiority over the enemy. Too often, though, soldiers have had trouble perceiving the importance of their unit's assignment and, as a result, of their own duties in the unit, because they have not been given the supplies they actually require. Quite often, the unit leader's reassurances have been insufficient, because 'regardless of how logical and well-meaning the explanations may be for the unit's shortages, soldiers will evaluate their role and their unit's mission on the basis of their own perceptions and no one else's'.³²

Moreover, it also entails 'training them to become seasoned soldiers who could survive on a battlefield, because they are technically, physically and mentally proficient'.³³ Thus, soldiers may often become embittered with their military leadership due to training restrictions that are often justified by politically motivated budget cuts, because they know that such restrictions could rapidly get them killed in battle due to their lack of expertise of certain combat scenarios and operations.

Furthermore, survey research of Israeli veterans from the Lebanon War showed that the feeling of loneliness (i.e. lack of support given by a tightly knit combat unit) was the best single predictor of combat stress reaction and that the best predictor of loneliness was low officer support.[34] Thus, combat leadership, particularly at the unit level has become even more important due to the fact that modern warfare, particularly urban warfare, requires the dispersal of numerous physically isolated units requiring small and autonomous actions based on tactical ingenuity.

Gibush – societal crystallisation

Various studies have also shown that unit cohesion and *esprit de corps* not only strengthen the unit's level of morale, but also act as 'a powerful preventive measure against psychiatric breakdown in battle and as a "generator" of heroic behavior among the unit's members'.[35] This was particularly substantiated during the early stages of the 1973 War in the Golan Heights theatre of operations:

> Members of IDF tank crews who were well acquainted with one another and had trained together were more combat effective, and, despite equally intense battle, had fewer psychiatric casualties than members of tank crews who were not well acquainted, and, though equally well trained, had not trained together.[36]

Whereas, though, such cohesion and *esprit de corps* are developed only during military service in other Western armies, in Israel such solidarity has been a product and reinforcement of the collectivistic nature of Israeli society and, thus, is already in part present before conscription takes place. In effect, Israeli society has been socialised into a cohesive society based on the principle of *gibush* (crystallisation), which 'traces its historical roots to the communal *utopia* of socialist Zionism'.[37] According to Eyal Ben-Ari:

> The *gibush* metaphor implies ... [that] the internal strength and solidity of both the individual and the group flow from the unifying sense of belonging, of being securely together 'in place'. The social ideal of *gibush* involves an emphasis on the undifferentiated collectivity – on joint endeavors, on cooperation and shared sentiments, on solidarity and a sense of togetherness.[38]

This process of crystallisation, thus, carries on as the members of a unit meet up yearly for their reserve service and often becomes the source of strong friendships, if not, brotherliness. Such unit cohesion in turn creates strong incentives to continue fighting, because the combatant ultimately will fight in order to ensure that he will not let down the other members of his unit.

The general acceptance and understanding by society that military service is an essential element in the maintenance of Israel's security and existence as a state within the Middle East region, and that such service is supposed to be shared by most members of Israeli society, are strong motivational factors as well. This is especially due to the case, as we shall see in the following two chapters, that the IDF was set up, by David Ben-Gurion, to be a 'people's army', which would also have civic and nation-building functions as well. Consequently, another social aspect enhancing unit cohesion is 'linked directly to broad, societal agreement about the citizen's duty to serve in defence of the nation … Soldiers must be aware that their society will exact penalties … for deserting' and will exact considerable social penalties for dereliction of duty.[39] As shall be seen in the following chapters, in the Israeli case, such penalties have for the most part been quite onerous.

According to Jesse Gray, 'soldiers have died more or less willingly, not . . . for any abstract good but because they realize that by fleeing their post . . . they would expose companions to grave danger. Such loyalty to the group is the essence of fighting morale'.[40] As such, it is important to create such cohesive units because during combat the enemy will always try to 'target the human bonds that the commander has so diligently prepared'.[41] If the commander has not developed unit cohesion beforehand then the unit's combat effectiveness will crumble under the pressure of considerable attack.

Again, Samuel L.A. Marshall's study of World War Two (WWII) US infantrymen led him to conclude that, 'men do not fight for a cause but because they do not want to let their comrades down'.[42] In Israel, this is particularly the case with the reservist corps. From the extensive interviews carried out in Israel, I would go as far to suggest that most Israeli reservists who report for reserve duty, not only do so because they feel a duty to protect Israeli citizens, but also because they do not want to let their comrades down and face their criticism the next time they report for reserve duty.

However, the growing lack of cohesion, which gained momentum due to reservist absenteeism and conscientious objection after the Lebanon War as well as the deep societal changes (particularly post-Zionist trends) brought about by economic development, would prove factors that would affect unit morale, reserve duty absenteeism and refusal to serve in the Territories, once the *Intifada* began and particularly during the Oslo peace era.[43]

Existential threat perception

Despite such negative trends, as well as the overall effects of attrition caused by the two *Intifadas*, the IDF has managed over the years to carry out its main duties on the ground by relying without too many difficulties on relatively enthusiastic conscripts, on the stability of the professional corps and, most importantly, on the high sense of duty of combat reservists. In spite of the numerous difficulties the IDF has confronted over the last 20 years due to, among other things, defence budget cuts, the growing inequality of the reserve service burden in the IDF reservist system, ethical and political dilemmas associated with the COIN campaigns in the Territories (and until May 2000 in Lebanon), both its commanders and soldiers have continued to perform relatively well – at least on a tactical level – against Palestinian insurgency.

Contrary to Gray's argument that soldiers do not fight for any 'abstract good' (i.e. ideology), this book will show that their desire and ability to continue fighting and carrying out their missions have, in fact, been affected appreciably by their unique *ideological* perception of the Arab–Israeli and, more recently, of the Israeli–Palestinian conflict, especially during the *Al-Aqsa Intifada*. The IDF soldier has been motivated traditionally to serve within the IDF and to protect the state of Israel and its citizens by the reality and perception that the IDF plays the most important role in not only protecting the territorial integrity and security of individual Israeli citizens, but also in maintaining the state's actual existence from Arab aggression. Thus, as the guardian of the Jewish collectivity's existence in the Middle East, the IDF soldier has often been motivated to serve and protect the state of Israel even when carrying out unconventional and morally questionable duties.

The view that Arab states posed, in fact, a strategic threat to Israel's existence through its conventional armies, due to the asymmetry of forces, resources, manpower and intentions between Israel and the Arab nations, was until very recently a clear component of the national security consensus. As such, national agreement on the need to allocate significant time and resources for the protection of the state, particularly through the establishment of *universal* military service was widely shared due to this collective perception that Israel faced an existential threat even during periods of relative quiet. Indeed, since the level of motivation is directly proportionate to the degree of importance of the individual and collective interest at risk, 'it is the perceived urgency of that interest that determines the price the individual and the entire polity are willing to pay in order to achieve it'.[44] The fact that Israelis saw – and many still see today – their existence at stake, played and still plays a significant factor in their motivation to both serve and fight within the IDF.

Although guerrilla and terrorist attacks were considered a major irritation to Israeli security, they were not considered existential, that is 'basic' security, threats. In any case, because they were seen as part of the greater Arab campaign to destroy Israel they were dealt with various hard-hitting COIN strategies that often resulted in the disproportionate use of punitive force. Such operations received the full support of the Israeli population as terrorist attacks caused significant disruption and fear to Israeli civilian life.

However, as shall be discussed below, the view that Palestinian insurgency was a threat to Israel's existence due to the intercommunal nature of the conflict was propounded adamantly once the *Likud* government,[45] led by Menachem Begin and influenced heavily by Ariel Sharon, came to power in 1977. Any major low-intensity violence carried out by the Palestinians, particularly within the Territories, would be deemed as an existential threat. Such an outlook lowered the threshold for Israel's decision to retaliate and use major force against Palestinian insurgency not only during the Begin era (1977–83), but also during the *Al-Aqsa Intifada*. It also influenced the combat motivation of most of the IDF, despite the domestic controversy surrounding the ideologically biased perception of low-intensity insurgency (particularly terrorism) as an existential threat.

Many within the IDF, given their militaristic viewpoint, came to accept the view that Palestinian terror and guerrilla warfare posed an existential threat to Israel. This was in spite of the fact that, for the most part, such tactics were used by the Palestinians as a means to gain statehood within the Territories, the maintenance of which, over the years following 1967, eroded Israel's national security consensus. This erosion in the national security consensus brought about an increase in conscientious objector cases amongst IDF personnel over the last two decades.

Mission accomplishment

In any case, at the primary or individual level there are other factors that provide soldiers with high levels of morale and combat motivation. In fact, these are, 'for each soldier, a goal, a role and a reason for self-confidence'.[46] Rather than fighting for a very abstract cause, the soldier needs to achieve specific and tangible goals in order to maintain high combat motivation. This is why in the IDF's case the operational objectives take precedence over the manner in which operations are carried out. Indeed, as shall be seen below, the IDF's traditional emphasis on directive control (i.e. mission command) gives, in principle, subordinates right down the chain of command the greatest possible freedom of action to achieve a mission's objectives.

In combat operations, the criteria for judging whether or not the goal has been obtained are often relatively unambiguous – 'conquer the objective and stop enemy troops from advancing. However, [in operations other than war] it is often very difficult to understand what constitutes mission success'.[47] One former IDF commander has stated that:

> Then the target was a hill, a fortification, an enemy military base and the cost was measured in terms of casualties, loss of weapons, etc. Today the definition of objective has been expanded to include such intangibles as image and public opinion.[48]

26 *Combat motivation*

Problems regarding the actual nature of the IDF's mission and its overall objectives in the context of its COIN campaign will be explored later on in the book.

Self-confidence

Furthermore, a soldier's role and self-confidence are both developed through the extensive training the soldier is put through as well as the combat experience gained through the various (successful) battles or military operations, which in the Israeli soldier's case has been a life-long and extensive endeavour. Thus, training is a key ingredient to increasing or maintaining the combat morale both at the individual and unit levels, because it is there that unit cohesion is built before combat troops go on any military operation. Marshall has noted that 'tactical unity of men working in combat will be in the ratio of their knowledge and sympathetic understanding of one another'.[49]

Extensive training also averts the soldier from losing control of his martial faculties and duties when the extensive chaos created by the fog of war ensues. Such training needs, however, are becoming more difficult to satisfy for reservist-intensive armies, such as the IDF, which train one month a year, if at all. This is due to the fact that the technical and interpersonal skills needed by the twenty-first century soldier in order to carry out sub-conventional military operations within urban or other civilian scenarios are much greater. Unless conscripts, reservists and professionals are thoroughly trained, they will lack the necessary military skills to tackle such scenarios, but also the necessary cohesion, which is so vital when coming to grips with the moral dilemmas of operating in civilian settings. The continuous state of alert and fatigue as well as the constant friction between soldier and the Palestinian population, could affect the soldier negatively through attrition and burnout and possibly lead to his moral deterioration. The book will attempt to overview such instances of friction in the latter chapters and see to what extent they have affected the forces involved in day-to-day operations within the Territories.

Moreover, whilst underlining the seriousness of conscientious objection in Israel, consideration is given to how the majority of its armed forces involved on the ground coped with military duty in the Territories and carried out their duties earnestly. The IDF's cultural ethos of *bitsuism* strongly influenced the way soldiers and officers perceived the conflict – as militarily necessary in the first *Intifada* and as an existential threat in the second *Intifada*. The desire to perform duties in the Territories 'militarily' even when on constabulary duty reduced the dissonance between what troops were trained to do (i.e. fight wars) and what they actually did (i.e. control the local population). As Eyal Ben-Ari shows, this was particularly the case during the first *Intifada* when the asymmetry between IDF and Palestinian violence was great.[50]

In spite of the controversial phenomenon of conscientious objection during the current *Al-Aqsa Intifada*, the perception of Palestinian violence as an existential threat galvanised the majority of the IDF forces to conduct counter-terror and COIN operations, which often went beyond the call of duty and occasionally caused significant collateral damage as well as instances of excessive violence that resulted in counterproductive strategic results.

Nevertheless, the IDF has continued to sustain this emphasis on tactical hyper-initiative that has often been strategically counterproductive particularly during the initial phases of each *Intifada*. Rather than limiting violence, reprisal operations escalated the Israeli–Palestinian conflict. As will be argued in the book the IDF's tradition of *bitsuism* together with its inability to adapt its strategic doctrine, order of battle and use of personnel to the challenges of low-intensity warfare have made it quite difficult to achieve a victory in the Israeli–Palestinian conflict. Until a political option was seriously pursued with the Palestinians both with the Oslo Accord during the first *Intifada* and with the Road Map for Peace initiative during the current conflict the constant use of the military to quell Palestinian insurgency led to a situation of attrition rather than its actual defeat.

3 Political–military relations

The Israeli security doctrine as well as the IDF's operational structure developed in order to tackle the various types of threat Israel faced over time. Such developments were significantly shaped by the founding father of the modern state of Israel, David Ben-Gurion. This chapter will demonstrate the extent to which Ben-Gurion helped mould the IDF into a *professional* army, established its basic institutional arrangements, and influenced the nature of Israeli political–military relations. In order to analyse Ben-Gurion's influence on Israeli political–military relations as well as their evolution, this chapter will provide an analytical account, as well as certain historical and descriptive examples which underline the dynamism of these political–military relations. The need to consider these political–military relations before exploring the evolution of Israeli national security doctrine is crucial, because according to Moshe Lissak, 'all security doctrines ... have implications regarding ... relations between military and political elites..., especially when the military leadership itself is primarily responsible for initiation and formulation of the security doctrine'.[1]

The birth of the IDF

Although the starting point when studying the IDF focuses on the pre-independence security structures, because 'the modern army of Israel [in effect] sprang from the security structures of the pre-independence pioneer movement of the Jews in Palestine' at the beginning of the twentieth century,[2] due to space limitations, this chapter will focus on political–military relations in Israel following the establishment of the IDF in 1948. Suffice to say that David Ben-Gurion since the early 1930s played a crucial role in developing the pre-state *Hagana* (Defence) militia and eventually the IDF into a professional military subject to the guidance and control of the civilian political echelons.[3]

War preparations before Israel's declaration of independence and the 1948 Arab–Israeli War brought about, in fact, the development of a much stronger and more centralised military machine. Shortly after the declaration of the state of Israel's establishment, the government approved on 26 May 1948 the 'Israel Defence Forces Order'. The Israel Defence Forces Order helped set up the legal foundations for the *Zva Hagana le-Israel*, the 'Israel Defence Forces' (*Tsahal* – IDF), which prohibited 'the establishment and maintenance of any armed force other than the Israel Defence Forces'. This was essential, according to Ben-Gurion, because it would guarantee 'a unified army ... answering to one government and one supreme command'.[4]

By disbanding the pre-state right-wing *Lehi* (*Lohamei Herut Israel* – Fighters for the Freedom of Israel) and *Etzel* (*Irgun Tsvai Leumi* – National Military Organisation) militias, the *Hagana, and* the elite *Palmah* (*Plugot Mahatz* – Assault Units) as well as subordinating the IDF military command to the government's political direction by the end of the War of Independence, Ben-Gurion was able to create the semblance of a professional army that was responsible to the government alone and not to this or that political faction. Ben-Gurion, indeed, defined the professional and national role and standing of the military on 27 October 1949 in the following manner:

> The military does not determine the policy, the regime, the laws and the government-rulings in the state. The army itself does not even determine its own structure, regulations and ways of operation, nor does it decide upon peace and war. The military is the executive branch, the defence and security of the Israeli government.... The military is subordinate to the government, and is no more than the executor of the political line and the orders received from the legislative and executive institution of the state.[5]

In order to implement clear civilian control of the IDF, after the establishment of the state, the MOD was given the responsibility, amongst other things, for purchasing and producing weaponry required by the IDF. This responsibility included the planning of the defence budget and controlling defence expenditure, researching and developing new weaponry, managing the IDF's manpower requirements and for helping with the state's settlement and development efforts. The ministry's director general was independent of the army, directly appointed and subordinate to the defence minister.

Furthermore, the fact that Ben-Gurion was both the Prime and Defence Minister helped him direct the structure and ethos of the IDF and of Israel's security approach as well as the overall composition of the defence economy. Ben-Gurion 'assumed the policy-making function of "head of war" whilst [the IDF] Chief of Staff was delegated the operational function of maintaining and training the army'.[6] Such direction influenced, in turn, the nature of political–military relations in Israel, as shall be seen below.

The IDF as nation-builder

Ben-Gurion did not view the military only as a security provider. The fledgling Israeli state needed all the help it could get in order to develop its infrastructure. The armed forces took up many extra-military functions, 'because they [were] thought to have the suitable organizational capabilities, the necessary manpower, and the technology to carry out ... "national tasks" most effectively'.[7] Ben-Gurion stated at the *Knesset* (Israeli parliament), in June 1950, that the IDF 'must be not only a fortress of security for the state, but because of the historic reality of ingathering the dispersed Jewish communities, the army must be the crucible of national unity'.[8] Immigration at this time was of particular significance.[9] One way of achieving greater national cohesion within such a diverse immigrant community was by introducing educational activities run almost exclusively by the IDF for immigrants and eventually for all serving officers.[10] Further education opportunities were gradually introduced in order to 'develop and nurture [the] soldier who [would have to] not only be a good soldier, but also a good citizen and a better person and human being'.[11]

Ben-Gurion believed that it was essential for Israel's existence to create facts on the ground by building new settlements, particularly in the newly acquired territories. 'The term "conquering the wasteland" [*keebush hashmama*], common in the 1950s, was assigned to the immense project of land settlement.'[12] The military also played a large part in the settlement effort by teaching the necessary agricultural skills to members of a special pioneering military unit, known as *Nahal* (*Noar Halutzi Lohem* – 'Fighting Pioneer Youth').[13]

Mamlachtiut

As an instrument for building the nation, Ben-Gurion made sure that the IDF was the first institution to undergo the process of nationalisation or *mamlachtiut* ('statism'). This process led in general to an increasing formalisation and bureaucratisation of the nascent state institutions, which previously had derived their power and legitimacy from political parties and voluntary groups, which assisted them in establishing the *Yishuv*. According to Ben-Gurion's view, the three main characteristics that encapsulated the principle of *mamlachtiut* were: 'the general interest, compulsion and independence'.[14] According to this principle, the state's citizens were obliged to give precedence to state interests over particularistic concerns; their participation in the process of state-building was obligatory, particularly in the military sphere; and such interests and participation were simultaneously the responsibility of all citizens in order to maintain the existence and independence of the state of Israel. Consequently, the responsibility of running the state was transferred from the parties and the pre-state organisations to the state itself and to *all* its citizens.

Due to the fact that the concept of *mamlachtiut* entailed the depoliticisation of the armed forces, various legal initiatives were carried out in order to uphold it. The *Knesset* enacted on 8 September 1949 the 'Defence Service Law', which established the three-tier military service system of conscript, permanent and reserve military service. Despite the introduction of universal conscription Ben-Gurion clearly stated in early 1950 that 'the IDF, although maintaining strict discipline ... and being based on [conscription], is basically built on pioneering voluntarism' and defined 'the permanent army [cadres as] an army of volunteers'.[15] Despite the huge penalties a draftee must suffer if non-compliant to the military service call-up, draftees at the age of 17 still receive until today a communiqué, which tries to impress upon them the *voluntary* nature of military service. The communiqué, in fact, reads: 'Draftees are called to the flag according to the law but come as volunteers.'[16]

Notwithstanding the huge personal sacrifices that conscript and reserve military service entailed, the majority of the population accepted it because of the perceived Arab threat that Israeli society believed it faced, especially in relation to the asymmetry of forces that existed between Israel and its Arab neighbours. Moreover, the general perception that military service was based on universal conscription made sure that Israeli civilians shared such a burden equally and, thus, helped avoid any resentment towards any free-riders on the part of those carrying the defence burden.

The only major exemption from military conscription that Ben-Gurion allowed was for those *Haredim* (Ultra-Orthodox Jews) who were devoted to the full-time study of the Jewish Bible in the *Yeshivot* (Jewish Rabbinical academies of higher learning), and for religious women. Given their small numbers at first, such an exemption was not contested. However, as we shall see further on in the book, with the growing inequality of military service and of the reservist burden since the early 1990s, complaints and calls for their conscription from those serving increased. The Israeli Arab minority was exempted from serving in the military for security reasons.

In addition, the burden of military service was accepted by the majority of the Israeli population, because of the rewards that such service brings about. Contributing to the state's security 'defines the extent to which an individual is "in" the social-evaluative system of Israel'.[17] In fact, due to the centrality of security in Israeli political, social and evaluative discourse, 'participation in security tasks, especially in combat roles, is itself a reward since individuals partake in the "charisma" of the central value system', embodied by *bitchonism* ('securitist orientation'), which is explained below. Moreover, it is 'the state itself, through the army, [which has] constructed [the security] "consensus"' and continues to perpetuate it through every generation via military service.[18]

Consequently, the level and extent to which one participates in defending Israel determines one's socio-economic and political status: the greater the effort the more likely one will be at the centre of the Israel value system. Generally speaking, the closer one served to combat or elite units and the greater the rank one achieved during military service, the greater the chance he (and to a lesser extent she) had in moving up the Israeli socio-economic ladder following conscript or regular service. Ben-Gurion and his successors encouraged this by rewarding the military elite with prestigious post-retirement employment posts within government or other prestigious state institutions as shall be seen below.

Political–military relations

The 1949 Security Service Law allowed army personnel to be members of political parties, but did not allow them to engage in active politics. The 1951 *Knesset* Elections Bill restricted election propaganda in army barracks and its 1958 amendment, furthermore, called for the resignation of senior officers wanting to stand for election 100 days prior to an election. Despite this, party meddling and participation in all spheres of the state did not cease.

Although Ben-Gurion's rhetoric spoke of the need for the army to be *super partes* and subject to civilian control, he, with the cooperation of his party, worked ceaselessly and secretively to dominate the security sphere by appointing politically sympathetic officers within the IDF and likeminded bureaucrats in the Defence Ministry. Ben-Gurion, furthermore, fully exploited his powerful position to exercise political patronage for the purpose of carrying out his plans of *depoliticising* the armed forces and of carrying out the reforms necessary for a second round of war with Israel's Arab enemies. What 'depoliticising' actually entailed was the staffing of the armed forces with sympathisers of Ben-Gurion's *Mapai* (*Mifleget Poalei Eretz Israel* – Land of Israel Worker's Party) and of his policies in particular. In fact, 'the civilian departments of the burgeoning Defence Ministry in the early days were deliberately staffed by *Mapai* or apolitical (but personal) loyalists referred to as *mishelanu*, or "one of ours"'.[19] Ben-Gurion, furthermore, took particular care in his chief appointments of Chief of Staff (COS), Head of Operations and Head of the Manpower Branch, who respectively had the crucial responsibilities of implementing the general strategic, operational and personnel set-up of the IDF.[20]

Obviously, such activities persuaded military personnel that in order to progress in the military or find meaningful employment after leaving the military, it would be wise to support *Mapai* in exchange for its largesse. Indeed, finding meaningful employment after a military career in the IDF was particularly crucial, because of the IDF's policy of high officer turnover – also known as the 'purge' system – which deliberately limited the number of years an officer could serve in the IDF. Ben-Gurion, with the assistance of the then COS Moshe Dayan, developed this system with the aim of maintaining the IDF leadership full of young, innovative and daring officers who would strive to enhance the IDF's standard of excellence. Such a turnover system was also set up so as to preclude the development of any corporatist tendencies and, hence, to preserve the IDF's ethos and constitution as a politically neutral and professional 'people's army'.

Consequently, most career officers retired by their early to mid-forties and were encouraged to start a second civilian career.[21] Due to the fact that career officers knew this to be an unshakeable reality they made extensive efforts to sustain formal and informal contacts with the political, public and private sector elites who would eventually offer high-level employment on the basis of such elite networking acquaintances as well as on the basis of the military elite's managerial credentials and overall charismatic popularity. Moshe Lissak and Daniel Maman demonstrated the importance of such networks by carrying out a comprehensive research on 120 members of the military elite (rank of Colonel and above) who were discharged between January 1973 and January 1983. They showed how crucial their relationships to the political, public and private sector elites were in influencing their success of gaining employment after retirement from the military. More astoundingly, Lissak and Maman found that many of the generals' relationships with the civilian elite were 'traceable to shared military service, rather than to their positions in an elite' *per se*.[22] Ultimately,

> The openness of the communication channels between the [military and civilian] elites ensured continued civilian control of the military elite and [functioned] as a safeguard against the formation of a military clique ... [because it helped] foster awareness among senior officers in uniform that the channels of military–civilian communication are open, thereby thwarting any tendency within the military to insulate itself...[23]

Furthermore, the civilian influence of reservists is dominant. The fact that the IDF is constituted by two-thirds of reservists and that these reservists are in constant contact with the much smaller professional cadre prevent it from becoming corporatist and distanced from civil society. Although the professional cadre works within the military framework and workspace, their spatial and ideological distance from civil society is minimal. Due to the fact, for example, that professional officers do not live in barracks or bases (except when on operational duty), but are fully integrated in civilian neighbourhoods, reduces the physical and psychological barriers that other armies tend to develop.

The 'parachuting' of generals into government and politics

Another practice, which Ben-Gurion's *Mapai* established during the early 1950s, was the 'parachuting' of retired generals into *Mapai*-led successive governments. For example, when Yigal Allon, the youngest general in the IDF was demobilised in 1949, he was elected to the *Knesset* on the *Adhut Haavoda* (Unity of Labour) list in 1955 and in 1961 was appointed Labour Minister by Ben-Gurion. Moshe Carmel, another general, released from the army in 1950, was elected to the *Knesset* on the same list in 1955 and was subsequently appointed Transport Minister by Prime Minister Moshe Sharett. Lt. Gen. Moshe Dayan, released in 1958, was elected to the *Knesset* in 1959 on the *Mapai* list and was appointed Agriculture Minister. In the subsequent decade, there was no significant further entry of IDF officers into politics, but shortly after the Six Day War the custom was readopted.

The practice of 'parachuting' generals into government, and in politics in general, became especially ubiquitous after the lightning victory of the 1967 Six Day War. The prestige of the IDF and its commanders was at its historical zenith. Politicians, consequently, wanted to capitalise on generals' electoral and charismatic assets. Prime Minister Golda Meir not only maintained in her successive governments Moshe Dayan, Yigal Allon and Col. Pinhas Sapir, but also appointed Haim Bar-Lev as Minister of Trade and Industry shortly after retiring as the IDF COS.[24] However, the most outstanding historical example of the phenomenon of 'parachuting' occurred in 1969 when Ezer Weizman, a former air force commander and IDF chief of operations, was appointed within 24 hours of his official retirement from the IDF as the Minister of Transport by *Herut*, a right-wing coalition partner of Golda Meir's government.

Other parties were also keen to adopt the policy of political recruitment and 'parachuting' of generals for the purpose of politically cashing in on the quasi-mythological popularity of the Six Day War veterans. They did so in order to present their party as the ultimate expert, in and guarantor of, security at a time when security had become even more central in Israeli public opinion and political discourse due to the War of Attrition (1969–70). Even after the debacle of the 1973 War and the consequent gradual erosion of the IDF's status in Israeli society due to the IDF's intelligence mishap prior to the conflict, amongst other things, political parties continued to recruit former military professionals.

When the *Likud* won the 1977 elections, Menachem Begin at once surrounded himself with former generals, because he was still viewed by many as lacking legitimacy due to his party's lack of governing experience and lack of military officers within its ranks. He therefore appointed Moshe Dayan, a member of the Labour faction, to the Cabinet as Foreign Minister, even though he did not require his vote to obtain a coalition majority. He offered Ezer Weizman and Ariel Sharon respectively, the Defence and Agriculture portfolios. Moreover, when the Democratic Move for Change joined Begin's government, Lt. Gen. Yigal Yadin became Deputy Prime Minister, and Maj. Gen. Meir Amit, Transport Minister. 'These former generals, most of whom had come from the very heart of the Labor movement ... accorded Begin and his government the legitimacy they lacked.'25

Lieutenant Generals Ehud Barak, Amnon Lipkin-Shahak and Shaul Mofaz are the most recent examples of top military personnel being 'parachuted' into the inner circles of government shortly after retiring from their military careers. Shaul Mofaz, in fact, almost five months after retirement, was appointed in November 2002 by Sharon as Defence Minister without either being a *Likud* member or member of the *Knesset*. Such appointments have in recent years created a certain amount of wariness on the part of, mostly left-wing, politicians who see the immediate co-option of generals into government posts as anachronistic and undemocratic.

During Shaul Mofaz's oath of office ceremony, on 4 November 2002, MK Tamar Gozansky of the left-wing *Hadash* party said, 'we are sick of generals, one after another. Enough is enough.' In addition, *Meretz* leader Yossi Sarid stated that 'in "normal countries chiefs of staff are not appointed as defence minister" to ensure that the country does not appear to be run by a junta'.26 The controversy surrounding this latest 'lightning' appointment of a senior retired IDF officer led finally in July 2005 to the approval of legislation, proposed by *Likud* MK Yuval Steinitz, Chairman of the Foreign Affairs and Defence Committee, that would prevent a Maj. Gen. or Lt. Gen. from retiring from military service and immediately getting a government position. Senior military figures would have to wait at least two years before running for the *Knesset* or for prime minister. Its approval led Steinitz to state that 'a two-year cooling off period is a blessing to Israeli democracy, on the one hand, and a blessing to the IDF, on the other hand, because it stops, or at least slows down the politicisation of the senior officer ranks in the military and security services'.27

After almost 50 years of political appointments of high-ranking retired IDF officers, Israeli politicians have come to the conclusion that such appointments run the risk of politicising even further security decision-making within the IDF at a time when the national security consensus regarding the future status of the Territories has become highly controversial and fraught with uncertainty.28

Ben-Gurion's security imperative

Ben-Gurion's blatant political activism within Israel's security structures between 1949 and 1965 was due to the fact that, since the first cabinet was formed in 1949, he laid down two conditions for participation in any of his coalitions: Cabinet decisions had to be passed by majority vote, and all coalition partners were collectively responsible for all cabinet decisions. Hence, these two principles made sure that 'a negative vote or abstention [in the *Knesset*], without prior cabinet approval, made it possible for the cabinet to force the resignation of the offending minister' and could lead to the break up of the coalition government itself.29 Such possibilities enabled

Ben-Gurion and future prime ministers, particularly those such as Menachem Begin and Ariel Sharon, to keep a tight leash on the ministers participating in the various government coalitions, both within and without their own party.

Moreover, Israel's perception of being under a constant state of siege gave Ben-Gurion ample reasons for his freedom of action and ability to influence security decision-making and policy. Ben-Gurion was, in fact, able to exploit Israel's *bitchonist* ('securitist') orientation. According to Baruch Kimmerling:

> The major premises of this orientation are that the Jewish state is involved in a battle for survival with its Arab neighbors and that a major military defeat would mean its annihilation. The primary means to prevent this destruction is maintenance of absolute and permanent Israeli military superiority.... The Israeli state is regarded as the ultimate authority for determining the organisation, location, duration of [the military].[30]

Anything that dealt with security, which was open to interpretation, could be co-opted by the inner circle of the government, which in military affairs was personified by Ben-Gurion. Moreover, plenty more was put under the security umbrella, because Ben-Gurion 'perceived the term security in its analytic rather than in its spatial sense. The security sphere, for him, included not only military organisations, but also anything associated with the survival, defence and development of Israel.'[31] This very pervasive 'securitist' orientation is one of the conspicuous features of Israeli society, which Uri Ben-Eliezer defines as a 'nation in arms'. According to Ben-Eliezer, a clear attribute of a 'nation in arms' is, in fact:

> Cooperation between the military and political echelons. This is based on a common view that political problems have to be solved by force and on a tendency to see the military route as the preferred and most efficient way to solve conflicts and disputes among nations.[32]

As Uri Ben-Eliezer demonstrates in *The Making of Israeli Militarism*, the creation of a 'nation-in-arms' – which is characterised by a blurring of the distinction between army, politics and society – in Israel during the 1950s established a working relationship between the military, the political echelons and society, whereby a significant portion of the state's human and material resources were mobilised for military purposes. Moreover, the 'securitist', or as Ben-Eliezer states 'cultural militarism' (the propensity by the *whole* of society to use the military for solving diplomatic and political problems), enabled the IDF to exercise significant influence on security-related decision-making matters without it having to intervene directly into politics or carry out a military putsch.[33]

Even foreign policy was seen as secondary to defence policy and, thus, fell quite often under the remit of the defence minister, his ministry officials and the upper IDF echelons. For example, during the preparations with France and Britain leading up to the 1956 Suez War, COS Moshe Dayan and MOD Director General Shimon Peres were the main diplomatic negotiators, as opposed to Foreign Minister Moshe Sharett. Senior military officers often joined and substantially influenced crucial diplomatic negotiations during the 1974 and 1975 disengagement agreements and in the 1990s during the Israeli–Palestinian Oslo Peace Process, because of the security implications stemming from such agreements.

Indeed, due to the lack of civilian strategic planning capabilities in Israel, the IDF's Strategic Planning Division as well as the Military Intelligence Division, have traditionally played a central role in the political–security decision-making processes of Israeli politicians. The IDF Military Intelligence Division, in particular, has been not only Israel's main information-gathering body responsible also for analysing Israel's strategic situation, but it has also been 'the centre of strategic and indeed political thinking in Israel's policy making process'.[34]

During the Oslo process the IDF was heavily involved in the policy-making process as well as in the actual negotiations with Palestinian security and political leaders. Prime Minister Yitzhak Rabin, for example, appointed Maj. Gen. Amnon Lipkin-Shahak, deputy COS, to lead the delegation to the diplomatic negotiations with the Palestinians. Two other generals, moreover, were appointed to head two of the delegation's subcommittees. Maj. Gen. Uzi Dayan, the IDF's Head of Strategic Planning, led the military subcommittee whilst the IDF's coordinator of activities in the Territories, Maj. Gen. Danny Yatom, led the subcommittee for civilian affairs.[35] Position papers were drafted by the Strategic Planning Division, approved by the chief of staff and became recommendations put forward to the political leadership echelon.

The Defence Ministry has often dictated foreign policy sometimes by pre-empting the Foreign Ministry's diplomatic efforts with hasty military action. For instance, when David Kimche retired after six years of service as Director General of the Foreign Ministry in 1986, he 'showed how much he resented the way the Defence Ministry dictated foreign policy' and cited two noteworthy examples of such interference: the first was when Israel bombed the *Osiraq* Iraqi nuclear reactor in 1981; no one at the ministry knew about it. The second case was the Lebanon invasion 'in which he said the Foreign Ministry had been excluded from the planning and was never asked about policy or information control'.[36]

Thus, the security sphere has not been subject to the same 'set of considerations, norms, and game rules that were common practice in all other public fields'. Ben-Gurion believed that 'professional considerations only, and not political ones, would determine defence policy, and defence matters would be under the jurisdiction of professionals only – the military command'.[37] Ben-Gurion's decision to assign defence matters *in strictu sensu* into the hands of the military command, whilst maintaining the civilian echelon's formal primacy over defence policy, was a way of avoiding the direct involvement of the military in the nation's political realm or the actual seizure of power by the military.

Nominal civilian control of the military

In spite of Ben-Gurion's overall strategic oversight of the military, substantial freedom of manoeuvre was left in the hands of the military echelon. This was possible because of Ben-Gurion's confidence in his military subordinates; after all, he had handpicked them since the IDF's establishment. Such freedom of manoeuvre was possible because of the weak political oversight of the military. In reality, in spite of the fact that civilian, i.e. political, control of the military was a core principle of Ben-Gurion's conception of a professional army, Ben-Gurion made sure that such control was only nominal in order for his personal influence on the military to remain undisturbed.

Hence, Ben-Gurion made sure that parliamentary control of the military, via its Foreign Affairs and Defence Committee was formal rather than real – its decisions were not binding on the military, especially in regard to the defence budget. In addition, the nature of the government's, and in particular the defence minister's, institutional relationship with and actual control of the IDF General Staff was purposely left ambiguous, and thus, hinged on the personal rapport between the incumbents of such bodies. Consequently, the lack of civilian oversight and the 'monopoly of strategic planning by the planning branch of the IDF General Staff' led the political leadership to increasingly rely on the military's strategic assessments and options.[38]

Such ambiguity and reliance on the IDF was acceptable so long as Ben-Gurion remained at the helm of the political and security establishment, because of his obsessive focus on security and overbearing charisma, which limited the IDF's capacity to take any autonomous or conflicting decisions. However, this state of affairs would prove highly problematic when less appealing and powerful figures took over Ben-Gurion's job. They had to deal with an army whose prestige and, thus, self-assertiveness increased, especially after the lightning victory of the Six Day War in 1967.[39]

So, without the appropriate political oversight mechanisms in place, once Ben-Gurion was out of the political equation, military activism and consequent tensions between the military and political command echelons were bound to occur, particularly during times of crises when the IDF was needed even more by the state to reduce the level of violence on the ground as was the case during the 1967, 1973 and 1982 Wars.

The Six Day War 'waiting' period

Prime Minister Levi Eshkol was at the centre of the Six Day War waiting period crisis, because he was seen as indecisive by the military during the three weeks prior to the conflict.[40] On three separate occasions relations between the Eshkol government and IDF generals were significantly strained, because of Eshkol's 'waiting' policy. The first incident occurred on 25 May when Prime Minister Eshkol paid a visit to the Southern Command with Yigal Allon and met the commanding officer, Brig. Gen. Yeshiyahu Gavish and the three division commanders, Brig. Gens. Ariel Sharon, Israel Tal and Avraham Yaffe. During the meeting a sharp altercation occurred between the government ministers and the officers who overtly questioned the cabinet's decision to delay further the order to commence an attack. On 28 May when the government had decided to postpone the decision to go to war, COS Yitzhak Rabin asked Eshkol to justify his decision to the high command. At the meeting some of the generals used language unsuitable for military personnel subject to civilian control. The third confrontation occurred when IDF Chief of Operations, Brig. Gen. Ezer Weizman went into the Prime Minister's office, ripped off his rank insignia and threatened his resignation if Israel did not go to war immediately.[41]

As the possibility of a conflict loomed and Eshkol's government continued to waver, public demands from the IDF leadership and eventually from the Israeli public for the replacement of Eshkol by Moshe Dayan as defence minister – given his well-known hawkish reputation – became more vocal. The generals were for the first time in Israeli history openly discussing the political appointment of politicians to the government in power; this was something previously unthinkable. They were also openly discussing and defining the political–strategic objectives of the Six Day War as they went along. Despite the gravity of such actions, the overwhelming victory silenced any doubts as to the political or legal appropriateness of such a popular plebiscite-like appointment by the military and the general public and of the generals' influence on the overall decision-making process. Further encroachments were more than likely to occur, as they did during the subsequent 1973 War.

1973: the battle of the generals

During the *Yom Kippur* War, civil control of the military turned full-circle due to the fact that many generals-turned-politicians after the Six Day War were now called back to military posts in the field. Indeed, after two days of disastrous tactical choices, Moshe Dayan decided to appoint Lt. Gen. (Res.) Haim Bar-Lev, a former chief of staff (1968–72), member of the ruling Labour Alignment and Minister of Trade and Industry, as the Southern Command Commander. However, the fact that Bar-Lev had had professional and personal disagreements with Sharon over the nature of the Bar-Lev defence system to be implemented in the Sinai shortly after the Six Day War complicated things still further.[42]

Political (and personal) rivalry between Sharon and Bar-Lev overtook professional–military considerations as the war progressed. Even Sharon's relations with his immediate superior, Maj. Gen. Shmuel Gonen, were complicated by the fact that, until a few months prior to the conflict, Sharon had led the Southern Command for three years. When he was called up on *Yom Kippur* he had to serve on his old front under his former direct subordinate Gonen. Relations between Sharon and his superiors became so acrimonious that Sharon was quoted as saying to Bar-Lev during the conflict itself, 'I am commander of 15,000 troops and I have no time to screw you now because I have to screw the Egyptians. I have no time to fight with you politically, but when the war is over you will have to wear helmets.'[43]

Sharon found himself repeatedly disobeying orders and justifying such insubordination by declaring that the orders handed down to him were politically motivated. On 20 October, for example, when ordered by Gonen to recapture a strongpoint on the Suez Canal, Sharon went over the heads of his superiors by appealing to Defence Minister Dayan to cancel the order; Dayan conceded. Moreover, the political row continued between Sharon and Bar-Lev after the war. Despite such insubordination, Sharon justified his actions in a *Ma'ariv* interview in January 1974 by stating that:

> Yes, even in the last war. I tried to carry out instructions.... When I receive an order I treat it according to three values: the first, and most important, is the good of the state.... The second value is my obligation to my subordinates, and the third value is my obligation to my superiors. I wouldn't change the priority of these three values in any way.[44]

Obviously, Ben-Gurion's conception, mentioned above, of the army being 'subordinate to the government, and is no more than the executor of the political line and the orders received from the legislative and executive institution of the state' was substantially discredited by some generals who, during the 1973 War, judged themselves to know better than politicians what was best for the state. Such violations had to be resolved.

The Agranat report

The Agranat Commission was set up in order to investigate the reasons for the heavy setbacks Israel suffered during the initial stages of the conflict as well as the various instances of misconduct carried out during the war, particularly in regard to disobeying orders. The commission submitted a report in April 1974 that led to the resignation of the COS David Elazar and other senior officers.

The report, amongst other things, found that in the opening days, strategic and field intelligence was almost absent,[45] that there was a general lack of discipline in the ranks and that mobilisation took longer than it should have taken. Maj. Gen. Zeira, the Chief of Israeli Military Intelligence, Zeira's deputy, Brig. Gen. Aryeh Shalev and Lt. Col. David Gedaliah, Chief Intelligence Officer of the Southern Command were consequently discharged.[46] The Agranat report particularly displayed concern regarding what it called 'non-compliance of operational orders' particularly in connection with the Southern Command, that is, the Command with most general-politicians.[47]

The Agranat report, more importantly, 'discovered that there [was] no clear definition of distribution of authorities, obligations, and responsibilities in matters of defence ... and of the relationship between the political leadership and the high command of the IDF'.[48] In order to obviate such confusion, the '1976 Basic Law: The Army' was legislated. It reiterated that 'the Army is subject to the authority of the Government' and that 'the Chief of the General Staff is subject to the authority of the Government and subordinate to the Minister of Defence'.[49] Despite the Agranat Commission report's stern warning regarding the lack of clear and delimited roles in matters relating to defence and the legislation of the '1976 Basic Law: The Army', other matters gained more prominence. The Agranat Commission's lack of criticism towards the political leadership echelons, which played a major role in the *Yom Kippur*'s debacle, became the centre of the public's attention and controversy.

The legislation did nothing to eliminate the confusion regarding civilian control over the military. The role, authority and responsibilities of the primary actors remained the same. That is, they remained subject to the personal make-up of the three major actors in the defence policy and decision-making sphere: the prime minister, the defence minister and the chief of staff.

Ariel Sharon and the 1982 Lebanon War

It was apparent that not delineating the level of civilian control over the military left political–military relations subject to interpretation as well as possible abuse from the military or political echelons. In the case of the Lebanon War, it was the civilian Defence Minister Sharon who took 'personal control of the entire strategic planning apparatus of the IDF and subjugated the military involvement in the formulation of national security policy to his own will'.[50] Sharon was, in fact, continuously breathing down COS Lt. Gen. Rafael Eitan's neck and frequently bypassing him in order to give direct orders to Eitan's subordinates. Similarly, COS Lt. Gen. Eitan (1978–83) was often blamed for acting the same way with Maj. Gen. Amir

Drori who, as Commander of the Northern Command, was responsible for conducting the campaign in Lebanon. Eitan was regularly seen riding along with his subordinate's spearhead units on the Lebanese battlefield. Many other cases of inter-rank command interference occurred during the Lebanon War.[51]

Such micro-management even from a highly regarded and experienced general such as Sharon could not be tolerated. Various attempts were made by the military to reduce Sharon's overbearing control during the conflict. For example, 'more than 100 top Israeli officers, including everyone above the rank of Brig. Gen., met behind closed doors with COS Rafael Eitan on 24 September [1982] to complain about Sharon'.[52] Such attempts proved unsuccessful because Sharon was able to conjure up almost full support from Begin's Cabinet, which lacked any other security 'heavyweights'. This was mostly done by presenting partial or even erroneous reports, which left most of the cabinet in the dark with respect to the conflict's ultimate goals and the costs entailed in order to achieve them. Although Sharon managed to deceive some of his cabinet colleagues, it was not done without causing substantial political controversy. Energy Minister Yitzhak Berman, for example, resigned three months after the invasion into Lebanon had commenced. Years later he recalled Sharon's manipulative strategy by testifying that:

> *We never discussed the final goals or the strategy of the war.* I resigned when I realized we were already in Beirut and had no idea where to go from there.... I reached the conclusion that the Cabinet was not receiving accurate or correct briefings.... Why weren't we informed in advance? [emphasis mine].[53]

Even Begin's over-reliance on Sharon's military expertise had a limit. Tired of Sharon's long sequence of unilateral military decisions and *fait accomplis* by August 1982, Begin vented his frustration at Sharon by saying at a government cabinet meeting, 'you are the government's representative to the army and not the army's representative to the government'.[54] The Lebanon War proved ultimately to be 'a colossal failure of civilian oversight of strategic planning'.[55] One man, with the collusion of COS Eitan, was able to drag Israel into one of its most politically and militarily costly wars without the full knowledge of the civilian leadership echelons.

New tensions between the civilian and military spheres

The various instances whereby the boundaries set up by Ben-Gurion between the civilian and military spheres were violated caused political–military crises that were manageable due to the resilience of the Israeli polity. Indeed, such crises never seriously put at risk the democratic nature or institutions of the Israeli state. The *bitchonist* consensus helped

Political–military relations 43

maintain a general balance between the tendency to over-militarise the Israeli polity or over-politicise the military sphere.

However, the explosion of the *Intifada* and the subsequent political and ideological controversies resulting from the increasingly costly continuation of the occupation, the gradual growth of socio-political schisms stemming from the Israeli–Palestinian peace process and the rebirth of the terrorism-based *Al-Aqsa Intifada* overstrained political–military relations in Israel. As shall be seen in the subsequent chapters drastic, and often eclectic, changes in Israeli–Palestinian relations since the mid-1980s have affected not only political–military relations, but have also significantly changed civil–military relations at the societal level. Such changes in turn have influenced the IDF.

As a matter of fact, organisational changes within the IDF, which have been brought about by the 'revolution in military affairs', the trend towards sub-conventional intercommunal warfare in the Israeli–Palestinian conflict and the growing desire of Israeli society for extra-security (post-military) needs at the expense of the security imperative, have augmented the possibility of tensions between the military and civilian spheres, which might have, in turn, impinged on the combat motivation and effectiveness of the IDF. Horowitz has emphasised three of such major sources of tension:

> 1. The tension between military professionalism, which is oriented toward segregation of the military from society and military participation in decision-making on issues pertaining to national security interests; 2. The rivalry over priorities in resource allocation between national security needs and domestic political demands; and 3. The incompatibility of military authoritarianism and of violence with the egalitarianism and pacifist tendencies prevalent in modern democratic societies.[56]

The following chapters will look, amongst other things, at how events over the last 15 years have affected the nature of political–military and civil–military relations and look at whether or not the sources of the tensions listed above have actually influenced the combat effectiveness and morale of the IDF. Before doing so, it is important to have a clear understanding of the Israeli national security doctrine, which has guided Israeli security decision-making and policy choices over the last 50 years.

4 National security doctrine

Despite the fact that 'the term "strategy" needs continual definition',[1] strategy, or security doctrine, is defined as 'the art of distributing and applying military means to fulfil the ends of policy'.[2] Furthermore, a security doctrine 'establishes the principles that guide the design of military force structure and operations, [which are used to link] defence policy and national strategy ... on the one hand, and the operational plans of the armed forces on the other'.[3] 'Policy, then, [should] permeate all military operations, [because it is] the political aim [which] remains the first consideration.'[4] Strategy is crucial in pursuing a state's political objectives through the use of the military instrument. Yet, in order to pursue such political objectives, it is not always necessary for a state to wield the military instrument by going to war. The threat of using the military instrument, whether explicit or implicit, is normally sufficient to obtain a state's foreign policy goals. Furthermore, other non-military coercive means are available.[5]

When analysing Israel's national security doctrine it is essential to understand that there is no *formal* doctrine in the sense of 'a close-knit, well-formulated aggregate of security principles' or in the sense of a binding, unitary and formal document.[6] Israel's security doctrine, in fact, is:

> In part an oral doctrine and in part a formal, written one. Its scattered contents [are] included in various laws; decisions by the *Knesset* (Parliament) and government; and standing orders, such as high command and General Staff directives and the training manuals used by the various arms of the Israel Defence Forces.[7]

Despite the fact that 'there has never been an official Israeli security doctrine',[8] and that it has been mostly 'the product of the knowledge gained through a process of trial and error' on the battlefield,[9] according to Maj. Gen. (Ret.) Israel Tal, 'the patterns of strategic thinking which serve as the basis for Israel's security concept were formulated for the most part in the period between the end of the War of Independence and the Sinai Campaign of 1956'.[10]

Israeli security doctrine assumptions

It was David Ben-Gurion's security assumptions that contributed most in establishing not only the foundations of Israel's national security doctrine, but also Israel's civil–military relations. Such security assumptions contributed profoundly to Israel's overall security-oriented culture (i.e. '*bitchonism*'). At the same time, 'the organizational culture of an army is a reflection of the nation from which it springs....' Hanson W. Baldwin notes that what he describes as a military philosophy 'grows from the minds and hearts, social mores and customs, traditions and environment of a people'.[11] With the exception of the Menachem Begin (1977–83) and Ariel Sharon eras (2001–present), such a security culture has for the most part remained intact and 'any changes [to it have been] more in the nature of glosses, amendments, and appendixes than qualitative or structural sea-changes'.[12]

Furthermore, the assumptions underlying Israel's national security doctrine have remained largely constant throughout Israel's long history of conflict with its Arab neighbours. These security assumptions, outlined by Ben-Gurion and shared by the majority of the Israeli population, played a crucial role not only in the development of the Israeli security doctrine, but also in helping successive Israeli governments justify the almost total mobilisation of the state's manpower and material resources for the purpose of providing security to its citizens both on a collective as well as individual level.

Existential threat

Ben-Gurion's first assumption was that in regard to the Arab–Israeli conflict the very existence of Israel was at stake. He, in fact, stated that:

> In our case it is not only a matter of securing our independence, our territory, borders, the regime – but securing our very physical existence. Our enemies do not conspire only against our territory and our independence; we should have no delusions in regard to this matter. They intend, as many of them have openly said, to throw us into the sea: put simply, to annihilate every Jew in the Land of Israel.[13]

Hence, all Israeli thought on national security starts from the principle that Israel is entangled in a conflict for its very survival. This consensus covers disparate beliefs and politics within Israel and affects every aspect of Israeli foreign and security policy decision-making. 'The threat to a state, as perceived by its population, is therefore of considerable significance in the development of conditions encouraging the formulation of a national security doctrine.'[14] Such doctrine, furthermore, is formed by internal political processes in which the state and society negotiate, under the limitations of the geo-strategic environment, over the extent of military participation required of the citizen.[15]

The pre-eminence of national survival as the essential goal of both military strategy and diplomacy is a given in Israeli policy and decision-making, due to the awareness that Israel is in an unending state of 'dormant war' even when it is momentarily not involved in actual hostilities. It has always been the belief of the top Israeli military and political echelons that 'Israel must deploy her forces so as to be able to hold her ground *in a state of no war and no peace* with alternating periods of tension and relaxation' [emphasis mine].[16] Thus, diplomacy is subordinate to strategy rather than vice versa. This is due to the fact that the menace to Israel's continued existence is perceived as being both perilous and looming. Such a rule was laid down by Ben-Gurion who stated that 'the minister of defence is authorized to determine defence policy, whilst the job of the foreign minister is to explain that policy'.[17]

For the Israeli political leadership, in fact, diplomacy is a means for the political handling of the Arab–Israeli conflict, a handling *always* based in any case on military–strategic calculations. This strategic-based perspective reveals a militaristic predisposition: making sure that military means – provided through large defence budgets – are sufficient for the Arab–Israeli conflict taking precedence over any real efforts to find instead a resolution to it, because 'Israel's independence and its continuing survival are bound up with the history [...] of the IDF'.[18] 'A closed tautological circle is thus created whose arguments feed on themselves. This justifies exploiting the military advantage to the hilt',[19] often at the expense of finding a political solution to the Arab–Israeli conflict, even though Israel has declared on innumerable occasions that it desires peace. Such peace, understandably, could not come at the expense of the state's and the individual's security. Pursuing any viable peace options with a very limited number of Arab states was not realistic for Israel until after the 1973 War.

The Israeli population's general perception of the Arab–Israeli conflict as existential has quite important consequences in terms of how the conflict must be solved or, at least, weathered.[20] The fact that the state of Israel was set up, indeed, to provide asylum and protection to the Jewish people led those responsible for security to render threats to the state of Israel equivalent to threats against the Jewish people as a whole. 'This reinforced the tendency to see the threat to the national collectivity as a physical threat to the individual.'[21] The perception of the conflict as being existential plays a very strong part in augmenting the IDF soldier's combat motivation as well as in facilitating the IDF reservist's decision – as reserve duty is officially and legally a *voluntary* convention – to continue training for war as well as serving one or more times a year within the reservist system for the sake of protecting Israel from any current, potential (or even imagined) threats.

The general acceptance and understanding by society, that military service is an essential element in the maintenance of Israel's security and existence as a state within the Middle East region, and that such service is supposed to be shared by most members of Israeli society, have been strong motivational factors. This is especially due to the case, as seen earlier, that the IDF was set up by Ben-Gurion to be a 'people's army', which would also have civic and nation-building functions.

Conventional – as well as non-conventional threats since the early 1980s – were dubbed as 'basic' or 'fundamental' security (*bitachon yisodi*) threats. Fundamental security threats became the main preoccupation of the Israeli security doctrine since its establishment. Lower-intensity type violence, such as guerrilla and terrorist activities were considered to be 'current security' (*bitachon shotef*) threats. 'Current security' threats were dealt with firmly by the IDF in order to maintain deterrent credibility. However, they were not deemed enough of a threat to distract considerably the IDF's focus on and preparation for conventional and, subsequently, unconventional threats (in terms of training, budgetary allocation, weapons procurement programmes, etc.). As a result, 'Israel's deterrent posture with respect to low-intensity conflict ... has been less precisely formulated.... To deter low-intensity threats Israel has adopted a strategy of lesser finesse by 'consistently promis[ing] to retaliate disproportionately'.[22]

Israeli counter-terrorism

Since its creation, the state of Israel has had to deal with waves of terrorist activity at its borders, in the Territories,[23] and inside Israel itself. Palestinian and other Arab *fedayeen* elements were intent in carrying out small-scale cross-border terror raids into Israel during the early 1950s. Indeed, 'in 1950 there were 50 civilian casualties, 97 the following year, and 182 in 1952'.[24] Such cross-border terror operations were carried out in order to cajole the IDF into retaliating. For the Palestinians such retaliation would hopefully, in turn, escalate tensions between Israel and its Arab terrorist-hosting neighbours to the point of bringing about a full-scale war, which would with any luck redress the Arab nations' and Palestinian people's defeat of 1948.

Israel initially attempted to impede such terror raids through diplomatic channels, using force solely to fend off attacks within its own territory. Yet, in 1953, when such actions proved fruitless, the Ben-Gurion Government authorised reprisal raids. According to Michael Walzer, these are 'appropriate to periods of insurgency, border strife, cease-fire, and armistice'.[25] Such reprisal raids were often carried out into neighbouring states. Their main rationale was that of deterring Arab governments from aiding and hosting any terrorist groups bent on attacking Israeli civilians and civilian installations. However, in 1955, it was clear to then COS Lt. Gen. Moshe Dayan, that:

48 *National security doctrine*

> We cannot guard every water pipeline from explosion and every tree from uprooting. We cannot prevent the murder of a worker in an orchard or a family in their beds. But it is in our power to set a high price on our blood, a price too high for the Arab community, the Arab army or the Arab government to think worth paying.[26]

Thus, from its inception, Israeli counter-terror policy was well aware that terrorism could not be fully eradicated. Counter-terrorism could only lower the effects of terror to a tolerable level whereby Israeli civil society could function normally, despite the grave risks it faced and still faces today. Such a limited counter-terror goal was due to the fact that Arab terror has predominantly been viewed by Israeli politicians and security officials as a tactical rather than strategic threat. For example, when addressing the *Knesset* on 21 October 1985, the late Defence Minister Yitzhak Rabin, stated that terrorism 'hurts, it is annoying and disruptive, but it does not constitute a threat to the country's very existence'.[27] Deterrence by punishment was the Israeli counter-terrorist method adopted during the early years of its fight against terror.[28] This method has not really changed since the early 1950s.

Despite the inability of terrorism to threaten the existence of Israel, the security establishment did not refrain from addressing the threat head-on. Since the 1950s, Israeli counter-terror operations have been motivated by three factors. First, they have been principally counterforce assaults on terrorist forces, centres and installations. Second, they have normally caused collateral damage given that terrorist bases have been commonly situated in civilian areas. Indeed, although Israel has often tried to reduce any collateral damage, it has argued that people living close to terrorist infrastructures and who back or tolerate terrorist operations must anticipate Israeli counter-terror attacks. According to Israeli policy-makers, the risk of collateral damage would possibly weaken the civilian population's desire to shelter, collaborate with terrorists or even tolerate the presence of terrorist organisations within their communities. Lastly, Israeli counter-terror attacks have normally been carried out in the sovereign territory of a neighbouring Arab state and have been planned to pressure the target state into withdrawing support for terror groups stationed within their territory.

By 1967 Israeli counter-terror policy was firmly established. It was generally defined as a strategy of retaliation and prevention based on deterrence. Counter-terror operations were generally reactive and between 1968 and 1969 were primarily focused on the Palestinian Liberation Organisation (PLO) bases formed in areas bordering the Israeli–Jordanian ceasefire lines. Following the exile of Jordan-based PLO operatives to Lebanon after their failed coup d'état fiasco against the Hashemite Kingdom in September 1970, IDF counter-terror operations focused mostly in South Lebanon. By then, Israel was not only carrying out special

National security doctrine 49

task force reprisal raids, but also targeting PLO bases through small-scale aerial and artillery bombardments.[29]

Furthermore, defensive measures were also undertaken at quite an early stage of Israel's fight against terror and guerrilla infiltrations. Israel built up fortified outposts along its borders, created minefields all along easily accessible crossing routes and supported these outposts and minefields with lightly armoured patrols, all in order to stop the Arab terrorist's access into Israel. Over the years the IDF's ' "perimeter defence system" continually expanded to incorporate such assets as ultra-sophisticated electronic equipment, maritime and airborne reconnaissance, border fences and patrol roads'.[30] This integrated perimeter defence system, however, was not able to stem all cross-border terror attacks over the years, but nonetheless proved essential in lowering the number of overall successful terror attempts. As shall be seen in the chapter on the *Al-Aqsa Intifada*, the security fence, the building of which began in late 2002, proved to be very effective in offsetting terror attacks within Israel, originating from the Territories in spite of the fact that it is not yet fully operational.

Defensive strategy and the operational–tactical offensive

From the operational perspective the conflict is believed to be a given. From the ideological point of view the conflict is considered to be imposed upon Israel. This has led Israel to believe that it has 'resorted to defence only and, despite its fundamental abhorrence of everything touching war and violence'.[31] In fact, Israel relied strongly on the purity of arms concept in order to convince its citizens that Israel's military strategy was morally justifiable and righteous. According to one former paratrooper:

> The purity of arms is the moral guideline for behavior in the Israeli army. Its emphasis is on restraint, on compassion, and its bias is in favor of human life. Soldiers who loot or mistreat prisoners or civilians violate the idea.[32]

The purity of arms concept, in effect, portrayed the Israeli soldier as a moral human being whose wielding of military power was strictly prompted by intentions of self-defence.

The Israeli national consensus regarding the use of military force, furthermore, is fuelled by the assumption that Israel *always* maintains the political and strategic defensive in any particular operation, even when the army presupposes that operation to be offensive. As Yigal Allon has stated, 'the moral and political aim of Israel's strategy [is] self-defence, to achieve this her armed forces [have] to be prepared to take initiative in carrying out decisive offensives in the event of any attack'.[33]

Maintaining the political–strategic status quo

This perception of being under an existential threat is based on the asymmetrical nature of the Arab–Israeli conflict: the Arabs can convert military and operational superiority and success into strategic success. That is, they could ultimately resolve the conflict by obliterating Israel from the face of the earth. Israel, on the other hand, ultimately cannot decide the conflict's outcome through military means alone. Ben-Gurion clearly stated this fact in saying that, 'Israel can win a hundred battles yet its problems will not be solved; but if the Arabs are victorious only once, it will mean our end'.[34]

Hence, Ben-Gurion's second assumption was that ultimately 'Israel will not be able to resolve the Arab–Israeli conflict through military means' alone,[35] but only be able to maintain the status quo until a political resolution is reached with its Arab neighbours. The IDF would be the main instrument in maintaining such a status quo until the Arab parties would cease to use any violence and decide to negotiate diplomatically instead.

The conviction that the conflict was imposed on Israel by Arab intransigence and hostility and that such a conflict could not be won purely on a military basis has often led to the unwillingness of the political echelons to deliberate seriously on the war aims of Israel. According to Efraim Inbar, the political echelons have abstained from dealing with the crucial issue of the objectives of war despite the fact that constant preparations for war devour a substantial part of the state's energy. 'Under circumstances where survival seems to be at stake and where the political culture displays a rather fatalistic attitude towards war, little intellectual energy is left to think about the goals of the coming war.'[36] Israel Tal reiterated this reality at a lecture at the National Defence College on 25 March 1978 by stating that:

> Since we lack a formal, declared war aim, we can only rely on a natural intuitive war aim that requires no proof and is understood by all as a question of existence. Israel has no positive war aims. Its objective in war is to neutralize the danger to its existence.[37]

Although such lack of political direction was not so problematic during the 'conventional era', such a deficiency has been much more costly during the two *Intifadas*. As John Nagl argues, 'undue focus on military action clouds the key political realities which can result in a military-dominated campaign plan'.[38] The disproportionate emphasis on military means for the maintenance of the status quo and the political echelon's inability to find adequate political alternatives to the two conflicts during their initial stages have led to the prolongation of the conflicts themselves. In effect, relations between the civilian and military leaderships during periods of protracted conflict, such as during the two *Intifadas*, are normally tense.

Armed forces such as the IDF are built upon the spirit of the offensive and on the 'mission command' ethos based on tactical initiative. Yet they are used by the political echelons for strategic goals such as deterrence based on reprisal raids. These forces end up overextending their initial operational and tactical objectives. This, in turn, usually escalates the level of violence rather than reducing it. Ze'ev Drory explains that the source of such tension lies in the different organisational goals that the political and military establishment have:

> The military echelon has its own aspirations and needs. Internal forces are generated which are activist, vigorous and targeted toward action and operational success. To the military, it sometimes seems as if political considerations are foreign to its *raison d'être*.... Moreover, to the military, creating and maintaining a record of operational success stands above any other consideration.[39]

As shall be seen, however, when analysing Begin's and Sharon's understanding of the Arab–Israeli conflict and on the consequent use of military force, both believed that the military means could yield substantial political outcomes, if not, victory. However, the lack of a clear definition of what constituted 'victory' during the crises they dealt with as prime ministers heightened further tensions between the upper military and political echelons.

Quick battlefield decision

Israel's limited staying power has forced it to have to rely on developing its assault power and on using its military adroitness to deter the Arab states and, if the occasion arose, provide a swift military decision on the battlefield in order to minimise the human and material costs that Israel would suffer in a major military confrontation.[40] In order to impose a battlefield decision on its Arab adversaries, Israel would need only to 'paralyse the enemy's military nerve system [which is] more economical in operation than pounding his flesh' (i.e. destroying its entire order of battle).[41] The need for a quick and effective battlefield decision was also necessary in order to enhance Israel's deterrent posture. This would be achieved operationally by penetrating as quickly as possible deep into enemy territory and attacking its enemies' main centre of gravity.

By doing this, Israel would ultimately discourage the enemy from continuing hostilities against the marauding IDF. The necessity of ending hostilities as quickly as possible and within conditions favourable to Israel was particularly crucial, because of the risk of superpower or United Nations (UN) intervention, which could have thwarted Israel's attempt at achieving its strategic objectives. According to Shimon Peres, 'hovering over all of Israel's wars in the past was the shadow of ... intervention, directly or indirectly, in order to prevent a full-fledged strategic decision'.[42]

National security consensus over Israel's strategic aims and control of the Occupied Territories

Israelis, however, have been far less unanimous about the territorial aims and outcomes of Israel's wars. Initially, the wars were fought out with the purpose of repelling any major threat to the state's security, but as military operations unfolded successfully, territory was seized as a result of the IDF's operational successes. Right-wing factions have traditionally maintained that territory seized whilst fending off a threat to security was in fact a retroactive fulfilment of a 'historic right' to *Eretz Israel ha-sh'leyma* (the complete Land of Israel) as envisaged in the Bible.[43]

Also, between 1967 and 1973, the maintenance of the newly acquired Territories of the West Bank and Gaza Strip, Golan Heights and the Sinai was justified by right-wing parties on the basis that by holding onto such a vast amount of land the threat of war would be removed. Given Israel's newfound strategic depth, pre-emptive operations or wars would become less likely. Despite the fact that the 1973 War disproved such assumptions, the argument for maintaining the Territories was still upheld. The main justifications for their maintenance changed, however.

Whereas in the past the maintenance of the Territories was seen as a way of protecting the Israeli heartland from the invasion of conventional armies, after the 1973 War, the main justification began to focus on the threat of terrorism. Right-wing factions, which eventually came to form the *Likud* party in 1973, argued that 'terrorism was conceived as the main danger to personal security.... If the territory were to be relinquished, there would be no personal security for anyone.'[44] The view by right-wing parties that terrorism could be a major threat to Israelis' personal security, as shall be seen below, eventually evolved into the belief that terrorism could pose an existential threat to the state of Israel itself. This had far-reaching consequences. Consequently, holding the Territories was essential for personal security. Moderates saw, instead, the captured territory as a 'bargaining chip', which would be relinquished if peace settlements with its belligerent neighbours were successful. In any event, most Israeli policy before the rise to power of the *Likud* party in 1977 considered territory as essential to resolving threats against Israel's existence and improving its security situation.

Furthermore, even amongst proponents of a 'Greater Israel' concept who were in favour of expanding Israel's borders, many established their territorial claims on the vital security role of those territories captured in 1967 rather than on any historic rights to the land. In fact, 'the notion that the country can be overrun, or cut into two, by an invading army within hours, is an important part of this discourse'.[45]

Although circumstances have changed dramatically since such a notion was first enunciated, the belief that Israel could suffer a conventional attack that could threaten the heartland of Israel and, thus, pose an existential threat in the future is still part of main Israeli discourse and plays a major role in its national security doctrine. Notwithstanding the fact that Israel has peace treaties with both Egypt (since 1979) and Jordan (since 1994) and that Syria, now as well as Iraq, no longer pose any serious threat to Israel at least from conventional forces, we shall see that the IDF continues to prepare its forces preponderantly on the basis that such conventional (and non-conventional) threats in the long term will re-emerge.[46]

The asymmetry of forces and strategic depth dilemmas

According to Dan Horowitz, the perception of the threat as being existential was not merely based on the awareness of the gravity of the Arab–Israeli conflict and the improbability of its peaceful settlement. It was also affected by the asymmetry of forces and resources between the two opponents and by the disputed borders that so severely constricted Israel's margin of security. Consequently, Israel's security assessments replicated a strategic inclination towards the solution of two crucial dilemmas: the dilemma of the asymmetry of forces and that of strategic depth. This twofold dilemma had no easy solution.[47] As stated by Yitzhak Rabin, 'because Israel lacked strategic depth, the IDF had an iron-clad rule that the war must be fought on the enemy's territory and that the enemy's forces must be defeated as quickly as humanly possible'.[48] Ben-Gurion clearly stated, as early as 1948, that geography demanded Israel 'apply the rule: he who strikes first wins the battle. Otherwise Israel would be overwhelmed.'[49]

Thus, two central dilemmas had to be resolved on the battlefield in terms of achieving operational and tactical objectives in the shortest time feasible. The first dilemma was whether or not to rely on detailed planning rather than on improvisation. The second dilemma was whether or not to encourage control over the resourcefulness of its forces. The IDF decided to promote 'mission command' principles (see below) and rely on both the resourcefulness and improvisation of its forces by decentralising authority. It allowed the relatively lower ranks of command to make tactical decisions on the ground without having to request security authorisation from the higher command echelons – who always maintained optional control over the mission – unless such a decision went against the general operational intent of the mission. Adherence to the objective rather than to the specific tactical plan was deemed more important given that both the 'fog of war' and the great fluidity of the battlefield often required local and effective improvisation. 'In the field, in battle, matters would be decided by the combatants [and] it would be the commanders in the field who would tell [the IDF chief of staff] what could and what could not be done.'[50]

An elastic structure of command, control and communications does not just save resources on forces; it also has the propensity to be less vulnerable to the demands of war than a more rigorously ordered system. It is

54 National security doctrine

not as vulnerable to shock tactics and deception by the enemy, a clear advantage in the confusion of battle. A highly versatile, offensive strategy places great strain on the command, control and communications systems of both sides, but is more debilitating for less flexible structures, such as the Arab armies. Consequently, this Israeli advantage has led to the Israeli predilection for a mobile and offensive war over a static and defensive one.

However, how was the IDF to conduct such an operational offensive as an organisation principally consisting of reserve forces? Until the early 1950s the IDF managed to rely on intelligence warnings regarding the enemy's intentions, early mobilisation of reserve forces and the absorption of any initial enemy attack by outpost defence units should intelligence warnings fail. However, as the IDF developed its operational and tactical offensive capabilities and ethos as its reprisal raids against *fedayeen* infiltrations continued, such measures came to be perceived as insufficient. The IDF, in fact, in the mid-1950s adopted the doctrine of pre-emption, during Moshe Dayan's term as chief of staff, in order to avoid the situation of not being able to mobilise its reserve forces in time to defeat any imminent attack.

The IDF's operational posture was also the result of Israel's national security doctrine, which overall was defensive in nature. The IDF's offensive operational posture was, in fact, intended to end fighting as rapidly as possible given Israel's strategic emphasis on defence. Israel's incapacity to completely overpower its adversaries made it indispensable for the IDF to achieve a clear battlefield decision/victory, so that Israel could maintain its overall preventive status quo strategy. Ending a war without clear operational achievements would represent a strategic failure. In both the 1956 Suez War and the 1967 Six Day War the IDF pre-emptively attacked and employed a major blitzkrieg offensive through the use of the armoured corps, mechanised infantry and support of the air force. Their success was not repeated during the War of Attrition or during the 1973 War. Both wars were initiated by its Arab enemies and did not result in either rapid or unambiguous victories. Despite this, the IDF did not modify its strategic concept and 'at the operational level [it significantly increased] the number of heavy armored formations and accelerated the effort to develop tactical patterns of penetration'.[51]

Furthermore, 'the necessity for short wars derives from political and socio-economic considerations'.[52] The fact that in order to fight wars, Israel relies heavily on its reserves would prove to be economically costly if such reserves are called up for an extended period of time. Moreover, Israel has always been very sensitive to its own casualties.[53] It, thus, has specifically developed a strategy that tends to diminish as much as possible the likelihood of heavy casualties by reaching a battlefield decision in the quickest time possible. This would enable low casualty rates, the demobilisation of reservists and, consequently, the resumption of the economy, as well as mentioned earlier on the forestalling of superpower or UN intervention before IDF gains on the battlefield were achieved.

National security doctrine 55

Consequently, in order not to permit the enemy to realise his political goals without attaining a victory on the battlefield, Israel has often tried to avoid wars of attrition by attempting to escalate them. Israeli dislike of drawn-out engagements was articulated on many occasions.[54]

Defensible borders

However, during the interlude between the cessation of the Six Day War and the *Yom Kippur* War, Israel adopted a strategy of 'defensible borders'. The seizure of new territories following the Six Day War gave Israel in-depth defence for the first time and provided natural defensive barriers such as the Jordan River, Suez Canal and the West Bank mountain range. This radical change of circumstances led to the revision of the Israeli security doctrine's concept of pre-emption. By adopting the concept of 'defensible borders', Israel would base its protection 'on a strong topographical posture composed of natural obstacles, capable when properly defended of resisting a modern land army, and suitable for the mounting of a major counteroffensive'.[55] The new cease-fire lines were seen as providing Israel with the ability to absorb an initial blow before conducting a major counter-offensive. This concept was perceived as being a better solution to the strategic depth dilemma than that of pre-emption. In 1969 Israeli diplomat Abba Eban defined these as 'borders which can be defended without a pre-emptive initiative'.[56] It released Israel, consequently, from the diplomatically problematic undertaking of commencing war, given its new ability in absorbing an Arab attack.

However, the decision to adopt a strategy of 'defensible borders' through the creation of the Bar-Lev Line on the east bank of the Suez Canal basically eliminated Israel's advantage in manoeuvre warfare and cost many lives due to the fact that both the isolated strongholds along the canal as well as the lines of communication between them were subject to Egyptian artillery bombardment and ambushes.[57] Israel, confident of its newfound strategic depth, was willing to actually absorb the first blow from the enemy, something unheard of until then. The concept of defensible borders created the traditional circumstances for a strategy of passive defence, which

> had profound implications for the IDF's military doctrine, one of whose sources of strength was an intangible, motivational component – initiative, leadership improvisation, ability to exploit opportunities, and tactical flexibility. In the static defensive alignment formed after the Six Day War, these components lost much of their advantages.[58]

This proved almost fatal during the initial stages of the 1973 War. The Egyptian surprise attack put the IDF in a distinctly unusual and difficult defensive posture. The IDF had not, since the 1948 War, permitted their

56 *National security doctrine*

Arab foes to initiate hostilities. Furthermore, the defensive proclivity was based upon a system of fortifications on both fronts that could be outflanked and cut off by the enemy.⁵⁹ As a result of nearly disastrous experiences during the 1973 War, Israel reverted back to its traditional stance of conventional deterrence based on pre-emption.

The qualitative edge: the IDF soldier

Another basic assumption of the Israeli concept of security is the equation of 'quality versus quantity', which recurs incessantly in Israeli perceptions of the quandary of the balance of forces and resources vis-à-vis the Arab states. Ben-Gurion was well aware of such a dilemma when stating that Israel's 'emphasis on quality, in the absence of quantity, is not only desirable in itself but is also forced upon us by the size of our country, the size of our manpower, the scale of our resources'.⁶⁰ The concept of 'quality' in the Israeli security doctrine reflects the tendency to exploit all existing resources more effectively than the enemy. In fact, by attempting to fully utilise the 'Israeli soldier's technological literacy to exploit the "force multipliers" with which the IDF's arsenal' equips itself,⁶¹ the IDF is able to make do with relatively smaller forces. In order to develop such force multipliers Israel has always strived to 'emphasize leadership and demanding exercise training, [to] promote on the basis of competence, to maintain a relatively young and aggressive officer corps, and to insist in forward leadership'.⁶²

The Israeli qualitative edge was also based on the fact that Israel was able to build up a more socially and economically developed society. As was seen earlier on, Ben-Gurion made sure that the IDF would be a 'people's army', which could be used to integrate and educate its citizens.⁶³ Consequently they would not only function better within the IDF, but also within the Israeli economy and society in general. The importance of maintaining its qualitative edge has remained a constant axiom of the Israeli national security doctrine. When interviewed in August 2003, then National Security Advisor, Ephraim Halevy still maintained that:

> The future of Israel depends on maintaining the qualitative edge in the field of weaponry, technology, and also the qualitative edge in the area of manpower. We must have the best and we must have the brightest. *If we don't we will die.* That is what maintains our superiority over our neighbours [emphasis mine].⁶⁴

With more developed and efficient infrastructure and manpower capabilities the IDF would be able to use its full potential during hostilities and, thus, would be able to concentrate its strength where the battle would be decided.

A 'people's army'

The full utilisation of Israel's relatively small manpower recruitment base led to its adoption of a 'people's army' based on a 'three-tiered structure': the *Sherut Keva* (Permanent Service Corps) – a small core of permanent service personnel which constitute the backbone of the military organisation; the *Sherut Hova* (Compulsory Conscript Service) for *all* 18-year-old Jewish, Druze men and Jewish women who must serve respectively for three and two years;[65] and the *Sherut Miluim* (Reserve Service) comprising all demobilised conscripts, who until recently have been called up annually for 45 days of active duty (men until age 48, women until age 26, unless exempted by marriage or children).[66] Gen. Yigal Yadin defined Israel's reservists as 'regular soldiers who were on leave eleven months of the year'. The most eminent example of the optimal utilisation of manpower in support of the qualitative edge is the Israeli reservist system, which forms about two-thirds of the total available force structure of the IDF and which considerably diminishes the implications of the large demographic asymmetry between Israel and the Arab states.[67]

In order to conduct war the IDF has relied heavily upon the committed contribution of reservists to fulfil its manpower needs and wartime objectives. Consequently, the morale and will to fight in the rear influences the combat motivation and efficacy of reserve forces in the combat zone, due to their close linkage and attachment to civilian life. Because of this, the lack of a national security consensus is capable of affecting 'the motivation and thus the combat performance of the units'.[68]

The principle of mission command and organisational ethos of *bitsuism*

Another factor that has enhanced Israel's qualitative edge over its Arab opponents in combat operations has been based on the IDF's reliance on operational flexibility and tactical initiative. This, however, could cause difficulties in the control and synchronisation of large operations. On the other hand, an operational method that fully exploits the fluidity and confusion of the battlefield entailed an even greater pressure on the less-flexible Arab command organisation.[69]

Given the rapid changes of battlefield conditions and the general occurrence of the fog of war during combat, operational flexibility and tactical initiative based on the 'mission command' ethos can be the crucial factors for success in any military confrontation on the ground. The mission command ethos emphasised in the IDF is the dedication to the objective instead of to specific (and rigid) tactical plans. Mission command is essentially 'a decentralized style of command relying on initiative, the acceptance of responsibility and mutual trust.... The underlying requirement [for mission command] is the fundamental responsibility to act, or in certain circumstances to decide not to act, within the framework of the commander's intent.'[70]

Mission command relies on mutual understanding in that subordinates need to have a lucid insight of their commander's intent so that when situations, which have never been envisaged or trained for before deployment, arise in the field, his subordinates are able to carry out the task without necessitating further guidance from their commanding officer or aborting the mission altogether. Ultimately, it is the task of the leader to determine clearly what constitutes mission success, particularly in the case of LICs at the lower end of the spectrum of violence, as it is often in such settings that troops find it difficult to comprehend what the mission actually is.

Mission command also depends on the delegation of responsibility from a superior to his subordinates when making crucial decisions during an operation. Without such delegation of responsibility, continuous interference by the commander in the execution of a particular mission in order to reduce the risk of making an operational error may damage his subordinates' self-confidence and, consequently, may stifle his subordinates' initiative. Obviously, a leader can only allow such delegation if he has been able to equip his subordinates with the appropriate tools to obtain the mission's objective.

Finally, mission command entails the acceptance of risk. Mistakes will happen and unless they are due to gross negligence, commanders should allow for them and not punish their subordinates for acting on their leader's intent, despite the risks involved in taking such an intrepid course of action. Without allowing for mistakes, and the associated risks, there can be no improvement as 'a necessary condition for learning is an atmosphere of openness to change, patience towards mistakes, encouragement of initiative and passing on the responsibility to the operational forces'.[71]

Thus, 'Israeli strategic planning leaves the greatest possible freedom for the commanders in the field … as long as they maintain and achieve the objectives assigned to them'.[72] According to Douglas Bland, in the traditional allocation of roles between the civilian and military echelons, officers treasure ' "the principle of tactical autonomy", the right to command forces in operations without civilian interference'.[73] However, as we shall see below, this autonomy is costly to maintain if armed forces are not cognizant of the actual strategic aims given the political–strategic effect that even minor tactical decisions can have in LIC scenarios.

Israeli dominance in this area of command and control is the product of a mixture of societal factors, military doctrine and organisational culture. A dominant aspect in the IDF's organisational culture, in fact, is *bitsuism*. *Bitsuism* is derived from the Hebrew verb *Levazea*, which means simply 'to do'. A person who is a '*bitsuist*' (a performer) is a doer who is capable of carrying out and completing many tasks swiftly and successfully.[74]

This cultural feature emerged as a result of Israel's fragile strategic situation and as a result of a doctrine that emphasised qualities such as aggressiveness, initiative and a high operational tempo. Throughout its history, unlike many other armies around the world, the IDF has never enjoyed long periods of calm when it could purely concentrate on force development and training. As a result, IDF commanders developed the habit of focusing on short-term tactical threats almost on a daily basis rather than on long-term strategic issues, force preparation and planning.[75] The continuous need to carry out a growing number of operational missions – often at the expense of training and other activities – made the actual ability to carry them out a dominant organisational value in the IDF. Gradually, this value became detached occasionally from objective environmental pressures leading to the execution of some missions that in reality were not necessary. Carrying out many missions became a dominant value in itself and even if missions were not the result of external threats, they were often initiated by the unit itself.

At a first glance, it seems that the *bitsuist* value, which corresponds with initiative and risk-taking, is exactly what is needed for mission command to be realised. Yet, mission command is the function of a delicate balance of ingredients. If one is taken out, the whole system may fall apart. The opposite side of initiative in the mission command equation is the capacity to learn, plan, reflect and adapt creatively. The intellectual capacity to decide whether or not to abort, change or continue a specific mission within the larger context under ever-changing circumstances is a critical capability subordinates and commanders alike must possess.

However, as we shall see later, due to the very different nature of contemporary LICs the *bitsuist* ethos may have reduced the IDF's capability to exercise mission command effectively. The *bitsuist* tendency has had serious effects on the strategic outcome of mere tactical operations during the two *Intifadas*.

Milkhemet ein breira – wars of no choice

Finally, the sensation that the Israeli soldier was fighting for his state's very existence and that there was no other alternative but to fight, developed the concept of *milkhemet ein breira* (wars of no choice).[76] The concept of *milkhemet ein breira* was a product of the combination of two collective memories shared by the population of Israel: 'on the one hand, the living memory of the Holocaust and on the other, the recognition that the state of Israel, the only sovereign home of the Jews, was surrounded by Arab states waiting to take advantage of any Israeli weakness'.[77]

This concept, which originates from Biblical times, has been one of the most important motivating factors for the Israeli soldier as well as a means for justifying Israel's decision to use force. The Holocaust created a sense of anxiety and fear amongst the Jewish population that needed to be righted with the state of Israel and the protection that it could provide to the Jewish nation. Ben-Gurion stated his and the Israeli state's determination at providing such security to its citizens by proclaiming:

> The people of Israel in their own land will not be like sheep led to the slaughter. What Hitler did to six million Jews … no other oppressor will do this to Jews who are free and rooted in their native land.[78]

This assumption more than any other has affected Israel's perception of the threats it has faced and the way it has addressed them since its establishment. The perception that Israel has been under an existential threat has also been applied to cases in which Israel was clearly involved in fighting asymmetrical conflicts where it visibly had the upper hand, as shall be seen in the following chapters.

5 Land and the rise of the LIC struggle

Strategic depth versus land for peace

Since the signing of the 1979 Israeli–Egyptian peace treaty, public debates in Israel over the necessity of strategic depth have centred on the West Bank. The assumption, until very recently, has been that 'Israel's main geostrategic weakness was the coastal plain facing Jordan, which was the "soft under-belly" of [Israel's] posture'.[1] The West Bank, consisting of Judea and Samaria, extends along the 'soft underbelly' of Israel, so termed for its proximity to the country's most crucial strategic centres. Thus, demilitarising the West Bank of weaponry and forces was deemed essential by those who maintained a moderate stance on the issue of strategic depth. Hawks, in contrast, argued that Israel must retain military control over the whole of the West Bank.[2]

Hawks rejected separating sovereignty from military control and aimed to annex the Territories, which they considered strategically crucial. Moderates, on the other hand, differentiated between a political border and a security border. These conceptual divergences have been the foundation of the debate over the benefits of maintaining settlements in Judea, Samaria and the Gaza Strip. Following the Six Day War, the area under Israeli control stretched beyond the minimum required for self-defence. As a result, military/pragmatic concerns lost their supreme standing and became, at least in part, subject to political and ideological influence. The lack of a national security consensus over the future status of the Territories extended from the political–ideological realm into the military–strategic realm:

> Recognition of the dependence of strategic decisions on politics and ideology undermined the autonomous standing of the defence establishment, which in the past had been able to formulate security doctrines and policies acceptable to holders of disparate and even opposing political views.[3]

The dissolution of the national security consensus, triggered following the 1973 War, gained momentum. Once the peace treaty between Israel and

62 *Land and the rise of the LIC struggle*

Egypt was achieved in 1979, the possibility that the IDF would have to fight concurrently on two fronts became less of a reality. These negotiations justified public debate over national security issues, especially on the necessity of maintaining territories seized after the Six Day War for the purposes of strategic depth. Before 1973 large-scale public participation in the domestic debate concerning strategic issues was restricted to the inner circles of the security establishment. Since then, 'foreign policy in Israel has become the most salient source of division and debate in the political process'.[4] The reduction of the consensus on the national security issues was also affected by Israeli domestic politics. The 1977 elections, in fact, brought an end to 29 years of Labour party hegemony and the rise of the *Likud*.

Israeli strategic doctrine during the Begin–Sharon era

Indications that Israel's national security doctrine was changing became apparent initially with Ariel Sharon's appointment as Defence Minister by Prime Minister Begin in August 1981. The new conception of the Israeli security doctrine, developed by Sharon, denied the traditional status quo approach, which involved the restrained employment of military force within the framework of defensive strategic and political objectives. Given the growing threat of Palestinian attacks from South Lebanon since the early 1970s, the call for the creation of a buffer zone in order to protect Northern Israel from PLO artillery and rocket attacks as well as from terrorist infiltrations gained momentum.

The amended concept of security that brought about the Lebanon War no longer aspired to thwart threats to Israel's existence through the use of defensive measures, nor was it based on Israel's self-perception as a status quo state. War 'was accorded wider scope and transformed into an instrument, which aided in the realisation of political objectives' unconnected to any concept of deterrence.[5] Such a change in security policy led to sporadic large-scale raids by air, sea and land against the growing PLO terrorist and guerrilla infrastructure in South Lebanon. These culminated in the two-month long 'Litani Operation' in 1978 and ultimately escalated in 1982 into a major three-year war and the subsequent 15-year occupation of South Lebanon.

Despite the fact that Operation Peace for Galilee's stated aim 'was to remove the [Palestinian] terrorists from firing range of the northern border, approximately twenty-five miles',[6] the war's actual aims were the following:

> To strike hard at the PLO [Palestinian Liberation Organisation] militarily and politically and thereby enable dictation of the Israeli autonomy plan on the West Bank, to wipe out the Syrian stronghold in Lebanon [...], to change the balance of interethnic power in Lebanon

[...], and bring about a peace treaty ensuring Israel's hegemonic status in Lebanon.[7]

The assertive use of the IDF in order to achieve Sharon's ambitious objectives undermined the only war aim, which had traditionally formed the core of the Israeli national security consensus. That is, the suppression of any threat to its existence through the use of the IDF. Prime Minister Menachem Begin, Defence Minister Ariel Sharon and IDF COS Rafael Eitan came to believe that the relationship between military strength and political influence was a proportional one. Accordingly, Israel's strategic concept was no longer to be defensive, but overtly offensive. Israeli power would no longer be designed for the purposes of deterrence, as had been the case in the past. In Begin's eyes, the Lebanon War was conducted in order to prevent a more costly and bloodier war in the future. Begin had stated his desire to curb the number of Israeli casualties as one of the most crucial incentives for initiating 'the war out of choice and for not leaving the initiative to the adversaries'.[8] In Begin's words, it was a 'war of choice', as opposed to previous wars of 'no choice' that Israel was confronted with. This was the exact opposite of the previous concept, which saw the avoidance of war as a win-win situation. Thus, this conception had two major consequences. It entailed greater autonomy on the part of the defence establishment in planning and employing force. It also changed Israel's cost–benefit analysis regarding the use of force for the purpose of achieving its political objectives. Traditionally, Israel *only* instigated a war in the face of an existential threat. Israel's new offensive strategy under Begin, however, not only evaluated military risks vis-à-vis issues of survival, but also against political gains stemming from the decision to use force.[9]

It was evident that the expansion of operational goals, which emerged from a substitution of a defensive for an offensive conception at the strategic level, augmented the price and threat of war. The fact that avoiding war was no longer the prime political benefit opened up the doors to Israeli military and political adventurism: for example, the annexation of the Golan Heights, the bombing of the Osiraq Iraqi nuclear facility in 1981, and Israel's supposed aggressive Cold War warrior stance are just some examples of such adventurism. Accordingly, the use of the IDF in the Lebanon War was characterised 'by an excess of force and overwhelming superiority in firepower. The enemy was to a certain extent outgunned rather than outmanoeuvred, pounded into submission instead of being outflanked, and crushed by siege instead of being overwhelmed by a war of movement.'[10]

From interstate to intercommunal warfare

The Lebanon War also constituted overall a novel perception of the Arab–Israeli conflict. According to Horowitz, in the past, the Israeli governments' interstate outlook of the Arab–Israeli conflict led to the interpretation of any major threat from the armed forces of the Arab states as a major threat to Israel's 'basic security', whilst the threat of terror and guerrilla warfare carried out by Palestinians had been, until then, perceived a less acute 'current security' threat that did not amount to a *casus belli*.[11] The main difference with the rise of *Likud* to power was predicated on the distinction that its members drew between accentuating the ideological, ethnic and intercommunal nature of the conflict as opposed to its interstate one.

Until the elections of 1977, Israeli governments had always underlined the regional and interstate character of the Arab–Israeli conflict, whilst seeking simultaneously to lessen its intercommunal, ideological and, to some extent, ethnic nature. This enabled Israel to draw a distinction between current and basic or existential security issues. Existential security threats, that is, conventional warfare threats, required a strong IDF response, such as pre-emptive attacks in the form of a full-scale war. On the other hand, current security threats were considered 'no more than a nuisance',[12] and were normally punished with limited force in the form of commando reprisals.[13]

However, by perceiving the PLO (and other Palestinian organisations) for the first time as an existential threat and not only as a terrorist irritation and, thus, by ascribing most vocabulary relating to the intercommunal conflict to the sphere of existential security issues, Israeli policy-makers lowered the threshold for conflict to a level that ultimately made going to war a much greater probability. The Lebanon War was not only a 'war of choice', but it was also the first war engaged principally against the Palestinians instead of an Arab state. The perception of the intercommunal conflict, involving usually low-intensity terrorist and guerrilla attacks, as an existential threat to the state of Israel became an ideologically contentious issue; it reduced even further the national security consensus within Israeli society – particularly regarding the issue of when the use of force against the Palestinians was deemed as justified.

As shall be seen further on, Ariel Sharon's reaction to Palestinian terror and guerrilla violence during the first three years and one-half of the *Al-Aqsa Intifada* was based on his fundamental conviction that he had 'always seen terrorism as a strategic threat, not a tactical threat'.[14] Such a conviction, which under *siege conditions* (that is under constant Palestinian guerrilla and terrorist attacks) was shared by a large portion of the Israeli population, created a situation in which any 'serious discussion of political options that could ameliorate the violence'[15] was cast aside for the purpose of fighting Palestinian aggression head-on. Paradoxically, though, and despite the fact that Israel had adopted a more offensive strategic doctrine during the Begin era, operationally the IDF, 'for the first time, adopted in the Lebanon War, a policy of moderating both the nature and the pace of assaults. This policy change involved, sometimes using indirect as opposed to direct assaults, [and often involved] considerable disapproval from officers in the field.'[16]

In spite of the efforts to produce a truly combined-arms strategy after the errors of the 1973 War, a chronic shortage of infantry led to a structural separation between infantry and armour, and between mechanised infantry and armour, thus leaving forces vulnerable to the numerous guerrilla ambushes carried out by both the PLO and Syrian forces. A systematic predilection for firepower over manoeuvre and the avoidance of conducting night operations – which the IDF was famous for carrying out in the past – also led the IDF to behave on the ground in a very static manner, thus, delaying operational plans set out by the General Staff and division commanders, who were also culpable of interfering with tactical manoeuvres and decisions at the brigade and battalion levels. Such interference, together with the confusion brought about by the continual rotation of commanders from one command front to another during the war, led to the IDF's inability to achieve most of the goals set out by Ariel Sharon's more ambitious and aggressive 'Big Pines' invasion plan.

Moreover, the shifting in the Israeli national security doctrine from the interstate to the internecine levels of the Israeli–Palestinian conflict ultimately affected two areas: '(1) in the operative-military sphere it lowered the threshold at which Israel will go to war, thus increasing the chances of war breaking out over internecine tensions, such as in response to terrorist activity.'[17] In fact, Israel's record of COIN tactics since 1985 underlines its greater propensity to enact reprisal raids against terrorists which have taken the form of large aerial and artillery bombardment campaigns, which, as shall be shown below, have had little deterrent effect on terrorist groups both in Lebanon and in the Territories; '(2) In the political/strategic sphere it emphasized the political, internecine aspect of the conflict, thus reducing the chance for an interstate territorial compromise in the West Bank and Gaza Strip.'[18]

Thus, the Lebanon War 'was a turning point, since it brought in its wake cracks in the broad Israeli consensus which in the past had granted almost automatic legitimacy to every instance of the use of military force by the security' establishment.[19] This exploitation of circumstances dictated Israeli security and defence policy as long as Ariel Sharon served as minister of defence. The political effects of the Lebanon War on the *Likud*, in any case, were felt even with the departure of Ariel Sharon. In fact, 'at the beginning, 67 per cent of the Jewish population supported [the Lebanon War]; by the end only 15 per cent. The political cost to the *Likud* was a 14 per cent drop in electoral strength in 1984 ... and a consequent sharing of power in a national unity government' with the Labour party.[20]

After the resignation of Defence Minister Sharon, due to the controversy surrounding the *Sabra* and *Shatilla* massacres of September 1982, there was a return to 'war when it is only essential' policy. However, it became clear that 'where guerrillas, terrorists, and civil resistance were concerned, battlefield decision [became] an almost irrelevant notion'.[21] The Lebanon War and the two *Intifadas* proved that the formerly high correlation between battlefield decision[22] and the attainment of the war objectives[23] had almost disappeared. The conduct of the war in Lebanon was, in fact, affected by the propensity of the IDF to use conventional military thinking. According to Richard Gabriel, the IDF during the Lebanon War provided a clear example of an army which had prepared itself for the last war it had fought, 'only to find itself facing battle conditions radically different from those it had prepared for'.[24]

The Shi'ite challenge in Lebanon

The old rules of war of conventional deterrence by punishment had to be changed. Despite the IDF's greater reliance on technology and stand-off battle platforms, the number of Israelis killed was quite high. Furthermore, the IDF kill ratios were rather mediocre. One of the major ironies of the Lebanon War was that the IDF, which had since the *Yom Kippur* War developed a large military force, was not able to apply its new combined-arms strategy given the fact that both the nature of the war and the terrain made such a strategy useless.

The IDF managed ultimately to drive out the Palestinians from South Lebanon and Beirut. However, during the war the IDF – which did not really have a 'hearts and minds' strategy in place – managed to arouse the fury of the Shi'ites from South Lebanon, who with the assistance of Tehran and collusion of Syria, established in 1982 *Hizbullah* (Party of God), a radical Islamic umbrella organisation intent on driving out the IDF from Lebanon through the use of terror and guerrilla tactics. *Amal* (*Afwaj al-Muqawama al-Lubnaniyya* – The Lebanese Resistance Brigades) had already been established in 1974 during the Lebanese civil war and was also intent in driving out the IDF from Lebanon. The resistance put up both by *Hizbullah* and *Amal* proved to be fearsome as well as deadly. Their use of human terror suicide bombers and evermore increasingly effective guerrilla attacks produced, between 1982 and 1985, 'the deaths of some 650 IDF soldiers and the withdrawal of the IDF' to the South Lebanese Security Zone.[25]

The IDF's retreat in May 1985, to 45 km from the Israeli–Lebanese border, as well as the establishment of the 850 km^2 'security zone', which ran for 70 km from Al Bayyadah on the Mediterranean coast, eastwards to the slopes of Mount Hermon, actually increased the level of violence within this area. Although the north of Israel initially became quieter after the establishment of the Lebanese 'security zone', clashes between the IDF and its ally, the South Lebanese Army (SLA, *c.*2,000+ militia trained, funded and armed by Israel and initially composed of a majority of Christian Lebanese) and *Hizbullah* increased dramatically.[26] The Lebanese quagmire continued, despite the official ending of the Lebanon War, and

Table 5.1 IDF personnel killed by *Hizbullah* attacks, 1992–98

Year	IDF personnel killed
1992	13
1993	12
1994	21
1995	23
1996	27
1997	39
1998	24

Sources: Michael Eisenstadt, '*Hizballah* operations: past patterns, future prospects', *Policy-Watch 197*, 7 May 1996, *Washington Institute for Near East Policy*, www.washingtoninstitute.org/templateC05.php?CID=1076 (accessed 5 May 2005) and Nicholas Blanford, '*Hizbullah* attacks force Israel to take a hard look at Lebanon', *Jane's Intelligence Review*, vol. 11, no. 4 (April 1999), p. 34.

proved even more challenging given the new dimension of the conflict. The area, jagged, riven by ravines and chequered with craggy mountains and hills, was the perfect setting for classic guerrilla terrain warfare, for which Israel was not really prepared despite its initial experiences of this form of warfare during the Lebanon War.

During the first decade, for example, *Hizbullah*, which initially conducted suicide human-wave attacks in which it lost many 'martyrs', began to improve its operational capabilities with the assistance and training of the elite Iranian Revolutionary Guards Corps (IRGC). During the early 1990s, *Hizbullah* began carefully planning hit-and-run guerrilla raids against IDF and SLA outposts scattered around the 'security zone', as well as on their patrols.[27] These attacks, which increased dramatically in tempo and lethality from 1990 onwards, exacted quite a significant toll on IDF (and SLA) personnel (see Table 5.1).

Israel's counter-guerrilla strategy in South Lebanon

According to Shmuel Gordon, Israel's counter-guerrilla strategy and operational doctrine vis-à-vis the threats originating from Southern Lebanon comprised five interconnected elements: (1) passive defence; (2) active defence; (3) offensive operations; (4) deterrence; and (5) negotiation and diplomatic efforts.[28]

'Passive defence' comprised defensive measures in order to defend Israeli civilians from *Katyusha* rocket attacks and other guerrilla missile attacks. These constituted forward position strongholds entrenched in the South Lebanon Security Zone, high-tech fences with electronic sensor capacities on the Israeli–Lebanese border, hospitals, psychiatric care and civilian support services, such as police and fire-fighting services, within the target areas in northern Israel. The core of Israel's passive defence measures was the high-tech security fence, which contained various early-warning and detection systems.

'Active defence' constituted limited operations such as infantry and special forces patrols and ambushes, which attempted to 'search and engage' *Hizbullah* squads within the security zone, in order to intercept any potential infiltrators wanting to conduct rocket attacks from within the security zone against northern communities in Israel, or against units stationed within the zone itself.

'Offensive operations' were those missions that involved IDF forces penetrating areas beyond the security zone. This aspect of Israel's counter-guerrilla strategy was intended to take the initiative and force *Hizbullah* to redirect its concentration and efforts towards defensive tactics. The Israel Air Force (IAF) played a crucial role in these offensive operations as they often involved air operations against *Hizbullah* infrastructure, training camps and the targeted killing of guerrilla leaders and members.

Although the main goal of these operations was that of enhancing Israel's deterrent image in the region, Israel's retaliatory operations gradually lost their deterrent effect, particularly as the lethality and effectiveness of *Hizbullah* increased during the 1990s. At the same time, the IDF's operations became more cautious from the point of view of protecting its troops, but more imprudent given its growing reliance on artillery and aircraft bombardments, which often resulted in collateral damage. As a result of the growing lethality of *Hizbullah* attacks and lack of success of regular IDF patrols and retaliatory operations in deterring them, the IDF initiated two vast air and artillery attacks in South Lebanon: on 25 July 1993, 'Operation Accountability'; and on 11 April 1996, 'Operation Grapes of Wrath'.

'Operation Accountability'

'Operation Accountability' was initiated following two major attacks on Israeli targets. On 28 June 1993, *Katyusha* rockets launched by *Hizbullah* caused civilian casualties in the town of Kiryat Shmonah, whereas during July, attacks in the South Lebanon Security Zone by Ahmad Jabril's Popular Front for the Liberation of Palestine – General Council Command (PFLP-GC) and *Hizbullah* caused the deaths of nine IDF soldiers. The Rabin government, consequently, set out to conduct a major retaliatory operation in order to deter further attacks. Given the fear of suffering significant casualties with a ground forces incursion, Israel decided to carry out the operation by artillery and aerial bombardment. The primary goal of the operation was to destroy *Hizbullah* headquarters, training and launch sites as well as the homes of its leaders. The secondary, and more controversial, goal of the operation was to conduct bombardments within and around Lebanese civilian population centres in order to disrupt civilian life and force the local population's displacement from the South

Land and the rise of the LIC struggle 69

Lebanon area. Israel hoped that with such a displacement the local population would turn against *Hizbullah* and retract its active and passive support for its forces and operations. Israel, furthermore, hoped that the Lebanese government would actively crack down on *Hizbullah* with such a move.

'Operation Accountability' (25 July–31 July) led to the Israeli bombardment of over 30 Shi'ite villages, the death of 147 civilians and the exodus of 350,000 people towards Beirut.[29] The operation, rather than achieving the aims stated above, actually alienated the local population and hardened *Hizbullah*'s resolve in fighting the Israeli occupation of Lebanon. *Hizbullah*, in fact, responded in kind with *Katyusha* attacks causing the death of two and wounding of 13 Israeli civilians from Kiryat Shmonah.[30]

Although an oral agreement was arrived at following the operation, whereby Israel agreed to desist from attacking civilian targets in Lebanon, whilst *Hizbullah* promised to stop firing *Katyusha* missiles into Northern Israel, nothing stopped *Hizbullah* from conducting attacks upon IDF/SLA forces within the security zone. This was quite ironic in that 'Operation Accountability' was ordered initially due to *Hizbullah* attacks on IDF forces in the area. Consequently, *Hizbullah* actually increased its strikes against Israeli targets (see Figure 5.1). Israel also replied with evermore hard-hitting retaliatory strikes involving often extensive collateral damage that had a negative effect given international, domestic and media condemnation.

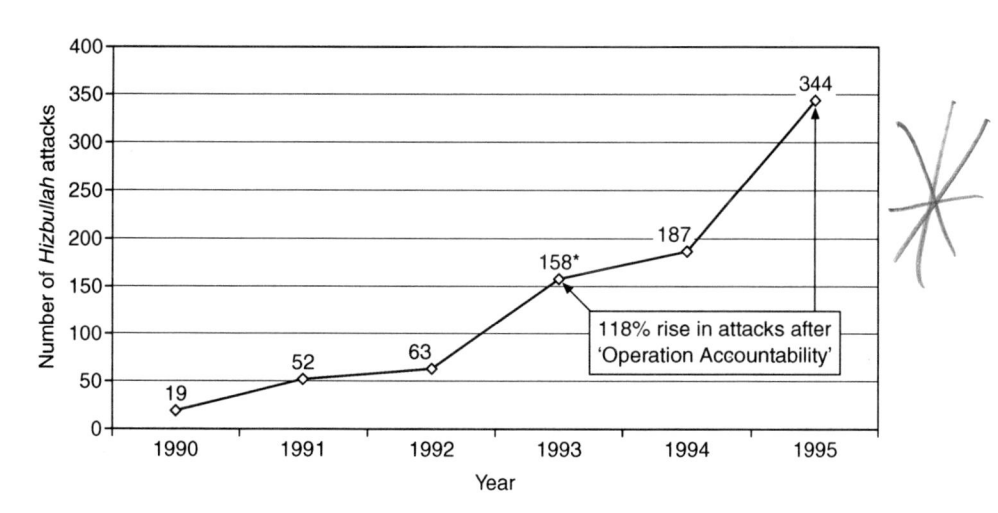

Figure 5.1 *Hizbullah* attacks against Israeli targets, 1990–95 (source: Michael Eisenstadt, 'Hizballah operations: past patterns, future prospects', *Policy Watch* 197, 7 May 1999, Washington Institute for Near Coast Policy, www.washingtoninstitute.org/templateC05.php?CID=1076 (accessed 5 May 2005)).

Note
Excludes attacks conducted during 'Operation Accountability'.

Operation 'Grapes of Wrath'

The tit-for-tat escalation culminated once again in April 1996. During the month of March, attacks, perpetrated both by *Hizbullah* and *Amal*, took the lives of six IDF soldiers, including one officer. The Israeli response on 30 March was the artillery shelling of the village of Yatar. It resulted in the death of two civilians. *Hizbullah Katyusha* rocket attacks followed further Israeli artillery barrages. Finally, the Israeli government approved an IDF operation, dubbed 'Grapes of Wrath' in response to the growing number of *Katyusha* attacks in Northern Israel. The aim of the operation was again, to obtain the total termination of rocket attacks by *Hizbullah*, as well as damage the popular support for *Hizbullah* amongst the Lebanese population.

During the 16-day intense retaliatory operation, Israeli pilots conducted 600 air strikes with fixed-wing aircraft and helicopters; also, artillery units fired over 25,000 shells into Lebanon. As a result, 154 civilians were killed in Lebanon, and another 351 were injured.[31] Precision-guided munitions were fired by the IDF in order to destroy *Hizbullah* headquarters, training sites, *Katyusha* launchers and mortars in the Security Zone as well as buildings and houses in the suburbs of Beirut. The IAF also bombed a power station in the outskirts of Beirut in order to pressure Lebanese Prime Minister, Rafiq Hariri, into suppressing *Hizbullah* activities. In spite of the use of precise munitions, extensive collateral damage went hand-in-hand with the IDF's retaliatory strikes.

Three major incidents marked the IDF's failure to avoid collateral damage in its bombardment of the South Lebanon during Operation 'Grapes of Wrath': a helicopter gunship attack on an ambulance in the village of Mansouri on 13 April that killed two women and four children; another helicopter gunship attack on a house in the village of Upper Nabatiyeh on 18 April that killed nine civilians, including a newborn baby, six children and their mother; and the artillery barrage in Qana.

During the operation a very tragic incident occurred, on 18 April, when the IDF responded to a *Hizbullah* attack launched close to the United Nations Interim Forces in Lebanon (UNIFIL) base near Qana. Lebanese civilians had gathered in the base in order to seek refuge during IDF bombardments. Nonetheless, IDF artillery shells hit the base, killing 4 UNIFIL soldiers and over 100 Lebanese civilians. The episode was denounced internationally and strengthened even more *Hizbullah*'s position in Lebanon.

Of the total 639 *Katyusha* rockets fired into Israeli territory during Operation 'Grapes of Wrath', about 28 per cent (81 rockets) were fired on 14 April, the day after the Israeli helicopter gunship attack on the ambulance in Mansouri that killed six civilians. The day after the attacks in Upper Nabatiyeh and Qana that resulted in over 100 civilian deaths, *Hizbullah* fired 90 rockets against Israeli targets.[32] Rather than deterring

Hizbullah rocket attacks, IDF retaliatory operations actually escalated them. Finally, on 27 April, a cease-fire agreement, similar to that reached in 1993, was attained between the two belligerent parties. Israel would refrain from attacking Lebanese villages suspected of harbouring *Hizbullah* operatives, whilst *Hizbullah* would stop launching attacks against Israeli civilian targets. It also set up a Monitoring Committee to oversee the agreement, which was monitored by representatives from Syria, France, the USA, Israel and Lebanon.

In summary, the gradual modification of the Israeli national security doctrine became evident both in the 1993 Operation 'Accountability' and in the 1996 'Operation Grapes of Wrath'. In these two operations the principle of transferring the war to the enemy's territory was substituted by the concept of transferring fire to the enemy's territory instead. The fear of suffering major IDF casualties led to the new approach involving the use of advanced technology, mainly in air power and artillery, to attack targets rather than the use of ground forces such as infantry and armoured units.[33] Although such tactics were not used during the first *Intifada*, due to the relatively low level of violence that the Palestinians used to voice their opposition to the continuing control of the Territories by Israel, as we shall see in Chapter 7, the use of conventional bombardments was again used during the *Al-Aqsa Intifada*. Rather than lowering the level of violence, the IDF, as it had done in Lebanon, increased it and radicalised even further Palestinian opposition to the occupation.

Ultimately, Israel was embroiled in a 15-year war of attrition, where it attempted to wear down *Hizbullah* forces and protect its citizens in the north of Israel. However, the IDF was not prepared to fight against this new form of low-intensity warfare carried out by non-state organisations such as *Hizbullah, Amal* (and eventually within the Territories, *Hamas, Islamic Jihad* and the stalwart PLO).

The chapters analysing both *Intifadas*, furthermore, will show how the IDF's difficulty in providing a military response to the growing Palestinian national consciousness and political–military activism had, to some degree, deleterious effects on IDF combat motivation and possibly caused 'a profound trauma in the security consciousness of Israelis in general'.[34]

6 The *Intifada*

As seen in Chapter 4, the Israeli security doctrine mostly focused on responding to conventional threats from Israel's Arab neighbours. Even solutions to sub-conventional threats, such as the terrorist infiltrations of the *fedayeen* during the 1950s, or the high-profile hijacking or kidnappings of the 1970s and 1980s, were carried out as conventional retaliatory attacks in the former case, and special commando salvage operations in the latter case. The fact that Israel was more concerned with existential security threats than with current security threats, understandably influenced the way in which Israeli strategic doctrine was formulated and operationalised and the way in which the IDF prepared itself for major military contingencies.

However, with the explosion of the *Intifada* in December 1987, Israel would confront a considerable threat to its control of the Territories. The source of such a threat was not to be found in the power of missiles, tanks and airplanes, but in the power of a civilian rebellion, which would eventually drag all of Israel – its leadership, its armed forces and its citizens – into a diplomatic, domestic but most of all, a moral quagmire. The *Intifada* would, in the space of six years, do what no Middle Eastern army or Palestinian terrorist organisation had been capable of doing over the previous 40 years: it would bring the, until then, most revered Israeli institution, the IDF, to its knees. It would also shake the ideological foundations of the state and damage further the national security consensus. But 'perhaps the most conspicuous result of the *Intifada* [was] the restoration of Israel's pre-1967 border, the famous Green Line, which had disappeared from Israeli maps and consciousness as early as 1968'.[1] Until the outbreak of the *Intifada*, 'there seemed to be a mental block in Israel'.[2] Such a collective mental block tended to ignore the existence of the Territories and of the plight of the Palestinian people.

Moreover, not only did the *Intifada* catch Israel by surprise in terms of its timing, virulence and longevity, but the *Intifada* also demonstrated the fact that the IDF could not rely anymore on its outdated and irrelevant mode of strategic thinking, which concentrated on interstate conventional warfare. Indeed, the Lebanon War had already presaged the IDF's strategic and tactical inability at winning decisively this new form of conflict: the intercommunal (or, as stated earlier, internecine) conflict.³ The *Intifada* magnified this new form of warfare as well as its deleterious effects on the IDF and Israeli society. In fact, the *Intifada* was to seriously challenge the operational effectiveness, deterrence capability and prestige of the IDF. Some argue it has yet to recover fully from its effects. This chapter will consequently look at the causes of the *Intifada* and its effect on the IDF. Before doing so, the chapter will briefly look at the central role the IDF and other Israeli security services had in maintaining the occupation and control of the Territories prior to the outbreak of the *Intifada*.

The military government in the Territories

After the overwhelming victory in the Six Day War, there were few in Israel that believed that the occupation of the newly acquired 70,000 square kilometres of land would become permanent. When asked by the American journalist Joseph Alsop how long the occupation would last, former Minister of Defence Moshe Dayan clearly replied that 'it would be for no more than two to four years' and in terms of the nature of the occupation that '[*Israel*] *must not interfere*, become involved, issue permits, make regulations, name administrators, become rulers. *For if we do, it will be bad for us*' [emphasis mine].⁴ Moshe Dayan was well aware of the fact that armies of occupation faced potential crises of legitimacy, which, according to Yoram Peri, 'can stem from the harm done to its professional character ... and which are: 1) the loss of its political neutrality; 2) a crisis of self-image and self-identity; and 3) damage to its relationship with the civil society'.⁵ However, despite such fears, the Military Government (MG) was established over all the Territories shortly after the war ended. Despite the rhetoric of non-interference, Palestinian dissension would not be tolerated. In fact, on 10 November 1967, Moshe Dayan stated at a Defence Ministry meeting that:

> Let the individual know that he has something to lose. His home can be blown up, his bus licence can be taken away, he can be deported from the region; or the contrary: he can exist with dignity, make money, exploit other Arabs, and travel in [his] bus.⁶

The crisis scenarios envisaged by Yoram Peri did not occur in the Israeli–Palestinian conflict until the *Intifada* began. This was because of the relative Palestinian quiescence and collaboration experienced within the Territories during the first 20 years of Israeli occupation. 'Granting of services was often made conditional upon agreement to collaborate with the authorities, including the police and the *Shin Bet* (*Sherut haBitachon haKlali* – 'General Security Services', GSS).⁷ The Palestinians in the Territories had pinned all their nationalist hopes on the other Arab states, on the exiled Palestinian Liberation Organisation (PLO) and its splinter groups to liberate them. Hence, the MG and the IDF, in particular, faced no major resistance from local Palestinians.

Thousands of Palestinians became local civil servants working for the occupying administration's offices and found proper jobs in Israel, thus creating Palestinian economic dependency on Israel. Most Palestinian trade became highly dependent on Israel. For example, already 'by 1968 Israeli exports to the West Bank constituted 76.8 per cent of its total imports',[8] whereas 'in 1986 they represented 89.4 per cent of their imports ... [this was] encouraged by the high level of protection enjoyed by Israeli goods in this "common market" with the Territories rather than any real comparative advantage of Israeli goods'.[9] Moreover, a large number of Palestinians were employed in Israel through the practice of labour exchanges. Consequently, 'in 1970 [Palestinians] made up 12 per cent of the total labor force [from] the West Bank and Gaza. In 1974, it was 32 per cent; in 1986, it was 36.3 per cent.'[10]

The strangling bureaucracy that developed in the Territories compounded the effects of Palestinian dependency. Paradoxically, the occupation and its institutions were funded by the 'occupation tax', which 'during the twenty years ... estimated at a conservative figure of US$800 million'.[11] The Palestinians were basically funding the Israeli occupation, albeit under the threat of a 'stick and carrot policy' which left them no other choice but to comply. Permits and overall administration on issues such as housing, finance, water, transport and agriculture had to be issued by the MG. However, such control was carried out by the Arab employees of the MG in order for the IDF to avoid direct contact and, hence, any friction with the local population.

The principle of minimal contact, initially formulated by Moshe Dayan, came 'not only out of concern for the welfare of the Palestinians, but also to limit the manpower requests' on the IDF, which had to focus on training and preparing for conventional warfare.[12] Additionally, even local nationalist Palestinian *notables* were more intent in gaining favours from the MG and in flaunting their social prestige than on pursuing viable political solutions to the Israeli occupation. Thus, 'the mediating activities of Palestinian communal leaders ... had provided a kind of cushion or buffer between the Israelis and the Palestinian rank and file that enabled people to go about their daily lives with a minimum of direct contact with the occupation'.[13] By the early 1980s, however, this working relationship was beginning to fall apart.

Consequently, 'a relatively modest military presence (and pervasive links of economic dependency) seemed, for two decades, sufficient to maintain physical control of the Territories'.[14] Until the *Intifada* had erupted, only one brigade of several hundred conscripted and reserve soldiers had preserved security throughout the whole Territories. Most of the preventative and repressive work was carried out by the GSS. The GSS's role was to gather intelligence about any terrorist or nationalist organisation and to uncover and incapacitate them by using a vast network of Israeli agents and Palestinian collaborators. The *Shin Bet*'s presence and efficacy was so great that its interrogators 'achieved an 80 per cent confession rate' and had 'success in preventing about 90 per cent of attempted terrorist actions'.[15]

Furthermore, until the eve of the *Intifada* any moral crisis within the IDF did not occur. This was due to the painstaking efforts made by the Israeli government to legitimise the occupation since 1967 within Israeli domestic and international politics. In any case, there was already a national consensus in Israeli society regarding the necessity of the IDF to remain in the Territories due to their role of providing much-needed strategic depth. Furthermore, the fact that the occupation was to continue until a political solution was found, not only helped maintain the perceived transitory character of the occupation, but also the necessity of holding onto it as a bargaining chip for future negotiations; such a perception helped legitimise Israeli occupation and maintain the national security consensus.

Another legitimising factor for Israel was to 'administer the Territories at the lowest cost possible ... by maintaining stability and order'.[16] As long as the military presence remained a low-key affair, due to Palestinian passivity, the need to physically enforce the occupation remained absent and, thus, politically, economically and morally tolerable. The first coordinator in the Territories, Maj. Gen. (Ret.) Shlomo Gazit, demonstrated amazing foresight, long before any major disturbances broke out in the Territories, when explaining Israel's need of a 'deluxe occupation' in order to avoid a complete breakdown of the national consensus regarding continued occupation:

> The world of today finds it politically difficult to come to terms with the continuing retention of occupied area ... As the disquiet increases in such an area ... the political, international, Islamic and Arab opposition to the occupation will increase ... *From a moral point of view, it is difficult to suppose that the Israeli society could come to terms with the need to implement cruel, repressive measures to maintain order in the Territories.* The Israeli society has become used to the widest support of public opinion regarding the policies and operations of the security forces; in light of this, the repression of civilian unrest ... would be most difficult to come to terms with.... If public opinion in Israel doesn't come to terms with what is being done in the Territories, we will not be able to remain there for one additional day [emphasis mine].[17]

For 20 years the IDF and associated security services were more than able to cope with the occupation, because of the relative calm and order that

Table 6.1 Jewish settlers in the West Bank, 1976–86[1]

Year	Total	Absolute increase	% increase on previous year
1976	3,176	–	–
1977	5,023	1,847	58.1
1978	7,361	2,338	46.5
1979	10,000	2,639	35.8
1980	12,424	2,424	24.2
1981	16,119	3,695	29.7
1982	21,000	4,881	30.3
1983	27,500	6,500	30.9
1984	44,146	16,646	60.5
1985	52,960	8,814	20.0
1986	60,500	7,540	14.2

Source: Meron Benvenisti, *1987 Report*, p. 55.

Note
1 Different Israeli government ministries provide different settler population figures due to their distinct *census* methodologies.

presided in the Territories, as well as due to the support of Israeli public opinion. Israel was able to maintain the status quo, which in the Territories' case 'signified a policy of avoiding any long-range decisions concerning [their] future'.[18] Israel was then able to focus on the major conventional threats arising from Egypt, Syria, Jordan and Iraq, in accordance with its strategic doctrine, and wait until a better political arrangement regarding the Palestinian population could be found. Such a political arrangement, though, would have to take account of the facts created on the ground, mainly, the expropriation of occupied/disputed land in order to carry out the rapid growth of Israeli settlements, which increasingly irritated the local Palestinian population (see Table 6.1). Indeed, 'by 1992 approximately 55 per cent of the total land area of the West Bank and 30 per cent of the Gaza Strip had been appropriated by the Israeli government'.[19] Clearly, the growing number of settlements and settlers could only appear in Palestinian eyes as Israel's desire of reinforcing the status quo by permanently annexing the Territories and frustrating any chances of ever relinquishing the land back to a future Palestinian state.

The *Intifada* explodes

The whole status quo was overthrown dramatically as the *Intifada* broke out on 9 December 1987 during a funeral-protest ceremony in the large *Jabalya* refugee camp adjoining Gaza. The event that sparked the funeral-protest, and consequently the uprising, was the accidental death of four Palestinians caused by an IDF tank-transport collision with a truck bringing back Palestinian workers from Israel the previous day. The Israeli army entered the camp in order to pacify the stone-throwing revolt and ended up killing a 20-year-old youth, which then aggravated the situation. The demonstrations spread like wildfire from the Gaza Strip to the West Bank.

Despite the fact that the uprising caught the Israeli public and its leadership by surprise, the birth pangs and the causes of the uprising had much deeper roots in the Israeli–Palestinian conflict. The traffic accident and the consequent Palestinian deaths 'were the spark rather than the real cause of the uprising.... But such was the tension ... that even a traffic accident was sufficient to trigger a big explosion.'[20] The tension had built up over the years, despite Israel's belief that it was pursuing a 'benign occupation' that raised Palestinians' living standards and taught them democratic values; things which according to Israeli apologists, the 'despotic' occupations of their former rulers (i.e. Egypt and Jordan) had been unable to provide. In reality though, the Israeli 'benign occupation' was anything but benevolent in the Palestinians' eyes.

First, the relative economic growth and welfare, which the Palestinians had initially benefited from with the occupation had all but disappeared and eventually evolved into a '"parasitic but complex two-way relationship" in the areas of land, water, labor and export markets ... [and which masked] the problem of structural underdevelopment'.[21] The inability to have any say on their economic condition only exacerbated the Palestinians' sense of desperation and political impotence, which in turn encouraged nationalist emotions to proliferate in the Territories. Indeed, 'the particular work experience of this population group, in addition to the realities of their daily lives in the Territories [gave] rise to a particular consciousness and identity'.[22] By 1987, this coalesced the whole Palestinian nation into a united opposition force against Israeli occupation.

It was, therefore, more than likely that the uprising would flare up in the Territories where, by 1987, 'unemployment was running at 50–60 per cent' and living conditions in most refugee camps were dreadful.[23] Indeed, it was only understandable that 'the explosion should occur in *Jabalya*, where some 60,000 people [made] their home in conditions of appalling poverty, overcrowding, and filth'.[24]

Despite the rhetoric of ruling the Territories democratically, full use was made of an arbitrary detention measure introduced in Palestine during the British Mandate by the British Defence (Emergency) Regulations of 1945. According to such regulations, individuals could be detained without charge or trial for a period of six months; furthermore, such detentions could be renewed every six months an indefinite number of times.

Hence, the Israeli MG was able to detain indefinitely any suspect without any legal representation or judicial hearing, for that matter. Quite often, such detainees were subject to interrogations involving torture and subject to humiliating living conditions. Such detentions were already common practice as early as 1970; in that year alone 'there were 1,131 administrative detainees'.[25] Furthermore, in 1967, the practice of the deportations of political activists, uncooperative notables and anyone

78 *The* Intifada

affiliated directly to the PLO was already in place. In fact, 'Palestinian sources estimate that at least 1,156 people were deported between 1967 and 1978'.[26]

The application of the Defence (Emergency) Regulations effectively introduced into the Territories a dual legal system. That is, a system which contains both the military and civilian court systems. Consequently, Jewish residents of the Territories have been, almost without exception, prosecuted in civilian courts under civilian law. On the other hand, Palestinians, under Israeli occupation, have been customarily prosecuted in military courts under the much harsher Defence (Emergency) Regulations. Such a dual system could only compound the sense of injustice and lack of trust that Palestinians felt towards the Israeli occupation.

Furthermore, two years prior to the outbreak of the *Intifada*, Israeli security provisions in the Territories, under the direction of then Defence Minister Yitzhak Rabin, were already described as the 'iron fist' policy. Such a policy included, amongst other things, deportations, house demolitions, collective curfews and press censorship. 'Between January 1985 and November 1987, 43 Palestinians were deported and during the year immediately prior to the outbreak of the *Intifada* at least 20 people died as a direct result of actions of the [IDF].... 180 suffered injury, 157 were imprisoned without trial under administrative detention, eight people were served with deportation orders, and 132 buildings were demolished or sealed.'[27]

Apparently, the political situation in the Territories was warming up. This was due in part to the increasing radicalisation of local Palestinians who had grown frustrated at the fact that the PLO had been in disarray following its exile to Tunis in December 1982, and the suffering of various setbacks, including the IAF raid on the PLO's Tunis headquarters in September 1985. Matters had to be taken into their own hands. Between April 1986 and May 1987, 3,150 cases of violent demonstrations took place, of which 1,870 incidents concerned rock-throwing, 600 related to cases of roadblocks and burning tyres, and there were 665 occurrences of flag hoisting, leaflet distribution and painting of slogans in favour of the Palestinian nationalist cause. During the same period, 65 episodes occurred concerning firearms, explosives and stabbings, and 150 involving petrol bombs.[28] Nonetheless, the Israeli authorities did not predict the looming civilian revolt (neither did Arafat for that matter). So, as long as the cases of nationalist defiance were perceived by the Israeli authorities as individual and sporadic endeavours, the MG did not have to modify its *modus operandi* in any major way. Such activities were not thought to seriously challenge the Israeli occupation. As one reservist put it:

> My first regular duties in the Territories were very quiet – in 1984–5. There was some stone throwing and the perception was that the Palestinians were not capable of doing anything. The perception was that if they see an Israeli soldier, they will hide away, they will run away.

One platoon was sent [to Tulkarem] and we were asked to march up and down the town three times, so that they would all see the red berets and the red boots and the city would get quiet and that is what happened basically. We were very, very arrogant when I think about it.... Next time we went to the Territories – it was already the *Intifada* – the story was very different.[29]

Such Israeli perceptions of Palestinian nationalist defiance were erroneous. They did not seem to comprehend the new nature in which local Palestinians were beginning to *vocalise* their disaffection with the Israeli occupation. The new form of violence was becoming much bolder and spontaneous, in the sense that it was becoming much more symbolically rebellious (for example, cases of civil disobedience were steadily increasing), locally initiated by politically unaffiliated protesters. Violence was beginning to be carried out in broad daylight and even, cheekily, in front of the Israeli security forces. Meron Benvenisti underlines this change of Palestinian tactics when statistically comparing the number of organised and planned acts of terrorism to spontaneous violent protests during the decade preceding the outbreak of the *Intifada*: 'The ratio of terrorist/spontaneous acts was 1:11 between 1977–84, 1:16 in 1985, 1:18 in 1986. This ratio indicate[d] a new phase in Palestinian resistance and the intercommunal strife.'[30]

The spontaneous and widespread manifestation of this new form of Palestinian protest was down to the fact that, since the early 1980s, most Palestinian communal *charitable* associations, as well as any sympathisers of terrorist organisations, were being targeted and legally disbanded. Such a course of action was *de jure* possible due to various legal amendments, introduced by the *Likud* government of Menachem Begin in the summer of 1980, a government which was intent on smothering further independent national Palestinian political articulation and organisation, following the Israeli–Egyptian peace treaty.

For example, on 28 July, the *Knesset* passed the Law of Associations, which superseded the previous legal framework established by the Ottoman Associations Law of 1909, regulating public and private associations. Such associations, which could comprise trade unions, civil rights organisations, social welfare charities and so on, were forced to re-register under new Israeli legislation, but any association 'concerning which "there [was] reasonable ground to conclude that ... it [would] serve as a cover for illegal actions or objectives" [would] not be registered'.[31] The fact that the legality of an association's actions and objectives was open to very broad Israeli interpretation, the withdrawal of almost any troublesome (read 'nationalist') association could be carried out summarily, albeit under the politically correct guise of the law.

Furthermore, the *Shilonsky* Amendment to Article 10 of the Israel Nationality Law (1952) allowed the Interior Minister to 'abolish the Israeli citizenship of any person who has committed an act that constitutes abrogation of loyalty to the state of Israel'.[32] The major question arising from such an amendment, though, was how could disloyalty be defined? Was any future legitimate questioning of government policy in the Territories, on the part of Israeli Arab citizens, or liberal Israeli Jewish citizens to be considered an act of disloyalty towards the state of Israel? The most draconian measure, however, was the Amendment to the Prevention of Terrorism Ordinance (1948), which basically equated any outward expression of sympathy, such as singing slogans or anthems, exhibiting banners, emblems, etc., towards any terrorist (read 'nationalist') organisation as almost an act of terrorism. Such an act would be punishable for a term of up to three years' imprisonment.[33] Due to this measure, IDF units often found themselves wasting a lot of time trying to force either the perpetrators of such acts, or innocent bystanders when necessary, into removing nationalist emblems and banners amongst Palestinian towns and refugee camps. This often resulted in cat-and-mouse games between Palestinian youths and IDF units involved in this farce.

With such legislation, the MG had free reign to pursue any dangerous individual or association that was even remotely affiliated to the PLO or any other of its splinter groups. Any high-profile leader or association was rendered severely susceptible to Israel's numerous COIN measures, such as deportation, detentions, bans and so on. Accordingly, any local protest would have to take on the form of a spontaneous and mass civilian uprising, because of Israel's effectiveness in rendering impotent any major nationalist organisation.

It was only two months after the spontaneous uprising began that a popular underground leadership was formed and began to call itself the Unified National Leadership of the Uprising (UNLU). The UNLU distributed leaflets calling for the escalation of the uprising and gave precise instructions and directives dictating the activities of the Palestinian local population.[34] As shall be seen below, most of the violence and civil disobedience became such a generalised phenomenon that 'the continuation of the uprising in spite of the detention of thousands [was] an indication that the *Intifada* [was] a social movement rooted not in traditional patron-client politics, but in a network of local community organisations and activism' whose leadership would prove hard to emasculate due to its hydra-headed configuration.[35] Thus, 'one woman screaming "*Allahu Akhbar*" (Allah is great) [could on occasion] bring 1,000 to 2,000 people out into the streets within minutes'.[36]

Nevertheless, shortly after the UNLU was formed it became clear to the IDF that it was under the influence of the PLO. Thus, the only way the IDF could really punish the evasive UNLU was to target instigators, terrorists, well-known PLO supporters within the Territories, and PLO members who were perceived by Israeli intelligence to be managing the *Intifada* from abroad. For example, on 16 April 1988, Israeli Secret Service agents killed Abu Jihad, *Fatah* leader, deputy commander of the PLO armed forces and who was considered to be 'the main architect of the *Intifada*'.[37] Besides the traditional hit squads of the *Shin Bet* or the *Sayeret Matkal* (General Staff Special Forces Unit), two new 'units of Arabists [were formed] – one for the West Bank [*Duvdevan* Unit], one for the Gaza Strip [*Shimshon* Unit] – whose task was to go after individual suspects and arrest or kill them' by infiltrating the local population through their Arab guise.[38]

First tactical reactions to the *Intifada*

When the *Intifada* began, Defence Minister Rabin, who was scheduled for a diplomatic visit to the USA, did not bother staying in Israel in order to oversee the IDF's initial COIN reactions to the uprising. He went off on his diplomatic mission to achieve a new conventional weapons package deal, as he did not see any difference between the new disturbances and the previous ones. He considered conventional deterrence to remain as Israel's number one strategic priority at that time. Upon his return, Rabin as well as Israel's 'military and political establishment took several months to grasp the strategic significance of the new challenge'.[39] Consequently, the *Intifada* continued to be considered by the Israeli military and political leadership a 'current security problem, for which standard operational procedures would suffice to restore the status quo within two or three weeks'.[40]

As a result, the traditional way of responding to any violence in the Territories was by the IDF's use of live ammunition at a relatively long distance from the actual source of the commotion, whenever such violence was deemed life-threatening. This initial response, however, led to an exponential rise in Palestinian deaths. In the 'first month of the uprising (9 December–8 January) 26 Palestinians were killed'.[41] Such a heavy-handed approach aggravated the uprising, for the disparity in the use of force between the Palestinians and the IDF only strengthened the Palestinians' resolve to continue the uprising. It also reinforced its moral standing before international opinion vis-à-vis Israel. Such a heavy-handed approach contrasted heavily with the Palestinian tactics of 'sticks and stones'.

Even Defence Minister Rabin was willing to admit that '85 per cent of all violent activities, which are the lifeblood of the *Intifada*, are incidents of stone-throwing [and that] an additional 10 per cent involves roadblocks, with and without burning tires, and [that] five per cent of the violent activities are stabbings or fire bombs', underlining the asymmetry of force between the IDF and the Palestinian protesters.[42] Consequently, the traditional view, which had so helped Israel maintain its self-image as a righteous nation that used force only in self-defence, against much greater and virulent Arab aggression, had dissolved in a matter of weeks. A role reversal occurred between Israel and its Palestinian subjects: Israel was now the Goliath, whereas Palestinians became the weaker, yet braver and morally 'righteous' David.

This did not mean that the nature of Palestinian violence was not meant to kill. In fact, 'between December 1987 and February 1989, 12 were killed [and] more than 1,280 Israelis – about 830 soldiers and 450 civilians – were injured, some of them critically'.[43] However, as Hebrew University of Jerusalem Professor of Law Mordechai Kremnitzer aptly put it, 'the fact that they don't throw grenades truly embodies the moral strength of their actions' was perceived by many Israelis to be true.[44]

Accordingly, in order to reduce the number of Palestinian deaths, a new tactic was adopted in January 1988 whereby a massive incursion of IDF troops[45] was brought into the Territories in order to come into close confrontation with the demonstrators and carry out Rabin's infamous policy of 'force, might and beatings'.[46] At the same time, the army command doubled reserve duty from 30 to 62 days. The weapon of choice adopted with this new policy was the plastic and fibreglass truncheon, which was introduced in March 1988, because the traditional wooden ones kept shattering too easily on Palestinian bodies. Furthermore, rubber bullets and tear gas were introduced, but proved ineffective in dispersing rioters.

Indeed, in August 1988, plastic bullets, which had an effective range of 100 metres and, thus, kept IDF troops at a safe distance from the reach of stones and Molotov cocktail bombs were introduced. This was done in order 'to reduce the soldiers' frustration … [for] it was demonstrated that the use of clubs, CN and CS gas and rubber bullets was insufficient when confronting stone-throwers at a range of 30–50 metres'.[47] Within such a distance IDF troops became highly vulnerable to any form of projectile hurled at them from the rioters.

Plastic bullets, when fired within 70 metres of the intended target, were capable of shattering a person's bones and could be lethal. 'According to an Israeli military spokesman's statement issued on 22 January 1989, in the five months that plastic bullets had been in use, the bullets were responsible for about half the fatalities of that period, with 47 Palestinians dying from wounds inflicted by them and 288 suffering injury.'[48] It is clear that the new measures introduced still caused many deaths and only worsened the IDF's domestic and international image of being an army that conducted itself on the basis of the 'purity of arms' principle.

The IDF became the target of ferocious criticism on the part of the Israeli Left and the international community. Because of its heavy-handed approach, new guidelines regarding the IDF's rules of engagement [ROE] were set in place in order to obviate such criticism. In February 1988, the IDF published a dispatch detailing the rules of required conduct by the IDF troops in dealing with the uprising. According to the IDF dispatch, force was generally permitted in order to quell riots and any resistance to arrest.

Force could not be used after the dispersal of a demonstration or during the custody of a demonstrator. The IDF was also prohibited from destroying property for the sole purpose of punishing or humiliating the activities of the Palestinian demonstrators.

Moreover, guidelines for opening fire at rioters became highly restrictive and would be sanctioned 'only when necessary to escape a life-threatening situation'.[49] Such guidelines, however, proved very hard to follow, due to the IDF's frustration borne out of the difficulty in suppressing the various disturbances in the Territories, as the ROE often proved to be irrelevant to the situation the soldiers on the ground faced.

The destruction and sealing of properties and deportation orders as punitive measures could only be officially sanctioned by the area commanders. They, nonetheless, increased during the apex of Palestinian violence (1988–89), but diminished once Palestinian demonstrations began to peter out at the end of 1990 (see Table 6.2 and Table 6.3).

According to Aryeh Shalev's statistical analysis, as the *Intifada* carried on, 'the deterrent effect of demolitions and deportations deteriorated significantly.... Indeed, demolitions [and deportations] were transformed into a stimulus to further escalation of resistance to Israeli rule.'[50] The ineffectiveness of such deterrent measures was partly due to the fact that the IDF was unable – or unwilling – to carry out such measures to the extent that they would have proven too costly for the Palestinians to actually carry on with their rebellion. Other non-military measures enacted by the

Table 6.2 Demolition of homes, 9 December 1987–91

Year	Demolitions	% difference on previous year
9–31 Dec. 1987	1	–
1988	149	148.0
1989	162	8.7
1990	118	−27.1
1991	46	−61.0

Source: 'Demolition of houses', *B'Tselem*, www.btselem.org (accessed 27 July 2002).

Table 6.3 Sealing of homes, 1988–90

Year	Sealings	% difference on previous year
1988	79	–
1989	97	18.6
1990	74	−23.7
1991	34	−54.1

Source: 'Demolition of houses', *B'Tselem*, www.btselem.org (accessed 27 July 2002).

MG, which proved also to be unsuccessful were, *inter alia*, the cutting off of electricity and of telephone communications, the imposition of limits on money being brought in from Jordan, the banning of agricultural harvesting and commerce and the imposition of economic restrictions in general.

Because of the vast number of Palestinians involved in the riots, large-scale curfews on whole villages and cities and, on occasion, closures of all the Territories were imposed in order to stop Palestinians from going onto the streets where most of the violence was perpetrated and in order to avoid any overspill of the uprising across the Green Line. Furthermore, schools and universities – traditionally seen as the breeding ground of nationalism, rather than centres of education – were also closed down periodically.

Such restriction of Palestinian movement was attempted in order to quell the riots and civil disobedience *per se*, and to facilitate the movement of IDF troops, *Magav* (*mishmar hagvul* – Israeli border police) units and GSS agents around the Territories. With the uprising, Israeli security personnel found it increasingly difficult to carry out their preventative and retaliatory operations as they became the target of rock- or Molotov-throwing defiant youths or found physical as well as human barricades all over the alleyways, streets and highways of the Territories. These closures had the opposite effect of what the IDF intended, for they increased the Palestinian youth's process of national indoctrination and radicalisation. As Joe Stork put it:

> The military can command that the schools open or close, but they cannot determine which serves their purpose: when open, they provide points of assembly for demonstrations and the like; when closed, the children take up subversive subjects such as Palestinian history and geography in the classes set up by the local committees.[51]

The gross limitations of such punitive measures were down to the fact that the UNLU as well as the Palestinian population in general, coalesced in solidarity vis-à-vis Israel's attempts at strangling the uprising. In fact, 'people ... set up local committees to handle distribution of foodstuffs in curfew and siege conditions, to organize guard duty in villages, to promote local agricultural projects' and so on.[52] Collaborators, in addition, were persuaded to give up collaborating with the occupying forces either through communal ostracism or outright death threats (and executions in the case of such threats being deliberately ignored), which were in large part carried out by *Intifada* shock forces such as the Black Panthers, Red Eagles and other groups. According to the IDF spokesperson, 942 Palestinians were killed by other Palestinians on suspicion of collaboration between 9 December 1987 and 30 November 1993. The Associated Press put the total at 771.[53]

The declining morale of IDF troops

According to Defence Minister Rabin, '60 per cent of the stone-throwers in the Territories [were] children aged 14–16'[54] and that such youths were able to make a mockery of the IDF's ineffective COIN operations, such as 'standing on rooftops and urinating on IDF troops patrolling in the streets below'.[55] This behaviour began to adversely affect the IDF's level of self-control, restraint and professionalism. Such mockery was also possible because 'according to press reports, the local population was well versed in the IDF's regulations for opening fire and regarding restrictions on soldiers' resort to violence, and exploited this knowledge' to their advantage.[56] Hence, many soldiers felt that trying to *fight* youthful stone-throwers was a futile activity. One squad commander recalled how useless he felt when capturing young insurgents:

> I remember in the Qalandia Camp, young children were throwing rocks and we were running after them. I caught a child and brought him to the [platoon] commander. The commander looked at me and I at him; it is like you cannot do anything. You caught him and now what? In the first *Intifada* you had to run, back and forth, after young children. How could you not be frustrated?[57]

Notwithstanding the IDF's dispatches, 'shooting deaths of Palestinian youths sometimes occurred as visceral reactions by soldiers to stone-throwing and other incidents. Vandalism of personal property and the firing of toxic gas into enclosed spaces often reflected frustration, vindictiveness and deep-seated anger. [Additionally], soldiers beat up Palestinians to "let steam off".'[58]

With the mounting of domestic and international criticism regarding the violation of guidelines under which force could be used, COS Lt. Gen. Dan Shomron (1987–91) was forced to admit, in an interview in March 1989, that because of the difficulty of the IDF troops in dealing with rioters, the guidelines left a 'grey area' within which each soldier had to use his own judgement. COS Shomron was, in effect, passing the buck of responsibility to the men on the ground rather than taking on the duty of setting down clearer deadlines. One Israeli army reservist cynically described what such a 'grey area' actually entailed:

> Every battalion works out its own set of norms.... Every battalion commander is the sovereign of the area (under his command). Every company commander is the *mukhtar* [i.e. village chief/elder] of a village or two, and every soldier manning a roadblock is a little god. He decides what to do: who will be allowed through and who won't be.... The best description I can find for what's going on there is total chaos.... There are simply no rules governing the

implementation of orders, behavioral norms, and methods of punishment.[59]

In any case, if the IDF's rules of engagement were grossly violated, complaints could be filed with the Military Legal Advisor. Thereafter investigations would be carried out and if the investigation found out that a soldier had departed from the mandatory norms of conduct, legal proceedings would be opened against him within the Military Advocate General. However, as one soldier put it, it would be very hard for comrades-in-arms to report on ROE violations given their close ties of friendship and comradeship:

> If you, for example, had to shout 'stop or I'll shoot,' but only shot without warning, nobody would tell you, 'you did not shout'. And even if somebody saw that you did not do the right thing, obviously, there would be a cover-up. Nobody is going to take somebody that spends so much time with you in that environment and who is basically serving his country and tell him, 'listen, you did not shout first before you shot, therefore, we are going to put you on trial'. It does not work like that.[60]

Although many minor violations were ignored and not reported, quite a few indictments were filed against IDF troops throughout the *Intifada*. The Chief Military Prosecutor has provided statistics which show that 'from the outset of the Palestinian uprising until the end of 1992, 168 indictments were filed against 241 IDF personnel: 54 officers, 183 regular troops, and 4 civilians employed by the IDF. In court decisions handed down, as of December 1992, 194 soldiers were found guilty of the charges brought against them and 23 were acquitted.'[61]

Such prosecutions, despite the fact that they partially vindicated the moral and democratic nature of the IDF, had an adverse effect on the local troops' conduct. The fear of being demoted, dishonourably discharged or even of serving prison terms had on numerous occasions dissuaded Israeli soldiers from carrying out their assigned duties to the point that in cases where the use of force was obviously needed in a specific situation, such soldiers desisted from taking the required security provisions for fear of overstepping the limits of legitimate use of force and subsequently being held legally responsible for their deeds. The growing fear of being prosecuted led some soldiers to cynically state that they could 'not serve without an "attached lawyer"',[62] which proved, according to Martin Van Creveld, that 'the acronym LIC ... really stood for lawyer-infested conflict'.[63] One soldier recounted his experiences regarding other soldiers' fears of avoiding carrying out ROE:

> There were people saying, 'why the hell should I shoot right now. I can get into a lot of trouble, so I won't shoot'. They [stone-throwers]

would run away, nothing happened and then I would be able to finish my shift and go back to sleep or whatever.[64]

Due to such fears many of the soldiers and officers involved in the *Intifada* clearly began to suppress their traditional ethos of initiative and aggressiveness when carrying out their mission. Others, however, reacted the opposite way.

Such caution often aggravated other IDF soldiers' frustrations and led to many more cases of 'savage behavior by the troops, of 15-year-old boys being thrown off speeding army cars, of heads being knocked against steel shutters, of beating of innocent bystanders' and so on.[65] However, in most cases, if Palestinians held in custody did not use any violence, IDF soldiers tried to carry out their duty without imposing punitive measures on their prisoners. One *Givati* NCO recollected how his undercover unit arrested riot instigators:

> We had undercover units basically in t-shirts from the waist up and you drove around in cars and raided into a crowd of rioters, jumped up and grabbed whoever was leading it. We handed them over to whoever we had to, the prison authorities. We weren't allowed to beat them. If they had any marks on them, they were set free. So, they were in relatively good condition when they got in. It was nothing, except if the guy hit back, he got the shit kicked out of him. If he didn't, okay, we arrested him and took him in. If they were very young, we took them home and the parents would beat the crap out of them, because of the fine they would get.[66]

To be sure, there were attempts on the part of various members of units perpetrating such punitive measures to stop or protest against them. Such protests, though, were often ignored and left the more morally disturbed soldiers a choice of either not taking part in such actions or in becoming a conscientious objector. Many comments echoed a soldier's statement regarding the effects of Rabin's policy of 'force, might and beatings' on their level of morale: 'The more I break other people's bones, the more I am broken myself.'[67] And yet many continued to go on with their assigned duties for the sake of obeying orders and sticking to the mission.

Increasing demoralisation

As the *Intifada* progressed, it was clear that the IDF would be unable to single-handedly quell the uprising. New groups, particularly Islamic ones, began to operate in the Territories in response to IDF COIN operations, which had until then only radicalised Palestinian youths. For example, in February 1988, the Islamic Resistance Movement, *Hamas* (i.e. 'courage' or 'bravery' in Arabic), was formed and operated in competition with Islamic

88 *The* Intifada

Jihad. As the IDF proved unable to quell the uprising, it was only natural for Defence Minister Rabin to declare by early 1988 that 'you can't rule by force over one-and-a-half million Palestinians ... and saddle the IDF with a mission that is outside its proper function'.[68]

Demoralisation within the IDF took root when it became obvious that the politicians under whose orders the IDF functioned could offer no answers to the uncertainties about present policies or the future of the conflict. Differences of opinion between the *Likud* and Labour parties, who formed the National Unity Government, led to ambiguous policy instructions and major strategic indecisiveness. Under such political conditions, the best the IDF could achieve was to buy time for the political echelon to proceed without pressure, in order to attain political solutions to the Palestinian problem. This did not spare the IDF from criticism from both sides of the political landscape.

'Politicians constantly attempted to make political capital of the *Intifada* at the expense of the army, the COS, and the defence minister',[69] either by stating that the IDF was not doing enough or was being too tough, depending on what side of the political spectrum such critiques came from. On top of such 'establishment' criticism, peace activities, run, for example, by Peace Now and *Gush Shalom* (Peace Bloc) mushroomed exponentially in order to protest against the occupation as well as the IDF's operations in the Territories.[70] On the other hand, right-wing groups such as *Gush Emunim* and the *Yesha* Council of Jewish Settlements not only criticised the IDF's 'soft' tactics, but frequently took matters into their own hands through retaliatory vigilantism.[71]

Such criticism of the IDF had already occurred to a lesser extent during the Lebanon War, albeit mostly from the dovish political camp and various peace groups, but not from right-wing groups. When commenting on the demoralising effect domestic criticism of the state's and the IDF's strategic objectives has on troops, one commander at the end of the Lebanon War, stated:

> We try hard to instil in our soldiers motivation, pride, proficiency. But when they go home on leave everything turns around. Instead of reassurance they get a slap in the face. And these soldiers who work so hard become depressed ... *Eighty per cent of our problems with the troops would disappear had there not been a public debate in the rear* [emphasis mine].[72]

With the *Intifada*, however, criticism sprung up from all quarters of Israeli life. This demoralised many troops serving in the Territories. It also led senior officers to defend the IDF publicly, given the Israeli public's growing meddling in the IDF's conduct within the Territories. In an army radio interview the IDF's Chief Education Officer, Brig. Gen. Nehemia Dagan, stated that:

The Intifada 89

> If this society wants to struggle, the way is first of all to struggle against the correct punching bag, which is not the IDF.... The IDF has begun to feel that it has been placed in the field in order to carry out a task and suddenly everyone in the country knows best.[73]

Despite the fact that the West Bank commander, Maj. Gen. Amram Mitzna, could brag at the beginning of the *Intifada* that 'he could count Israeli resisters on the fingers of one hand', a few months after such a brash comment the first cracks in the IDF began to appear.[74] Indeed, 'over 450 reservists signed an ad that *Yesh Gvul* [i.e. There is a limit] published in Israeli newspapers on 3 June ... [publicly committing] themselves not to serve in the Territories'.[75] Ironically, later on that year, a conference on the morale problem of the IDF was organised by reserve soldiers and commanders from the left-wing *Kibbutz HaArtzi* movement, to which Mitzna belonged. The soldiers published a booklet called *Si'ah Lohamim 1989* (Soldiers' Reflections 1989). It centred on interviews with those who had served in the Territories, thereby exposing the intimate feelings and fears of the traditionally coarse Israeli soldier. Defending their abhorrence of the IDF's conduct in the Territories the booklet stated that:

> There is nothing to be ashamed of if they say about us, 'we shoot and we cry'. When ... you are obliged to perform duties which are against your conscience, against your education and your worldview, and when you don't know whether you will accomplish your mission from the military point of view, it is not a disgrace to cry.... A spokesman for those participating in the meeting warned Gen. Mitzna: 'We have reached a moment of truth, a moment in which the army must listen to us.... *We are reaching the limits of our abilities*' [emphasis mine].[76]

Such statements became gradually more vociferous and regular. Many troops were, in fact, quite demoralised. Such demoralisation became almost inevitable, because most of the positive factors affecting troop morale and combat motivation dissipated with the uprising's continuation. Indeed, if one looks at the grievances expressed in the previous quote of the Soldiers' Reflections 1989 booklet, it is clear that it touches on various morale factors that were negatively affected by the *Intifada* COIN tactics adopted by the IDF.

First, soldiers were obliged to perform duties which were against their conscience, education and worldview. Obviously, the belief that the Israeli soldier fought according to the principles of never letting the Holocaust happen again, of *milkhemet ein briera* and of *tohar haneshek*, that is on the basis of pure self-defence and of 'preserving humanistic norms in combat, refraining from unnecessary bloodshed, and avoiding, at all cost, harming civilians in general and women and children in particular',[77] were shattered. Despite attempts to introduce non-lethal weapons and anti-riot methods, insinuations about Israeli soldiers now being 'Judeo-Nazis' began appearing in the Israeli press. Furthermore, a *kibbutz* soldier, reflecting many other soldiers' similar opinions, wrote bluntly in an Israeli newspaper that 'there is no purity in the club and no morality in tear gas'.[78]

Such moral dilemmas were particularly pertinent to the IDF units carrying out infantry duties, because it was the infantry that bore the brunt of the *Intifada* and because it was the infantry that had to come into close proximity with the enemy. This new form of warfare could not entail a high level of firepower. Instead, it involved direct contact with a hateful and much weaker enemy. The morality that resulted in this conflict was of a different nature to the one faced in previous conflicts. As one infantry soldier put it:

> I think that you can find a morality of war [*moosar milkhama*] among other forces, but for infantry soldiers it is much more complex. When you fire a shell in a tank, or when you cast a bomb from a plane you don't have a concrete connection with whom you hit. [But] in the infantry you do have this concrete connection, more than others.[79]

Moreover, soldiers' parents were unwilling to remain silent when witnessing the violation of the democratic and humanistic values instilled in their children's upbringing and their consequent demoralisation:

> We *refuse* to accept the fall in the values upon which we have educated our children.... Service in the Territories has shaken the *moral immunity* of the soldiers and affected the motivation of the best of our youth to serve [emphasis mine].[80]

Defining the mission

The lack of clear, stable and effective rules of engagement caused much frustration in the IDF's lower ranks. What proved even more exasperating was the general confusion both within the lower and higher IDF echelons of what really constituted the IDF's mission vis-à-vis the Palestinian uprising in the Territories. The head of the Central Command, Maj. Gen. Amram Mitzna, stated in early 1989 that 'it is not the policy or the order that is confusing, but the mission. That is confusing from every point of view.'[81]

Whereas during the first few months of the *Intifada* the IDF was expected to completely restore the status quo ante, by mid-September 1988, then Defence Minister, Yitzhak Rabin, stated that the IDF's mission was to first of all 'attain a significant abatement in the level of violence, a situation of relative calm, and second, ensure that the civil administration functions'.[82] The Israeli government expected the army to at least bring calm and to reduce violence in the Territories to a bearable level before a political solution could be found. The various National Unity Governments (1988–92) were unable to reach a diplomatic agreement with the Palestinians five years into the uprising.

Such a 'policing' mission was alien to the IDF's history and was, furthermore, hard to measure in terms of what constituted success or mission accomplishment from a military point of view. Despite numerous calls by the IDF, for greater strategic guidance from the political leadership, the IDF was on the whole left to its own devices. Many within the IDF blamed the political leadership for its failures due to such lack of guidance. Just before retiring as the head of the Israeli Air Force, Maj. Gen. Avihu Ben-Nun stated in December 1991 that, 'today, the IDF is not getting political guidance on issues pertaining to security concepts. Anarchy develops.'[83]

Many soldiers on the ground did not have a clear sense of their military objective, because of the political echelon's indecisiveness and lack of leadership both at the strategic level, but more importantly, at the tactical level. Lt. Col. Ilan Malka recollected his experiences as a platoon commander during the first *Intifada*: 'In the first *Intifada*, many [upper echelon commanders] did not support us or trust us as nobody knew what was happening.'[84] Such lack of direction could only but demoralise the troops serving on a daily basis in the Territories.

The IDF tried to adapt, through a process of trial-and-error, to Palestinian low-intensity violence. Such adaptation, however, proved to be very complicated, given the IDF's traditionally conservative approach to changing its security doctrine. The IDF was challenged by the *Intifada*, in that it was forced to assume a *modus operandi*, which diverged considerably from typical Israeli military doctrine. The *Intifada* made it clear that it could not be smothered with a single conclusive strike. As a result, the IDF had to conduct its COIN operations 'within an overall strategic framework of attrition'.[85]

Thus, Israel found itself fighting a war of attrition, which was something of an *anathema* to its strategic doctrine and which proved demoralising for the IDF. The IDF was accustomed to short, goal-oriented military operations, which normally entailed the elimination of a clear and present threat and, in the case of the major wars fought previously, the seizure of tangible assets, such as land and the resources therein. As Uri Dromi, then editor of the IDF officer's magazine *Ma'arachot*, commented, when analysing the IDF's aimlessness, 'the *Intifada* is a slap in the face for the IDF.... The result is a little of this and a little of that – the worst of possible compromises.'[86]

Another morale factor that was adversely affected, was the IDF troops' level of self-confidence. To be sure, the IDF was still one of the most professional and powerful conventional armies in the world. However, in accordance with its strategic doctrine, the IDF's military preparedness and professionalism was geared towards conventional threats. The *Intifada* was a completely new form of warfare, for which the IDF was neither psychologically nor tactically equipped. Elite brigades, which were trained to fight and defeat an armed enemy, found themselves now carrying out policing and riot control operations, for which they were totally untrained.

According to then Head of the IDF's Central Command (March 1991–March 1993), Maj. Gen. Danny Yatom, the extensive use of IDF units in policing duties throughout the *Intifada* severely curtailed the IDF's training opportunities. The *Intifada* raised issues of how to allocate the IDF's limited resources of time and manpower to training for the two different threats (i.e. conventional and sub-conventional) the IDF's ground forces were dealing with at the time:

> Firstly, it was very difficult to divide resources, time, units for those two missions, which in many aspects, are contradictory, because if you wanted to prepare a unit for the next war, you should have given the unit the time and the assets [necessary] to conduct large-scale manoeuvre exercises, but if at the same time you needed the units to be deployed in Judea and Samaria [i.e. the West Bank], the units were no longer able to conduct the regular training programmes. So, no doubt there were many disturbances.... No doubt, many training programmes shortened and in many cases we had to just stop some of them.[87]

Despite their lack of familiarity with this new form of warfare and their growing lack of self-confidence, it was only towards the end of the *Intifada* that the IDF's Command and Staff College began to teach low-intensity warfare tactics. In any case, the *Intifada*, in general, disrupted a significant portion of the IDF's standard training regimen and led some commentators to speculate on the degradation of even the army's conventional capabilities. Thus, Martin Van Creveld of the Hebrew University of Jerusalem wrote, regarding the IDF, that 'what used to be one of the world's finest fighting forces is rapidly degenerating into a fourth-class police organisation'.[88] One soldier, for example, stated that 'doing police duty [had] destroyed all I had achieved as a soldier in the IDF. Messing with civilians, children, women, the elderly, you know...'.[89]

Finally, the growing lack of unit cohesion, due to the weakening of the Israeli collectivistic ethos and growing individualism brought about by huge economic and, hence, societal changes that began in the early 1980s, also weakened troop morale as well as the soldiers' traditional coping mechanisms, which actually relied on strong unit cohesion.[90]

Coping with demoralisation

The right to conscientious objection is not legally recognised; men refusing to fulfil military duties in Israel face severe penalties. According to the

1986 National Defence Service Law, failure to fulfil military duty is punishable by up to two years' imprisonment, whereas attempting to evade military service is punishable by up to five years' imprisonment. Similarly, refusal to perform reserve duties is punishable by up to 36 days' imprisonment, the sentence being renewable if the objector refuses at each reserve duty call-up. In addition, what can be even more difficult for the conscientious objector, are the social and economic costs felt in Israeli society (until very recently) after having served his prison sentence. Indeed, conscientious objectors 'who lack documents are often regarded with suspicion. For instance, they may find it difficult to get employment ... and they can be refused loans by credit institutions.'[91]

In many cases, numerous soldiers demoralised by the *Intifada* went about their military service because they deemed the consequences of conscientious objection too high. After extensive interviewing, Liebes and Blum-Kulka came to the conclusion that military service, despite demoralisation, was possible due to the coping mechanisms soldiers adopted, consciously or unconsciously, during their multiple tours in the Territories. Besides outright refusal, the most common coping mechanisms found amongst the interviewed, in order to reduce the dissonance between their duty to serve and the moral dilemmas stemming from such duty, were either by 'redefining self, army, or [the] *Intifada* ... in order to justify obedience [or by adopting] "negotiated actions"'.[92]

Thus, in the former case, soldiers would emphasise their duty as IDF soldiers in order to comply with the various morally questionable orders given by their superiors, thereby withdrawing into a state, which soldiers refer to as 'small head' [*rosh katan*], i.e. relinquishing thought and responsibility.[93] Such a phenomenon was compounded by the fact that during the extended period in which the *Intifada* carried on, many units, particularly reservist ones, had served numerous times within the Territories and had dealt with the same enduring problems. Not only did the burden accumulate, but it also affected many within the IDF. According to Rabin, 'as many as 250,000 IDF troops had experienced service in the Territories at one time or another between 1987 and 1993'.[94]

The protraction of the conflict service in the Territories, even if not questioned from a moral basis, began to become a concern of burden accretion and attrition. Maj. Gen. (Ret.) Yatom acknowledged the affects of attrition that reoccurring service gave rise to:

> There is a risk that for the tenth or eleventh time young soldiers come with their battalion to secure the area of Hebron or Ramallah and for the eleventh time they face the same problems of confronting mobs, confronting civilians and standing at a roadblock for long hours. It has a negative effect on youngsters and the friction is very tough and the general situation affected the sensitivities of a human being. The burden accumulated.[95]

In other cases, soldiers would try to change or restructure their external reality in order to reduce their moral dissonance. This was commonly done by 'avoiding any contact with the confrontational aspects of the *Intifada* altogether through manoeuvring with the system'.[96] That is, they would try and come to some arrangement with their commanding officer or appeal to the *Valtam* (Committee for Coordination of Release from Reserve Service), so as not to serve on the 'frontline' of the *Intifada* or avoid service in the Territories altogether. This option became very widespread. One IDF refusenik recounted how commanders on the field tried very hard to accommodate potential conscientious objectors by offering alternative and less controversial missions, in order to avoid their refusal to serve from becoming a public, and thus, political statement: 'The colonel who tried my case did everything in his power to avoid sentencing me.'[97] In his case, though, he declined any alternative offers.

According to 'Ishai Menuchin [by the end of 1989] ... more than 2,000 soldiers either refused or requested not to serve in suppressing the *Intifada* and were subsequently dismissed by their commanders'.[98] Many commanders during the *Intifada* (and during the Lebanon War), preferred rather to ignore or sweep under the carpet the problem of conscientious refusal, by transferring objectors to other posts or duties instead of going through time- and resource-consuming disciplinary procedures.[99] Subsequently, such arrangements became more clandestine and, thus, statistics on them are not available. The lack of statistics on this phenomenon became so common that it became publicly known as '*sarvanut afora*' ('grey refusal') or 'partial objection'.[100]

The greatest coping mechanism used by the majority of the IDF soldiers and officers on the ground was that of focusing on getting the job done – that is, of achieving the immediate tactical mission – without really reflecting too much on the legitimacy or moral dilemmas associated with their COIN actions. In fact, whilst the conundrums presented by the *Intifada* were not disregarded completely by the IDF, the upper echelons of the military establishment did try 'to deflect a soldier's attention away from a self-examination of the legitimacy of his actions to a consideration of a job well-done. What became important was not the morality of the task itself, but how well it was carried out.'[101]

Although the IDF was and still is considered to be a 'people's army', mostly composed of conscripts and reservists, the IDF nonetheless has always stressed the value of professionalism, which is considered to be an essential element for units to achieve a particular mission. This entailed avoiding, within the unit, overtly political discussions that might impinge on achieving the unit's objectives. When asked about the political considerations or the moral dilemmas involved in operations that were carried out in the Territories, one company commander stated:

> I don't see a big difference between me as a left-winger and another officer who serves with me or under me; it's a profession, it's clean, it's very difficult to understand, but it is a profession like any other profession. I consider myself a professional officer and I do what I do from a professional point of view. I have no other considerations. I don't think about my beliefs, I don't think about my ideology. I do what I do, because I trust the system and I do what the system asks me to do according to my judgement and within the limitations of the power that I have.[102]

Soldiers and commanders were encouraged to evaluate their performance on the basis of whether the mission of a particular COIN operation was achieved (this usually meant the quelling of disturbances around the Territories). Serg. Maj. (Res.) Hachmov confirmed that 'in those days the commanders did not like to talk about it [i.e. the morality of their actions]; it was all about the assignment and mission and that was it. If they saw someone who looked a little uncomfortable, they would let them go on leave for 48 hours, come back and then everything would be ok.'[103]

Hence, the traditional *bitsuist* tendency – that is, the proclivity towards achieving immediate short-term and tactical military solutions to particular security threats at the cost of long-term planning and strategic foresight, as explained earlier on, was reinforced in many during the *Intifada*.

Even though the conflict involved mostly popular expressions of discontent and low-level violence, many within the IDF, at least implicitly, began to view the uprising not as a question of civil disobedience and unrest, but rather as a military issue. This *bitsuist* tendency led IDF personnel to perceive their current security operations – which were clearly policing actions – instead as military ones, to the point where the language used to describe them, as well as the approach to the particular mission's objectives were clearly military. Consequently, many soldiers did not perceive their treatment of the Palestinian population as excessive, because their perception was based on the fact they were *only* carrying out their military duty. An IDF survey at the beginning of 1988 showed, in fact, that although 65 per cent of the respondents believed that they had conducted themselves 'coarsely' toward the Palestinians in the Territories, 70 per cent of them perceived their actions to be fair and proportionate.[104]

Military sociologist Eyal Ben-Ari recounted how some of his unit members coped by re-conceptualising their duties in military terms during reserve service, despite the fact that both their equipment, which was issued before their missions began, as well as the language used during their pre-deployment briefings, belonged to the domain of policemen. As they began to serve in the Territories, they adopted traditional military terms like *nikui shetach* (mop-up), which was used in the past to convey the 'elimination of pockets of enemy resistance in a given area', but was now being used to denote the clearance of '"civilian" (i.e. Palestinian) roadblocks, stones, tires, PLO flags, or demonstrators'. Other military words such as 'deployment (*prisa*), breakthrough (*pritza*) into houses, raids (*peshita*)' and so on were used to describe other IDF police actions.[105]

More importantly, Ben-Ari narrated how the standards by which units in the Territories were evaluated by their superior officers were employed in regard to regular army duties. For example, a unit would be appraised by whether or not it had done '"clean work" (*avodah nekiya*): that is, operated with minimal damage to "our" forces, efficiency, smooth execution, and no delays in the designated timetable'.[106] Thus, the implicit perception by many of the *Intifada* as a military conflict facilitated the carrying out of police duty actions, which under normal circumstances would have proven ethically questionable.

Such a perception also allowed many non-infantry units to view the *Intifada* as an opportunity for learning new infantry-based skills, such as carrying out foot and jeep patrols, check-point duties, and search and arrest operations, etc. As the IDF began to involve a greater number of IDF forces in the Territories, armoured and artillery corps units, for example, began participating in regular current security duties that had been, until the outbreak of the *Intifada*, the sole domain of the infantry and paratrooper brigades and the Border Guard. The exposure to new military skills and duties, notwithstanding the climate in which they were carried out, had a positive effect on the motivation of such units, at least initially. According to Lt. Col. Hadass Ben-Eliyahu, 'a sort of environment developed in which soldiers saw great purpose in what they were doing as they were able to learn all sorts of new jobs and competencies, which they saw as a very positive experience'.[107]

The self-perception by Israeli soldiers and officers, that they were carrying out military duties in the Territories, however, did become more common and easier to develop, given the growing level and nature of violence that the Palestinians were using as the *Intifada* progressed. Statistics provided by the IDF showed that between 1991 and 1993 the number, by and large, of major riots diminished (by as much as 45 per cent on the West Bank) and the frequency of knife, firearm and grenade attacks by organised groups of Palestinians increased (by as much as 60 per cent in the Gaza Strip).[108]

In spite of the attempts to avoid demoralisation through these coping mechanisms, close and violent contact with local Palestinians led to a process of their dehumanisation, which in turn led to a growing hatred of them. As one soldier put it: '[the *Intifada*] caused me to feel disgust toward the Arab population and to reinforce my feeling that they have no business within our state'.[109] The dehumanisation tended to facilitate the various punishments many soldiers imposed on the Palestinian population.

Many soldiers came to abhor this state of affairs, especially when confronted by colleagues who would boast about their violent exploits. One soldier commented: 'I saw the effect on the soldiers who dealt with the civilians: a lowering of their moral standards, conceit about beating up an Arab kid.'[110] Such empathy also led many soldiers to question the Occupation *per se* and led them to support Palestinian self-determination.

Such coping mechanisms were unable to stop Israeli soldiers from suffering psychological burnout. One survey, which interviewed a significant sample of IDF officers that had direct contact with the *Intifada*, showed that 'seventy-two per cent of them suffered stress by it'.[111] It was, therefore, not surprising that the highest number of conscientious objectors in the history of the IDF, until that point, would arise during the *Intifada*. The absolute number of full conscientious objectors still seemed low, however, that is, only 300.

Relatively speaking, the number of conscientious objectors was double the amount that came across during the Lebanon War, whilst before then there were no major cases of conscientious objection. More astonishingly, 'in contrast to the war in Lebanon, when refusals were made after the soldier had already spent time at the front, now they were refusing even before being sent to fight the *Intifada*'.[112] Whereas in the past refusals were carried out mostly by members on the fringe of Israeli society, during the *Intifada* the elite, that is the traditional backbone, of Israeli society became the spearhead of the conscientious objectors' movement.

According to Ruth Linn's survey, the typical *Intifada* objector was 'a secular, thirty-year-old *Ashkenazi* (i.e. a Jewish of Central and European origin) Israeli male, who lives in a city, is married with children, is highly educated, and is a member of the liberal professions ... [and appears] to be a political individualist'.[113] As for their military background they tended to be committed and experienced combat soldiers. Linn, indeed, discovered that '(27 per cent) were experienced military officers, (73 per cent) were dedicated to the army, had participated in previous wars in combat roles (since 1967), and had spent at least one stint of reserve service in the war in Lebanon and/or the Territories prior to their decision to refuse'.[114]

The fact that these conscientious objectors had such great combat experience, were a traditional pillar of Israeli society and yet were the most morally affected by the *Intifada* could only emphasise the seriousness of this new conflict. It also revealed the war-weariness of Israeli society in general. The *Intifada*, moreover, led to the eventual recognition on the part of Israeli society and of Rabin, that the Palestinian people and their need for self-determination, as well as the future status of the Territories, had to be addressed before radical Islamic terror groups, such as *Hamas* and the Palestinian Islamic *Jihad* could gain even more influence within the Territories and beyond.

The Oslo Peace Accord

The Oslo Peace Accord suggested a way out of the *Intifada* predicament. Developments within the PLO, as well as within the Middle East, during the late 1980s and early 1990s proved propitious for a diplomatic resolution of the Israeli–Palestinian conflict (and also of the greater Arab–Israeli conflict). Although the Lebanon War had not achieved most of Ariel Sharon's ambitious strategic aims, it did significantly weaken the PLO's operational capabilities and, more importantly, its direct ties with and influence over Palestinian nationalist efforts within the Territories. After all, the PLO, in 1982, had fled hastily from Lebanon to Tunis.[115] The Lebanon War drove the PLO towards the diplomatic route. This ended up in the PLO's historic decision, in November 1988, to accept a 'two-state solution' to the conflict enshrined in the 1947 UN Resolution 181, as well as UN Resolutions 242 and 338, as the basis of such a solution. Even more astoundingly the PLO declared in December 1988 that it would renounce terrorism as a means of obtaining Palestinian statehood.

Despite such developments, the Shamir government's lack of trust of the PLO, given its terrorist track record together with the *Likud*'s ideological aversion towards the creation of an actual Palestinian state, in what it considered to be territories belonging to *Eretz Israel*, did not result in any major development. This was also the case during the Madrid peace process, which was launched in October 1991 under the auspices of the USA.[116] The US at the time was enjoying the benefits of its new global hegemonic status (given the collapse of the Soviet Union) and Middle East regional support (given the United States' leadership role in liberating Kuwait from the 1990 Iraqi invasion during the Gulf War).[117]

Such a conference was possible due to the fact that for the first time in Middle East history, Arabs (by providing logistical, economic, diplomatic support and even armed forces) and Israelis (by not intervening in the 1991 Gulf War despite Saddam Hussein's SCUD attacks against Israel's heartland) cooperated together with the USA to rectify Iraq's invasion of Kuwait. Such cooperation and the USA's newfound role of superpower hegemon made it easier for the Bush administration to pressure both Israel and the Arab states to find a diplomatic resolution to the Arab–Israeli conflict.

The fact that the PLO had sided with Saddam Hussein during the Gulf War had led it to diplomatic isolation and to the verge of bankruptcy. The PLO's budget got cut in half virtually overnight as payments originating from the Gulf States stopped. Consequently, 'PLO financial support to the West Bank and Gaza Strip dropped from $120 million in 1989 to approximately $45 million in 1992'.[118] This led to the drastic reduction or even cancellation of various social welfare, medical and education programmes. In addition, Saudi Arabia and other Persian Gulf states began funding and supporting *Hamas* as a demonstration of their irritation with the PLO's *faux pas* during the 1991 Gulf War. Consequently, *Hamas* was able to gain even more political support and to begin challenging the PLO's leadership hegemony within the Territories.

Although no major agreement was reached via the Madrid conference peace initiative, it did achieve a major historic watershed by bringing together Israeli, Syrian and Jordanian-Palestinian delegations to the same table. It also laid the foundations for future bilateral negotiations between Israel and Syria and between Israel and the PLO (that led to the Oslo peace initiative).[119]

These developments together with the election, in June 1992, of a Labour government under the leadership of Yitzhak Rabin, who had campaigned on a peace platform during the elections, made the prospect of peace with the Palestinians (and other Arab states) more realistic. Rabin, in fact, began to fear that without some form of peace settlement with the PLO, which had shown signs of moderation and compromise since the late 1980s, *Hamas* would eventually gain ascendancy over the PLO and then prove impossible to negotiate with, given its completely rejectionist stance towards the existence of Israel in the Middle East.

The opportunity for meaningful negotiations following the faltering Madrid peace conference process with PLO-affiliated representatives, arose almost by chance when Deputy Foreign Minister, Yossi Beilin, appointed his colleague, Yair Hirschfeld, a political science senior lecturer at Haifa University, to conduct a series of unofficial and secret meetings with PLO member, Abu Ala, under the auspices of Terje Larsen, the director of the Institute for Applied Social Sciences, a Norwegian think-tank. Between January 1993 and August 1993 the Israeli team (which gradually began to include close aides to Peres and Rabin) and Palestinian team met on several occasions and were able to come to a historic compromise without any serious pressure or interference.[120]

The similarity between the September 1978 Israeli–Egyptian Camp David Accords and the 'Declaration of Principles on Interim Self-Government Arrangements' (in short, 'Oslo Accord') was striking. Both, in fact, envisaged a solution to the Israeli–Palestinian conflict by creating a Palestinian self-governing authority for an interim period of up to five years, until both parties would agree on a permanent solution to the status of the Territories. The Israeli and Palestinian architects of the Oslo Accord, which was officially signed by Yitzhak Rabin and Yasser Arafat on the US White House south lawn on 13 September 1993, were able to set up a peace negotiation process. The process would make significant concessions, albeit without 'any guarantee ... as to the nature of the final settlement between the two parties'.[121] Most importantly, the accord entailed the mutual recognition of each other's existence and right to live side by side.

The Oslo Accord represented the abandonment of a Palestinian all-out struggle against Israel until its destruction as laid down in the 1968 Palestinian National Charter. It also entailed the Israeli recognition of the Palestinians as an actual nation as well as their right to 'govern themselves'.[122]

The interim process would involve the transfer of power and responsibilities to the Palestinians in the Territories by establishing self-rule in the Gaza Strip and the West Bank town of Jericho. It also entailed the relinquishing to the future Palestinian Authority (PA) of the control of five specific spheres of government: tourism, social welfare, health, direct taxation and culture and education.

An agreement regarding the election of the Palestinian Council, members of which would be elected via democratic elections, would specify the structure and authority of such a council and would be negotiated during the initial stages of the interim process. Whilst the responsibility for security at international border crossings with Egypt and Jordan and for Israeli settlers in the Territories would remain in the hands of the IDF, the newly formed PA would be allowed to create a strong police force in order to maintain public order, internal security and, most importantly, fight terrorism.

As a result of the interim process, there would be cooperation between Israel and the PA leading to a decrease in any mutual suspicions and ill-will, which had stopped both sides from reaching a diplomatic agreement in the past. At a certain stage the process would hopefully lead to a final status agreement relating to the permanent status issues of refugees, settlements, final security arrangements and borders as well as the status of Jerusalem.

However, the success (as well as eventual downfall) of the Oslo Accord relied on the fact that the whole interim process was seen as a confidence- and security-building measure that relied on ambiguity in order to be tolerated by both parties' populations and opposition parties. The Oslo Accord was purposefully vague due to the fact that both parties were not prepared to discuss the most serious matters at stake, and that even Rabin was not at the time prepared to admit the reality that the Oslo process would some day lead to the creation of a Palestinian state. The Oslo Accord stated that 'the outcome of the permanent status negotiations should not be prejudiced or pre-empted by agreements reached for the interim period', basically encouraging both Israelis and Palestinians to interpret the agreements obtained in a way that was fitting for them.[123]

Thus, the Oslo Accord, 'by its very nature, made it a logical imperative for both sides to work outside the Oslo framework in order to establish new "facts on the ground"' given that whatever would be achieved during the Oslo Peace Process would not be binding with regard to the final settlement.[124]

Israel and the PA developed a *modus vivendi* and achieved significant interim agreements (such as the May 1994 Gaza-Jericho Agreement, the October 1998 Wye River Memorandum, etc.) throughout the Oslo process. As it could not lead to Palestinian autonomy in the designated 'A' (Palestinian security and administrative self-government) and 'B' (Palestinian administrative self-government) areas in the Gaza Strip and the West Bank,[125] their respective positions vis-à-vis the final status issues remained at loggerheads. The ambiguity of such an accord enabled each party to interpret the agreement according to their liking and benefit.

The Israelis consequently continued to build settlements within the Territories in order to create new 'facts on the ground', whilst the PA, fearful to some degree of an internal civil war, but also as a cunning resort to pressure Israel to make greater concessions during the extended interim negotiation process, did not seriously try to fight terror and terrorist groups within the areas under its control.[126]

As the Oslo Peace Process progressed, often under the encouragement, if not pressure of the USA, so did terrorist attacks against Israel and Israeli settlers as well as Israeli military and, on occasion, settler reprisals against Palestinians suspected of being terrorists.[127] Despite periods of relative quiet, the Israeli–Palestinian conflict exploded a few months after the Camp David II negotiations, when both Israel and the PA failed to reach agreement on the final status issues.

Although this came as a shock to Israel, the USA, and the rest of the world, clearly the writing had been on the wall since the start of the process, in spite of the euphoria resulting at first from the DOP signing. Both Israeli and PA leaders and their respective spokespersons had re-iterated innumerable times, for the benefit of domestic and international public opinion, the maximum extent to which they would have made concessions relating to the final status issues. What had been set up as a confidence- and security-building measure, that would have led hopefully to a final status agreement over the Israeli–Palestinian conflict, had led instead to greater distrust, mutual recrimination and ultimately another round of bloody intercommunal warfare as will be seen in the next chapter.

7 The *Al-Aqsa Intifada*

The *Al-Aqsa Intifada*, like the previous *Intifada*, did not explode because of one simple incident. Ariel Sharon's visit to the Temple Mount Mosque, on 28 September 2000 was the purported reason or event, which sparked the second *Intifada*. However, PA Chairman Yasser Arafat, together with other Palestinian leaders – not to mention terrorist organisations – had already called for a second major round of violence against Israel. This was because of the failed Oslo Peace Process final-status talks at Camp David in the summer of July 2000, although this could have finally brought about a Palestinian state in almost all of the Territories.¹ By the time the Taba talks were underway, in December 2000, Palestinian violence had escalated to guerrilla warfare.²

The PA had learnt, during the Oslo Peace Process (1993–2000), that the alternate use of negotiations and violence could bring about significant Israeli concessions. Indeed, Yasser Arafat's lack of cooperation in fighting terror during the Oslo era was somewhat encouraged by the fact that both the Rabin and Peres governments (1992–96) disassociated the peace process from reactions to terrorist attacks against Israel. That is, the peace process continued, despite Israeli threats of stopping it altogether, even after mass-murder attacks in Israel. Moreover, the PA believed that it would be possible to achieve, through the use of violence, what *Hizbullah* had achieved, through guerrilla warfare, in Lebanon in May 2000: that is, the full unilateral withdrawal of the IDF from the Territories without the need for any formal peace agreement. The Israeli unilateral withdrawal, dubbed Operation 'Early Dawn', had been a serious blow to Israel's deterrent posture and had proved a major galvanising factor for a second uprising in the Territories. Indeed, Marwan Barghouti, a senior leader in the PLO *Fatah Tanzim* paramilitary organisation, stated in early 2001 that 'the thinking of the entire new Palestinian generation is influenced by the experiences of our brothers in *Hizbullah* and by Israel's retreat from Lebanon.... I must say that Israel's withdrawal from Lebanon was indeed one contributing factor to the [*Al-Aqsa*] *Intifada*.'³

Advanced plans for re-igniting the uprising were being made throughout late summer/early autumn of 2000, so as to put pressure on Israel, if and when the final-status negotiations faltered. As in the past, 'Arafat's ultimate strategic objective was to force a situation under which the international community would impose a solution on Israel, forcing it to fulfil most, if not all, Palestinian aspirations.'[4] Yet, Palestinian violence initially took the form of rioting and mass demonstrations, as Arafat was still willing to negotiate with Prime Minister Ehud Barak under duress. Sporadic terrorist attacks during this period normally comprised of Palestinians opening fire at Israeli vehicles or murdering settlers in the West Bank. Nevertheless, the IDF's response was significantly robust in spite of the Barak government's desire to reduce the level of violence whilst still pursuing negotiations with the PA.

During the first few months of the *Al-Aqsa Intifada* the Barak government had adopted the dual strategy of continuing negotiations with the PA, whilst allowing the IDF to conduct 'restrained' preventive and retaliatory operations. Such a policy of restraint, most importantly, forbade the IDF from entering PA-controlled 'A' areas. The IDF's conduct, however, was often more aggressive than Barak had intended. This was due to the IDF's intent on carrying out its operations 'on the basis of purely military considerations'.[5] As a result, the IDF managed to kill a large number of Palestinians within quite a short space of time and this, in turn, led to an unintended intensification of violence. According to Col. Yossi Kupperwaser, at the time a Central Command intelligence officer, the IDF managed to fire, during the first months of the *Al-Aqsa Intifada*, over 850,000 5.56 mm bullets – 1.3 million bullets when including the Gaza Strip.[6]

The strong IDF reaction was also due to the fact that both the senior military (e.g. then COS Shaul Mofaz, Deputy COS Moshe Yaalon) and political (e.g. PM Ehud Barak until February 2001, PM Ariel Sharon and Defence Minister Binyamin Ben-Eliezer after February 2001) echelons had come to the conclusion that the failed Camp David and Taba peace negotiations were solely the fault of the Palestinian Authority. They believed that this failure was due to Arafat's intransigence on key final-status issues such as the right of return of Palestinian refugees and sovereignty over (East) Jerusalem and so on. The IDF's excessive response at the start of the *Intifada* was also calculated not only to suppress the uprising, but also to compel the Palestinians to admit defeat.

Despite the fact that official intelligence briefs throughout 2001 claimed that Arafat and the PA leadership were still interested in obtaining a viable state through diplomatic negotiations, the Israeli leadership and eventually society came to believe that there was no Palestinian peace partner and that Arafat was really intent on using the Oslo Peace Process to destroy Israel. This interpretation of events was expounded actively by the former Military Intelligence head of research division, Maj. Gen. Amos Gilad (1996–2001), during numerous *Knesset* Defence and Foreign Affairs Committee as well as cabinet security meetings before and after the Camp David talks. This version of events enabled Barak – and subsequently Sharon – to completely blame Arafat for the Oslo Peace Process' failure. It also led a greater section of Israeli society to lose faith in the Oslo Peace Process.[7]

In the face of significant Israeli concessions during the Camp David II talks and the growing use of guerrilla warfare tactics, as well as terrorist attacks against Israelis both within and beyond the Green Line, Labour Prime Minister Ehud Barak was ousted from power by the hawkish Ariel Sharon of the *Likud* in February 2001. The majority of the Israeli population was tired of making concessions to the PA whilst at the same time absorbing growing terrorist attacks from *Hamas* and Palestinian Islamic *Jihad*, increasing numbers of members of the Palestinian Security Service (PSS)-affiliated militias (e.g. *Tanzim*, Force 17), the PLO-affiliated *Al-Aqsa* Martyrs Brigades, and eventually the PSS itself – which was paradoxically set up by the Oslo process and manned mostly by PLO-*Fatah* members and sympathisers in order to combat Palestinian terror. Indeed, *Shin Bet* statistics show that during the first two years of the *Al-Aqsa Intifada*, out of the 145 suicide bombers '52 were *Hamas* men and 35 belonged to *Islamic Jihad*, whilst 40 belonged to *Fatah*'.[8]

Despite being called the *Al-Aqsa Intifada*, the second *Intifada* was not, apart from the first five weeks (that is, until November 2000), a popular uprising. Furthermore, according to Mamduh Nufal, a personal adviser to Yasser Arafat, the PA's role in the outbreak and maintenance of the *Intifada* was crucial. In early 2001, he stated that 'this current movement is distinguishable from the first *Intifada* and is perhaps unique altogether. From the beginning, this movement was led and accompanied by the forces of the PA. It is not a mass movement divorced from the Authority.'[9]

Indeed, in this current conflict, the term '*Intifada*' is a misnomer, because the nature of the violence used by Palestinians has been of a different kind. The *Al-Aqsa* militants used blatantly 'different tactics and weaponry, transforming a civil uprising into an urban guerrilla war' and terror campaign.[10] As shall be seen below, this radical transformation in the level of violence used by the Palestinians posed serious tactical, as well as legal, dilemmas on IDF personnel during the *Al-Aqsa Intifada*, particularly regarding rules of engagement and proportionality of force.[11] When underlining the stark difference between the danger IDF soldiers faced in the first *Intifada* and *Al-Aqsa Intifada*, Lt. Joshua of the 7th Armoured Brigade stated:

> The job of one of my commander's brothers, who participated in the 1987 *Intifada*, was to go and throw stones back at the Arabs! And now, going into Gaza without three tanks, two bulldozers and five armoured personnel carriers is unimaginable.[12]

According to then COS, Lt. Gen. Shaul Mofaz (1998–2002), at the very beginning of the *Al-Aqsa Intifada*, 'Israeli fire during the *Intifada* ha[d] not resulted in massive Palestinian civilian casualties', because he had told his 'soldiers to count to ten before they return fire'. He had also attributed low

Israeli casualties to the fact that 'we prepared the military for this confrontation. We trained and bought equipment for low-intensity conflict. We invested in armour for individuals and vehicles.'[13]

Former IDF spokesman, Brig. Gen. Ron Kitri, stated that the numbers of Palestinian casualties were relatively low, particularly when looking at the number of incidents in which they had initiated attacks on Israeli troops and civilians. Brig. Gen. Kitri added that the low numbers of Palestinian casualties were mostly due to the fact that 'after the [Hasmonean] "tunnel riots" of September 1996, the army trained sharpshooters so that in any similar confrontation in the future there would be no indiscriminate firing. This controlled use of snipers, firing only at armed Palestinians, he argues, ha[d] kept Palestinian casualties down.'[14]

Despite the IDF's view that Palestinian casualties were very low at the start of the current *Intifada*, figures of casualties provided by the Palestinian Red Crescent Society (as well as the statistics on the amount of ammunition used by the IDF mentioned above) showed otherwise. The first month of conflict resulted in 141 deaths (mostly caused by live ammunition) and 5,984 casualties (caused by live ammunition, rubber/plastic bullets, tear gas, etc.) on the Palestinian side.[15] Israeli casualties, on the other hand, were significantly lower: around 12 fatalities and 65 casualties.[16] This was in part due to the fact that although IDF tactics, including the use of advanced protective equipment, reduced their own casualties to a minimum, the use of live fire as opposed to the very limited use of non-lethal weapons significantly augmenting the number of Palestinian casualties. Once the conflict escalated to guerrilla-type warfare and large-scale terror attacks, so did casualties on both sides, particularly on the Palestinian side, due to heavy Israeli retaliation, which escalated significantly as of December 2001 (see Table 7.1 and Table 7.2).

As the popular uprising phase did not achieve the Palestinians' desired results, which in the PA's case was that of gaining much better concessions on final-status issues, 'the *Tanzim* fighters began a guerrilla campaign' initially by placing gunmen amongst the Palestinian stone-throwing mob 'and later in ambushes, using snipers to kill Jewish settlers driving on main roads' of the Territories. Furthermore, the guerrilla campaign intensified into 'Lebanese-style roadside bombs, mortar attacks and large-scale

Table 7.1 Israeli casualties, 29 September 2000–9 August 2005

Casualties	Civilians	Security forces	Total
Injured	5,154	2,217	7,371
Killed	744	319	1,063

Source: Adapted from 'Israeli civilian and security forces casualties since September 2000', *IDF Spokesperson's Office*, www1.idf.il/SIP_STORAGE/DOVER/files/7/21827.doc (accessed 9 August 2005).

Table 7.2 Palestinian casualties, 29 September 2000–9 August 2005

Killed	Injured
3,659	29,035

Source: 'Total daily numbers of deaths and injuries – West Bank and Gaza', *Palestine Red Crescent Society*, www.palestinercs.org/crisistables/table_of_figures.htm (accessed 9 August 2005).

ambushes and shooting incidents',[17] which gradually began to be carried out by all of the Palestinian militias and terror groups.

Guerrilla tactics, such as the use of short-range rocket and mortar attacks, roadside bombings and sniping, were used particularly by *Hamas*, which had been influenced by *Hizbullah*'s tactics in Lebanon. Terrorist operational links had developed, in fact, between *Hamas*, *Hizbullah* and Iran during the 1990s. Following the signing of the Oslo Accords, Tehran started hosting various *Hamas* members for terror-related training sittings. Moreover, relations between Iran and *Hamas* improved dramatically following Sheikh Ahmed Yassin's visit to Tehran in March 1998.[18]

By the start of the current *Intifada*, further links between *Hizbullah*, Iran and *Fatah* elements of the PLO, such as the *Tanzim* and Force 17, developed. Under one operational umbrella, called the 'Return Brigades', these forces conducted attacks, which were textbook examples of *Hizbullah*'s repertoire in Lebanon.[19] *Qassam* rockets (named after the *Izz ad-din al-Qassam* Brigades, the military wing of *Hamas*), which were used by *Hamas* to bomb and terrorise Israeli settlements in the Gaza Strip, as well as neighbouring towns within the Green Line, were created with the advice of *Hizbullah*. Roadside bombs, which managed to destroy Israeli APCs and tanks, the videotaping of ambushes and of the 'living wills' of soon-to-be suicide bombers were also other *Hizbullah* tactics adopted by local Palestinian organisations.[20]

Military aid was also forthcoming from Iran. For example, in January 2002, Israeli naval commandos (*Shayetet 13*) intercepted and seized the *Karine-A* vessel, which was filled with more than 50 tonnes of weapons, including 12-mile range *Katyusha* rockets, LAW and Sagger anti-tank missiles, hand grenades, mines, machine guns, sniper equipment, ammunition and more than 2 tonnes of explosives.[21] Arafat's attempt at importing this large arsenal ultimately proved his undoing in the long term, as will be seen below. Indeed, henceforth, the USA perceived Arafat as compromised by terror and the Bush administration began to push for Arafat's removal as leader of the PA.

Suicide bombing attacks against purely Israeli civilian targets began to rise steadily throughout late 2001 and peaked during early 2002. Such attacks were carried out in crowded public transportation buses, street markets, cafés, night clubs and restaurants in order to kill as many Israeli civilians as possible. The intended effect of such attacks was to create enough insecurity in the Israeli population so as to paralyse their normal daily lives and, thus, convince them to pressure the Israeli government to retreat from the Territories.

The terrorist campaign was designed to force Israel to buckle under pressure – as Palestinians believed had happened for Israel in Lebanon. However, the Palestinian terror campaign had the opposite effect on both the Israeli leadership and population. In spite of the relative low-intensity nature of the conflict, a large proportion of the Israeli population perceived this *Intifada* as an outright war. This led Ariel Sharon, for example, to state in late 2001 in a televised address to his nation that 'a war has been forced upon us. A war of terror. A war that claims innocent victims every day. A war of terror being conducted systematically, in an organized fashion and with methodical direction.'[22]

Not only was the current Israeli–Palestinian confrontation interpreted as a war, but also as an existential one whereby Israel had 'no choice' but to defend itself against Palestinian aggression. In interviews, many within the IDF (regulars and reservists), confirmed the view that Israel was fighting for its existence. For example, Brig. Gen. Gershon HaCohen stated that 'we must understand that now we are struggling in a new way for the defence of our existence'.[23] IDF officers on the ground, furthermore, viewed Palestinian violence as an existential threat. They also perceived the motivation for such violence as completely different from that of the first *Intifada*. As one *Nahal* reserve company commander stated:

> Today it is harder for me to believe them [i.e. the Palestinians] that this is about their lives. They do not care about what will the next day be [like] for them. They care more about whether I am going to be here or not and this is a real threat on my life. It is no longer a movement of people that says, 'I want a better life'. It's more like, 'I want to destroy you'.[24]

Suicide bombing missions were also often initiated in order to avenge the death of Palestinian militants or terrorists at the hand of Israeli security forces. They were also often motivated by the need to avenge perceived abuses and collateral damage suffered at the hand of IDF operations in the Territories. The Israeli need to respond to such attacks due to its deterrence posture based on reprisals obviously led to a growing spiral of violence of tit-for-tat insurgency and COIN actions.

The Israeli response

With Ariel Sharon in power the Israeli response to escalating Palestinian violence became fierce. This was possible because the majority of the Israeli population hardened their resolve in wanting to combat Palestinian aggression. Whereas during the first *Intifada* an increasing segment of the

Israeli population had begun to favour a political solution over a military one, during the early years of the second *Intifada*, mainly due to the Palestinians' disproportionate use of terrorist and guerrilla tactics, Israeli public opinion shifted to the right. For example, '53 per cent of the sample in 1997 fully supported trading land for peace.... In the 2002 survey that percentage dropped to 37 per cent.' Moreover, favouring the military option, in 2002 '75 per cent believed that [the *Intifada*] could be controlled by military activity, with 23 per cent saying that it could be stopped altogether'.[25] Given Israeli public opinion's shift to the right after Camp David, support for tough military measures against Palestinian terrorism and violence in general was almost universal (see Table 7.3).

Furthermore, the military response was even greater than in previous Israeli–Palestinian flare-ups due to the increasingly bloody nature of Palestinian violence. The IDF introduced more of its major weapons platforms into the conflict together with the implementation of expanded counter-terrorism measures against the Palestinians in the Territories. Artillery barrages, naval bombardments, F-15I and F-16 aircraft as well as AH-64A Apache and AH-1 Cobra attack helicopters 'surgical' air strikes became commonplace, particularly after January 2002.[26]

The extensive and extended use of firepower during the second *Intifada* even led Israeli defence officials to admit that during Operation 'Defensive Shield', which took place in April 2002, as will be seen below, 'the amount of weapons and munitions used ... was more than had been used by the IDF over the last decade'.[27] This situation led to an emergency appeal to the US Department of Defense for more essential munitions to be used in the fight against Palestinian guerrillas and terrorists.

Moreover, former COS and Defence Minister, Shaul Mofaz, authorised, in August 2001, the use of the *Merkava* main battle tank (MBT) for the first time in the *Intifada*, reversing former chiefs of staffs' belief that using 'tanks against the Palestinians was detrimental to Israel's international

Table 7.3 Israeli public opinion on IDF military options

Until the renewal of talks with the Palestinians Israel should:	2001 support (%)	2002 support (%)	2003 support (%)
Eliminate (assassinate) those active in terror	89	90	92
Destroy home of families of terrorist	N/A	N/A	88
Use tanks and fighter aircraft against the Palestinians	71	80	79
Use closures and economic sanctions	68	73	72
Invade Area 'A' (i.e. PA-controlled areas)	57	72	76

Source: Adapted from Asher Arian, *Israeli public opinion on national security 2003*, p. 29.

Note
N/A = Not asked.

image'. Indeed, focusing on the MBTs' military performance (and on the need to protect IDF forces) rather than on ethical dilemmas, outgoing IDF Armoured Corps commander Brig. Gen. Udi Shani stated, in August 2001, that 'we don't exactly think it is a wise and an ethical way to operate tanks against the masses. But that's the way it is.'[28]

The use of major weapons systems brought about cases of excessive force and led consequently to the occasional acknowledgement of its disproportionate nature on the part of IDF military commanders. For example, in early October 2002, following an attack by Palestinian gunmen on IDF troops attempting to build a wall blocking Palestinian smuggling from Rafah into Egypt, an IDF tank responded with four shells, killing six Palestinians, including women and children. This incident led the commander of the army in Gaza, Brig. Gen. Yisrael Ziv, to concede that 'the army used an exaggerated amount of force. The tank fired four shells when one was enough.'[29]

The greater use of firepower by the IDF, as of early 2002, was possible due to the existence of tangible PA government and security buildings. Such assets were easy to target without causing too much collateral damage. However, as IDF Lt. Col. Gal Luft pointed out, as early as December 2001, 'the use of airpower [and by extension firepower] may be effective in degrading the PA's military infrastructure, but it is far less effective in detecting and eliminating squads of suicide bombers'.[30] The incessant pounding of PA targets at the start of the conflict was symptomatic of the IDF leadership's conventional strategic mindset, which until Spring 2002 called for the destruction of tangible targets rather than the interdiction of suicide bombers and attempts at lowering the tit-for-tat violence through more controlled measures.

The use of greater firepower and aggressive retaliation was also the result of the Sharon government's policy of making sure that the PA understood that 'the days are over when we [i.e. Israelis] were willing to negotiate in the morning and go to the funerals of terror victims in the afternoon' and that the Israeli government considered the PA to be fully responsible for the escalation of violence and terror during the *Al-Aqsa* conflict.[31]

The IDF, in fact, was able to prepare and respond tactically to the various Palestinian threats used against Israeli civilians and soldiers, particularly from the mid to late 1990s as the Oslo Peace Process degenerated into tit-for-tat low-intensity skirmishes and then eventually erupted, in November 2000, into a full-scale guerrilla and terror campaign. As seen earlier on, then COS, Lt. Gen. Shaul Mofaz, boldly stated that the IDF was ready for any confrontation with the Palestinians. Preparations had started soon after the 1996 riots. Colonel Gal Hirsh stated that in early 1997, then COS Amnon Lipkin-Shahak (1995–98), had told him: 'We must prepare for war and continue with the peace process; go there and help General Yitzhak Eitan, who was the Chief of the Central Command [i.e. the area responsible for security in the West Bank], help him to prepare

110 *The* Al-Aqsa Intifada

units for war.'[32] Until then the IDF's focus was on training its troops for major conventional warfare and, to some degree, for open-field guerrilla warfare in South Lebanon. According to Capt. (Res.) Shahar Amit, 'things started to change around 1996–7. We trained a lot more in simulations involving what we actually did in combat – use of smaller teams, more emphasis on NCO command, a lot more emphasis on the personal level and on small arms accuracy.'[33]

Israel's actual preparedness for the reality of urban warfare involving a very hostile, well-armed group of terrorist-guerrillas, entrenched in an extremely complex built-up and densely populated battleground, was severely tested. According to Capt. (Res.) Noam Wiener, until the Hasmonean tunnel riots, where live-fire on a large scale was exchanged for the first time since the start of the Oslo Peace Process between IDF and PSS units, the IDF had not prepared doctrinally and operationally for the type of violence it had been confronting:

> I could say militarily-wise and doctrinally-wise, I think the army was in denial, at least until 1996. By denial I mean that I remember specifically sitting in officer school and we talked about different types of battle – offence, defence and ambushes, retreat, pursuit of the enemy – we tried to think what arrests in the West Bank are, and they didn't really fit [into a particular category]. They're not offence, because you don't attack to withhold territory, they're not a raid, because it's not somewhere you go, attack and then retreat and try to make a maximum effect. I thought that it didn't match any of the regular military schemes, because it's not a military job, it's police work. On one level it was obvious that this was the army doing policing work, but on a doctrinal level it was never developed into anything at least until 1996. Until then, I think that the army tried mainly to fill in the gaps.[34]

In any case, despite the greater use of the IDF in fighting Palestinian insurgency and terrorism, in the first three months of 2002, over 170 Israelis were killed in terror attacks, 39 suicide bombing missions were carried out, 11 of which were intercepted by the Israeli security services.

Operation 'Defensive Shield'

Operation 'Defensive Shield', which was initiated in April 2002, in response to the late March 'Passover Massacre' suicide bomb attack,[35] was the first major Israeli urban warfare operation to be carried out since the siege of Beirut in 1982.

Following the *Seder* Night Massacre, on 27 March 2002, the Israeli government initiated a second stage to the conflict. Until then, the IDF had retaliated to terror and guerrilla attacks by carrying out short reprisal raids. As of April 2002, the IDF adopted a much more proactive stance. Once the

Israeli government viewed Israel as being in a state of war, a substantial increase in the size and depth of the IDF's military operations, 'including the mobilisation of 20,000 reservists' was ordered.[36] It adopted a more aggressive stance by trying to actively neutralise the terrorist infrastructure and by entering PA-controlled 'A' Areas and by conducting large preventive and pre-emptive operations, which Israel hoped would take 'the battle to the enemy, disrupt his plans, and confront the worst threats before they emerge'.[37]

According to COS, Lt. Gen. Moshe Yaalon (2002–05), Operation '"Defensive Shield" was the turning point of the IDF's transition to initiate Israeli action rather than reaction'.[38] The three-week operation's goal was to attack the infrastructure of Palestinian terrorism. Operation 'Defensive Shield' also came to symbolise the fact that Israel was going to take back the sole responsibility of its own security – something that it had begun to relinquish to the PA during the Oslo process. Brig. Gen. HaCohen explained it in the following manner:

> When we entered Jenin, we emphasized [the principle of] 'never again'; we are going to take back the responsibility for our security.... By entering Jenin we emphasized that we can take back our sovereignty, that we can take on the price of the struggle [and] that we are not afraid of being killed.[39]

Operation 'Defensive Shield' was initiated in order to perform major weapons seizures, the arrest of terrorists and their support network, the destruction of weapons factories and suicide bomb workshops, the targeted killing of 'ticking bomb' suicide bombers, and to gather the intelligence necessary to thwart future terror attacks.

In order to carry out such an operation, the IDF reoccupied Ramallah, Nablus, Tul Karem, Bethlehem and Jenin, and other cities in the West Bank. 'Operationally, this translated into the encirclement of a city and the slow cautious entry of infantry forces [normally a brigade, sometimes two of them], supported by tanks ... and by attack helicopters.'[40] The encirclement of the areas targeted before the entry of troops actually encouraged the chances of hunting down terrorists and guerrillas who had nowhere to run to.

The operation generated significant arrests of terrorist and guerrilla suspects, the partial destruction of the terrorist and guerrilla infrastructure within the areas targeted, and ultimately, yielded groundbreaking evidence of the level of the PA's connection to terrorist activity. Correspondence between the PA and terrorist groups, procurement requests for ammunition and bombs by terrorist groups, numerous rocket-propelled grenade launchers, short-range *Qassam* rockets, suicide bomber belts, amongst other things, were found in Arafat's *Mukata* compound in Ramallah alone (see Table 7.4).

The IDF encountered significant resistance in most of the Palestinian

Table 7.4 Weapons seized during operation 'Defensive Shield'

Type	Quantity
Kalashinkov rifles	1,949
Long rifles	2,175
Sniper rifles	388
M-16 rifles	32
Pistols	781
RPG launchers	9
RPGs	49
Mortars	6
Mortar bombs	13
50 calibre machine guns	93
Magazines	311
Nightvision equipment	121
Hand grenades	37
Ammunition crates	40
Rifles w/telescopic lens	81
Explosive charges	430
Explosives (kg)	30
Explosive belts	6

Source: 'Operation defensive shield summarized statistics', 28 March–17 April 2002, *IDF Spokesperson's Office*, www.idf.il/english/news/netunim_eng.stm (accessed 16 July 2002).

West Bank cities it entered (e.g. Qalqiliya, Nablus and Tul Karem), but encountered especially stiff opposition in the Jenin refugee camp where 15,000 poverty-stricken civilians lived in 600 square yards of condensed space. Around 300 Palestinian guerrilla fighters affiliated to the various Palestinian terrorist organisations (e.g. the PLO-affiliated *Al-Aqsa* Martyrs Brigade, Force-17 and *Fatah Tanzim*, as well as Palestinian Islamic *Jihad* and *Hamas*) were involved in the battle of Jenin. Snipers, mines and booby-traps were planted everywhere: inside cupboards, under sinks, inside sofas, in cars and dumpsters. 'On one street alone, an Israeli [D-9] bulldozer detonated 124 explosive charges, some weighing as much as 250 pounds.'[41] Similar to other armies' urban warfare doctrine, the Israeli army used overwhelming numbers in Jenin: there were approximately 100 soldiers for every Palestinian gunman.

Intelligence

The Israeli army was using overwhelming numbers. It also used most of its highly sophisticated weaponry and intelligence-gathering capabilities in order to maintain the initiative, something armies entering urban theatre of operations have always had trouble keeping, because of the high tempo and high level of confusion that urban battlefields usually create. Indeed, reiterating the importance of intelligence in the urban battlefield, IDF COS

The Al-Aqsa Intifada

Moshe Yaalon stated at an international conference on LIC warfare that 'creating intelligence dominance is a critical factor for managing and dominating the LIC environment. The qualitative intelligence provides the ability to realize military power properly and precisely.'[42]

Hence, the decision by the IDF General Staff to form, in April 2000, the Field Intelligence Corps, which fields combat intelligence-gathering units trained to gather tactical intelligence, and to provide it in real-time, to combat units during operations. This enabled information, through the increasing digitisation of its armed forces, to go faster to the troops and, in turn, reduce the element of Palestinian surprise attacks.[43] The improvement in the command, control and communication systems enhanced the IDF's ability to monitor ground operations and improved the provision of real-time operational intelligence to ground troops.

According to an AH-1S Cobra helicopter squadron commander, during the fighting the IAF 'kept four attack helicopters and two Searcher II reconnaissance Unmanned Aerial Vehicles (UAVs) overhead at all times to ensure commanders knew where their troops on the ground were'.[44] Human intelligence was also provided by *Mistar'aravim* (i.e. 'to become an Arab') units, who are trained to blend in with the local population, gather operational intelligence and sometimes conduct targeted killings. More importantly, and underlining former GSS Chief Ya'acov Peri's conviction that 'there is no substitute for a human source',[45] the GSS had begun by the end of 2000 a large recruitment drive for Palestinian collaborators given the fact that their use had diminished significantly since the start of the Oslo Peace Process.[46] Such collaborators were put to good use, particularly in the targeted killing of key terrorist leaders.[47]

Attack helicopters were used to pinpoint and eliminate hostile forces either by using snipers or missile attacks. As one Special Forces captain stated, for example, 'in Jenin, I was in a helicopter above everything. I saw it happening. We were snipers; from the helicopter we were supposed to locate a certain area and eliminate hostile elements.'[48]

Circumvention and 'swarm' tactics

Such intelligence-gathering efforts, which were initiated weeks prior to the IDF's entry into Jenin, were carried out in order to avoid most armies' traditional urban infantry 'attrition approach' tactics, whereby operations abide by the 'move, make contact, deploy, fire and manoeuvre model (usually along a linear axis)'.[49] The Israelis, on the other hand, 'were able to deploy out of contact with the enemy by selectively seizing small areas of the camp, drastically reducing exposure to enemy fire and maintaining momentum by only clearing as necessary'.[50] This could be done only through the prior accumulation and analysis of field intelligence.

Various small-unit infantry, armour and air force task forces 'swarmed' around the Palestinian forces from all directions, thus, successfully

114 *The* Al-Aqsa Intifada

integrating disparate units and proving their interoperability. Such 'swarm' tactics especially managed to confuse Palestinian guerrilla fighters and terrorists. According to Colonel Gal Hirsh:

> In one battle in the Nablus *Kasbah* in about 24 hours they lost more than 80 of their gunmen and they never could identify where we were. We used the air force, combined forces and new fighting groups. Even if they were inorganic forces, they became task forces that knew how to fight together.[51]

Moreover, when faced with dangerous alleyways full of booby-traps and snipers, IDF forces circumvented these by using D-9 bulldozers that were able to create alternative avenues of approach within buildings, albeit at the cost of significant collateral damage. Such circumvention and 'swarm' tactics were particularly used after 9 April 2002, when a suicide bomber detonated his explosive belt in a courtyard, where 13 IDF infantry soldiers were instantly killed. The need to avoid such targeted and lethal suicide bomb attacks, as well as heavy sniping against IDF personnel, led to this innovation. Despite the negative media portrayal, the use of D-9 bulldozers may have, in fact, reduced the potential for further Palestinian confrontation during the operation given that many fighters did not know how to cope when confronted by such machines. For example, in an interview detained Islamic Jihad militant, Tabaat Mardawi stated when the IDF sent in armed bulldozers, 'there was nothing I could do against that bulldozer. What could I do? Either surrender or be buried by the rubble.'[52]

Since Operation 'Defensive Shield' the IDF also learnt that in order to eliminate terror cells embedded in Palestinian towns and villages, it did not have to show overwhelming force. Such large-scale 'invasions' into Palestinian areas created considerable international outcry and negative media exposure.[53] The growing involvement of the media in military operations, as well as the media's increased effectiveness in diffusing information in real-time, regarding the IDF's handling of various military operations, posed serious challenges to the operational effectiveness of its forces involved in the LIC. Even prior to Operation 'Defensive Shield' senior IDF officers, such as Maj. Gen. Giora Eiland, then IDF Director of Planning, admitted that 'public opinion, like weather conditions, topography and intelligence information, must be thrown into the mix when evaluating the effectiveness of particularly military organizations'.[54]

Notwithstanding the fact that the greater presence of the media in the military operational theatre made the soldier on the ground more accountable and, thus, less prone to carry out abusive or illegal behaviour, other senior commanders understandably were not willing to compromise the safety of their own troops for the sake of maintaining a positive media image. Then head of the IDF's Armoured Corps, Brig. Gen. Avigdor Klein, acknowledged in an interview the important role of the media during the *Al-Aqsa Intifada*, but also added that:

> My mission is to prevent the Palestinians from achieving political goals through violence.... And since we face numerous threats each day from terrorists willing to die, we're not going to risk the safety of our troops in attempts to look better in front of the news cameras.[55]

Furthermore, the ambiguous nature of certain images led occasionally to the misinterpretation of the soldier's or the unit's legitimate conduct during his or their mission.

One sergeant from the *Nahal* Infantry Brigade voiced his concerns regarding the way the media had portrayed IDF operations he had participated in during Operation 'Defensive Shield' in April 2002:

> They were firing at soldiers coming down one of the alleyways. How do you explain to someone that the only way that you can take out a heavy machinegun – which is armour-piercing – is that you have to call in a helicopter and it has to be a pinpoint strike at that building? So you hit that top floor. Just the top floor is damaged and the people on the middle floor are fine. But a cameraman comes and shows that building. And suddenly it's a destroyed building and you are accused of having killed people.[56]

As a result of wanting to avoid such exposure, the IDF adopted 'low-signature' operations that were often not only more effective, but also domestically and internationally less controversial due to the stealth and rapidity with which they were carried out.

Continuous improvement of training capabilities and avoidance of non-combatant casualties

In spite of the operation's success, the death toll of both Israelis and Palestinians was perceived as too high. In order to reduce casualty rates through better preparation and equipment, the IDF launched a multi-million dollar programme in June 2002 to upgrade the IDF's Tze'elim National Training Centre in the Negev Desert. The centre provides Israeli soldiers with significantly better urban warfare training facilities. The digital urban warfare centre is modelled after Palestinian cities and provides various landscapes in order to train the Israeli combat soldier for all types of contingencies. It includes a downtown area, rural village section, market area with narrow alleys and urban outskirts. The centre was set up in order to train around 90,000 reservists as well as all conscript ground forces in urban warfare battle skills.[57]

Furthermore, attempts at reducing the number of non-combatant deaths during the *Al-Aqsa Intifada*, whilst not sacrificing the protection of friendly forces, led to three major weapons development efforts. The Israeli MOD commissioned, for example, the development of a high-speed automatic anti-sniper gun, called 'Believer', based on infrared thermal technology[58] as well as the 'Corner Shot' non-line-of-sight weapon system, both of which aim to reduce the soldier's exposure to enemy fire.[59] The IDF has, furthermore, purchased from Israel Military Industries, a new infantry weapon system called *Refa'im*, which enables the infantry soldier to launch grenades against targets beyond visual range. More importantly, the rifle 'features a self-destruct mechanism to avoid post-battle casualties'.[60]

In order to avoid killing civilians when targeting Palestinian snipers, which often have been used deliberately as human shields – crowds of women and youth demonstrating or rioting – the IDF decided to equip not only trained snipers, but also regular infantry with advanced optic sight scopes that have enhanced laser rangefinder capabilities.[61]

The IDF ground forces multi-year plan titled, '*Kela 2008*' (Katapult 2008), as shall be seen later on in the book, will significantly expand the IDF's infantry capability by adding five new light-infantry battalions, which will be based permanently in the Territories.[62] Their permanent stationing in the Territories will increase their tactical knowledge of the urban terrain and of the civilian population. Such knowledge and the greater number of infantry brigades will, in turn, reduce the stress soldiers usually suffer in urban warfare operations due to the greater turnover of rest periods that such soldiers will undergo. Not only has the reduction of stress reduced cases of IDF abuse vis-à-vis the Palestinian population, but the 'ongoing connection with a single specific area ... has greatly improved operational successes'.[63]

Ethical dilemmas

Moreover, the need to reduce cases of abuse by Israeli soldiers whilst carrying out security duties after Operation 'Defensive Shield', particularly at checkpoints and roadblocks, led to the development, by the IDF School of Military Law, of an ethical and operational code of behaviour. Such a code, which is based on 11 key rules of conduct, has been taught over the last four years to both regular and reservist ground forces units. It provides extensive role-playing exercises that deal with the dilemmas of how to operate security checks on civilians and civilian property and, more importantly, with the dilemmas of what rules of engagement are acceptable within heavily populated civilian areas.[64]

Tackling ethical problems has been a major focus of the IDF over the last few years, as it is precisely the ambiguity in LICs that led to cases of excessive force or abuse. Col. Roi Elcabets stated that:

> There has been quite an impressive advancement in this area. In the officer course we have just developed principles on how to lead in

complex situations. We have also developed a lot of lessons and examples of bad and good behaviour. They are dealt with in moral and professional terms.[65]

This, however, did not eliminate all cases of misconduct given the fact that soldiers at checkpoints, and elsewhere, have occasionally abused Palestinians, albeit more as a result of operational stress than malice.[66] One *refusenik* described how boredom or stress could lead to punitive behaviour or pedantic checks at checkpoints and roadblocks:

> As a soldier you are supposed to check cars at roadblocks, you can legally have the person come out of the car, frisk him completely, have him take the car apart and put it back together. The degree you do this depends on how bored you are, whether you have been relieved on time, or if breakfast is late, or that kind of thing. So, you can either just stop the car and ask for his ID ... or literally get him to do everything – this is legal. We are not talking about soldiers who are acting barbarically. It's human, but when you're human and you're upset, you take it out on yourself or you punch a pillow or wall. When you're a soldier in the West Bank, you take it out on the population. And then some soldiers are more violent.[67]

In order to reduce the number of such cases of abuse, a special Checkpoint Unit was formed in mid-2004, under the command of a lieutenant colonel from the Military Police Corps. The special Checkpoint Unit has operated over the past three years in all the security crossings along the security fence and within the Nablus area. The unit's members have been trained in carrying out routine checks through the use of advanced technological measures (e.g. biometric identification, luggage transparency machines and magnetic gates) in Arabic, and in civil rights issues in order to improve the conditions of Palestinians trying to enter Israel and to reduce especially the time spent by Palestinians at checkpoints.[68]

Improvements have been made to the security crossings on the Green Line. Roofs have been mounted above the whole length of the security checking crossing zones, restrooms and drinking posts have also been fitted and humanitarian points have been set up to provide medical assistance to those being held up at the security crossings.[69] Nonetheless, in spite of such improvements, the mere existence of checkpoints, roadblocks and other forms of population control have caused friction with the local Palestinian population. Consequently, attempts to reduce such friction as well as international and domestic disapproval led the IDF, during the course of 2004, to remove 13 security crossing checkpoints and 87 roadblocks. Hence, by June 2005 only 12 security crossing checkpoints and 66 roadblocks remained throughout the West Bank.[70]

Moreover, the IDF School of Leadership also holds residential workshops for combat units who would like to discuss their moral misgivings in a sheltered environment between operational deployments. Such discussions reduce tensions and the stress that is built up during their missions in the Territories. The head of the IDF School of Leadership, Lt. Col. Timna Shmueli, explains the crucial role that such sessions have played in the professional development of combat units during the current conflict:

> I think that our main role is to help them, to facilitate them. We convince commanders to take a break, to sit with the soldiers and talk about all the issues that during the war they cannot talk about. Because if you sit here for three days and think and analyse how you make your mission and let the soldiers speak out their dilemmas, their conflicts and so on, most of the time they have the solution.[71]

Although the IDF has focused heavily in the past on the professional and tactical competency of its small-unit leaders, clearly dealing with the two *Intifadas* has led to a realisation that the ability for the commander and soldiers to deal creatively with ambiguous situations in LICs is important. One IDF field psychologist emphasised this point by stating,

> You have to deal with civilians and your actions are really not a function of how well you deal with your weapon or how good your tactical thinking is. It is mostly understanding complex situations and being able to see two steps ahead [i.e. two levels of command above], thinking innovatively and creatively.[72]

In fact, all soldiers involved in LIC scenarios must make quick judgement calls that cannot be drilled into them through traditional training methods. 'To maximize military effectiveness [in terms of achieving the mission], leaders must empower soldiers to make morally informed decisions.'[73]

Combatants rarely have the time to consider the operational and strategic implications of their operations, because they are constantly operating during heightened crises, such as the *Al-Aqsa Intifada*. According to a former instructor of the IDF combat squad leaders' course, 'the whole moral code, moral conduct, is something that is inserted into training programmes from day one. As a young soldier we talked about it and we had lessons for it and as a commander I passed it onto my soldiers.'[74]

Despite the relative success in arresting or killing many terror suspects, whilst trying to carry out operations ethically during 'Defensive Shield', its follow-up – Operation 'Determined Path', and other subsequent ones, the method often used for apprehending terror or guerrilla suspects was that of the highly controversial 'neighbour practice'. The 'neighbour practice', in reality, was used repeatedly to get wanted men out of houses within highly populated Palestinian areas. This was despite assurances of the IDF to the Israeli High Court of Justice that such a counter-terror method would be eradicated. Basically, the 'neighbour practice' involved the use of the wanted man's neighbour as a 'living shield' for IDF troops, whereby he is sent to call on the suspect to come out. In spite of the fact that one officer argued that the ' "neighbor practice is a military method, an efficient and effective method".... Former Justice Minister, Yossi Beilin, called the practice "immoral and un-Jewish" and warned that [the Sharon government] "is teaching the army the worst practices, and *is turning the concept of purity of arms into slander*" ' [emphasis mine].[75]

Such methods were used in part due to the greater danger and violent resistance that IDF units faced during the *Al-Aqsa Intifada* when trying to apprehend terror suspects. Whereas during the first *Intifada* and during the Oslo Peace Process, the arrest of wanted Palestinian militants required small teams and faced minor resistance, Palestinian militants during the *Al-Aqsa* crisis would resist IDF arrest raids through fire-fights and often resorted to intricate booby-traps. One infantry reservist recalled how much more dangerous arrest operations became compared to those conducted during the mid-1990s:

> We went into Gaza city last year. The objective was to draw fire as a younger team of soldiers (conscript soldiers) would go in as they carried out a whole night of house arrests there. We went in, and something which until then I had not done before was to fire in a suspect place, to neutralise that area. What if a kid was hiding there? But you don't take chances. In Gaza, you don't take any chances. So many times in a 'routine' mission our people got killed.... In the past we used to go out to house arrests with 15 guys. We used to secure the house, sneak in, wake up the suspect and take him with us. Now, to do a house arrest, it is a battalion that goes in.[76]

Counter-terrorism's relative success

In any case, massive incursions into the Territories enabled the IDF and the GSS to find plenty of evidence of PA complicity with, and activity in, terror attacks and to obtain valuable intelligence. The incursions, furthermore, enabled the IDF to arrest and occasionally kill numerous incumbent terrorist martyrs, defined by Israel as 'ticking bombs' and gradually to reoccupy, by the end of 2002, the former autonomous 'A' Areas for the sake of security. Although such targeted killings substantially reduced the number of terrorist leaders, recruiters and engineers, they deterred to a much lesser extent, suicide bombing volunteers. Their use, until very recently, augmented rather than reduced the number of suicide attacks due to the tit-for-tat cycle that Israeli reprisal operations often brought about.

During the early stages of the conflict, for example, an attempt by Arafat to reduce the level of Palestinian violence, which was spiralling out of control due to *Hamas*' and the PIJ's increasing involvement, led him on

120 *The* Al-Aqsa Intifada

16 December 2001 to declare, during the first Israeli–Palestinian brokered cease-fire, on Palestinian TV and radio that anyone who broke his cease-fire orders would be punished. In spite of the three weeks of relative quiet, the IDF's targeted killing of Raed Karmi, a *Tanzim* militia local leader, radicalised *Fatah*'s outlook of the conflict and pushed it towards greater cooperation with *Hamas*, PIJ and other minor terrorist cells.[77]

Thus, many analysts, such as former head of the *Shin Bet*, Ami Ayalon (1996–2000), came to question Sharon's counter terrorism strategy by arguing that 'war against terrorism is part of a vicious cycle. The fight itself creates ... even more frustration and despair, more terrorism and increased violence.... [And that] it is not a fleeting battle that ends in either victory or defeat.'[78]

Notwithstanding remarks such as these, there were signs following Operation 'Defensive Shield' that the IDF's continuous sorties, reprisals and incursions into the Palestinian terrorist- and guerrilla-infested cities and refugee camps had some positive results. The number of terror attacks against Israeli civilians diminished. The frequency between suicide attacks was reduced considerably since the deterrent effects of the IDF's re-occupation of Palestinian-controlled West Bank 'A' areas finally came to fruition by 2003. During the months of November 2002 and January 2003 there was *just* one suicide attack, whereas December 2002 reported none. During the same three-month period, the IDF reported that 36 suicide missions were thwarted and in the first two months of 2003, 123 different terror attacks were prevented.[79]

There were no attacks in February; three in March; and only two in April. This was due to the fact that the Israeli security forces had been able to arrest over 150 (and kill a substantial number of) potential suicide bombers since the beginning of the *Al-Aqsa Intifada* and that Israel's security prisons incarcerated around 6,000 Palestinians suspected of terrorist activity or affiliation with terror organisations. Continuous Israeli security forces operations against Palestinian clandestine bomb factories led to a growing scarcity of military-grade explosives.[80]

Furthermore, with the completion of the first portion of the controversial, yet effective, security fence (which will be discussed below), by 2004 the IDF was able to thwart 432 attempted terror attacks. The number of suicide bombings that actually made it through to Israel dropped from 55 in 2002 to 'only' 11 in 2004 (see Figure 7.1).[81]

Such 'success', however, did not come at a low cost. It involved growing numbers of IDF incursions in areas, such as the Gaza Strip, whose Palestinian population was initially relatively less active in carrying out terror or guerrilla attacks against Israeli civilians or troops. Moreover, whilst incursions into the Gaza Strip were initially one or two-day tactical raids carried out on a sporadic basis (the Southern Command initially was very cautious about mounting raids deep inside Gaza), they became longer in duration, more frequent and involved greater numbers of IDF personnel and materiel.[82] As a consequence, *Hamas* terrorist activities originating from the Gaza Strip increased.

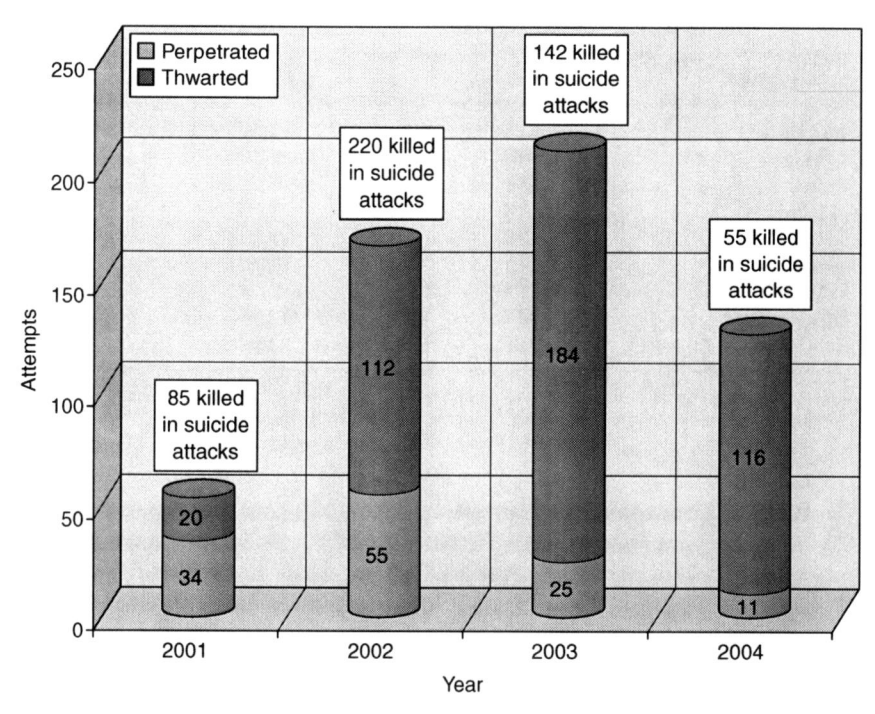

Figure 7.1 Palestinian suicide attacks perpetrated versus thwarted, 2001–04 (source: Adapted from 'Ebb and flow: summary of 2004', 19 April 2005, *IDF Spokesperson's Office*, www1.idf.il/SIP_storage/dover/files/6/37876.pdf (accessed 19 April 2005)).

The shift in public opinion, as seen above, enabled the IDF, since the re-occupation of the PA 'A' Areas with Operation 'Defensive Shield', to employ extensive coercive measures against the Palestinian population, including wide-ranging curfews (see Table 7.5), closures, house demolitions, the burgeoning of IDF checkpoints on many main Palestinian roadways in the Territories and the withholding of Palestinian tax revenue from the PA.[83] This 'stage of security control', dubbed 'Determined Path' (June 2002–May 2003) was directed at controlling Palestinian movement on the ground and, hence, at facilitating the apprehension, and possible assassination, of terrorists and wanted Palestinian insurgents hidden within the towns, villages and refugee camps of the West Bank.

In conjunction with more military-type operations – such as targeted killings, bombardment of PA and Palestinian terrorist infrastructure, firefights with Palestinian gunmen and so on – the IDF began, as of mid-2002, to take control of security matters on the ground throughout all of the Territories. Figures provided by the UN's Officer for the Coordination of Humanitarian Affairs (OCHA) in December 2003 showed to what extent

Table 7.5 Total hours of IDF curfews on major Palestinian population centres, 18 June 2002–25 January 2004

District/city	Curfew on	Curfew off
Ramallah	2,443	11,501
Nablus	4,640	9,376
Jenin	3,766	10,322
Hebron	5,828	8,093
Qalqilia	2,188	11,877
Bethlehem	2,625	11,416
Tulkarem	4,455	9,561
Total hours	25,944	72,145
Total days	1,081	3,006

Source: 'Curfew hours in cities starting June 18 2002 to midnight January 25 2004', *Palestinian Red Crescent Society*, www.palestinercs.org (accessed 28 January 2004).

the IDF was controlling the transport thoroughfares within the re-occupied PA 'A' Areas, in order to limit the mobility of potential terrorists. According to the OCHA report the IDF had set up, since the start of Operation 'Determined Path', '65 roadblocks, 464 mounds of dirt, 58 trenches and 95 concrete barriers'.[84]

The show of force, and widespread presence of IDF, and *Shin Bet* personnel in the Territories entailed more frequent contact with the Palestinian civilian population and, thus, greater chances of friction between soldiers on the ground and Palestinian civilians. Such friction, furthermore, possibly did wear out IDF forces involved in policing and COIN duties in the Territories as shall be seen below.

Escalation and the continual use of the military instrument without really seeking a diplomatic agreement, as occurred during the first three years of the conflict, reflected the purported understanding of Prime Minister Sharon, Defence Minister Mofaz and IDF COS Moshe Yaalon, that there could not be a political solution to the current conflict due to the Palestinians' intransigence and ultimate desire to destroy Israel.

Shortly after being appointed as new COS, Moshe Yaalon, stated in an interview with *Ha'aretz*, the major tenets of this view, shared by a large part of Israeli society, of Palestinian intentions and the nature of the Israeli–Palestinian conflict. Yaalon equated Palestinian terrorism with the nuclear threat and termed it as an existential threat due to the *Al-Aqsa Intifada*, which was not really about the Israeli occupation of the West Bank and Gaza, but rather of the actual recognition of the state of Israel's right to exist in the Middle East. He asserted that:

> The Palestinians have returned us to the War of Independence. Today it is clear that the state of Israel as a Jewish state is still an alien element in the region. It will take generations until various elements in

the region accept its existence. Therefore, we have to go back to the ethos ... of no choice.[85]

As the Palestinian threat was seen as existential and the Israeli state had no choice but to defend itself, the IDF, under the leadership of Sharon, Mofaz and Yaalon, set out to 'burn into the Palestinian and Arab consciousness that terrorism and violence will not defeat us [i.e. Israel] ... and that terrorism does not lead to agreements'.[86] For the first time in the *Al-Aqsa Intifada* Israeli political and security leaders labelled Palestinian terror as an existential threat. Nonetheless, other senior commanders did have a more nuanced perspective on the nature of the Palestinian terrorist and guerrilla threat. Then Head of Southern Command, Maj. Gen. Doron Almog stated, in fact, that 'the terrorism we face today is certainly a threat to our nation in terms of attrition, economic damage and our way of life.... But it's not the same type of existential threat faced by my parents' generation.'[87]

Nonetheless, the fact that Yaalon and other military and political leaders perceived the *Al-Aqsa Intifada* as a continuation of the pre-1948 Israeli–Palestinian conflict led them, consequently, to view the *Intifada* again as an intercommunal one. This perception had obvious consequences. As seen in Chapter 4, interpreting Palestinian violence as an existential and intercommunal threat, according to Dan Horowitz, lowers the threshold at which Israel will go to war. Hence, the outcome of such a view and of the need to 'burn into the Palestinian consciousness' the fact that terrorism would not bring about any strategic dividends was further military escalation.

This perspective, which was held strongly by the IDF General Staff at the start of the conflict, evidently led to tensions with the political echelon over how to conduct IDF operations from a strategic, operational (and sometimes) tactical point of view. For example, one member of the IDF General Staff stated publicly, in late December 2000, that 'the IDF intends to win in this encounter. *It is not ready to allow the political echelon, with its contradictory orders, and other considerations, to dim its victory*' [emphasis mine].[88] It also led to competition over resource provision priorities between the IDF's military needs and domestic political demands. Tensions over budgetary demands became even more common and led often, as shall be seen below, to upper echelon military personnel as well as ministers of defence to voice their concerns polemically in public.

This escalation, including penetration of IDF operations into areas initially left out of the conflict, were the result of their deep-seated belief that, as stated for example by Lt. Gen. Yaalon in *Yediot Ahronot* in August 2002, 'the only solution is to achieve an *unequivocal victory over the Palestinians*' and that such a victory would not come at a low price or immediately [emphasis mine].[89] However, according to Levitt and Wikas, 'counterterrorism is a form of conflict management, not conflict resolution'.[90] Thus, it is hard to see how the IDF alone would be able to impose an 'unequivocal victory' or political solution over the Israeli–Palestinian conflict. Col. Avi Peled agreed with this view in an interview by stating that 'the problem is that you cannot solve the terrorism problem just by military means. You can reduce the threat, you can defeat some of the terror organisations, but you cannot defeat the whole society, the whole community.'[91]

'Road map' for peace, PA power struggles and unilateral disengagement

Sharon acknowledged that 'it [i.e. terrorism] is not something that we can fight and destroy quickly. It takes time. It demands commitment and hard work...'. At the same time, knowing how deleterious an effect the protracted conflict could have on the operational capabilities and combat motivation of the IDF, Sharon by late 2002 was clear that he did not want it bogged down forever in the Territories: 'I don't want to sit in Nablus forever. I do not want to have our country mobilized forever to sit in Nablus.'[92]

The opportunity for achieving some kind of agreement with the Palestinians, and the cessation of major terror and guerrilla attacks was presented by the 'road map' performance-based peace plan proposed by the so-called 'quartet', that is, the USA, the European Union, Russia and the UN.[93] The principles of the plan were first enunciated by US President George W. Bush in a speech, on 24 June 2002, in which he called for a two-state solution of the Israeli–Palestinian conflict. In exchange for independent statehood, the PA would be required to not only fight terrorism, but also carry out significant democratic reforms. Israel, on the other hand, would be required to facilitate the establishment of a reformed Palestinian government and end (as well as reverse) settlement activity in the West Bank and Gaza Strip.

The Road Map peace plan would be carried out in three phases, between mid-2003 and 2005: (1) End of Palestinian violence, establishment of Palestinian political reforms (initially by appointing a new leader through democratic elections) and the removal of Israeli settlements; (2) Establishment of an independent Palestinian state; (3) Achievement of final-status agreement on issues such as final borders, the status of Jerusalem and the fate of Palestinian refugees and remaining Israeli settlements. The progress of such a plan would be subject to the compliance and efforts of both parties in satisfying their respective Road Map obligations. After the appointment by Yasser Arafat of the first-ever Palestinian Prime Minister, Mahmoud Abbas (also known as Abu Mazen), on 19 March 2003, the US released the road map's details on 30 April 2003 and oversaw the first Sharon–Abbas summit in Aqaba, Jordan on 4 June 2003, whereby both leaders publicly declared their willingness to uphold the Road Map principles.

However, days after the summit, the Israeli failed attempt to kill *Hamas* leader, Abdel Aziz Rantisi with helicopter air strikes in Gaza, on 10 June, led to a re-conflagration of the conflict and, on 11 June, to a Palestinian suicide bomb attack on an Israeli bus, which caused the deaths of 17 passengers and bystanders. Pressure from the newly appointed Prime Minister Abbas led, on 29 June, to a unilateral, but tentative, cease-fire (*hudna*) between the PA and the four major Palestinian terrorist groups: Islamic *Jihad*, *Hamas* (three-month cease-fire), *Fatah* (six-month cease-fire) and the Democratic Front for the Liberation of Palestine. This cease-fire, which rapidly broke down, was seen by the Israelis as a ploy for such factions to re-group and recover from the IDF's incessant COIN operations – after all, Israel's COIN measures by mid-2003 were beginning to have a major attritional effect on Palestinian guerrilla and terrorist units.

Further meetings between Sharon and Abbas took place during the summer of 2003, but Abbas, exasperated by Arafat's attempts at limiting his ability to govern and reform the PA, tended his resignation to the Palestinian Legislative Council on 6 September. Arafat's close associate, Ahmed Qurei (also known as Abu Ala), was appointed as Abbas' successor in early October 2003. However, a few days following his appointment, Prime Minister Qurei threatened to resign due to a clash with Arafat over the control of the PA's security forces, which were unable, if not unwilling, to fight terrorism just as Israel was unwilling to limit the construction of new settlement homes.[94]

As a result of continued Palestinian violence and the Road Map's lack of progress, on 23 November 2003, Prime Minister Sharon had told his cabinet that he was planning to take 'unilateral steps' as a goodwill gesture to the Palestinians, but had not decided what those steps would be. Consequently, Sharon, who believed that only with improved security could the Road Map succeed, announced on 18 December 2003 at the annual 'Herzliya Conference on the Balance of Israel's National Security', that Israel would initiate 'the unilateral security step of disengagement from the Palestinians'.[95]

The Disengagement Plan (*hitnatkut*) was to be centred on the total withdrawal of Israeli settlements and security forces from the Gaza Strip (and to a much lesser extent from the West Bank), the redeployment of IDF forces along new security lines and the inclusion of various Israeli West Bank settlements behind an intricate 650 km-long security fence – dubbed by the Israelis 'separation fence' (*gader hahafrada*) – that would follow roughly the contours of the 1967 Green Line. Such a disengagement plan would reduce, according to the Sharon government, the chances of friction between both the Israeli and Palestinian population, and forces in the Territories. More crucially, it would reduce the level of terror attacks originating from the West Bank.[96] Although Sharon reassured his audience that the 'security line will not constitute the permanent border of the state of Israel', he did warn that through the Disengagement Plan 'the Palestinians will receive much less than they would have received through the direct negotiations as set out in the road map'.[97]

The idea of building a physical obstacle between the Palestinian and Israeli populations was first suggested by Yitzhak Rabin in the early 1990s, as the number of terror attacks and violent incidents increased, both in Israel and in the Territories, in spite of the Oslo Peace Process. 'Rabin declared that Israel must "take Gaza out of Tel Aviv" that is, create two distinct entities so that the two populations could avoid what he called *chikuch* (friction)'.[98]

Such friction was a particular concern given the changing demographic composition of Israel and the Territories and the growing lack of trust between the two populations. For example, in the Gaza Strip alone the Palestinian population was 731,000 in July 1994, 1,054,000 in July 1998, and 1,225,911 in July 2002. The population in effect increased by almost 68 per cent between 1994 and 2002.[99] Consequently, the Rabin government built the Israeli Gaza Strip barrier in 1994, and in 1995 it set up the Shahal Commission in order to examine the feasibility of constructing a security barrier separating Israelis and Palestinians along the West Bank.

Netanyahu avoided the issue, as he was weary of creating, in effect, a security barrier that might jeopardise existing and limit future settlements in the West Bank. Prime Minister Ehud Barak revived Rabin's idea of creating a security barrier around the West Bank prior to the Camp David 2000 Summit, but was unable to implement it, given his electoral defeat in February 2001. Nonetheless, when Sharon entered office Barak warned, 'When there are 70 dead Israelis, you can resist the fence, but when there are 700 dead Israelis, you will not be able to resist it.'[100]

The security fence was approved by the defence cabinet in July 2001. It was initially conceived, however, for the purposes of preventing illegal entry into Israel of Palestinian workers along three major areas (Jerusalem, Tulkarem and Um el Fahem). Once the terror campaign by the Palestinians increased considerably after December 2001, the Sharon government understood that only a contiguous fence along almost the whole of the Green Line could reduce, if not halt, terror attacks in Israel. The initial route was approved by the defence cabinet in June 2002, and partially modified on the basis of the 30 June 2004 Israeli High Court judgement.

Legal challenges to the construction of the security fence

Petitions from Israeli human rights organisations (on behalf of Palestinian communities affected by the security fence) to the Israeli High Court of Justice led it, in February 2004, to state that the fence was not illegal for security reasons, despite the fact that the security fence was being constructed partially on occupied/disputed territory. The High Court, however, did order the Israeli government to reroute a 30 km portion of the existing and planned security fence.[101] During the same month, the International Court of Justice (ICJ) hearings began, at the request of a December 2003 UN General Assembly resolution, in order to provide an advisory (i.e.

non-binding) ruling on the legality of the security fence. In spite of the fact that the PA is not a member of the court, it was allowed to make a submission to the court. The ICJ, furthermore, allowed 56 countries from the Organisation of the Islamic Conference, as well as the 22 members of the Arab League, to make submissions to the court against Israel, even though none of these states were affected in any way by such a fence and despite the fact that Article 36 of the ICJ's Statute requires that disputes can only be presented before the ICJ with the consent of all parties.[102]

Israel, understandably, did not consent to the ICJ arbitration. The ICJ, nonetheless, on 9 July 2004, ruled (almost unanimously) against the security fence, calling for its removal and for the compensation of any Palestinians who had been so far affected by it. The right of self-defence, on the basis of Article 51 of the UN Charter, which was invoked by the Israelis in support of the construction of the security fence, was rejected by the ICJ advisory opinion. The ICJ, in fact, believed that such a right could only be invoked against threats emanating directly from states, rather than from sub-state actors. Presumably, the news of the growing trend towards sub-state violence and terror since the end of the Cold War – and particularly after 11 September – had not yet reached The Hague.

Local protests carried out by Palestinians, Israeli and international human rights activists – who dubbed the security fence 'apartheid wall' – have been quite common and have led, occasionally, to violent clashes resulting in injury on both sides of the fence. On one occasion protests against the security fence in Gaza led to the death of British International Solidarity Movement activist, Tom Hurndall. Hurndall was shot in the head by an IDF soldier on 11 April 2003 and died subsequently on 14 June 2003. After significant calls for justice from his parents, an IDF military court, two years after Hurndall's death, found the accused soldier guilty of the charges of manslaughter, obstruction of justice (two charges), submission of false information, solicitation of submission of false information, and conduct unbecoming.[103]

In spite of such Palestinian and international opposition, as the suicide terror attacks increased, Israeli popular support for the construction of the security fence increased accordingly. Tel Aviv University's Tami Steinmetz Peace Index recorded 83 per cent support for the security fence from the Israeli–Jewish public in October 2003. Such support remained high – 84 per cent in February 2004 – in spite of strident Palestinian and international opposition to it, most of which was either voiced in the media and in courts.[104] More significant internal protests, as shall be seen in the following chapter, occurred in relation to the disengagement's main goal to dismantle all the settlements and to redeploy all *local* IDF forces from the Gaza Strip. The number of right-wing conscientious objectors and protesters, as the disengagement process gained momentum, increased. Furthermore, it showed to what extent the national security consensus on the maintenance of the Territories had deteriorated.

128 The Al-Aqsa Intifada

Ongoing violence

More than 100 Israeli checkpoints in the Territories became prime targets by terrorist groups, to the degree that 'Israel's army chiefs were reappraising the value of such outposts that were leaving soldiers "like ducks in a shooting gallery"'. For example, on 3 March 2002, 'a lone sniper using a WWII-vintage bolt-action carbine from a hilltop adjacent to Ramallah killed 10 Israelis and wounded four during a 30-minute attack. The assassin, after firing only 25 shots, escaped unharmed'.[105]

Such incidents became increasingly commonplace in the Territories. Here it shall be recalled that the growing number of Israeli casualties brought about by guerrilla ambushes on outposts became one of the factors that led to the Israeli withdrawal from Lebanon. In order to avoid a similar amount of casualties from such static posts within the Territories and in order to carry out more dynamic security sweeps, 'a commission of inquiry established [in late 2002] that the IDF should reduce the number of permanent roadblocks and opt for more spot checks set up without warning', because as one IDF officer put it, 'you can't carry out your functions inside a bunker'.[106]

IDF infantry units were not alone on the receiving end of Palestinian ambushes. Armoured personnel carrier (APC) and tank patrols also were subject to bloody ambushes, which in turn led to further IDF reprisals in the areas where the ambushes were perpetrated. For example, on 14 February 2002, three soldiers were killed and another was wounded when an explosive device detonated under the underbelly of a *Merkava Mk3* tank on the Karni–Netzarim road. On 14 March 2002, three soldiers were killed when their *Merkava* tank drove over a bomb on that same road. On 5 September 2002, an Israeli soldier was killed and three others wounded when their tank drove over a bomb near Kissufim. Another incident involved the killing of four other Israeli soldiers on 15 February 2003, when an explosive device detonated under their M-60 '*Magach*' tank a kilometre south of the settlement of Dugit in the northern Gaza Strip.[107]

The growing number of terror and guerrilla attacks originating from the Gaza Strip led to a series of high-profile targeted killings of leading *Hamas* figures, including *spiritual* leader Sheik Ahmed Yassin, on 22 March 2004, and on 17 April 2004, *political* leader Abdel Aziz Rantisi, who had just recently replaced Sheik Yassin as leader of the *Hamas* movement.

Yet, on 11 and 12 May 2004, two APCs of *Givati*'s '*Dolev*' combat engineering battalion, which was conducting an operation aimed at destroying *Hamas* metal workshops involved in the manufacture of *Qassam* rockets, were destroyed in two separate attacks. These resulted in the deaths of 11 soldiers. The remains of the six soldiers from one of the APCs were dispersed by the large explosion and were paraded by the local Palestinian population in front of Arab television networks, including *Al-Jazeera*.[108]

The parading of mutilated bodies caused an outrage in Israel, eventually leading to a large operation in the Zeitoun neighbourhood of Gaza City and in Rafah, dubbed Operation 'Rainbow', which began on 18 May 2004 and ended on 23 May 2004. The aim of the operation was to destroy the terrorist infrastructure, weapon smuggling tunnels, and *Qassam* rocket missile equipment, which had been used increasingly by *Hamas* terrorists to bomb civilian settlements and towns within and beyond the Green Line. According to Brig. Gen. Shmuel Zakkai, then commander of IDF forces in Gaza, during the operation the IDF had 'killed 41 terrorists, found and destroyed 3 tunnels and a hole, used for digging a tunnel, arrested terror activists connected to the building of tunnels [and] demolished 56 structures',[109] which were used for preparing explosives or harboured gunmen during the actual operation.

Many roads in Rafah were damaged due to the fact that many of these were booby-trapped with explosives. IDF D-9 armoured bulldozers were used to remove the asphalt in order to dig up and detonate these explosives, which were placed all over the city's nodal links. Nonetheless, it was inevitable that innocent civilians became homeless, given the extensive demolition of homes carried out by the IDF, during these, and other operations, particularly in the Gaza Strip in the last months leading up to the unilateral disengagement.

However, as the IDF's and *Shin Bet*'s increasingly effective onslaught on Palestinian terror progressed, the nature of the Israeli–Palestinian conflict changed. This was particularly the case in Gaza, where the conflict had become an '"over/under" conflict, with mortar shells and *Qassam* rockets being fired or tunnels being dug under Israeli settlements and IDF bases'.[110] The IDF, between 2003 and 2004, uncovered 80 tunnels in the Gaza Strip. It also saw an exponential growth in Palestinian surface-to-surface missile attacks during 2004, despite Operations 'Rainbow' and 'Days of Penitence' (see Figure 7.2 and Figure 7.3).

Thus, Palestinian groups within the Gaza Strip not only began targeting the IDF whilst it conducted its regular military operations, but it also began attacking actual IDF bases and outposts by constructing large underground tunnels rigged with explosives, which were detonated usually by suicide bombers. For example, in late June 2004, an underground explosion at the 'Orhan' outpost near the Gush Katif junction killed one, and wounded five other IDF soldiers. *Hamas* and *Fatah*'s *Al-Aqsa* Martyrs Brigades both claimed responsibility for the attack, which was intended to avenge the killing of both *Hamas* leaders, Yassin and Rantisi.[111]

Despite the targeted killings of *Hamas* leaders, Rantisi and Sheikh Yassin, *Hamas* was undeterred. Even after Operation 'Rainbow', *Qassam* rocket attacks increased. Following the death of two Israeli children, aged three and five, after a *Hamas Qassam* rocket attack on the town of Sderot, on 29 September 2004, the IDF initiated another major retaliatory operation, called 'Days of Penitence', within the towns of Beit Lahia, Beit Hanoun and the Jabalya refugee camp. These areas were used repeatedly as launching sites for *Qassam* rocket attacks.

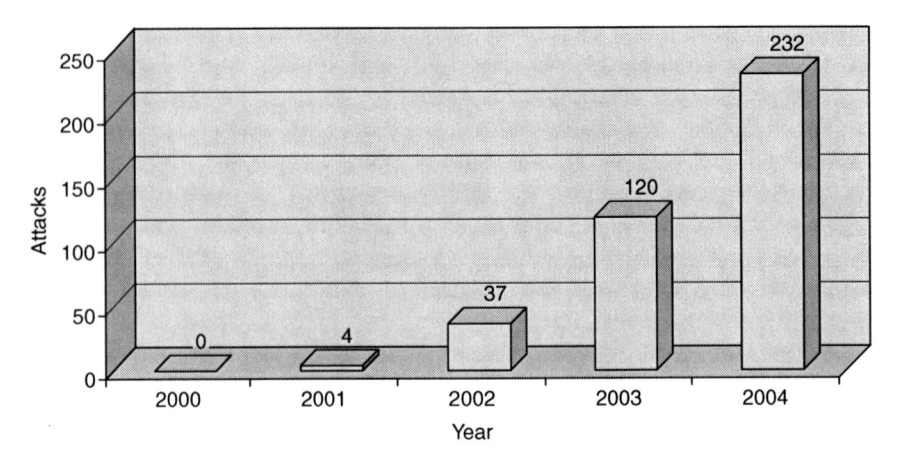

Figure 7.2 Qassam attacks on Israeli targets, 2000–04 (sources: Arieh O'Sullivan, 'IDF: 44% fall in terror victims', *The Jerusalem Post*, 30 December 2004; 'Four Years of conflict: Israel's war against terrorism', *Israeli Ministry of Foreign Affairs*, 3 October 2004, www.mfa.gov.il/NR/rdonlyres/9D70B198-BB04-481F-8C3B-1D4DD0F8BF93/0/Four YearsofConflict.doc (20 December 2004)).

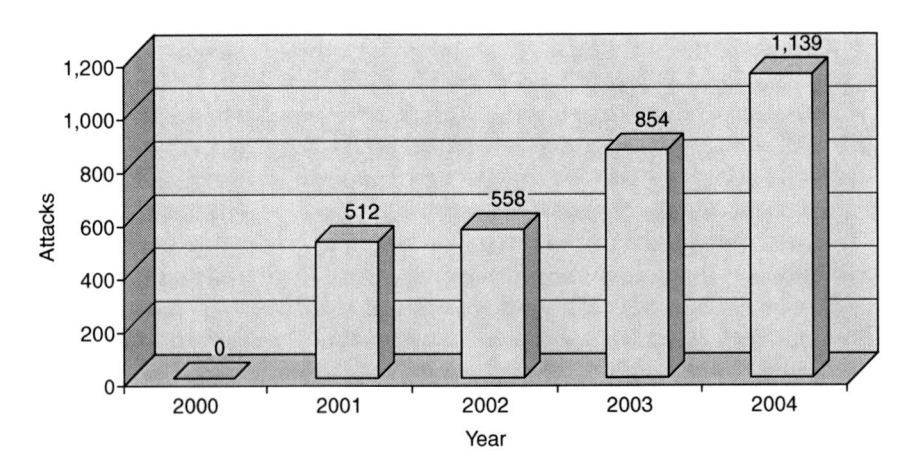

Figure 7.3 Mortar shell attacks on Israeli targets, 2000–04 (sources: Arieh O'Sullivan, 'IDF: 44% fall in terror victims', *The Jerusalem Post*, 30 December 2004; 'Four years of conflict: Israel's war against terrorism', *Israeli Ministry of Foreign Affairs*, 3 October 2004, www.mfa.gov.il/NR/rdonlyres/9D70B198-BB04-481F-8C3B-1D4DD0F8BF93/0/Four YearsofConflict.doc (20 December 2004)).

Operation 'Days of Penitence' was the largest IDF incursion into Gaza since the start of the *Intifada*. It also stood out quite disturbingly from other previous large-scale operations by the fact that it was named, planned and initiated by the Gaza division headquarters rather than by the General Staff or Southern Command. Brig. Gen. Shmuel Zakkai came to the conclusion that given the upsurge in *Qassam* rocket attacks following the Jewish New Year (*Rosh HaShana* – 16 September 2004), the IDF had to enter the launch areas in the Gaza Strip once again. 'The General Staff was asked only to approve a reinforcement in the form of the *Golani* reconnaissance battalion.'[112]

The aim of the operation was to improve Israel's deterrence vis-à-vis the *Qassam* and mortar squads within the northern Gaza Strip. Sharon, furthermore, had stated that once the operation had begun it would carry on indefinitely, that is, until *Hamas* attacks would cease. The brigade-level operation (consisting of the *Givati* reconnaissance battalion, the *Golani* reconnaissance battalion, an armoured battalion and an engineering battalion) was conducted over 17 days and managed to destroy nine *Qassam* rocket cells, a dozen bomb-laying squads, eight anti-tank rocket launchers, whilst suffering *only* 16 casualties, including one soldier killed on the first day of the operation. Over 50 per cent of the fatalities amongst the armed Palestinians were due to helicopter gunship attacks.

The significant increase in the use of the Israeli Air Force's UAV and helicopter gunship fleet, during Operation 'Days of Penitence', marked a qualitative change in the IDF's counter-terror operations in Gaza. The ground forces, in effect, manoeuvred under continuous airborne cover, which not only eliminated Palestinian threats on the ground, but also provided real-time intelligence for the ground forces in the vicinity.[113] Forces on the ground, however, caused considerable damage. By the end of the operation the IDF had killed 100 Palestinians, including 27 children, injured over 400 and destroyed large portions of the local infrastructure.[114] Nonetheless, many of the Palestinian casualties during the operation were caused by Palestinian gunmen using the civilian population as human shields and hiding amongst civilian quarters.

Excessive force and rules of engagement

In any case, even preventive measures, such as the omnipresent curfew, whose objective according to the IDF 'is to prevent terrorists from planning and executing attacks on Israeli citizens', led various IDF units to use *excessive force*, that is by using live fire even in non-life-threatening situations.[115] In October 2002, for example, a commander of an IDF unit that hit five civilians in one day, admitted, during his explanation of the incident to the head of the Central Command, that 'the soldiers were becoming lax about open-fire orders'. As a result, the head of Central Command had issued strict open-fire orders, particularly at roadblocks where 'firing is no longer permitted ... unless there is a definite threat to the soldiers' lives'.[116]

132 *The* Al-Aqsa Intifada

Although there were attempts to impose stricter rules of engagement, there was also growing criticism for the degree of permissiveness allowed by the IDF. For example, 'in the first *Intifada*, soldiers needed authorisation from an officer with the rank of major general to enter a mosque, whereas now they hurl smoke grenades into mosques as a matter of course'.[117] One squad leader explained his experiences whilst doing reserve duty in Nablus in March 2001:

> Every night there were shootings from inside Nablus on us. We were on top of a hill and we just did whatever we wanted over there. And I found myself doing really stupid things like shooting and trying to blow up a gas station in the middle of Nablus, shooting on a mosque and shooting on houses.[118]

One reason for this escalation is that Palestinian terrorists and guerrillas were more prone to use religious sites unscrupulously for their own protection, as was the case during the occupation by Palestinian militants of Bethlehem's Church of the Nativity during April 2002. In addition, according to international law, such sites if used for military purposes become legitimate military targets. Regardless, the cost in terms of public domestic and international opinion, however, should have been taken into account by the IDF before imposing a siege on the Church of the Nativity in Bethlehem.

As with the first *Intifada*, the standard operating procedures regarding the use of live ammunition became muddled as the *Al-Aqsa Intifada* progressed. Due to the fact that the IDF labelled the uprising in the Territories as 'an armed conflict short of war', the circumstances under which live ammunition could be used by IDF ground troops were broadened substantially. Indeed, 'the renewed definition of the state of affairs ... created a situation in which [even] breaking up demonstrations is considered a wartime activity, justifying the use of firearms'.[119] Nonetheless, this contradiction between the definition and the actual perception of the nature of the conflict by commanders on the ground led to confusion amongst the ground troops. One reservist recounts:

> During debrief arose the question of whether every armed Palestinian is life threatening. Eventually, no definite answer was given and it was left up to the serviceman's judgement. As to breaking up demonstrations, no instructions were given.[120]

Moreover, subsequent to an investigation regarding fire orders, Chief of Investigating Military Police, Col. Mikki Barel stated, when commenting on the discrepancy between the command and its actual implementation in the theatre of operations, that 'there is confusion around the fire orders.... [And that] it's like kindergarten children playing "pass the message on" – each giving the message their own interpretation.'[121] Whereas, in planned missions (such as targeted killing or search and arrest operations), ROE were clearly stipulated and rehearsed beforehand, routine operations were often the source of this confusion. According to Lt. X:

> Once you are out on a daily routine and you hear different rules of engagement; that is when it is confusing. That is when you lose your direction. They [i.e. his subordinates] wake up – they are exhausted – and we get the command from high up, and in a second it changes, and you change it in your head, and you are giving it to soldiers who are on shifts: 'Wait, today [the ROE] are? He is shooting at me, what do I do today? Do I shoot to kill or do I shoot to hurt him or do I back off?' So, it was complicated. I felt the complication right at the beginning, around a month and one-half, two months into the *Intifada*. *Everything was very organized, just when it got down to the bottom line, when the soldier has to pull the trigger, it was complicated* [emphasis mine].[122]

Despite the confusion of the IDF's rules of engagement, attempts were made on the part of the IDF to maintain the level of professionalism and morality, for which it had been renowned in the past. Indeed, commanders 'carried out thousands of inquiries in the field and the findings [were] passed on to the Military Advocate's Office'. As a result, there were, by early 2003, 'over 230 cases, regarding different criminal acts.... Investigations by the Military Police ... led [by mid-2003] to the filing of charges against about 30 soldiers and officers.'[123] In spite of the IDF's attempts at enforcing strict rules of engagement, the IDF's international and domestic image has suffered substantially since the start of the *Al-Aqsa Intifada*.

Curfews, house demolitions and closures have constantly been a problem for Israel's image, both domestically and internationally. During both *Intifadas*, the IDF became the focal point of consistent outcries of condemnation, despite its belief that such measures had a deterrent effect on the Palestinian population. Even when conscious of the humanitarian problems related to such preventive/punitive measures, the IDF often could not compromise the security of its citizens. Then Coordinator of Government Activities in the Territories, Maj. Gen. Amos Gilad, highlighted the dilemma of needing to balance Israel's security needs with Palestinian humanitarian conditions:

> It is very difficult to solve this contradiction between terror, on one side, and humanitarian assistance, on the other. For example, to ease the daily life of Palestinians we must open the roads between cities, but the moment we do that, we are hit with terrorist attacks. Similarly, without the IDF presence in the Palestinian cities, we would be suffering a totally unacceptable toll of casualties.[124]

IDF officials, furthermore, claimed that such measures had a significant deterrent effect, at least if viewed from a long-term perspective. One senior officer stated to *Ha'aretz* that, 'demolishing a house is a grave penalty for the family. It is not merely an economic blow. A home has emotional value which cannot be restored' and, thus, leads family members to dissuade or even to physically stop potential *shahidim* (martyrs) from committing a suicide bomb attack.[125] The extent to which house demolitions deterred Palestinian terrorists from committing acts of terror is questionable, though, given that the pinnacle of terrorist attempts committed during the *Al-Aqsa Intifada* tended to correspond to the height of IDF counter-terrorist house demolition activities as well.

Not only were house demolitions used for punitive or deterrent purposes (see Figure 7.4), many were carried out in conjunction with major IDF incursions into PA areas, given that Palestinian fighters and terrorists often used such dwellings for cover or ambush opportunities during such IDF COIN operations (see Figure 7.5). Such measures, although intended to protect IDF forces, often resulted in extensive collateral damage and large cases of civilians becoming homeless (see above: Operations 'Rainbow' and 'Days of Penitence').

Collective measures such as the curfew were sometimes the only option, because according to the Israeli army spokesperson, 'the cynical use of the freedom of movement by the terrorists prevents us from relieving the burden on the civilian population'.[126] However, many others stated that such collective measures did not have much of a deterrent effect, but had actually galvanised the Palestinian population. Zuhair Kurdi, a journalist with Hebron's *Al Amal* TV station, argued somewhat rhetorically that, 'the legal father of the suicide bomber is the Israeli checkpoint, whilst his mother is the house demolition'.[127]

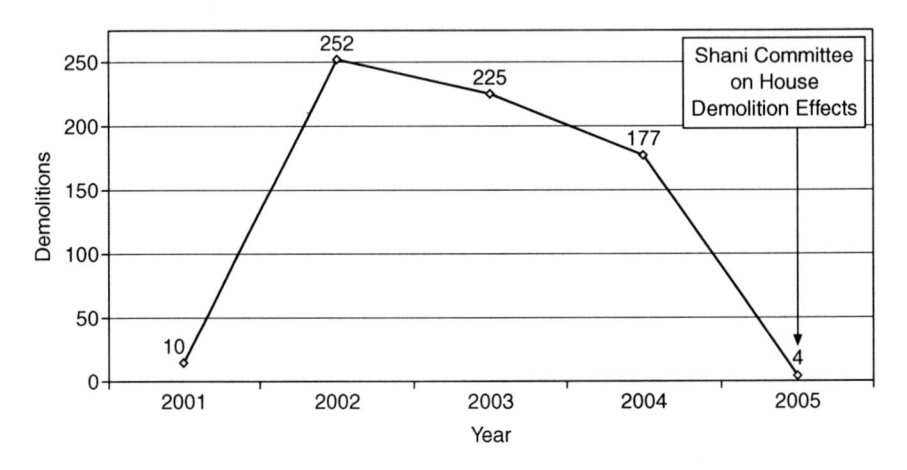

Figure 7.4 IDF house demolitions of Palestinian homes in the Occupied Territories for punitive purposes, 2001–05 (source: 'Statistics on punitive house demolitions', *B'Tselem*, www.btselem.org/english/Punitive_Demolitions/Statistics.asp (accessed 25 January 2005)).

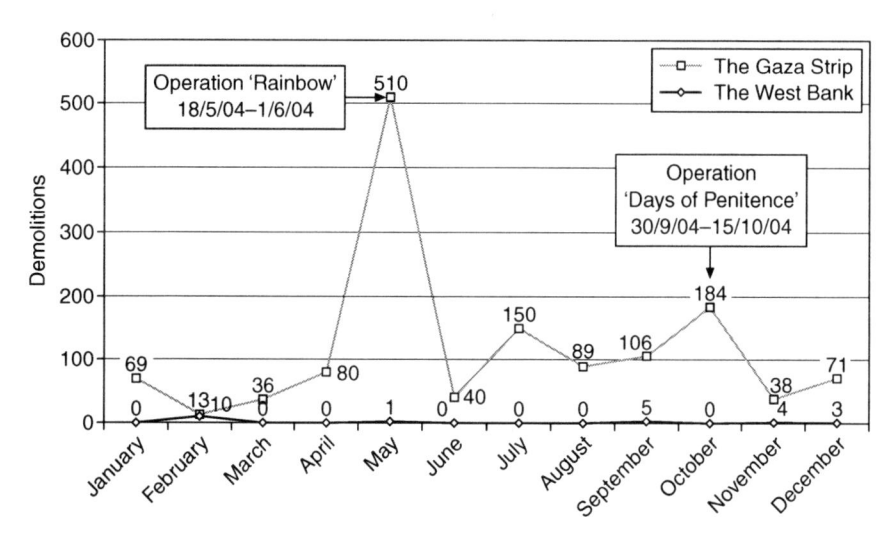

Figure 7.5 IDF house demolitions of Palestinian homes for alleged military purposes, 2004 (source: 'Demolition for alleged military purposes', *B'Tselem*, www.btselem.org/english/Razing/Statistics.asp (accessed 25 January 2005)).

Conscientious objection during the *Al-Aqsa Intifada*

As in the previous *Intifada*, such measures notably affected the morale and combat motivation of noteworthy sections of the IDF forces. The consequences of such demoralisation become clear when looking at the conscientious objection phenomenon during the second *Intifada*. From the start, the number of conscientious objectors gradually augmented. Most of those who refused were 'selective' conscientious objectors. That is, on the one hand they refused to serve in the Territories, whilst on the other hand they continued to express the desire to defend pre-1967 Israel.

A major factor that galvanised the conscientious objection movement, since the beginning of the *Al-Aqsa Intifada*, was the publication, on 25 January 2002, of the 'Combatant's Letter' by the group *Ometz Le'sarev* (Courage to Refuse), which comprised initially 53 signatories. By late 2005, the number of signatories had increased to 629, whereas the total number of other active objectors was around 1,700.[128] According to the signatories of the Combatant's Letter, the fight going on in the West Bank and Gaza Strip is seen as 'a "War of Settlements"', whereby an entire people is being dominated, expelled, starved and humiliated in order to maintain the occupation of territories, which 'are not Israel and that ... are bound to be evacuated in the end'.[129] Consequently, the signatories of the letter refused to serve in the Territories. All were willing to serve alternatively within the 1967 Green Line, because they perceived themselves to be patriots and Zionists willing to protect the state of Israel, but not the settlements in the Territories. As one *refusenik* argued,

> Security is essential, but it's not a justification for whatever the IDF is doing in the West Bank ... There is a justification for the existence of the state of Israel, and that existence depends on having an army and, hence, I'm willing to be part of that army, but I am not willing to partake in whatever it's doing in the Occupied Territories.[130]

The signatories of the letter believed that all the Territories were under illegal occupation and should be liberated. For example, one signatory, Noam Livne, a lieutenant in the Engineering Corps, accused the settlers of being '200,000 citizens [who] are holding the other 9 million [Palestinians and Israelis] hostage in a violent bloodbath that has continued for 35 years'.[131]

Furthermore, many of the *Intifada*'s conscientious objectors believed that *all* military operations carried out in the Territories were illegal and as such the soldier could not carry out such operations. They based their decision to refuse 'illegal orders' on the Israeli Supreme Court's verdict of 1958, which stated that 'on certain orders the black flag of manifest illegality flies ... A soldier has not only the right but also the duty to disobey such orders.'[132] The Israeli Supreme Court's verdict was pronounced in regard to a curfew, imposed in October 1956, by Border Police, who shot and killed around 50 civilians from the Israeli Arab village of Qafr Qassem as they returned home from work unaware that their village had been placed under curfew at the start of the Suez War. Many soldiers disagree with the conscientious objectors' stance, but argue that it is possible for a soldier to refuse to obey certain commands above which there 'hangs a black flag'. However, many conscientious objectors, such as Infantry Serg. Maj. Avner Kokhavi, believe that 'one big black flag hangs above all military activities in the Occupied Territories'.[133]

Such a position starkly contrasts with that taken by most conscientious objectors of the first *Intifada*. Then, most conscientious objectors campaigned for a political settlement, which did not necessarily entail complete withdrawal from the Territories and the dismantlement of *all* settlements. Now, objectors clamoured for drastic measures for the sake of ending the occupation regime. *Ometz LeSarev* activists claim that the occupation 'undermines those principles of moral justice ... prevents the attainment of peace ... and endangers Israel's existence', because it eats the very soul and fabric of Israeli society.[134] As one *Yesh Gvul* activist put it, 'we understand today that the price of the occupation is loss of the humane image of the IDF and corruption of the entire Israeli society'.[135]

The call for such a radical 'solution' to the *Al-Aqsa Intifada* has been brought about by various factors. First, the number of settlers has doubled over the last 15 years and consequently has resulted in the consistent growth and new developments of settlements in the Territories.[136] Such settlements have been the main source of tension between the Palestinian and Jewish communities, who are ruled by two different legal systems, and treated in a biased manner by the Israeli administrative and security apparatuses (negatively in the Palestinian case, positively in the Jewish case). Israeli sociologist Baruch Kimmerling argues that such double standards are so rife that 'Israel has ceased being a democratic state and become a *Herrenvolk* democracy [within which] part of its subjects (citizens) enjoys full rights and another part (non-citizens) enjoys none'.[137]

Second, as a result of such tensions and the visceral hatred of the Palestinians towards settlers and their settlements, their inhabitants have often been the main target of terrorism, guerrilla raids and missile attacks carried out by Palestinian militants. This has added to the burden of protecting such settlements – even illegal ones (by Israeli legal standards) – on the IDF itself.

Many conscientious objectors – who come from within the 1967 Green Line as well as serving IDF troops who are not keen, in general, to serve in the Territories – believe that the IDF should not be protecting settlements. Many question the maintenance of settlements in the Territories for ideological reasons, whilst others do so for purely economical and military reasons. For example, some minor settlements such as that of Morag in the Gaza Strip, which until recently had around 200 inhabitants, required a battalion to protect it properly. Maj. (Res.) Rami Kaplan, a former leading figure in the group *Ometz Le'sarev*, expressed his views on defending settlements and on what effect this had on the landscape of the territories as well as on the operational preparedness of IDF units:

> The thing that influenced me or troubled me more than the moral aspect was the political aspect or the total uselessness of doing what we do there, because I saw that when I came to Gaza everything was becoming more and more fortified and it reminded me very much of Lebanon. We fortified ourselves, brought in more tanks and more units. For example, once shots were fired at agricultural workers on a kibbutz. So, the day after we send in a company from *Givati* still in basic training – they didn't know anything. I saw this and understood the reasons why basic training of conscripts have been cut; and for what? For this shooting? So, tomorrow in another sector there will be another shooting and they will send in another company.... This [i.e. Gaza] is a fortress with more soldiers than people living there.[138]

These conscientious objectors consider such settlements to be the source of tension between Israelis and Palestinians and do not deem their military efforts to be protecting Israel proper. Major Kaplan has argued that 'we [the IDF] are not defending Israel there – exactly the opposite. We are defending the settlements.... I think being in the territories as a soldier is not defending my family in Tel Aviv.'[139] They ask why defend settlements, which are the source of the conflict? Why serve in the Territories when their main concern is protecting their families who mostly live within the 1967 Green Line?

Furthermore, the IDF has been taking part in very large and perilous counter-terror and counter-guerrilla operations. Such operations have bogged down many units within the Territories. The ongoing presence of the IDF within the Territories, especially when carrying out spot checks, patrols and enforcing checkpoints, has inevitably led to the IDF's close encounters with many Palestinian civilians. This close contact has been the main demoralising factor of the current conflict, for although the IDF has undergone greater low-intensity warfare training, it has still not been thoroughly equipped or trained to deal with the civilian components of the conflict.

Instances of IDF–civilian clashes have been a strong inducement in compelling soldiers to become conscientious objectors, because of the guilt they have suffered after carrying out acts on civilians that are contrary to their moral conscience. Amit Mashiah recounts an instance that strongly affected his decision to become a *refusenik*:

> 'There was an old lady who ran to me and spat in my face. It's a dangerous situation. You've got your soldiers behind you seeing you've been spat in the face and what do you do?' Mashiah asks. He tells ... that he 'shoved her real hard', and says it was worse for him to shove her than it was to have been spat upon. 'It was a terrible thing to do', he says.[140]

Furthermore, as in the case of the first *Intifada*, the exact number of conscientious objectors during the *Al-Aqsa Intifada* has been hard to estimate due to the secretive nature of the IDF. Nonetheless, in early 2003, different conscientious objection groups in Israel estimated that 'more than 2,000 people [had] declared their conscientious objection since September 2000. More than 1,100 cases [had been] well documented.'[141]

Combat motivation during the *Al-Aqsa Intifada*

And yet, the phenomenon of conscientious objection from left-wing opponents of the occupation was smaller than that of people willing to fight and serve within the IDF during the current *Intifada*. This motivation to serve was instigated by various factors. First, the view and perception that Israel is under existential threat and that it is using its armed forces for defensive purposes against Palestinian terror and guerrilla warfare were shared generally by large segments of the Israeli population. Some, such as *Shin Bet* Chief Avi Dichter, came to equate the Palestinian terror campaign with the Holocaust.[142] According to Col. (Res.) Dr Efraim Kam,

> There is a feeling here in Israel that we are fighting for our home.... It does not mean that most Israelis support long-term occupation. But

whatever the view on the future of the Territories is, in one thing we are almost united: that we are fighting against terrorism.[143]

A large portion of the population was in favour of using military force against the PA and terror/guerrilla groups. According to Col. Gal Hirsh, Arafat had actually put Israel 'back into the Zionist incubator' and strengthened Israel's resolve to protect itself, rather than collapse under terror and guerrilla attacks, as *Hizbullah* leader, Sheikh Hassan Nasrallah, had predicted erroneously after Israel's retreat from South Lebanon in May 2000. Col. Hirsh also pointed out that, 'Lebanon is not Judea, Samaria and the rest of Israel'.[144] Israel was perceived to be protecting its homeland once again, as a result motivation remained high. Many troops shared the view held by Capt. Dan Goldfus that,

> We are defending our country, we are defending our life here in Israel and we do not take pleasure in going in the middle of the night, entering a house where there are women and children in order to arrest a terrorist. I do not take pleasure in it, but I do what I have to do to carry out the mission of fighting terrorism.[145]

Ben-Gurion's traditional security assumption, that the IDF uses its forces solely for defensive purposes against existential threats, was restored *fully* after the assumption had gone into disrepute during the first *Intifada*. The perception that Israel was facing an existential threat and that the IDF was being used as a defence against this threat, according to Eyal Ben-Ari, fitted well with 'their [i.e. IDF soldiers'] professional self-image as being soldiers rather than policemen'.[146] One former general put the threat of terrorism into perspective when comparing it to the former conventional wars the IDF, and Israel, had faced:

> I think that the youngsters, those officers, they presented it [i.e. terror] the way you present it [i.e. as existential], because they are not acquainted personally with the large scale wars that we were involved in my generation. They do not understand the full meaning of it and *probably this is something that they are educated upon by their leaders in order to motivate them, but it is not an existential threat* [emphasis mine].[147]

Second, the IDF was able to reduce the political implications of the left-wing *refusenik* movement by downplaying the phenomenon. This was done, as in the first *Intifada*, by unofficially allowing for grey refusal (at the lower command echelons) and, more crucially, by avoiding the court martial of staunch objectors. Such trials would have led to greater exposure of the *refusenik* movement's causes in the media, political and public domains, whereas the repetitive incarceration of objectors during each reserve call-up, for 28 days (or more), was deemed punitive enough by the IDF command echelons.

In any case, the general Israeli population has always frowned upon refusal to serve in the IDF for moral and even political reasons. A public opinion survey conducted by Asher Arian in 2003 confirmed this view. The survey found that 75 per cent of the respondents believed that a soldier could not legitimately refuse to serve in the Territories. In light of the disengagement, 73 per cent of the respondents also said that soldiers should not disobey orders to evacuate settlers.[148]

The lack of moral support towards conscientious objectors is down to the fact that most believe that, given the democratic nature of the Israeli state, opposition to security policies decided upon by the Israeli incumbent government should be voiced through democratic and legal means, especially by those who serve in the IDF (professional, conscript or reservist). Rather than through conscientious objection, most Israeli citizens reckon that IDF personnel should, as soldier-citizens, voice their concerns through the electoral process.

Furthermore, with terror on the rise in 2001 and 2002, the average Israeli was more interested in security provision than in the upholding of universal ethical values. During this initial period, combat motivation remained high even within the reserves, despite the increasing inequality in the reserve duty burden.

At the same time, there was a noteworthy increase in the motivation of new recruits to serve in such units. According to the IDF, 'motivation to serve in combat units [rose] by seven per cent since 2001' and at the end of 2002 it was at '84 per cent'. 'Of the 14,000 new recruits drafted for service in the IDF over [the month of April], 6,500 of those [would] serve in combat units.... 72 per cent [of which would] serve in land-based units.' The IDF attributes the growth in induction motivation to serve in combat units to 'the fact that the IDF is engaged in fighting against Palestinian terror [that] raises the motivation of the new recruits to be part of the units that are determining the outcome of the war'.[149] According to an IDF survey carried out at the Tel Hashomer Induction Centre on the November 2004 conscript intake, 91.3 per cent of recruits for field units asked to serve in combat units.[150] However, rates of induction motivation have always tended to be high in the IDF, particularly regarding combat units, because of the prestige and mystique associated with military service in combat units. Such statistics, thus, do not confirm any major shift in induction motivation within combat units.[151]

Grey refusal

These induction statistics may be misleading if taken on their own, because they do not take into account recruits that have already been able to opt out from serving in the IDF by taking advantage of the various psychological and physical exemptions available to them. Many grey refusals have been possible because of the recruits' ease in obtaining profile '21' and profile '24' exemptions.

A '21' profile normally means health-related problems disqualify a recruit from military service, whereas a '24' profile can also mean that the recruit is not educated or comes from an underprivileged background. Moreover, a '24' profile is often used by a psychologist to discharge a recruit because of his 'unsuitability'. Such exemptions are normally granted by military doctors and psychologists during the initial induction process and do not reach the military courts. Such exemptions, furthermore, help avoid potential *refuseniks* from publicly and, hence, controversially declaring their refusal to serve in the IDF. A report published by Derby University in July 2004 indicates that '30 per cent of all inductees refer to the mental officer at the induction centre. 16 per cent are discharged during their first year of service, 70 per cent of which are due to emotional problems.' The IDF claims, however, that the total figure of inductees that refer to army mental health officers is *only* 25 per cent.[152]

Hence, since the Oslo Treaty, there has been a gradual upsurge in the rate of those receiving psychological exemptions. Indeed, according to the 2002 State Comptroller's Report:

> In 1998, 3.62 per cent of those exposed to the draft were exempted from service on psychological grounds. In 2000, the rate increased to 3.95 per cent; by September 2001 when such data was next gathered, the rate had already swelled to 4.05 per cent.[153]

The relatively small number of outspoken *refuseniks*, during the second *Intifada*, was described by Ishai Menuvhin, spokesman for *Yesh Gvul* and a major in the reserve IDF, as only the 'tip of the iceberg'.[154] The relative ease with which new recruits have gained '21' and '24' profile exemptions, the constant reduction of conscripts called up for military service, the growing desertion rates on the part of reservists and the general downsizing and budget-cutting of the professional force, supports this statement, which points to a possible decline in the principle of the 'people's army' within Israeli society. These trends as well as the costs incurred during the *Al-Aqsa Intifada*, will be analysed in the next chapter.

8 Strategic impasse

The costs of the conflict

The IDF incurred significant expenses stemming from the uprising, which have had several negative consequences on both the IDF's financial autonomy and operational capabilities. Maj. Gen. (Ret.) Uzi Dayan cautioned as far back as September 2002 that the struggling Israeli economy would be incapable of backing the military campaign against the Palestinians for much longer. He estimated that conflict was costing Israel about $3 billion annually.[1]

Since the start of the *Al-Aqsa Intifada*, the economy declined noticeably. Whereas in the first three-quarters of 2000 the Israeli economy flourished – it grew by an impressive 7.4 per cent – in 2001 Israel registered negative growth of 3.2 per cent (see Figure 8.1). It was the first time since the depression of 1953 that Israel experienced negative growth. The unemployment rate, which stood at 8.8 per cent on average in 2000, reached almost 11 per cent in 2003 (see Figure 8.2).[2] Although such economic indices can be accounted for in part by the global economic slowdown at the end of 2000, Palestinian terrorism did have a considerable negative effect on key Israeli economic sectors such as agriculture, tourism, construction and exports to the PA areas.

Due to the economic crisis, the IDF reported 'a 60 per cent increase in the number of applications for army careers in 2002',[3] which reinforces the argument put forward by Stuart Cohen and Dan Horowitz, that over the last two decades, for many Israelis an army career has become more of a profession than a vocation and has possibly become the second best option to take if there are no better offers from the highly developed Israeli market economy. The alleged lack of a vocational ethos has also led some to argue that the defence establishment's leaders have, over the last decade, 'attained their positions as bureaucrats, as technocrats – not as creative commanders'.[4]

Despite the 5 billion Shekels (US$1.1 billion) budget supplement allocation to the IDF in order to face the insurgency, calls for greater scrutiny by the Finance Ministry over defence spending were being made by the political

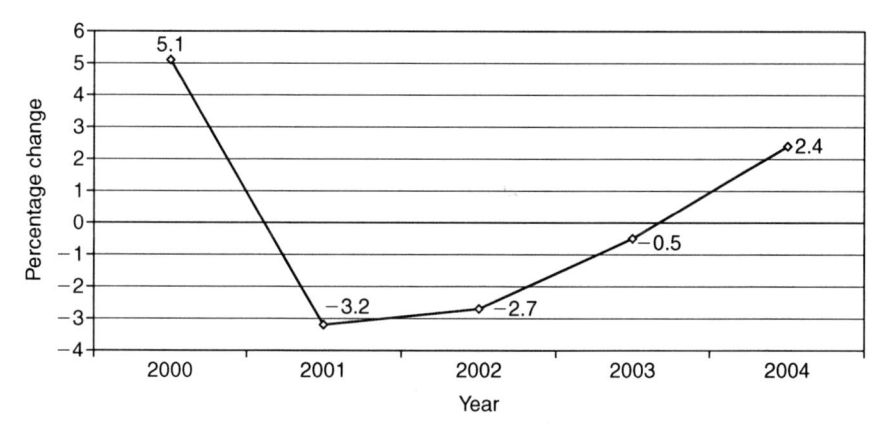

Figure 8.1 Israeli GDP per capita growth, 2000–04 (source: 'Economic Trends in Israel', August 2004, Israel Ministry of Finance, www.mof.gov.il/research_e/trends2004e.pdf (accessed 15 April 2005)).

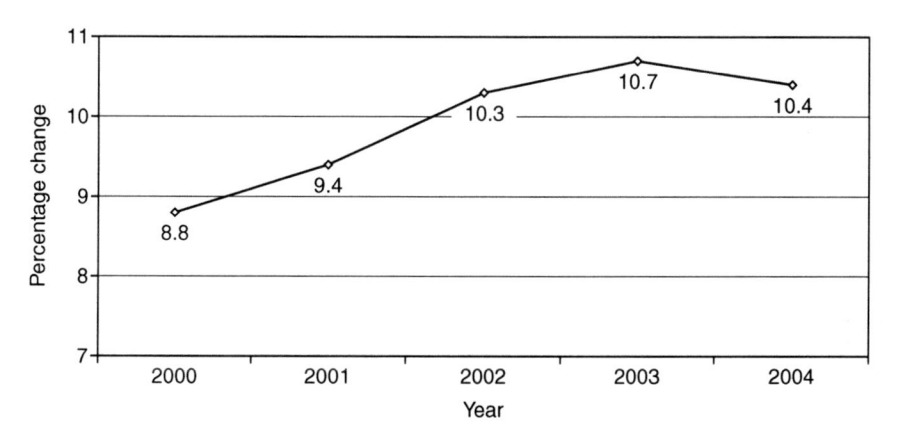

Figure 8.2 Israeli unemployment rate, 2000–04 (source: 'Economic Trends in Israel', August 2004, Israel Ministry of Finance, www.mof.gov.il/research_e/trends2004e.pdf (accessed 15 April 2005)).

establishment. This was quite a new development in terms of civil–military relations relating to defence budgetary politics. Nonetheless, following the extensive budget cuts of the 1990s, because of the peace process, the supplement was perceived as insufficient, to the point that former Defence Minister Ben-Eliezer argued, possibly on a rhetorical note, that 'we cannot cut back on defence unless we want to face a catastrophe'.[5] Such fears were repeated by his successor, Defence Minister Shaul Mofaz, who deemed the government's proposal for NIS (New Israeli Shekel) 4.1 billion (around US$939.9 million) in defence cuts for 2004, as 'too drastic and intense'.[6]

Weapons and training programmes curtailment

The reductions in defence funding together with the increased costs and number of personnel involved in fighting terrorism, guerrilla attacks and general rioting led to the freezing of various IDF weapons development programmes, to the curtailing of significant benefits given to the professional army and it considerably disrupted the IDF's training regimen.

The equipping of infantry soldiers with the new *Tavor* assault rifle and the development of the new generation *Merkava Siman 4* MBT was delayed on numerous occasions due to budgetary uncertainties, despite vociferous calls from the IDF Ground Forces Command to boost their production.[7] The IDF also made plans to cut down 'by about 25 per cent' the time it permitted career officers to study whilst serving in the army and in March 2003 it decided 'to cancel vacation programmes for combat soldiers', which play a crucial role in restoring soldiers' motivation after stressful or long deployments.[8] Moreover, the cutting of the defence budget by NIS3 billion for 2003, due to then Minister of Finance Benyamin Netanyahu's financial austerity programme, were described as 'a dramatic event' and even led to the closure of some IDF field units

The reduction of such career benefits has been part of a larger attempt by the IDF to cut costs, relating to the professional officer's second career prospects. Such cost-cutting efforts are, in effect, being implemented in the hope that the IDF is planning to augment the retirement age of career officers, because the investment to make them marketable after early retirement has become too prohibitive, notwithstanding the recent economic crisis.

Most of the conscript and professional army has been required, since the re-occupation of PA 'A' Areas, in mid-2002, to remain in the Territories almost continuously throughout 2003 and 2004. IDF senior officers had already warned the political echelon that 'military exercises [would] be reduced to a minimum.... The practical meaning of this is that the standing units of *Golani* or the Seventh Armored Regiment [would] have no more than two to three weeks training a year.'[9] Additionally, the 'time taken to qualify an infantry soldier [would] be reduced from 14 to 10 months and the course of training for elite units ha[d] been halved to one year'.[10] Due to the budget cuts, according to Maj. Gen. Yiftah Ron-Tal, all training exercises for reservists were scheduled to be cancelled in 2004.[11]

These drastic training cuts, together with the constant use of ground forces units on routine security missions, had quite significant consequences on soldiers' combat readiness. Serg. Maj. (Res.) Jonathan Javor stated that 'once I started doing tours and doing less training, I realized that my skills deteriorated. I realized that I was not fit and accurate [i.e. target]. On my last training exercise I just saw how my skills had completely gone.'[12]

The lack of sufficient and relevant LIC training affected the performance of IDF troops in actual ground operations to the point that a number did not really develop satisfactory operational capabilities. Whatever training regimen the IDF has in place to cope with intercommunal warfare, many soldiers until very recently were not trained to cope with the type of contact they had with the hostile civilian Palestinian population.

Quite a few suffered demoralisation as a consequence and were compelled to become conscientious objectors as a result of their inability to overcome the ethical dilemmas of enforcing curfews, roadblocks and other collective and punitive measures. These were not the usual praxes of an army whose moral standing is based on the purity of arms concept. Armoured Corps Staff Sergeant and conscientious objector Tal Belo stated that 'they [the IDF] taught us to fire our rifles, to set up ambushes, jump from an airplane, carry our gear, run, fall, run again. They forgot to teach us to talk, cry, and forgive ourselves.'[13]

The reduction in essential training programmes is not a new phenomenon. The Israeli State Comptroller had already warned, in the late 1990s, that this phenomenon had been increasing since the late 1980s, that is, since the start of the first *Intifada*:

> Until 1988, all combat units underwent training exercises every year. Beginning in 1989, the frequency of training exercises was reduced from annual to bi- and tri-annual. In 1998, the proportion of reserve combat units participating in training exercises fell to 20 per cent.[14]

There were already a few, poignant, cases in which certain units suffered casualties on the field because of their lack of operational preparedness. An attack on 19 February 2002 at the Ein-Ariq checkpoint by two Palestinians led to the deaths of an officer and five soldiers, the injuring of the seventh unit member, whilst the eighth, a sniper, hid and made no attempt to help out his comrades. The investigation showed that the soldier who survived the initial attack did not fight back, the wounded soldier, who pretended to be dead, did not call for assistance once the attackers had left and that the squad was lacking in preparation for its mission.[15]

Even more shockingly, poor preparation, hasty tactical planning and inadequate equipment were noteworthy factors in the loss of 13 reserve soldiers in the battle of Jenin, in April 2002, during Operation 'Defensive Shield'. According to an IDF inquiry, there were grave blunders in the planning, command and control of this battle. The IDF inquiry discovered that the commanding officers neglected to carry out appropriate battle planning and found that the two commanders in charge of the operation's management in Jenin, 'Division Commander, Brig. Gen. Eyal Shlein, and the Brigade Commander, Col. (Res.) Didi Yedidya, did not enter the camp area during the nine days of fighting that preceded the fatal ambush'. In addition, several senior officers involved in the battle contended that 'it was a mistake to send reservists on such a complicated mission', because of the reservist Brigade 5's lack of experience in house-to-house combat. Finally, the bereaved families' own inquiry discovered that the equipment

146 *Strategic impasse*

was also unsuitable – 'the soldiers had ordinary flak jackets instead of ceramic ones and were using long-barrelled M-16 rifles that were awkward for manoeuvring through the narrow alleys of the refugee camp'.[16]

When interviewed, a Brigade 5 company commander who had spearheaded one of the units entering the Jenin refugee camp during Operation 'Defensive Shield' corroborated such allegations by affirming that 'this was not like what we were trained for. It was something else, because on every corner, on every house there were bombs, booby traps, people with bombs on them [i.e. suicide bombers], mines.'[17] Other complaints were voiced by units of the elite Battalion 50 of the *Nahal* Brigade when soldiers, who were sent in October 2004 into Gaza for a major two-week operation aimed at rooting out *Qassam* launching sites and dubbed 'Days of Penitence', fought in major urban skirmishes without ceramic flak jackets.[18]

Despite the fact that the protection of one's soldiers should be an elementary principle for any armed forces, particularly in an urban environment teeming with booby traps and enemy snipers, and that it constitutes a key factor in maintaining combat motivation, the IDF struggled to fully protect its soldiers due to ongoing budget cuts (these are addressed in detail below). Although the IDF's Army Headquarters budget for combat equipment for the Territories was scheduled to increase in 2005 by 400 per cent (3,000 extra units), Colonel Nir Solomon, Head of the Strategic Planning Branch of the Strategic and Organisation Department of the Army Headquarters, justified the shortage of such an essential piece of equipment by stating that 'we would have wanted that every IDF soldier should have a bullet proof vest, but it is not realistic'.[19]

One IDF reservist philosophically justified such lack of essential equipment, as just how things worked in the IDF: 'Other than the air force, this is an army that is held together by masking tape and rope and there is always a lack of equipment.'[20] A more appropriate explanation, however, would be the IDF's ongoing preoccupation with conventional and non-conventional warfare, and its bias towards the acquisition of state-of-the-art and highly sophisticated weapons platforms, which have put a serious dent into the defence budget. The Israeli Air Force alone has ordered, over the past three years: 102 F-16Is ($4.5 billion), 24 Blackhawk helicopters ($400 million), nine Longbow attack helicopters ($500 million), three Gulfstream electronic intelligence aircraft ($350 million), and one fourth-generation Amos satellite ($200 million). Some have questioned the need for such equipment given the IDF's budgetary cuts and current involvement in LIC warfare within the Territories.[21]

The growing burden on IDF reservists

Due to budget cuts the defence establishment had to rely even more on reservists, however unprepared, in order to permit conscripts and professionals to carry out the IDF's minimum required training programme. Emergency

'Tsav-Shmone' (Order Eight) orders from the beginning of the Palestinian insurgency required many draft reservists to serve 43 days a year, as opposed to the 30 originally stipulated. Such a measure did not have the desired effect because of the growing desertion rates on the part of reservists. Figures showed that there had been 'an increase of 67.2 per cent' in 2002, compared to figures in the previous year (from 1,564 to 2,616).[22] Until Operation 'Defensive Shield' in April 2002, according to *Ma'ariv*, 'of the total pool of some 250,000 potential reservists, just 13,000 serve[d] the full reserve term of 26 days a year'.[23] Reservists for the most part evaded military service, due to the failing economic conditions of their families brought about by the general decline of the Israeli economy, and the increased reserve duty burden, which impinged on their civilian lives.

The increased reserve service burden, since the mid-1990s, has also led to an increase in emigration rates from Israel. However, emigration, due to the increased reserve service burden, did not grow very significantly during the *Al-Aqsa Intifada* due to the greater threat perceived by Israelis. This perception made it easier for combat reservists to continue serving despite the increasing and unequal reserve burden that they were personally shouldering. An earlier study by Yinon Cohen, on the causes of emigration from Israel, corroborates the fact that whilst a heavy reserve duty burden increases emigration – irrespective of internal socio-economic conditions – 'salience of the conflict attenuates emigration rates, but only during the period of relative consensus'.[24]

Calls for a minimum wage, even in the case of conscripts, became ever more frequent, though at the time of writing they fell on deaf ears. This was the case even though there were instances in the *Golani* Brigade, the 890th Paratroop Battalion and other infantry battalions where soldiers, amongst other things, 'need[ed] assistance in purchasing warm clothing and foodstuffs' and in spite of the fact that full-time Ultra-Orthodox *Torah* scholars received more from the state than active-duty conscripts.[25]

In addition, only '54 per cent of all Israeli men and women' were drafted in the IDF and when it came 'to the reservists ... only one-third of all men eligible for reserve duty actually served'.[26] This put a greater security burden on an increasingly smaller segment of Israeli society, which although more motivated, became increasingly resentful of those exempted from military service. Despite the increased burden on reservists – leading to troop demoralisation and extensive political debate over the years – not much was done to obviate the problem.[27]

A law, stopping employers from sacking somebody for performing reserve duties, was not strictly enforced, leaving reservists feeling that they were left on their own to both defend Israel and to pay personally for the price of this protracted conflict. According to the IDF spokesperson, 'there was a 35 per cent increase in the number of reservists who lost their jobs whilst on duty in 2002 as compared to the year before'.[28] It is easy to sympathise with *Baltam*[29] Chairman Ro'i Ron's statement that:

148 *Strategic impasse*

> It's incredible that a small group of reservists will continue risking their lives, getting wounded, suffering at home, at work, and at school, while the government does nothing to compensate them or make sure they aren't harmed. Instead, all they do is extend reserve days and grind down the reservist soldiers.[30]

Such resentment and the fact that, 'according to IDF projections, the number of those eligible for reserve duty who dodge service will increase to 50 per cent by 2008' led certain commentators to declare that 'the state is in an advanced stage of deterioration … due to the unravelling of social cohesion and inequality in the burdens imposed on the citizen'.[31] Such resentment has been compounded by the fact that many Ultra-Orthodox Jews (*haredim*) do not serve at all in the IDF and actually receive large benefits from the state in order to carry out their Biblical studies on a full-time basis. The exemption from military service of Ultra-Orthodox Jews was instituted by Ben-Gurion when the IDF was established in 1948. However, at the time, a few hundred *haredim* were exempted. Today over 41,000 are classified as '*toratam omanutam*', full-time *Torah* students on state benefit, which reservist activists claim should be spent on improving reserve duty conditions.[32]

Under pressure from reserve duty organisations and from sympathetic politicians, Sharon decided to establish a chief reserve officer position within the IDF in order to improve reservists' service conditions, as well as raise the profile and importance of reserve duty within Israeli society. A substantial part of Israeli society – which was caught up in the economic boom rather than in its usual obsession with security issues given the Oslo Peace Process – had, in fact, since *c*. the early 1990s, begun to view people going for reserve duty as '*freierim*' (suckers). These 'suckers' were deemed either too stupid to find a way of getting out of reserve duty or naïve enough to believe that reserve service was still a national-Zionist duty. Col. (Res.) Itay Landsberg, one of the founders of the Battalion Officers' Reserve Forum, stated that

> The only social circle that supports the soldiers that go to the army reserves is the first circle, which is the family – wife and kids. That is all. The other circles [such as that of] friends, work colleagues, university, society around him: they do not support him. You are a *freier*, a sucker. You are doing something that fucks up your life and if you go and do it again and again, you are a sucker. That is the image that most of the soldiers take with themselves when they come back from the [reserve] army.[33]

Thus, reserve battalion commanders, who are the highest-ranking reserve officers in combat units during times of peace, often found themselves organising reserve duty missions with considerable personnel shortages, working up to 180 days per year for the IDF on a voluntary basis. Reserve battalion commanders have considerable duties: 'they settle personnel-related issues, determine battalion norms, the battalion's organizational culture and the manner in which it functions'.[34] These duties are not compensated and often come at the expense of the reserve battalion officer. Reserve battalion officers were also burdened by the needs, and special circumstances, of their subordinates, which were often at a disadvantage vis-à-vis those not serving in the reserves. Calls for extra reserve service compensation, national insurance benefits, safeguards against penalisation at work (dismissal) and at university (repetition of year due to missing exams) became gradually more vociferous.

Reservist burnout

Reservists, according to Martin Van Creveld, were 'originally meant to be deployed only in emergencies.... But now, where the situation is neither full-out war nor peace, we run the risk of overusing them' and eventually subjecting them to fatigue and possibly burnout.[35] One symptom of this was a sharp growth in friendly fire and operational mishaps within IDF units. The IDF ascribes such a rise in the protracted exposure to the strains of combat that soldiers were suffering whilst fighting in the Territories:

> The IDF weekly journal, *BaMahane* said ... [that] there have been more than 100 accidents involving misfirings in the IDF this year [i.e. 2003], injuring seven soldiers. Last year, 37 soldiers were injured in similar incidents. Officers quoted in the article said, 'the fact that no soldier has died this year in a weapons-related accident is just a matter of luck'.[36]

Another problem arising from combat stress and burnout is the desensitisation of the soldier. One battalion commander has stated that 'this can lead to a weakening of one's moral sensitivities: you often stop seeing a human as a human but only as a potential terrorist'.[37] When commenting on the overall effect that military service had on IDF soldiers, Serg. Maj. (Res.) Yehuda Shaul, founder of *Shovrim Shtika*,[38] claimed that

> A situation in which 18 year-olds hold a gun and rule other people's lives is corrupting. It is a situation that just screws up your mind, your feelings, your ethics, and there is no way to pass through it without getting numb.... You just become apathetic to everything. You act brutal not because you see it as brutal. That is the only way to survive: you become an animal and you become addicted to the feeling of ruling over people and you enjoy it.... And that is the second you just start to play games [with Palestinian peoples' lives] at checkpoints for example.[39]

150 *Strategic impasse*

The Israeli human rights organisation *B'Tselem*, amongst others, has documented numerous cases of physical abuse carried out by IDF troops in the Territories. In the past the military appellate court decried such cases of abuse by IDF soldiers warning that 'bullying and other criminal acts sometimes cause vengeance, and vengeance can lead to further violence – a tragic cycle'.[40] After several duties in the Territories, Serg. Maj. (Res.) Amit Almog described his policing duties there in the following manner:

> It's really shitty work, because you see the suffering of the people and you can do nothing about it. You just learn how to hate them, you get the hate inside because that is the way they train you, to hate them. That is what everybody talks about and you treat them like animals. You really lose it; you lose your humanity a little bit over there. I don't think anybody likes it.[41]

The extensive use of reservists also strained many relations between ground troops and their commanding officers. Disturbingly, between 2001 and 2002, 'complaints concerning the relationship between soldiers and commanders jumped by 20 per cent'. Given the extensive use of reserve soldiers during 2002, the fact that 'the ratio of complaints coming from this contingent only grew by 10 per cent [i.e. from 2,305 to 2,535]' was an encouraging feature.[42]

Transformation?

As seen over the previous three chapters, during the last 20 years Israel has strategically and tactically responded to local Palestinian insurgency, which has evolved, from civil disobedience to outright terrorism and guerrilla warfare, particularly following the now-defunct Oslo Peace Process. Over the last 20 years, the Israel Defence Forces (IDF) has tried to transform its conventional-based and trained army, and to adopt low-intensity urban warfare strategies and tactics against violent rioters, guerrilla fighters and terrorists. This was particularly the case during the *Al-Aqsa Intifada*, which began in September 2000. Part of this effort to transform its order of battle and doctrine has been carried out through the IDF's current five-year strategic review and work-plan, dubbed '*Kela 2008*' ('Shot 2008'). This plan has been hailed as 'revolutionary', particularly in regards to the supposed perceptual changes the IDF General Staff has undergone in order to produce it. The core of the revolution is articulated in the 'decision to put the emphasis on the element of firepower (from precision weaponry rather than massed firepower) and less on manoeuvrability on the ground'.[43]

As a result, the IDF's security doctrine, which had focused on bringing the war to the enemy's territory, by capturing it with the use of large conventional forces through manoeuvre warfare, will try to emphasise,

Strategic impasse 151

instead, the use of precision weaponry, together with the significant exploitation of the IDF's intelligence capabilities, in order to reduce the sensor-to-shooter cycle. The increased use of precision firepower and intelligence, in turn, will lead to the reduction of forces, particularly within the Armoured Corps and the IAF. Significant organisational changes, discussed below, will also bring the IDF closer to the goal of becoming a truly multiforce and interoperable armed force.

The decision to adopt such changes has been influenced by the ideas on the changing nature of warfare, dubbed as the 'Revolution of Military Affairs' (RMA) and how such warfare should be conducted according to network-centric warfare principles. By carrying out effects-based operations (EBOs), mostly through stand-off precision firepower, against the enemy's critical centres of gravity, the armed forces using such operational methods is hopefully able to change the behaviour of the opposing armed forces and, hence, the behaviour of the target state without actually having to destroy/defeat it completely.[44]

However, I argue that rather than being revolutionary, changes to the IDF security doctrine have been reactive, in the sense that most of the changes the IDF is currently deciding to implement have been forced upon it, mainly due to large budgetary cuts. The changes, furthermore, perpetuate the IDF's emphasis on conventional warfare without really addressing the growing issues of low-intensity warfare from a doctrinal and strategic perspective. Such budget cutbacks have been especially dramatic since the beginning of the *Al-Aqsa Intifada* in spite of the rising costs that such a conflict has exacted on the overall defence budget.[45] Moreover, I contend that such changes could have already taken place earlier, but have not, given the conservative nature of the IDF strategic doctrine. Notwithstanding such criticisms, I will illustrate the strategic, operational and, particularly, tactical changes that the IDF – principally its ground forces – has undergone during the two *Intifadas* and is planning to undertake over the coming years.

Personnel

Budget cuts implemented by the Ministry of Finance over the last three years have been quite dramatic given the dire economic situation Israel has found itself in since the outbreak of the *Al-Aqsa Intifada*.[46] The IDF has had to first of all address personnel issues given the fact that in 2003, for example, '44 per cent of Israel's defence budget was allocated for human resources',[47] whereas in 1984, 'personnel costs absorbed 19.2 per cent of the defence budget'.[48] Hence, the '*Kela 2008*' programme's main goal has been 'to lower personnel costs to around 30 per cent' of the total budget.[49]

This would be done by reducing the number of career soldiers, initially by 6,000, through early retirement programmes in 2005. Such personnel reductions would also include a 10 per cent cut in senior military ranks: '14 of the 94 Brig. Gen.s [would] leave the army, as will 51 of the 470 colonels and 250 of the 2,500 lieutenant colonels'.[50] Further cuts have periodically been discussed in the *Knesset* Foreign Affairs and Defence Committee.

Moreover, in 2003 the General Staff decided to raise the retirement age by establishing a three-tier selection process for promotions, making it harder for an officer or non-commissioned officer to reach retirement, due to more stringent performance reviews at every 'selection gate'. If he or she does make it through the three selection gates, officers and NCOs will retire on average ten years later than officers and NCOs under the previous system set up by the late IDF COS Moshe Dayan, who in the 1950s was keen to create a young and dashing army through early retirement schemes.

Such measures will reduce the number of career officers who, after early retirement, receive large pension benefits whilst pursuing a second career in the civilian or political job markets. Such reductions have been deemed necessary, given that over the years the number of retired personnel has burgeoned considerably and has placed a large onus on the IDF defence budget.

Reserve corps reforms

Even more radical changes will affect the reserve system, which has traditionally been the backbone of the IDF and which provides the IDF with around two-thirds of its total manpower requirements. Created initially in order to fight against full-scale attacks from hostile Arab conventional armies through emergency mobilisation, IDF reservist units have increasingly carried out over the last 20 years, 'current security' operations, such as border patrols, checkpoint duties, curfew enforcements and counter-guerrilla operations. Such operations have often occurred at the expense of training for major warfare contingencies. The use of reservists was particularly prevalent during the first two years of the *Al-Aqsa Intifada*. However, according to the IDF Ombudsman Brig. Gen. Avner Barzani's annual report, even in the protection of settlements within the Territories during 2004, reservists received insufficient training for such duties, thus exposing them to danger.[51]

Their use has proved to be very expensive. Reservists are paid roughly according to their civilian salaries, which on average can be between 10 to 100 times more than that of regular conscripts.[52] Thus, the IDF has decided to limit reserve duty to a maximum of 14 days a year (70 days per three-year cycle for officers) – which will be devoted solely to training. It is not clear whether or not such limited call-ups, even if dedicated solely to training, will enable the IDF to maintain its combat readiness. This is because the technical and interpersonal skills needed by the twenty-first century soldier in order to carry out sub-conventional military operations within urban or other smaller civilian scenarios are much greater. Unless reservists (and conscripts) are thoroughly trained, not only will they lack the necessary military skills to tackle such scenarios, but also the necessary cohesion, which is so vital when coming to grips with the moral dilemmas of operating in civilian settings. The continuous state of alert and fatigue, as well as the continuous friction between soldier and the Palestinian population, could affect the soldier negatively through attrition and burnout and possibly lead to his moral deterioration.

The IDF has decided also 'to release 60,000 reserve soldiers aged 40 and over' and possibly to 'further lower the maximum service age to 36'.[53] Lowering the age of reserve duty has been especially crucial due to the fact that older soldiers tend to get paid more than younger ones. Their early dismissal, thus, has provided significant savings for the IDF.

Furthermore, as the increasing burden of reserve duty has fallen on dwindling numbers of reservists – particularly on combat reservists – over the last decade reservist advocacy groups such as *Baltam* and the Reserve Battalion Officers Forum have pushed the *Knesset*, MOD and the IDF General Staff for better reserve service conditions. Some limited steps have been taken to improve their service conditions – such as more equitable national insurance payments, the provision of better equipment during reserve duty, legislation of laws prohibiting the dismissal of employees due to reserve duty service, etc. An attempt to show appreciation towards and recognition of serving reservists also led to the establishment, in September 2004, of a 'Reservists' Day' celebration during the Jewish holiday of *Lag B'Omer* (The Counting of the Omer), which will be celebrated henceforth each year in May.[54]

In spite of the fact that reservists who do show up for duty feel that they are shouldering most of the reserve burden at the expense of their civilian lives, most of those who do report for reserve duty do so because they feel a duty to protect Israeli citizens and actually enjoy the camaraderie experienced during reserve duty.[55] They also do so because they do not want to let their comrades down and face their criticism the next time they report for reserve duty. After having skipped only one tour of reserve duty with his usual unit during Operation 'Defensive Shield', in April 2004, Staff Sergeant (Res.) Amos Harel explained how his unit comrades reacted:

> But once I got there this time, I got all kinds of looks from commanders, soldiers who were under my command and so on. They kept saying, 'Oh, we thought we would never see you here again' and so on and I was only absent for one tour which I did, of course, serve somewhere else.... People were a bit doubting for the first few minutes – 'where has he been?'[56]

However, the IDF General Staff has basically decided to deal with the reservist burden and budgetary shortfalls by shelving the reservist system altogether. The IDF, henceforth, will only call up reservists either in the case of a national emergency or for sporadic training opportunities. Col. (Res.) Itay Landsberg, a reserve battalion commander argued in an

154 *Strategic impasse*

interview that such little training would be insufficient for forces that would fight in a future war:

> Being prepared for war, you need to train the reserve units and you need to make them ready on the human side, on the equipment side, on the training side to fight wars. War is something different from what we are doing now in the Territories. To train an army reserve unit for war is something you have to work on for a few years, because if it has like ten days of training once a year or once every two years and it is doing missions instead, it will not be ready for war.[57]

Consequently, the traditional IDF notion of being a 'people's army' is being eroded slowly as greater numbers of reservists are being discharged from reserve duty obligations for financial reasons. Reservists are also being discharged, or not being called up, by the IDF because it recognises that most reservists are just not willing to make the sacrifice anymore. One IDF study conducted in the late 1990s showed that, if given a choice, most reservists would never report for duty and that out of 11 potential reservists, only 2 actually reported for duty. This finding stood in sharp contrast to a similar study, carried out in 1974, which showed that only 20 per cent of those surveyed were unwilling to do reserve duty.[58]

Eyal Ben-Ari, described the decision to dramatically curtail reserve duty in the future, not as revolutionary, but 'more a recognition of the situation as it now exists'. He added that

> It is no longer a 'people's army'.[59] Having said that, there is still a widespread commitment to the idea of a 'people's army' and any threat to that idea is not accepted lightly or, to put it more strongly, you have voices within the army and some outside the army resisting this kind of move.[60]

Training cuts

Furthermore, given the costs and problems associated with reserve duty, the bulk of 'current security' duties has been transferred over gradually, since mid-2003, to regular conscript units, albeit sometimes at the expense of their training schedules. Indeed, regular army conscripts, who used to spend their three-year conscription stint in 17-week rotations of training and operational deployment, have over the last few years been conducting operations almost continuously since the start of the second *Intifada*. According to then commander of the IDF Ground Forces Command (GFC), Maj. Gen. Yiftah Ron-Tal, 'instead of devoting half of their service for training, now [the IDF] can only allow ten weeks of training each year for the regular units'.[61]

In order to obviate such a lack of training, the IDF has established the concept of '"training through fighting" in which the junior commanders are required to use the time between operations for skills improvement'.[62] Such a concept will be operationalised mainly through the new practice of using mobile shooting training simulators as well as through the development of eight giant machines, which will simulate virtually every war zone with three-dimensional scenarios and dynamic targets.[63]

Although some GFC officers have stated that such simulators will considerably develop combat soldiers' abilities, according to the head of the training department at the GFC, Col. Ofer Segal, the main rationale behind their development has been to reduce the cost of live-fire training.[64] Indeed, such a cost-cutting measure has been implemented in spite of the fact that many other IDF officers believe that real live-fire exercises are far more effective in preparing a combat soldier for war.

Despite the increased load of 'current security' duties on conscript units, and the consequent reduction of their training regime, the IDF has begun devising a plan to shorten mandatory conscript service for men by four months – from 36 months to 32 months.[65] The reduction of conscript duty is the acknowledgement by the IDF of a safer strategic situation (at least from a conventional point of view), which Israel finds itself in since Operation 'Iraqi Freedom'. It is also the result of the growing realisation that greater incentives – such as payment and shorter terms of service – are needed in order to convince reluctant Israeli youth to serve in the IDF, particularly in non-combat units.

The IDF, as a result, intends to introduce financial incentives for any soldiers whose service will exceed the new conscript service timeframe.[66] Because of the reduction of reservists conducting 'current security' operations as well as dwindling conscript training opportunities, five mechanised infantry conscript battalions (*Kharuv*, *Lavi*, *Duhifat*, *Nachson* and *Shimshon*) were amalgamated, under the command of Col. David Menahem, into a division specifically designated for dealing with the violence stemming from terrorists, guerrilla fighters and violent demonstrators within the Territories of the West Bank and, until the Disengagement, the Gaza Strip.[67]

Structural changes

The extensive cutbacks of regular and reserve personnel have been possible due to the reduction of older weapons platforms particularly within the Armoured Corps and the IAF. Indeed, the upgrading of the *Merkava MK 2* and *3* and the introduction of the *Merkava MK 4* main battle tank (MBT), which because of its superior firepower and precision, as well as its communication capabilities, will allow the IDF to field smaller units based on the 'elementary cube' operational unit, 'or the smallest unit capable of autonomous manoeuvring and fire management'.[68] The enhanced capabilities of the new *Merkava MK 4* MBT will allow the Armoured Corps, within the next four years, to reduce the total number of its MBT units by 25 per cent, mostly through the disposal of the IDF's older *Magach 60* MBTs.

Moreover, such 'elementary cube' operational MBT units will be reinforced by infantry, engineer, artillery, intelligence and air force units (particularly helicopter assault units) and will enable the IDF to combine its combat elements to form flexible and mission-adaptive formations with joint-force capabilities. These moves, towards rapid and flexible joint-force formations, have been encouraged by the operational experiences of IDF units during the *Al-Aqsa Intifada*.

At the start of the *Al-Aqsa Intifada* the fast rotation and frequent breaking up of organic units was perceived by the military establishment to be problematic for these temporary units' cohesion. With time, these units managed, in fact, to adapt and develop 'ad hoc cohesion'. Recent studies on the IDF ground forces units, by Eyal Ben-Ari, led him to corroborate this:

> We found that many of these temporary units, these temporary formations worked together very well. So, if you go back to the classic literature [on unit cohesion and combat motivation] it shows that the will to fight is broken when units are not cohesive. We found actually that cohesion has to be maintained, but to a lesser extent [than what is argued in the classic literature]. Second, a crucial element of cohesion is trust. 'Swift trust' was developed on an *ad hoc* basis and sufficient enough to work together successfully.[69]

Hence, the IDF's decision to move forward with its plans to develop greater joint force capabilities was taken with '*Kela 2008*'. Indeed, the IDF's new operational doctrine of integrating multiple military branches will be possible due to the new 'Digital Ground Forces' (DGF) project, named '*Tsayad*' ('Hunter'). The DGF project will not only reduce the need for ground forces significantly, but will give better command, control and information, and decision-making, capabilities to all members of the IDF command structure through the use of fibre-optic technology by 2007.[70] Whereas, until now air, sea and land forces were under the control of the separate territorial commands (Northern, Central and Southern Commands), the DGF project supposedly will 'bring about the full integration of the air, sea and land forces under a unified control and command system'.[71]

There have also been numerous debates and plans over the possibility of transforming the IDF's traditional combat divisions – which are trained for all types of contingencies and are rotated periodically around all three territorial commands – into 'assignment-driven divisions, each to be attached to a specific region and trained in a limited array of scenarios'.[72] Such divisions would become more professional and proficient in the tasks they would be assigned to, given their greater specialisation. Such specialisation, which would reduce operational costs would, however, be achieved possibly at the cost of diminished operational flexibility.

Strategic impasse 157

Similarly, plans for merging the logistical activities of the three forces and *AMAN* (Military Intelligence) into one multi-force division have been underway. Such a division will decrease manpower of the standing forces by thousands, 'cut living expenses of the army by 20–30 per cent and will save at least $440 million to $665 million a year in the defence budget'.[73]

As for air combat support platforms, the IAF will continue to use and upgrade its extensive fleet of unmanned aerial vehicles (UAVs), its AH-1S Cobra and AH-64 Apache attack helicopter squadrons and will deploy in the coming years the Boeing AH-64D Apache Longbow. Such platforms have indeed proven their worth in counter-guerrilla and counter-terrorist operations within the Territories and, thus, will increase in numbers as the IDF's strategic doctrine and order of battle *gradually* adapts to low-intensity operations.

The IDF as a conservative organisation

Nonetheless, and despite the rhetoric of former IDF Chiefs of Staff, Dan Shomron, Ehud Barak and Amnon Lipkin-Shahak during the 1990s regarding the creation of a 'leaner and smarter' army, 'the partial changes so far [have been] typically "first-order" changes, aiming towards more (e.g. training) or less (e.g. length-of-service) of the same and presenting merely reactions to "nagging" demands'.[74] Changes in the IDF's training regimen and in its promotions and retirement policy for professional staff clearly have been reactions to budgetary constraints, whereas alterations to reserve duty patterns have been the result of reservist complaints as well as budgetary considerations.

The reduction of significant numbers of older weapons platforms has not been spurred by the IDF's goal of creating a 'leaner and smarter' army, but by the need to keep new weapons acquisitions programmes going, through the prior reduction of more obsolete platforms. Furthermore, such reductions are relatively small if the number of platforms, which is still present in the IDF's order of battle, is accounted for.

Thus, rather than being revolutionary, such changes have been relatively minor. In fact, the nucleus of the IDF ground forces has not changed very much in the past 30 years. The backbone of the army remains its armoured and mechanised forces, which have over 3,500 main battle tanks (MBTs), more than 10,000 armoured personnel carriers (APC) and over 5,000 artillery pieces.[75] Furthermore, calls for relying less on the operational mode of offensive manoeuvre warfare were already present in the mid-1990s and only now are being applied, albeit only partially.[76]

The considerable decrease of the conventional threat from Syria, whose order of battle has become obsolete since the Soviet Union's collapse in 1991, from Jordan due to the October 1994 peace accord with Israel, and, more importantly, from Iraq whose armed forces were obliterated by the US-led coalition in Operation 'Iraqi Freedom', have not been able to change some of the most essential assumptions underlying the IDF's new 'Kela 2008' strategic review.[77]

Former IDF Ground Forces Commander, Maj. Gen. Yiftah Ron-Tal, stated that the concept guiding the 'Kela 2008' strategic review was that 'the nature of our conflicts would still be the fight over territory'.[78] Such a statement obviously clashes with the 'revised' IDF strategic doctrine's guiding principle, which allegedly puts more emphasis on the element of firepower, rather than manoeuvrability on the ground. Indeed, given the growing saturation of the battlefield, which the IDF painfully realised in the 1973 *Yom Kippur* War, continuing to build an armed forces intent on offensive manoeuvre warfare does not seem after all that revolutionary, but almost orthodox. The IDF is still geared towards major conventional manoeuvre warfare.

Rather than revolutionary, changes to the IDF strategic doctrine have been – even prior to 'Kela 2008' – gradual. The IDF has always mixed 'persistent innovation … with a generally incremental and conservative approach that fits new techniques, inventions, or operational outlooks into a deeply rooted and relatively fixed military paradigm [i.e. strategic doctrine]'.[79] Real revolutionary transformation in the IDF strategic doctrine and in its force structure, in fact, cannot occur until the Israeli political–military leadership decides what strategic role the IDF is to play in the significantly altered strategic environment Israel actually finds itself in at the start of the twenty-first century.

Imposing increasingly greater budget cuts on the IDF will certainly force it to change – and sometimes improvise – its force structure and operational capabilities, but without strategic guidance from the political leadership, the IDF will certainly become a much 'leaner' and possibly less bureaucratic military organisation. However, whether or not the IDF will successfully become 'smarter' remains to be seen.

Furthermore, notwithstanding the extensive and relatively successful innovations in tactics, weaponry and training adopted in response to Palestinian attacks and the Israeli political echelon's decision to conduct low-intensity warfare *ad nauseam*, without seriously providing an alternative political resolution to the current Israeli–Palestinian conflict (until 2005), has shown that ultimately the IDF has not been able to achieve what it initially set out to do, which is to achieve victory over the Palestinian insurgency. Thus, the IDF has not been able to impose a battlefield decision on Palestinian insurgency efforts and has not been able to ultimately achieve strategic success during the last 20 years of the Israeli–Palestinian conflict, despite the belief by the Israeli political and military leadership that – at least during the initial stages of both *Intifadas* – such objectives could actually be achieved by the IDF.

In spite of the enormous difficulties in fighting Palestinian popular insurgency, terror and guerrilla warfare within the villages and cities of the West Bank and Gaza Strip, the IDF did manage to provide significant tactical and technological solutions to the Palestinian terrorist and insurgent threats, albeit often at the cost of collateral damage and cases of excessive force vis-à-vis the Palestinian civilian population. Such tactical success, however, did not yield strategic dividends due to the lack of political and strategic direction from the Israeli political echelons, as well as the political complexities surrounding LIC insurgency. The IDF was, however, able to achieve its traditional LIC goal, that of lowering the level of violence to the extent which Israeli politicians felt safe or strong enough to conduct diplomatic negotiations. Whether or not recent tactical successes will be used by the political echelons to arrive at a strategic solution to the Israeli–Palestinian conflict remains to be seen, especially in light of the Israeli perception that until late 2005, that is, until Yasser Arafat's death, there was no serious political negotiator on the Palestinian side.

Strategy

Strategy involves the employment of military forces to achieve a specific political goal. Since war is an instrument of politics, 'limited political aims result in the definition of limited war aims'.[80] However, as seen over the last two chapters, the IDF's application of conventional strategy and forces to low-intensity type conflicts has always been difficult. The 'intermingling with enemy forces, mixing with the civilian population, and extreme dispersion' have significantly challenged the IDF particularly within the urban arena of warfare.[81]

The IDF has struggled to deal with Palestinian insurgency since the end of the 1980s. Even though the IDF has been able to adapt its tactics, particularly since the late 1990s, to face Palestinian threats head-on within their towns, villages and refugee camps, it has had much greater difficulty providing a battlefield decision to the Israeli–Palestinian conflict. This failure was the result of the IDF's inability to adapt to and address strategically the Palestinians' increasing employment of low-intensity insurgency as a tool of national liberation, given the gross indecision and lack of direction provided by the Israeli political echelon, as well as the IDF's constant focus on short-term tactical solutions.

Moreover, such a goal was not obtainable: a strategic doctrine geared towards linear conventional threats, with clear parameters for what constitutes battlefield decision and victory, cannot be applied to low-intensity insurgencies, which need to be resolved not just by military, but also by political means. Almost four years into the *Al-Aqsa Intifada*, National Security Advisor, Maj. Gen. (Res.) Giora Eiland, still underlined, in fact, Israel's dilemma of winning in, and even establishing clear strategic goals relevant to the Israeli–Palestinian LIC:

> In these new kinds of conflicts ... how do you determine the strategic goal? What exactly do you want to achieve? During conventional wars it was quite simple to describe the goal, because everything was

defined in very clear, decisive terms and, consequently, easy to transform the strategic goal into military objectives. This was the case, because these military objectives were primarily very physical ones, like conquering a specific piece of land and destroying the enemy's capabilities. Now, what is the exact strategic goal and how do you transform this goal into clear objectives? To try to define the strategic goal in this kind of conflict is like trying to hold a jelly in your hand. The harder you squeeze it [i.e. the more you try to define it], the more it splits through your fingers.[82]

Israeli security strategy

As seen in Chapter 4, since the early 1950s, the IDF has customarily differentiated between two types of military operations: *bitachon shotef* ('current security') and *bitachon yisodi* ('fundamental security'). The former – which has been abbreviated usually to the term *batash* – includes responses to terrorist attacks, retaliatory raids and border skirmishes; the latter to big wars [i.e. conventional], real or potential.'[83] The Israeli strategic doctrine has traditionally focused on fundamental security aspects due to the greater nature of the threat stemming from a conventional war against Israel.

The basic assumptions underlying the Israeli strategic doctrine, which focused primarily on the Arab conventional threat, were: (1) That Israel was and will continue to live in a hostile environment, hence, the belief that it was confronted with wars of 'no choice' (*ein briera*); (2) That Israel was involved in a conflict in which it finds itself strategically inferior vis-à-vis its Arab enemies both in terms of manpower and resources; (3) That no matter how decisive results on the battlefield were, Israel would never be able to achieve complete strategic victory. Hence, Israel's general strategic goal has always been that of maintaining the status quo by deterring major attacks against it. The exception, in applying such a strategic goal, occurred unsuccessfully in the 1982 Lebanon War when force was used to root out the Palestinian Liberation Organisation's terror infrastructure in South Lebanon, and also to establish a friendly Lebanese government controlled by the Christian Maronite minority.

In the case of the outbreak of a conflict, returning to the status quo ante would be achieved through the attainment of a swift battlefield decision, which, as Avi Kober points out, is not synonymous with victory. In fact, 'battlefield decision can be defined in terms of negating the other side's combat capability, victory can be defined in terms of the correlation between what each adversary defines as its political and military war objectives ... and what it actually succeeds in achieving during that war'.[84] That is, once war is imminent, the defending armed forces will try to disrupt, as quickly as possible, the aggressor's military capability by attacking and disrupting the enemy's centre of gravity.

Indeed, the three pillars of Israeli strategic doctrine have been 'deterrence, early warning, and the winning of a decisive [battlefield] victory'.[85] These three pillars were called into question in light of the 1973 *Yom Kippur* War.[86] They have also proven quite difficult to operationalise when dealing with low-intensity type threats, which have increased over the last 20 years. Israel's deterrence policy, based on reprisals vis-à-vis sub-conventional threats and guerrilla or terrorist forces, has served 'as a means of redress, but has not, generally prevented recurrence of the provocation'.[87]

Despite the IDF's traditional focus on the conventional threat in terms of strategy, order of battle, manpower policy and training, the IDF has been, for the most part, involved in current security operations, particularly since the first *Intifada* (1987–93). Whereas at the beginning of the first *Intifada*, IDF and other security forces such as the *Shin Bet* were involved in anti-riot policing operations and arrests, towards the end of the first *Intifada* and particularly during the Oslo Peace Process (1993–2000), the IDF was used increasingly in counter-terror and counter-guerrilla operations.

Moreover, with the outbreak of the *Al-Aqsa Intifada* in September 2000, the IDF has been in constant operational use against terrorist and armed guerrilla fighters – many of which were trained, equipped and mobilised paradoxically under the auspices of the Oslo Peace Process in order 'to guarantee public order and internal security'.[88] Over the last 20 years, the IDF has also been increasingly involved in routine policing and anti-riot measures, some of which have had a preventative function, such as the widespread creation of checkpoints and the extensive use of military patrols, even though such measures have had a negative impact on troops. For example, according to Capt. (Res.) Shahar Amit, 'today standing in a checkpoint day in, day out, 12, 16, 20 hours a day makes you insane. It fucks you up in ways you cannot imagine.'[89]

The IDF has also resorted to measures that, although tactically effective, have had more of a punitive purpose and negative strategic results, such as the imposition of wide-ranging closures of the Territories and the enforcement of protracted curfews within Palestinian cities, towns and villages considered to be either hotbeds of Palestinian militancy or outright terror. The practice of demolishing the houses belonging to terrorists or to their closest relatives has also been considered, until very recently, successful by the IDF as a deterrent for other terrorist attacks, in spite of the censure expressed by human rights organisations, by the European Union and other states as well as by Israel's closest ally, the USA.

Nonetheless, many others have believed that such collective measures have not had much of a deterrent effect, but have actually incited greater instances of Palestinian violence. Indeed, in February 2005, a military committee set up by then COS Lt. Gen. Moshe Yaalon, and headed by Maj. Gen. (Ret.) Udi Shani, concluded that the punitive measure of demolishing the homes of families that included a terrorist was not effective and should be stopped. This conclusion was reiterated shortly thereafter at a *Knesset* Foreign Affairs and Defence Committee meeting by the Chief Military Prosecutor, Brig. Gen. Avi Mendelbiet who informed those present that the army was not going to resume the practice in the near future given its ineffectiveness.[90]

In spite of the pervasive use of IDF personnel and materiel, as well as the growing threat and lethality of Palestinian terror and guerrilla operations within Israel and the Territories, the IDF has not been able to critically address the predominant, and relatively new, low-intensity dynamic of the Israeli–Palestinian conflict from a strategic point of view. As seen above, even during the *Al-Aqsa Intifada* some Israeli military (e.g. the former COS and Defence Minister, Shaul Mofaz, and recently retired Chief of Staff Lt. Gen. Moshe Yaalon) and political leaders (e.g. former Prime Minister Ariel Sharon) had come to define as existential threats, what were regarded traditionally as current security threats (i.e. terror, guerrilla and riot violence). This was due to the fact that they came to perceive the conflict as an intercommunal, rather than interstate, one.

There has not been a major shift in the IDF's strategic approach vis-à-vis low-intensity-type conflict scenarios. The belief that the Israeli military could impose a battlefield decision, or even obtain victory, was shared initially by top officers of the IDF General Staff. Israel's conventional strategic goal of maintaining the status quo through deterrent retaliatory or pre-emptive measures has been erroneously applied to the contemporary Israeli–Palestinian conflict. Whereas in the past maintaining the status quo through deterrence was geared towards the conventional threat and, hence, towards the avoidance of a major conventional attack by Israel's neighbouring states, Israel's attempts at deterring Palestinian terror and guerrilla attacks have had the limited goal of reducing the level of violence and maintaining a status quo. This situation has become unbearable for the Palestinian population living in the Territories and has proved increasingly costly to Israeli society.

Preserving the status quo vis-à-vis the conventional threat was not only essential to Israel's existence, but was also a widely held principle of the Israeli national security consensus. Upholding the status quo in the Territories today has dramatically deteriorated the already meagre Palestinian standards of living. This is due to the extensive curfews and closures – which have denied the Palestinian people a viable economic base – as well as due to the rampant corruption of the Palestinian Authority. It has also eroded the national security consensus – particularly regarding the continued control of most of the territories seized during the 1967 Six Day War. In fact, with the first *Intifada* public support for maintaining the status quo decreased substantially in most sectors of the Israeli polity, except within the right-wing and national-religious camps. The *Intifada*, which underlined the intercommunal dimension of the conflict, led to a greater longing for separation between Israel and the local Palestinians.[91]

The continuation of the conflict has also led to a major economic crisis in Israel that has affected all major government budgets, Israeli living standards, and most crucially, the defence budget. A recent survey of 7,200 Israelis aged 20 and over, from all regions of the country, commissioned in late 2003 by the Central Bureau of Statistics, found that 35 per cent of the survey sample reported that their financial situation had deteriorated in the past five years.[92] Poverty levels as well as the socio-economic gap between rich and poor increased steadily over the last few years not only due to the slowdown of the Israeli economy, but also due to free market financial reforms and large budget cuts, which have curtailed the Israeli welfare state's support of the society's poor (see Figure 8.3).

Furthermore, the use of the IDF to lower the level of violence – as well as to convince the Palestinians that Israel will not negotiate under fire – has led to an over-emphasis on the operational and tactical use of the IDF. The use of the IDF has been a panacea for the lack of the military and political leadership's ability to come up with a new strategic paradigm that will bring about a strategic decision, vis-à-vis the problem of Palestinian terror and other forms of low-intensity violence. The political echelon's inability to develop a new strategic paradigm, given the experiences of the first *Intifada*, the 1991 Gulf War, and the changed strategic environment,

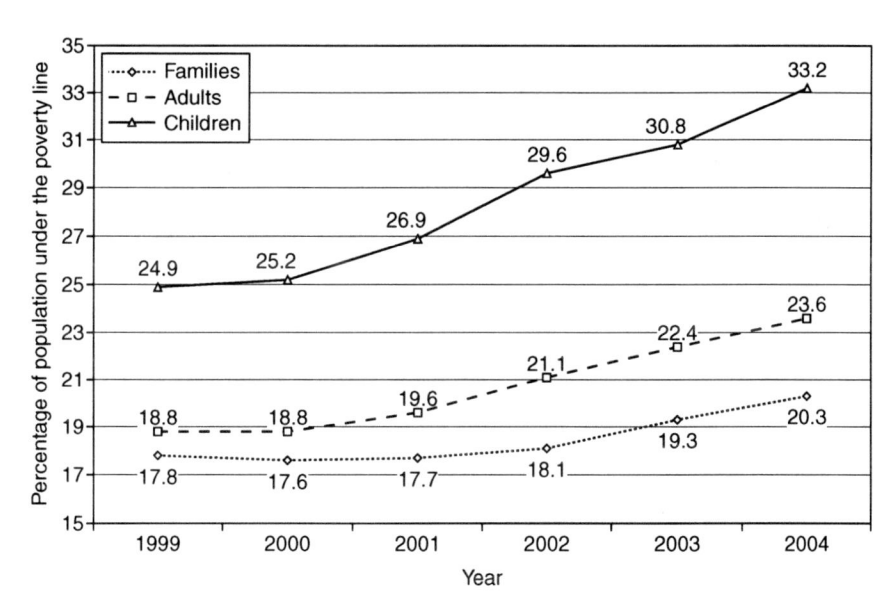

Figure 8.3 Percentage of Israeli population under the poverty line, 1999–2004 (source: Leah Achdut, Annual Survey 2000–2004 (Jerusalem: National Insurance Institute, 2000–04), www.btl.gov.il/English/btl_indx.asp?name=pirsumim/publications.htm (accessed 9 August 2005); Moti Bassok and Ruth Sinai, 'PM Sharon: The poverty situation will improve in the next year', *Ha'aretz*, 9 August 2005).

164 *Strategic impasse*

brought about by the Israeli–Palestinian and Israeli–Jordanian peace accords, was already voiced in 1998 by a *Knesset* sub-committee chaired by *Knesset* member Dan Meridor. The enquiry stated that:

> The Government of Israel, which is responsible for Israel's national security, has not conducted any substantial and comprehensive discussion regarding the national security policy and its applications.... We have not found any integrative and long-term thinking, examination or decisions. It is critical that such examinations be conducted at the national level, and not only by the military or the defence system.[93]

Until very recently Israel has been able to afford the price of not addressing the Palestinian problem strategically, because of the IDF's exceptional ability in providing rather effective short-term tactical solutions to all forms of Palestinian violence.

Bitsuism

The reason for the IDF's successful provision of short-term tactical innovations can be ascribed to the organisational culture and military tradition of the IDF, which has demonstrated 'at virtually every level of war (except, perhaps, the highest: that of strategy) ... throughout its history a proclivity for the dashing, the unusual or the creative solution to military problems'.[94] Indeed, within the IDF, preference for the pragmatic *bitsuist* ('doer') over the reflective thinker has led to the IDF's tendency to focus its energies in current security problems often at the expense of long-term vision and innovation. As one IDF field psychologist admitted recently in an interview,

> When I got my education in the officers' course, the most central value that you are educated on is 'complete your task'. There's nothing more important than completing your task. Now, this is one of the ten principles of war: stick to your mission. But the full commandment is 'stick to your mission as long as it is directed to the strategic goal'. Remember the goal of the mission, the aim. But Israel tends to forget the second half.[95]

A typical aspect of the IDF's *bitsuist* organisational culture is 'the concentration of effort on pressing day-to-day problems' whereby commanders are not really 'troubled by the war to come', but find themselves instead in a position where they want 'to be everywhere, to decide everything, to invest the maximum in whatever engages' them.[96] One battalion commander, for example, stated that in 2003 alone, he planned and executed over 240 missions throughout the year.[97] According to Col. Gil Barak, former commander of the Lachish training base, the IDF, in fact, 'has been operating on a five-months-in, three-weeks-out, five-months-in, six-weeks-out formula'.[98] The (token) time out is usually used for training, recreation, educational seminars or actual leave. Due to these working regimes many run the risk of burning out. Yet, as one interviewee remarked, 'luckily in Israel the service is only three years, not everybody has to do 25 years, because if we had soldiers having to do what they do today for longer, they would definitely be inhuman or they would all break'.[99]

Not only has the number of operations increased, but also the time spent preparing for them has diminished. Former head of the special forces unit, *Sayeret Egoz*, Lt. Col. Avi Peled, compared a typical special operation in Lebanon with that of one conducted in the Gaza Strip during the second *Intifada*:

> In a *Golani* commando operation in the south of Lebanon, they had three months to accomplish the mission. They had plenty of time to prepare models [of the operation], but today, you have to go every day. Every day you have an operation. You come back, analyse the mission within three hours and then go onto another mission within the same day.[100]

Such an operational tempo, clearly, raises the chances of units making a mistake and, thus, of causing collateral damage or even of incurring own casualties. It also reduces the chances of battalion – and by extension brigade and division – commanders to overview effectively the long-term strategic consequences that such operations may have on the Israeli–Palestinian conflict. It also reduces the possibility for the IDF to conduct training for formations greater than the size of companies, which raises serious readiness issues for division, brigade and battalion commanders.[101] The IDF, on any given week, has *c.* 20 to 30 individual platoons in training, given the fact that it can no longer spare its forces for battalion or brigade manoeuvres.[102] This has been particularly the case during the *Al-Aqsa Intifada* where, due to the growing lethality of Palestinian terror and guerrilla groups, and the increasing budgetary constraints, the IDF has had to improvise and make do with ever fewer resources, despite the growing number of military operations.

A negative aspect of the *bitsuist* tendency, within the IDF, is that higher command echelons, such as those consisting of brigade, division and General Staff commanders, tend to maintain the habit of improvisation, informal planning and short-term thinking, which they developed previously as combat officers.[103] Such improvisation even at the higher levels of the military – and political – echelons is consonant with societies that perceive themselves to be in a continuous state of conflict. Not knowing where the next threat will originate from leads the IDF to be on a constant state of readiness for the short-term, which impinges on its long-term planning. As Chris Demchak states, '*ad hoc* responses as a management style

166 *Strategic impasse*

are common throughout the wider society as a function of ... the widespread presumption that some kind of attack is always imminent in unpredictable ways'.[104]

Another aspect of the *bitsuist* ethos of the IDF is a marked aversion towards conceptual thinking as well as 'a demonstrated and declared anti-intellectualism' within its ranks.[105] Even Avi Kober's exhaustive content analysis of articles, published between 1948 and 2000 in the IDF's professional military journal, *Ma'arachot*, found that there were three main lacunae in Israeli military thought. First, of all the articles published, only 2.5 per cent (73) dealt with theoretical aspects of doctrine and warfare. Despite the important role that the three concepts of deterrence, early warning and battlefield decision play in the Israeli security doctrine, they received very little attention in *Ma'arachot* – only 3 per cent of published articles. Second, the majority of articles published in *Ma'arachot* focused on high-intensity conflicts despite the growing frequency and significance of LICs in the Israeli (and global) strategic situation. Third, the majority of articles related to tactical issues, whereas the number of articles touching on operational or strategic issues was very low.[106]

As seen above, the *bitsuist* tendency in the IDF also has often led to cases of excessive enthusiasm, and consequently, excessive collateral damage, on the part of the units carrying out their missions. For example, when securing areas, IDF units have often adopted, over the last decade, the 'stripping policy', that is, the razing of houses and uprooting of trees in order to preclude Palestinian gunmen from using them as cover when firing on them or Israeli civilians in the Territories. In spite of orders to the contrary during the *Al-Aqsa Intifada*, issued by head of the Civil Administration in the West Bank, Brig. Gen. Dov Tzadka, this 'stripping policy' occurred often. When asked why this happened frequently, Brig. Gen. Tzadka stated: 'They are given explicit orders ... but when I reach the place, *I find the forces in a state of hyperactivity. The soldiers and the commanders get carried away* [emphasis mine].'[107]

Furthermore, the IDF has often found itself conducting missions, which although tactically and operationally effective, have had negative political–strategic outcomes due to the significant collateral damage caused by overzealous units wanting to demonstrate their tactical prowess to higher echelon commanders. Besides the instances shown in the previous chapters, another clear example of such operational expediency was when the IDF conducted the targeted killing by an Israeli Air Force F-16 missile strike on Salah Shehade, a *Hamas* leader. The operation, in July 2002, resulted in the killing of 14 civilians, including nine children and even an official – and embarrassing – apology on the part of the former IDF Chief of Operations, Maj. Gen. Dan Harel.[108]

A slight break from such a tradition of overlooking the strategic consequences of day-to-day tactical operations was initiated by COS Moshe Yaalon, who after three years of advocating military force as a solution to

Strategic impasse 167

the Palestinian insurgency had come to understand that it would not be possible to achieve an 'unequivocal victory' through the IDF. Consequently, following his personal realisation that the IDF could not win the *Al-Aqsa Intifada*, Yaalon began to criticise the Israeli leadership's decision to use heavy-handed military operations against Palestinian terrorists, because of the substantial collateral damage caused when conducting such operations and despite the fact that they could have negative strategic consequences. In *Yediot Ahronot*, COS Yaalon was quoted as saying that, 'in our tactical decisions, we are operating contrary to our strategic interests'.[109] Due to his outspoken comments, disagreements over the disengagement plan as well as over other IDF missions led the Sharon government to veto Yaalon's re-appointment as chief of staff for another year, something which would have been approved as a matter of course, had he not expressed his *political* viewpoint in such an outspoken manner.

Collateral damage

The mission carried out in Jenin during Operation 'Defensive Shield' is a clear example of this. Despite attempts to use precision-guided missiles and highly trained snipers to eliminate Palestinian guerrillas, whilst avoiding casualties and major collateral damage, the extensive insertion of armoured and infantry elements into such a compact battleground did bring about approximately 52–3 Palestinian deaths – most of whom were combatants – and structural damage to over 100 homes. Most of the destroyed homes were either fully or partially occupied by Palestinian combatants and, thus, deemed legitimate military targets by international law.[110]

Nonetheless, as a result of such collateral damage, the IDF has, since Operation 'Defensive Shield', been able to map out most Palestinian cities by developing a system that divides 'the urban battlefield into precise increments and gives each building in a city ... an individual four-digit designation so both land and air forces know exactly which target they are trying to hit'.[111] Such detailed mapping and digital designation of Palestinian urban areas has helped reduce, appreciably, the cases of operational errors, which have often led in the past to extensive collateral damage.

If compared to past operations carried out by US forces at Hue City, Mogadishu, Panama City and by Russian forces in Grozny, the IDF did a good job given the fact that Operation 'Defensive Shield' enabled the IDF to seize, among other things, 396 wanted suspects, many weapons and explosives and led to the destruction of 23 explosives and weapons laboratories without causing the same levels of casualties and collateral damage other armies have caused when operating in similar conditions (see Table 7.4).

Operation 'Defensive Shield', successive IDF counter-terror operations, but especially the (so-far partial) construction of the security fence-wall reduced, by 30 per cent, the number of terrorist attacks committed against Israeli targets (from 5,301 to 3,338) and, by 50 per cent, the number of terror victims (from 451 to 213) between 2002 and 2003.[112] Moreover, according to a senior IDF officer, attempted suicide attacks were diminished by 75 per cent between mid-2003 and mid-2004.[113] Many Israelis have come to realise that the security fence along the West Bank has significantly improved their security situation. The Tami Steinmetz Peace Index survey, at the end of June 2004, found that a majority of 62 per cent of the Israeli population thought that the security fence had improved their sense of security, whilst only 4.5 per cent thought it harmed their sense of security.[114]

The re-occupation and control of PA 'A' Areas following Operation 'Defensive Shield' facilitated the monitoring and apprehension of suspected terror activists. The construction of the security fence gradually reduced the need on the part of the IDF to conduct high-profile targeted killings of 'ticking bomb' suicide terrorists. The greater use of intelligence-driven arrests, instead of targeted killings, which had galvanised rather than deterred potential terrorists, has been a much more effective tool at foiling Palestinian terror. A terror-stock model analysis of terror attempts following IDF targeted killings and preventive arrests between March 2002 and the end of 2003 showed that arresting suspected terrorists reduced the chance of further suicide bombings without encouraging the recruitment of more suicide bombers.[115] The arrest of suspected terrorists has become the Israeli security services' preferred counter-terror method given the wealth of intelligence that such arrests have provided. However, as corroborated in my interviews, the decision to safeguard one's own soldiers and security officers from harm has always been the determining factor of whether or not to carry out an arrest or targeted killing. That is, if the arrest of a suspected terrorist has proven too risky to carry out, then their assassination has been ordered instead.

The strategic impasse

However, such tactical and operational successes have not achieved any major strategic dividends, despite the belief of the higher political and military echelons to the contrary as seen above. Indeed, according to Brig. Gen. (Ret.) Shlomo Brom:

> On the tactical-operational level, the preparations were excellent, but the problem was, as usual, on the strategic level, because of the problem of how to prepare for it. Was it a preparation for a military conflict? Now in a military conflict you have very clear benchmarks for success. You have to – in blunt terms – kill as many of the other side and have as few own casualties as possible.... In this type of conflict there is a totally different benchmark, which should be built on

the analysis of how it can be stopped, not on how it can be won. Thus, in this type of conflict, my aim should be to minimize, as much as possible, my casualties and to minimize as much as possible my opponent's casualties, because killing breeds more killing.[116]

No matter how successful the IDF may have been at the tactical and operational levels, the Palestinians have been willing to continue conducting terror and guerrilla operations and to inflict suffering on the Israeli and Jewish settler population until they achieve a political resolution leading to national independence. Efforts on achieving 'victory' has been a constant problem for conventional armies that have conducted low-intensity campaigns, with much larger and better-equipped forces, against weaker and poorly equipped terrorist and guerrilla fighters.

Even when loss ratios have been considerably skewed in favour of conventional forces, irregular forces have historically gained the strategic upper hand on innumerable occasions. In Vietnam the loss ratios (including civilians) were 16:1, in the US' favour. In Algeria the loss ratios were 24:1, in the French forces' favour. In Afghanistan the loss ratios were at least dozens:1 in favour of the Soviet forces and in Mogadishu, during an 18-hour battle, on 3 October 1993, the loss ratio between US forces and Somali irregulars and civilians was 56:1 in the US' favour.[117] Yet, despite their military superiority, all such forces ended the conflict without achieving 'victory', as Israel did not when it left the South Lebanese Security Zone in April 2000 and has arguably not in the *Al-Aqsa Intifada*.[118]

9 Unilateral disengagement

After three years of relying heavily on the IDF to impose a military decision on the Israeli–Palestinian conflict, Prime Minister Ariel Sharon finally came to the conclusion that the conflict's stalemate would have to be solved on a political level. As was seen in the previous chapter, PM Sharon (and the majority of the Israeli population) did not believe that there was any credible negotiator on the Palestinian side. This belief was partially changed following Yasser Arafat's death on 11 November 2004, but reverted back to its original stance once *Hamas* won the Palestinian Council elections.[1] In any case, by December 2003, Sharon decided to progress with the Road Map peace initiative through unilateral disengagement.

Faced with a demographic time bomb, in that within Gaza 8,000 settlers lived amongst 1.5 million Palestinians, the large financial and human costs the IDF was facing in order to protect local Jewish settlers and the continuing pressure of Palestinian violence originating from Gaza, Sharon had surmised that remaining in Gaza was too costly for the state of Israel.

Already, Moshe Dayan, just after the Suez War had warned about the demographic, security and economic problems that the Gaza Strip would bring, should Israel occupy it:

> A situation could develop in the Gaza Strip whereby our present problems would appear minuscule compared to the economic, police and security problems we would inherit if we captured [the area] with its [masses of] refugees.... The next generation might ask us one day: why were you such fools to change a borderline that you could control with two infantry companies for this hornet's nest?[2]

The issue of demography was again one of the main factors leading to Israel's dismantlement of the settlements through unilateral disengagement. *MK* Danny Yatom stated that,

> In order to secure Israel as the only Jewish democratic state in the world we have to separate ourselves from the Palestinians, otherwise

we will find ourselves in an ocean of Arabs.... They will become the majority and, as time goes on, it will be more and more difficult to separate from the Territories.[3]

The friction and violent reality that the settlements in the Gaza Strip and West Bank were posing had finally superseded the ideological imperative and material benefits that settlements were intended to provide. The unilateral disengagement entailed the withdrawal of 17 settlements from the Gaza Strip and of four communities from the West Bank.[4]

Sharon's decision to dismantle and remove whole communities from the Territories was a great shock and blow to the settlement movement. He had been a champion of the *Gush Emunim* (Bloc of the Faithful) religious settlement movement.[5] Sharon's main goal in the Territories since the late 1970s was to build Israeli settlements throughout the West Bank and Gaza Strip in order to ensure that any future Palestinian Autonomy (set out by the 1979 Israeli–Egyptian peace agreement) would never become a sovereign state in the future. Through various government appointments, Sharon had carried out this goal unswervingly: as Minister of Agriculture (1977–81) in Menachem Begin's government, as Minister for Housing Construction (1990–92) in Yitzhak Shamir's government, as Minister of National Infrastructure (1996–98) in Benjamin Netanyahu's government and finally as Prime Minister from February 2001 until his unilateral disengagement decision.

Sharon's single-handed determination to carry out unilateral disengagement did not come at a cheap price, particularly on the domestic front. Most Israelis broadly supported unilateral disengagement because of the demographic problem and the fear that one day Israel would become a de facto bi-national state, should it continue to control all of the Territories. They did not, in fact, want to keep on controlling the lives of millions of Palestinians for the sake of maintaining the (more remote and difficult to protect) settlements within the Territories.

Despite the fact that Sharon had promised that the Gaza disengagement would not take place under Palestinian fire, preparations for the disengagement moved on as *Qassam* and mortar rocket attacks against settlement and Israeli targets increased.

As seen in the previous chapter, Operations 'Rainbow' and 'Days of Penitence' were used to restore Israeli deterrence vis-à-vis terrorist groups in the Gaza Strip. However, the fact that Israel was set on leaving the Gaza Strip and some communities of the West Bank without any real bilateral political arrangements with the Palestinians only encouraged groups such as *Hamas* and Islamic *Jihad*. These groups could not help but draw parallels between Israel's retreat from Lebanon, in May 2000, and the current unilateral disengagement. Thus, *Hamas* was planning large, post-pullout, victory celebrations (including the purchase of 30,000 uniforms) in order to express the message that the Gaza Strip withdrawal was the direct consequence of its military accomplishments over Israel.[6]

172 *Unilateral disengagement*

The scaling down, since late 2004, of IDF operations given Arafat's death and the restoration of Road Map negotiations with the newly elected PA President, Mahmoud Abbas, allowed Palestinian groups to recover their capabilities. This led COS Yaalon to declare at his last *Knesset* Defence and Foreign Affairs Committee meeting, shortly before retiring, that 'implementation of the disengagement whilst Palestinian groups are boosting their strength is a very serious problem'.[7]

Fears that Israeli towns within the Green Line would increasingly be the target of Palestinian rocket and mortar barrages (Sderot had already been the target of multiple *Qassam* attacks), following the disengagement, also grew. According to Col. Uzi Buchbinder, head of the Home Front Command's civil defence department, the implementation of the disengagement would leave, in fact, 46 western Negev communities exposed to *Qassam* rocket fire.[8] Despite fears of greater violence and the weakening of Israel's deterrence credibility, that the disengagement would possibly bring about, Sharon implemented his plans for unilateral withdrawal.

Domestic opposition to unilateral disengagement

Opposition from the right was very vociferous not only for security reasons, but more importantly, due to ideological motives. Opposition within the *Likud* party against Sharon's plan was particularly strident from *Likud* members of the *Knesset* and government, and from regular party members. On 2 May 2004 the *Likud* party held an internal referendum on the disengagement plan. PM Sharon, suffered a devastating defeat as party members voted against the plan by 59.5 per cent to 39.7 per cent.[9] Despite this defeat, Sharon decided to continue with his disengagement plan by seeking approval from his government cabinet and the *Knesset*.

Following the cabinet approval of the disengagement plan by a 14–7 majority, in early June 2004, members of the *Ichud Leumi* ('National Union'), Avigdor Lieberman, Benyamin Elon and Zvi Hendel, as well as two of the government ministers of the *Mafleget Dati Leumi* ('National Religious Party'), Effi Eitam and Yitzak Levy, resigned. This brought Sharon's base of support in the *Knesset* from 61 to 59 seats. Cabinet ministers from the *Likud* party, such as Finance Minister Benjamin Netanyahu, Education Minister Limor Livnat, Foreign Minister Silvan Shalom were also toying with the possibility of resignation given their disagreement with Sharon's plan.[10]

The settlement movement and their sympathisers carried out large protests against the disengagement plan. For example, on 25 July 2004, 130,000 settlers organised a human chain, 90 km long, of people standing side-by-side from the Gaza settlement of Nissanit in the Gaza Strip to the Western Wall in Jerusalem.[11] Some 100,000 protesters gathered in Jerusalem's Zion Square, on 12 September 2004, as well as outside the *Knesset* in January 2005. Prayer rallies, house visits to Israelis inside the

Green Line, to show the human cost of the disengagement, and other initiatives were adopted by the anti-disengagement movement throughout 2004 and 2005.

Regardless, preparations for the disengagement were hastened by the Sharon government. In order to ease the removal of settlers from the settlements marked for evacuation, a generous compensation bill was approved in February 2005. The compensation bill instituted a complex scheme of financial reimbursements, ranging from $100,000 to $270,000 with additional grants covering moving costs, up to six months' rent and a resettlement bonus for those willing to move to the development areas of the Galilee and Negev. The compensation was cover for the loss of land, assets and livelihood of those settlers who would leave voluntarily, prior to the mid-August disengagement deadline and the start of the forced removal of settlers from the Gaza Strip and West Bank communities.[12]

As of late June 2005, only 264 families had signed up for the generous compensation bill.[13] Many settlers ignored the evacuation administration, 'SELA' ('Assistance to Settlers in Gaza and Northern West Bank Administration'), which had been set up by the Evacuation and Compensation Bill in order to facilitate the whole process.

Evacuation operation

The actual evacuation was initially, and ironically, scheduled for 25 July 2005, the start of the three-week mourning period of *Tish B'Av*, which commemorates the destruction of the first and second Temples. Given their religious sensitivities, the start of the three-week disengagement process was moved to the day following the end of *Tish B'Av*, 15 August 2005. According to the evacuation plan, 18,000 police officers and 41,000 regular and professional IDF soldiers and officers would take part in the pull-out.

These forces would be deployed in six different security rings. The internal ring would be comprised of unarmed IDF personnel; the second ring would be used and manned by armed IDF personnel to secure the settlements and roads within the evacuated areas. The third ring would involve soldiers that would secure the evacuation routes and areas from possible Palestinian attacks. The fourth ring would conduct counter-terror operations in the case of Palestinian attacks. The fifth ring would be comprised of both police officers and soldiers assigned in blocking anti-disengagement protesters from entering the Gaza Strip, whilst the sixth ring would surround the outer Gaza Strip and consist of police patrols assigned to block the entry of unwanted vehicles in the Strip's vicinities.[14] Given the extensive use of the professional and regular corps in the disengagement, 17 reserve battalions would be called up by the IDF in order to cover the regular *batash* duties of the units involved in the disengagement process.

IDF operational and ethical preparations for the disengagement

The financial cost of the disengagement, during the first three years of its implementation, was estimated to be at around $460 million. Likewise, the legal, moral and operational complexity of the operation would be quite considerable. During 2005, forces scheduled to implement the evacuation participated in various training sessions, involving simulations and role-playing scenarios, given the expectation that significant violent and non-violent resistance would arise during the evacuation.

Moreover, due to the highly contentious political controversy surrounding the disengagement process and, even more so, the decision to use the IDF to transfer Jews forcibly from the settlements, the IDF Education Branch set out, from February 2005, to prepare IDF troops mentally and emotionally for evacuating settlers from the Territories. This was necessary as the use of the IDF for the disengagement was quite problematic.

The IDF had traditionally played a central role not only in protecting the settlements they were now going to remove, but they also had played an active part in building them.[15] To some, the radical and sudden change in its role, in relation to the settlements, was quite distressing. This was particularly the case for large numbers of combat unit soldiers and junior officers that were part of the national-religious camp.[16] Not only were they ideologically opposed to the disengagement, but quite a few either lived or had relatives in the settlements scheduled for evacuation. The IDF had been perceived to be a Jewish army protecting the Jewish people. To use it for removing Jewish people from what settlers and many of the national-religious camp believed to be part of *Eretz Israel* ('land of Israel') was believed to be tantamount to its destruction (*'hurban'*).[17]

The IDF Education Branch, consequently, had distributed over 4,000 'explanation kits' complete with videos, CDs and pamphlets to help commanders (from division to company level) prepare their soldiers for the evacuation process. The kits offered a framework for officers to open discussions with their soldiers on potentially difficult scenarios involving the evacuation process. A major emphasis was put on the obligation of the IDF to carry out missions that are not considered to be part of the national security consensus. Thus, the kits also opened up discussions on dilemmas over obeying controversial orders.[18]

Conscientious objection to the evacuation of settlers, despite official statements to the contrary, became a key preoccupation of the IDF in the 18 months leading up to the start of the disengagement process. In March 2005 the IDF distributed a 'disobedience guide' for commanders involved in the evacuation. It also set out the various disciplinary measures (e.g. dismissal of professional staff, possible court martial of conscripts, etc.) the IDF would implement against those who would disobey orders.

The severe reaction to any possible act of disobedience to the evacuation orders continued as the disengagement date approached and right-wing refusal gained a steady momentum. This momentum increased the IDF's fears of mass insubordination to the extent that the IDF labelled it an existential threat. IDF Manpower Division Head, Maj. Gen. Elazar Stern, stated, when commenting on right- (and left-wing) conscientious objection, that 'any kind of disobedience ... constitutes an identical threat to Israeli society ... and could endanger the IDF's continued existence and even the existence of the state of Israel as a Jewish, democratic country'.[19]

Although not an existential threat, the right-wing refusal movement did rise to prominence very rapidly and with great determination to stop the disengagement process. What distinguished the right-wing movement from the left-wing objectors of the current *Intifada* was that many of the potential objectors were not only reservists, but strikingly, also conscripts and professional personnel.

Furthermore, the political debate regarding refusal and unilateral disengagement was subject to much greater political controversy. Quite a few members of the *Knesset* and cabinet ministers were either explicitly calling for soldiers to refuse future evacuation orders, or criticising to such an extent the unilateral disengagement plan that refusal seemed to be the only logical answer to it. Politicians' challenges to the unilateral disengagement plan, and calls to refuse, led newly appointed COS Lt. Gen. Halutz (June 2005) to admonish public leaders against involving the army in political disputes, given their deleterious effect on civil–military relations: 'The calls that are being heard to disobey orders are putting an unbearable amount of weight on the shoulders of troops and commanders, and are threatening to dissolve the public agreement around the IDF.'[20] At the same time, other politicians insisted on the need to implement government decisions and to uphold the democratic nature of such decisions regardless of soldiers' personal and ethical misgivings.

Furthermore, the orders to carry out the future evacuation and the manner in which the Israeli government and *Knesset* came to decide the need for disengagement were questioned. Opponents to the disengagement had been calling for a national referendum, regarding the disengagement, since early 2004. A bill proposing this referendum had, however, been voted against in the *Knesset* in late March 2005.[21] Consequently, disengagement opponents believed that the disengagement plan had not received a sufficient popular mandate.

Accusations that the disengagement process was undemocratic, in spite of the fact that majorities in favour of it were obtained in both the government and *Knesset* votes, became widespread. Even cabinet members from the *Likud* party questioned the legitimacy of the disengagement plan. This led Sharon to come to loggerheads with several of his colleagues. Following *Likud* minister Uzi Landau's criticism of the disengagement plan, Sharon chastised him by stating that 'you say you are against refusal, but you say the government's decisions are illegitimate. It is the same as calling on soldiers to refuse. Your position endangers the maintenance of a democratic regime in Israel.'[22]

Right-wing refusal

Despite the General Staff's stark warning regarding refusal to obey evacuation orders, 34 Binyamin District Command reserve officers, most of whom came from the settlements in Samaria, wrote a letter in early January 2005 to their brigade commander, Col. Mickey Edelstein, demanding that the army could not force them to take action that violated their beliefs. Following meetings with the head of the Central Command, Maj. Gen. Kaplinsky, whereby the officers explained their intentions, all of them were dismissed from the reserves. This instance was quite unique in that none of the officers had disobeyed an actual order; they merely expressed their future intention to do so before being called up for reserve duty.[23]

Another initiative was headed by Noam Livnat, brother of Education Minister Limor Livnat. Livnat established the 'Defensive Shield' initiative, the aim of which was to derail the disengagement by gathering enough signatures of reserve and conscript soldiers willing to refuse the evacuation orders. The petition stated that 'we the undersigned are citizens of the State of Israel and serve in the army with pride.... We identify with rabbis who view the disengagement plan as a national disaster and we declare that we will not lend a hand to the plan.'[24] In early February, Livnat presented at a press conference his petition, in which over 10,000 signatures were collected, in the hope that the IDF would come to the realisation that they would not have an army to carry out the evacuation.

The growing trend towards religious refusal did strike alarm bells amongst senior figures within the national-religious camp who believed that the duty to follow orders in the IDF superseded personal views regarding the disengagement. Consequently, many (e.g. former Yesha Council Chairman, Otniel Schneller and a leading settler Rabbi, Yaacov Meidan, etc.) spoke out against the disengagement, but even more persuasively, against refusal at a public meeting in Jerusalem, on 26 January 2005. Maj. Gen. (Res.) Yaacov Amidror, former Military Intelligence research head, stated that

> It is hard to find a worse plan than the disengagement plan, except for one plan – the plan to refuse orders.... Despite everything, much worse than this terrible plan is to break the only instrument holding us together – the army – which protects the state of Israel.[25]

Despite such admonitions, in the months leading up to the disengagement, other reservists announced their refusal to serve in the disengagement process. In May 2005, 12 reservists from the Armoured Corps Battalion

925 announced their refusal to serve during the disengagement period,[26] a *Golani* infantry platoon commander from the regular army requested to be discharged, in May 2005, in order to avoid carrying out future evacuation orders,[27] and 12 conscript combat engineers were tried, in late June 2005, after threatening to refuse to take part in future settlement evacuations.[28] Another 12 regular soldiers, in July 2005, were arrested for refusing to participate in a test-run of the Gaza Strip closure. During the closure, these soldiers refused, in full view of their comrades, to block the entry at the Kissufim border crossing of hundreds of protesting settlers into the Gaza Strip.[29]

The fact that most of the objectors were religious soldiers who had gone through the *Yeshivat Hesder* programme led then newly appointed COS Lt. Gen. Dan Halutz, to declare publicly, in July 2005, that he was considering abolishing the *Yeshivat Hesder* arrangement between the IDF and the national-religious *yeshiva* movement.[30] With the exception of *Nahal* units (including the *Nahal Haredi* Battalion), since the establishment of the IDF, its leaders have tried to adopt 'manpower policies based on the principle of social integration, with very few military allocations reflecting the origins or affiliations of individual troops'.[31]

The concession made to the national-religious *yeshiva* movement since the mid-1960s, whereby religious recruits would serve intermittently for only two years in the IDF, whilst also studying the *Torah* for three years during different service periods, was quite a unique case in the IDF. It had also, by now, become controversial. Many within the IDF came to perceive the *Yeshivat Hesder* programme as dangerous, in that it produced a situation of dual loyalty amongst its members, either towards the state (and the IDF's commands) or the *Torah* (and its commandments). Such fears were compounded by the fact that since early 2005 some IDF military chaplains and reservist rabbis had been declaring their opposition to the disengagement.[32]

Yet, following the *Yeshivat Hesder* members' public uproar against Halutz's hypothetical declarations, he reassured them that their closure would not be an option, but that punishment for insubordinates would be severe. Halutz, in any case, ordered the disbanding of the company of *Yeshivat Hesder* students that had refused to remove protestors, in early July 2005, from the Kissufim crossing.[33]

Disengagement accomplished

And yet, when the unilateral disengagement finally began threats and fears of massive disobedience quickly dissipated. Preparations for such a massive operation, not only on an operational level, but also on a psychological level, enabled soldiers to cope with the 'trauma' of disengagement. Instances of opposition from certain elements of the settlement communities and from national-religious activists, who had managed to infiltrate the

Gaza Strip were relatively negligible. They consisted of verbal abuse, burning of property, barricading of synagogues and other communal buildings and some minor assaults on IDF and police personnel. Overall, *only* 320 soldiers and police officers suffered minor injuries during the week-long disengagement pull-out.[34]

Matters failed to escalate for the most part, because of the IDF's restraint and professionalism, even in cases that saw soldiers and high-level commanders (such as Brig. Gen. Gershon HaCohen) bear the brunt of the settlers' insults and, in some cases, physical assault. Moreover, the decision by most of the settlement community to cooperate with the IDF was based on the fact that it was still perceived by the settlement community, despite disengagement, to be a highly revered institution that, after all, had protected it during Israel's control of the Territories since 1967.

In total, only 600 anti-disengagement protestors were arrested during the operation and only a handful of soldiers ultimately refused to carry out the disengagement process. Indeed, the rapidity and fluidity of the whole pull-out took the IDF (and the whole world) by surprise. It also led IDF commanders to praise their troops. Head of the Southern Command, Maj. Gen. Dan Harel, for example, stated that the evacuating forces 'displayed amazing maturity, wisdom, judgement and restraint'.[35]

Just as the removal of settlers from the designated settlements in the Territories ran smoothly, so did the IDF's withdrawal from the Gaza Strip the following week. After 38 years of occupation, the IDF had finally relinquished any sort of control within the Gaza Strip. At the IDF's withdrawal ceremony at the Kissufim crossing, on 12 September 2005, the chief of the Gaza Division, Maj. Gen. Aviv Kochavi, defined it as 'the end of an era'. He also reiterated that 'the responsibility for what goes on inside is placed on the Palestinian Authority. Yet the responsibility over the security of Israeli citizens continues to be placed on our army.'[36] Although the IDF was relinquishing control of the Gaza Strip it did not opt out of the possibility of using force within it, should terror and guerrilla attacks continue to be launched from it.

Despite the success of the disengagement process, the political and moral repercussions of the disengagement process on the IDF may not be clear yet. The fact that a new online petition, calling against conscription, has been signed by hundreds of right-wing youths does not bode well for the IDF, especially given that the petition is expected to collect as many as 5,000 signatures.[37] More territorial concessions might increase this new phenomenon of right-wing refusal and become problematic for the IDF, which wants to continue to maintain the image that it still is a 'people's army' willing to defend Israel.

Although division over the national security consensus, particularly regarding the maintenance of the Territories, has been quite high over the last two decades, the fact that Israel is completely removing all forms of control over certain elements of the Palestinian population and the Territories will likely increase it. For the Right, relinquishing what they consider the land of Israel is tantamount to betrayal of the Zionist enterprise in Palestine, whereas for the Left (and even more so for the Palestinian Authority), Ariel Sharon's unilateral disengagement has not been sufficient for achieving peace with the Palestinians.

It is likely that the IDF will continue to be used to quell further Palestinian opposition and violence, particularly originating from *Hamas* and the PIJ. This will be done in spite of assurances from the PA that it will rein them in and continue carrying out democratic reforms, according to the Road Map peace plan. Whether or not the IDF will do so by using greater discretion in its use of force vis-à-vis the Palestinians and whether or not it will be able to remain above the political wrangling over the national security consensus between the Left and the Right remains to be seen.

However, as the book showed previously, without the necessary strategic and doctrinal changes needed to effectively address the Israeli–Palestinian LIC, the IDF will continue carrying out retaliatory operations that may inflame rather than limit the tensions at particularly sensitive junctures of the conflict. As for the IDF's ability to avoid being entangled in political and ethical disputes over Israel's right to remain in the Territories and conduct military operations, depends on how divisive such disputes become and to what extent conscripts, professionals and reservists use refusal to serve as a way of putting pressure on the Israeli incumbent government to bend policy to their particular ideological agenda. The fact that conscientious objection has become increasingly commonplace both on the Right and on the Left of the Israeli political spectrum, due to the controversy involving the Territories and the IDF's task there, will not facilitate the IDF's role over the coming decade before, hopefully, some form of diplomatic arrangement between Israel and the Palestinians will have brought about, at least, a state of non-war and, at most, the ever elusive peace.

10 Conclusion

This book set out to analyse the tactical and operational conduct of the IDF's COIN campaign during the two Palestinian *Intifadas*. This analysis was conducted in order to see to what extent armed forces, equipped and trained for the most part to fight major conventional warfare are able to adapt to LIC scenarios, ranging from unarmed revolt to an outright guerrilla and terror campaign. Whilst doing so, this book explored what effects fighting in complex, ambiguous, and sometimes politically controversial conditions had on the combat morale of the IDF units that operated in the Territories.

Initially, the book provided a historical background of Israeli civil–military relations and of the evolution of the Israeli national security doctrine. The reason for this was to explore the degree to which the Israeli security assumptions, civil–military relations, the IDF's organisational culture, as well as its basic structure and conduct, influenced its capacity to adapt to the recent Israeli–Palestinian LIC. When analysing the IDF's adaptation to the two *Intifadas*, the book focused especially on the ethical and operational dilemmas the IDF underwent given that, as argued in my introduction, such an analysis would have provided insight into what other militaries around the world have experienced, and will continue to experience, as they continue to fight the GWOT in somewhat similar operational conditions, and under a similar set of moral and legal dilemmas.

The IDF's record in its COIN efforts during the two *Intifadas* has had mixed results. During the first *Intifada*, the IDF struggled to come to grips with the Palestinian uprising. This was because the IDF was unprepared to carry out, what basically amounted to, constabulary duties against an unarmed civilian population that was demonstrating in order to gain independence from 20 years of Israeli military rule.

The large asymmetry between the Israeli conventional war machine and the Palestinian civilian demonstrator, domestic and international scrutiny and condemnation, together with the internal political questioning, tested both the effectiveness, as well the moral mettle, of the IDF units operating in the Territories. A military that had traditionally prided itself for its perceived superior ethical standards and for using its military might for defensive purposes *only*, was now employing its power for arguably repressive reasons.

The growing erosion of the national security consensus, concerning the maintenance of the status quo and of the Territories, together with the lack of political guidance, if not backing, towards the IDF led to increasing confusion regarding the actual mission the IDF was supposed to achieve. More crucially, for the units on the ground, there was more confusion regarding what rules of engagement were supposed to be applied against Palestinian insurgents. In the midst of these difficulties, many of the units involved in the IDF's COIN campaign became frustrated, stressed and demoralised. Individuals reacted to such problems either by trying to avoid direct contact with Palestinians through 'grey refusal' or by not showing up for duty (if they were fortunate enough to be reservists) or by outright refusal to serve.

Although many *refuseniks* proved to be more morally sensitive and sympathetic to the Palestinians' plight than the average Israeli soldier, most conscientious objectors refused to serve for political and ideological reasons. Most *refuseniks* perceived the occupation as illegitimate and, thus, military–security operations carried out in the Territories were considered similarly unlawful in that they ultimately perpetuated control over the Palestinian people rather than provide security to Israeli citizens.

Nonetheless, the majority of the IDF did continue to serve in the Territories. The *bitsuist* ethos enabled most forces to perceive their constabulary duties as military operations. Many soldiers and commanders were able to focus on achieving the immediate tactical goals of their missions and avoid having to question the legitimacy of their actions, given the belief that the IDF only used force for defensive and, thus, legitimate purposes. Not only did many of the units perceive their actions to be legitimate, but they also saw them as fair and proportionate given the belief that they were facing a 'military' threat. Others got on with achieving their missions by trying to avoid thinking about them, as one armoured corps platoon commander put it, when asked about the moral dilemmas faced in operations carried out in the Territories, 'usually what we are doing, we are not thinking about it ... [You] just don't want to think of it. [You] just do everything without thinking about it. You get by the day by not thinking about these feelings.'[1]

Given the lack of support from politicians, and to an extent, from the upper IDF command echelons, many other IDF units tried to avoid fully carrying out their duties due to the fear of undergoing legal prosecution or stiff military disciplining, should they make operational errors resulting in collateral damage or civilian casualties. The phenomenon of *rosh katan* became quite common. This was contrary to the IDF's tradition of carrying out duties with boldness and initiative until the mission was fully accomplished. The attritional effects on the IDF, which also led to cases of dehumanisation and abuse, as well as the growing understanding that the

Intifada could not be stopped by military means alone, led to the Oslo Peace Process. Although the Oslo Accords are considered a historical watershed in Israeli–Palestinian relations, they did not develop the desired confidence and trust between the two parties; neither did the Oslo process bring peace.

Despite the considerable challenges the IDF faced during the *Intifada*, it did not really try to apply the lessons learned during the uprising. The IDF did not modify the training, tactics and psychological preparation of its troops for a similar type of conflict in the future. One reason for this is that the political and military leadership in Israel initially hoped that with the Oslo Accords, constabulary and counter-terror duties within the Territories would increasingly be conducted by the Palestinian Security Services. This lack of transformation can also be explained by various factors relating both to the nature of civil–military relations in Israel and to the organisational culture of the IDF.

Given the lack of a civilian institution that is able to analyse and address comprehensively long-term threats to Israeli security, Israel has had to rely too often on the assessments and plans provided by the IDF. Although the political echelons play an important part in overseeing and deciding upon security matters, their dependency on the IDF has often led to either political indecision or over-reliance on the alternatives that the IDF presented them with, via such intelligence reports, or directly by the facts created on the ground by tactical units during operations. IDF intelligence and strategic threat assessments, moreover, have provided insight into what the next major threats or future war will be like. This, in turn, has influenced what war(s) the IDF should prepare for.

Due to the IDF's traditionally conservative nature in its strategic-level thinking, it has prepared preponderantly for major conventional manoeuvre warfare. Although this seemed like the optimum choice, given the existential threat that Arab conventional armed forces once posed, since the late 1970s the geo-strategic map in the Middle East has changed considerably. Peace with Egypt in 1979, the rise of intercommunal warfare with the Palestinians in the Lebanon War and in the Territories since the late 1980s, the growing sub-conventional threats originating from Lebanon since the mid-1980s and from the West Bank and Gaza Strip since the mid-1990s, peace with Jordan in 1994, the Oslo Peace Process with the PLO, as well as the weakening of Syria and Iraq during the post-Cold War era, did not bring about a change in the Israeli national security doctrine.

Because of the IDF's limited resources in relation to the multifaceted threats it tries to deal with, one can understand why it needs to focus on what it believes to be the greatest threat to Israeli security. Nonetheless, it appears that the conservative nature of the IDF has made it difficult for it to adapt to recent strategic challenges posed by the Israeli–Palestinian conflict. As seen in this book, even though the IDF adapted very well from a tactical perspective to the threat posed by Palestinian guerrilla and terror activities during the *Al-Aqsa Intifada*, as with the previous *Intifada*, it was still not able to impose a strategic solution on the Palestinian insurgency.

The IDF was unable, until early 2005, to understand the extent to which some of its tactical decisions and modes of operation had often had an escalatory, rather than restraining effect on the conflict. Missions were often carried out by units that did not understand the higher order intent and strategic outcome of their actions, which is required by mission command principles. The timing or strategic necessity of some operations did not always play a part in the IDF decision-making process. They were, in certain cases, conducted to increase the combat motivation of units through the creation of 'special' missions, which resulted in greater friction with the Palestinian population. In other cases, they were carried out because of the IDF's organisational ethos of *bitsuism*. Consequently, missions were often pursued beyond what was initially required of them. Without receiving the clear intent or desired outcome of such actions from the political echelons, the IDF was left practically on their own to 'develop their own plans, methods and even objectives [and] only knew one thing: that they should act and act forcefully'.[2]

Bitsuism has also traditionally influenced the way IDF officers, with some exceptions, have eschewed the intellectual exploration of 'big ideas' in warfare. Promotion in the IDF has often been on the basis of battlefield experience and prowess rather than on the intellectualism of the officer. Until recently, education and doctrinal thinking in the IDF often came at the expense of techno-tactical combat preparation and operational experience. Although this pragmatist bent is understandable in an army that has spent most of its existence fighting one threat or another, it did produce an organisational culture in which major strategic-level adaptation and transformation efforts have been at best gradualistic and more often non-existent.

Almost all IDF commanders, including the chief of staff, must join as recruits and get promoted on the basis of their (combat) abilities. This makes it difficult for the IDF to shift its doctrinal emphasis. Even its upper echelon commanders have been socialised, throughout their whole careers, to focus on day-to-day pressing (tactical) problems, rather than on long-term strategic re-organisation on the basis of the changing geo-strategic realities of the Middle East. Proof of this has been given by the IDF's most recent '*Kela-2008*' re-organisation plans that, as mentioned above, have been geared towards fighting major conventional warfare.

Both the civilian political echelon's lack of clear strategic guidance, together with the IDF's concentration on tactical innovation, made it difficult for the IDF to adapt an LIC strategy that would factor in effectively politico-strategic considerations, in the use of its forces in intercommunal strife within densely populated civilian areas. By early 2004, the IDF finally began to realise this. In February 2004 an IDF committee headed by Maj. Gen. Amos Yadlin, concluded in a report to the COS Lt. Gen.

Yaalon, that in spite of great tactical innovation and aggressiveness, Israel did not have a real strategy and was lacking coordination between the political and military echelons. It also concluded that, even though the true enemy was never really defined (i.e. Arafat, the PA or *Hamas*, etc.) and even with some latitude for manoeuvre, the IDF was not able to terminate the conflict (that is, win the war).[3]

The emphasis on providing military tactical solutions to Palestinian threats led to an almost complete oversight of a 'hearts and minds' strategy. This oversight happened because both Israel and the IDF, particularly during the height of the Palestinian terror campaign (2002–03), saw it as an existential war. Consequently, IDF units really did not see a 'hearts and minds' strategy as a viable option, given their main interest in stopping the terror onslaught originating from the Territories, in order to normalise civilian life in Israel and the settlements. Once suicide bombings became a weekly affair in Israel, the restraint and containment efforts shown by the IDF were set aside, in an attempt to defeat Palestinian terrorism as quickly and effectively as possible.

Clearly, the IDF did eventually lower the level of Palestinian violence in both *Intifadas*, but this outcome was more the result of attrition. It was also the result of the increasing likelihood that some form of political settlement would be achieved (i.e. Madrid Conference in the first *Intifada*; Road Map and Unilateral Disengagement in the *Al-Aqsa Intifada*). It is the case that the IDF and Israeli security services were able to dramatically reduce the level of successful Palestinian terror and guerrilla attacks in the *Al-Aqsa Intifada*. Together with the partial construction of the security fence, and the Israeli security and intelligence services' enormous efforts at dismantling the Palestinian terror infrastructure developed during the Oslo Peace Process, plus the *Al-Aqsa Intifada*, Israel was able to 'routinise' ultimately the effects of the conflict.[4]

Nonetheless, in December 2005, Lt. Gen. (Ret.) Yaalon, at the time a distinguished military fellow at a Washington, DC think tank, reiterated the fact that military operations cannot extinguish completely, the threat of terrorism: 'Strategic considerations in counterterrorist operations must account for the absence of an exclusively military "knockout" option against terrorism.'[5]

The IDF has been able to partially destroy the capability of the Palestinian terror network, but not the will of its members as well as supporters amongst the general population. Whilst trying to fight Palestinian insurgency, Israel has not only galvanised Palestinian terrorists' intentions but also spurred more Palestinians to support the leading proponent of terrorism in the Israeli–Palestinian conflict, that is, *Hamas*. *Hamas*' recent overwhelming Palestinian Council electoral victory is the reaction to many years of PLO incompetence and corruption. It is also a result of Israeli military policies in the Territories over the last five years. Many Palestinians, furthermore, have viewed *Hamas*' campaign, originating from Gaza, as a victory on their part, because of Israel's unilateral disengagement from the Strip in 2005.

As for the effects of the *Al-Aqsa Intifada* on combat motivation, the number of conscientious objectors and 'grey refusers' increased considerably in relation to the first *Intifada*. This was quite surprising. Despite similar operational circumstances in certain aspects of both *Intifadas* (e.g. checkpoint, border crossing duties, patrols amongst hostile civilian populations, etc.), the magnitude of guerrilla and terrorist violence carried out by Palestinian groups as of early 2001, and particularly as of early 2002, led most of Israeli society to perceive the conflict as an existential one. The rise of outspoken and politically active conscientious objectors was contained by the IDF's deliberate strategy of ignoring the phenomenon. Once the IDF learnt that punishing *refuseniks* only strengthened their cause, the IDF decided to marginalise the phenomenon by allowing their direct commanders to either allow them to serve in less ethically questionable posts, or by not calling them up at all for reserve duty. Since 1982, 'only 8 per cent of the soldiers who signed petitions and were committed to refusing to serve in Lebanon and in the Occupied Territories have been court-martialled'.[6]

The perception of being under an existential threat stopped the Israeli political leadership from seeking further political solutions to the conflict. It also led to its decision to 'unleash' the IDF. Most units shared the perception that Israel was under an existential threat and that Israel had no choice but to fight the war on terror. High combat motivation, together with the strengthening of *bitsuist* tendencies, given the nature of the threat sometimes led to overzealous operations, which resulted in cases of excessive force. Motivation remained high even amongst the IDF units that did not participate in 'special' missions. Instead, they mostly participated in *batash* duties, because they found it easy to view their constabulary duties as military and necessary ones – even more so than in the first *Intifada*.

This book has shown that despite the many factors determining the motivation/morale of combat soldiers and combat units, including those negatively affected, IDF morale as a whole did not suffer any major erosion. The ideological perception of both conflicts enabled IDF personnel to cope with ethical dilemmas and operational difficulties that could have negatively affected their combat motivation.

Ideology as the perception, as well as the narrative of the conflict has played a major role in motivating IDF soldiers and officers. If their perception of the conflict was seen by IDF personnel as unethical and politically questionable, then motivation to serve and carry out assigned duties lowered dramatically. Conversely, if IDF personnel identified their actions as militarily essential, especially if the existence of the state of Israel was ostensibly at stake (as was the case in the *Al-Aqsa Intifada*), then their motivation would remain comparatively high.

The implications of this are quite enlightening for states that are involved currently in the GWOT. Although Israel may be considered to be a unique case, in that the threat it confronts and the area in which its military operates lies at Israel's doorstep, if not in its heartland, rather than thousands of miles away and that its military is conscript and reservist-based, rather than constituted of professional volunteers, parallels can be drawn between Israel's occupation of the Territories and the US-led coalition's control/occupation of Afghanistan and Iraq, and between respective struggles to defeat (Islamic) terrorism.

Many Israelis have come to view their conflict with the Palestinians as an intercommunal one, in the context of globalisation and its effect on the narrowing gap between the centre and periphery in international relations, just as many within the Western world have come to view the GWOT as a clash of civilisations against *Al-Qaeda* and the states/societies supporting it. Although many have denied the plausibility of Samuel Huntington's book,[7] the language and standards by which Western leaders compare their societies' ethics, militaries' conduct, and general view of the role of religion in politics, in relation to those of the Islamic *Jihadist*, one can see how societal (i.e. civilisational in the global context) dimensions have gained prominence in the GWOT.[8] This has particularly been the case given that the distance between societies and their value-systems have narrowed significantly.

Additionally, those leading the GWOT at the time of writing (i.e. President George Bush and Prime Minister Tony Blair) have also interpreted 'conventional' terror as an existential threat. Consequently, just as the threshold for the use of major force has lowered in the Israeli case, it has also lowered in the case of the GWOT. In the past, major terror attacks did not warrant full-scale interventions/invasions. With Afghanistan and Iraq (and possibly Iran and Syria next),[9] a new trend has perhaps come into being.

The consequences for perceiving the war on terror as an existential and/or intercommunal war may be significant, not because of the question of whether or not the perception actually reflects reality, but whether or not it is shared by domestic constituencies, international public opinion and, most crucially, by the military forces involved in the COIN campaigns. If such a perception is shared, then the legitimacy and use of force become less problematic for governments that order such force, as well as for the military forces that have to carry out such duties.

However, if this perception becomes too far-reaching, the possibility of the GWOT moving away from a military and nation-building mission to a narrowly focused military campaign, similar to the campaign Israel carried out against the Palestinians over the last six years, may occur. This may indeed become the case if reactions to the GWOT continue to result in greater incidents of terror attacks, instability and the electoral victory of extremists within the Middle East.

11 Postscript
The Lebanon Summer War

The Second Lebanon War, conducted over the course of July–August 2006, magnified the IDF's various doctrinal and organisational deficiencies and incongruities that have affected it over the last two decades. As seen throughout this book the nature of Israeli civil–military relations, the conservative nature of the IDF in terms of its doctrinal, organisational and strategic adaptation to changing political–strategic realities have influenced the way in which it has been able to cope, on a strategic and sometimes operational level, with the threats Israel faces. The Second Lebanon War, in fact, proved to be so far the nadir of Israel's and the IDF's ability to deal with asymmetric threats that require more than just the occasional arrest, targeted killing or small-scale incursion. The much better equipped, trained and motivated *Hizbullah* fighters together with *Hizbullah*'s strategic use of missile warfare last summer proved to be a very challenging threat, which both the government and military of Israel struggled to tackle effectively.

The operational blunders and overall lacklustre performance of the IDF as well as the systemic indecisiveness displayed at the time by Prime Minister Ehud Olmert, then Defence Minister Amir Peretz and COS Lt. Gen. Dan Halutz as well as by many IDF upper echelon commanders have sent out shockwaves within the Israeli military and political establishments. The resignations of Defence Minister Peretz, COS Halutz, Northern Command head, Maj. Gen. Udi Adam amongst others as well as the establishment of numerous IDF-appointed and the government-selected Winograd Commission of inquiry, set up in order to investigate why Israel fared so poorly during the Second Lebanon War, have been but the initial materialisation of the domestic fallout instigated by the war.

The command and control, conduct and operational outcome of the IDF's offensive against *Hizbullah* in Lebanon following the killing of several as well as the abduction of two other soldiers, Eldad Regev and Ehud Goldwasser, by members of *Hizbullah*'s armed wing, *Al Muqawama* (Islamic Resistance) on 12 July 2006 led Israel to fail in achieving any major strategic goals. Prime Minister Ehud Olmert's government had set out these goals shortly after such abductions had taken place on Israeli

188 *Postscript*

territory.¹ This daring, yet unprovoked, *Hizbullah* attack involved the use of *Katyusha* rocket and mortar attacks on both Israeli military and civilian targets.

Weary of previous *Hizbullah* (and recent Palestinian) abductions and cognisant of the fact that limited responses by the IDF since its unilateral retreat from Lebanon in May 2000 had deteriorated Israel's deterrent posture in the region, both PM Olmert and Defence Minister Peretz, who have no real military experience or credentials, decided that Israel should react aggressively against *Hizbullah*. The Israeli initial response came in the guise of a precise and devastating IAF strike, which destroyed 59 of *Hizbullah*'s long-range launchers and Dahiye neighbourhood headquarters within 35 minutes. This strike, however, set in motion a tit-for-tat escalatory bombardment campaign between the IDF and *Hizbullah*, which lasted for the most part of the 33-day conflict.

Whilst the initial aerial assault eliminated, in fact, *Hizbullah*'s long-range rocket capability and, thus, spared Israel's central heartland from rocket attacks, the inability of the IAF to reduce the number of rocket attacks against Israel throughout the conflict led Israel's civilian and military leadership to desperately seek alternative solutions to the air campaign as medium- and, especially, short-range missiles were practically immune to Israeli air interdictions.²

Despite the availability of regular, and the initial mobilisation of reserve, ground forces, the IDF COS Dan Halutz, PM Olmert and Defence Minister Peretz were reluctant to order a significant ground assault, which in effect was necessary to eliminate the shorter-range, yet more portable and concealable, *Hizbullah* rocket launchers. This was due to two considerations. First, both the civilian and military leadership echelons feared that a major ground invasion would result in a large number of combat casualties and deaths. Second, COS Halutz was confident that a heavy air campaign would be adequate in compelling *Hizbullah* to stop its rocket barrages against Israel or at least, by targeting valuable Lebanese assets, convince the Lebanese government to move against *Hizbullah*. These assumptions, however, proved futile and went contrary to what the IDF had envisioned and prepared for in the case of a similar threat scenario from *Hizbullah*. According to the ex-COS Lt. Gen. Moshe Yaalon:

> In a scenario of the abduction of soldiers, exactly as occurred on July 12, the IDF was supposed to respond with an aerial attack and the mobilization of reserve divisions, which would act as a threat to the Syrians and to *Hezbollah* and would encourage Lebanon and the international community to take action to achieve the desired goal. If the threat itself did not achieve the goal, a ground move would have begun within a few days aimed primarily at seizing dominant terrain as far as the Litani River and the Nabatiya plateau. The ground entry was supposed to be carried out speedily, for an allotted time, without

the use of tanks and without entering houses or built-up areas. Because of our awareness of the anti-tank missile problem and our awareness of the bunkers and of the fact that the routes are mined, the intention was to activate the IDF in guerrilla modalities. That was the operational idea, that was the plan and that is how the forces were trained.... *Instead of sticking to the IDF's operative plan, they* [i.e. the military and political leadership echelons] *started to improvise. They improvised, improvised and then improvised again.* Instead of grabbing political achievements at the right moment, they went on with the use of force [emphasis mine].³

And yet until almost the very last stages of the conflict, and with the exception of a limited number of small Special Forces and other elite ground forces' raids into *Hizbullah* strongholds along the Israeli–Lebanese border, the IDF relied predominantly on stand-off firepower, rather than on a large-scale and assertive manoeuvre-based incursion in order to deal with the unrelenting *Hizbullah* rocket campaign. Indeed, over the course of the month the IAF carried out over 15,000 sorties, whilst artillery units fired over 150,000 shells against *Hizbullah* and Lebanese targets.

The extensive use of stand-off firepower, as noted earlier on, was based on the IDF adoption of RMA principles and practices over the last decade. By relying on precise, and not so precise, firepower the IDF hoped to compel its enemy to change its behaviour through quick and decisive effects-based operations. This, however, did not occur. Thus, only towards the end of the conflict when the UN Security Council had actually drafted a ceasefire resolution did Olmert agree to a large ground incursion up to the Litani River, around which most medium-range rockets were being fired from. The problem with this late decision to order a major invasion into Lebanon is that it was deficient of any strategic rationale given that it occurred only several hours before the ceasefire stipulated by UN Security Resolution 1701 came into effect on 14 August. It was, furthermore, a costly move that led to the deaths of a further 33 IDF soldiers.

The overall slow and hesitant IDF large-scale advance into Lebanon as well as its inability to reduce the number of *Hizbullah* rocket barrages were due to three main weaknesses. First, the indecisiveness and lack of direction from the upper political and military echelons led to the IDF's late and eventually slow deployment of ground forces in Southern Lebanon. The IDF's initial air, artillery and naval bombardment campaign was mostly the result of the COS Halutz's organisational bias for stand-off firepower provided by the air force. The IAF, in fact, carried out more than 15,000 sorties targeting over 7,000 targets in Lebanon. The Israeli Navy conducted over 2,500 bombardments off the Lebanese coast, whilst imposing a blockade of the Lebanese coast.⁴

Just like the US military, at the time of writing involved in its counter-insurgency campaigns in Iraq and Afghanistan, Israeli senior commanders have come to depend too much on firepower and hi-tech weapons systems for fighting terrorists/insurgents. Regrettably, these systems have proven to be relatively ineffective against guerrilla and terrorist insurgencies. The amount of ammunition and firepower expended against such a small and relatively weak enemy was criticised by many Israelis. According to *Yediot Ahronot* defence correspondent, Ofer Shelah, this situation was incongruous with the nature of the threat that the IDF confronted:

> Some of its basic ammunition was used so extensively (and uncontrollably) that stocks were exhausted and immediate supplies were required from within and outside Israel. A confrontation with around 1,000 men ... in a limited arena of less than ten kilometers in depth, without an enemy tank or jet, and with an adversary that barely launched any attacks ... brought Israel to a state reminiscent of the need for the airlift during the *Yom Kippur* War.[5]

Second, during the six years of ongoing counter-terror operations against the Palestinian terror and insurgency campaign, known as the *Al-Aqsa Intifada*, the IDF concentrated on refining small-unit tactics for conducting search and arrest operations and targeted killings. Moreover, the IDF spent considerable time and resources in enforcing curfews and closures throughout the Territories of the West Bank and Gaza Strip. Such operations improved the IDF's constabulary and special operations capabilities, but they severely impeded the IDF's training for non-urban guerrilla warfare and for preparing IDF units for large-scale joint-force operations.

For example, several infantry brigades that had carried out constabulary duties for long periods in the Gaza Strip were unable to coordinate artillery batteries and air cover during their advances against *Hizbullah* units in Southern Lebanon. Such coordination obviously was not needed when policing the cramped streets of Gaza City or Khan Yunis. Tank units that had grown accustomed to providing static firepower to infantry units operating in the Territories did not coordinate their movement with other units, move and shoot. In fact, many tanks remained stationary. This provided *Hizbullah* fighters armed with state-of-the-art anti-tank missiles with easy targets. Members of the 'Spearhead' elite infantry reserve brigade, on the other hand, did not know how to operate their own LAW anti-tank missile launchers and, thus, could not return fire.[6] Despite the fact that the new *Merkava MK 4* tank is considered one of the safest as well as deadliest tanks in the world, the IDF armoured corps suffered significant setbacks during its operations in Southern Lebanon. 'Twenty-two tanks sustained hits that penetrated their steel armour' leading to the death of 30 soldiers and officers and more than 100 casualties.[7]

Logistical problems also affected in part the operational tempo of certain missions and in particular the preparedness of reservist units. A lot of the combat equipment stockpiled in emergency stores for major combat operations was already being used for units operating in the Territories. Reservists from the elite *Egoz* unit, for example, were compelled to collect contributions from abroad after they were sent off into combat without flak jackets.[8] Some forward deployed units lacked basic essentials such as food and water. Reservist units lacked or had obsolete equipment, whilst some units experienced real trouble in achieving their mission due to deficiencies in basic logistical provisions. According to one soldier from the Alexandroni Brigade,

> [Their] [m]ission was to reach a position that controlled the coastal road.... But while it should have taken 36 hours, it took eight days.... We went as long as two-and-a-half days with daily rations of a can of tuna, a can of corn and a couple of pieces of bread – to share between four soldiers. So we got slowed up because 25 soldiers collapsed from dehydration and had to be evacuated.[9]

The reservist units' lack of training and essential equipment as well as the poor operational choices that ultimately led to the loss of 46 reservists appreciably eroded reservists' trust in the political and higher military echelon leadership capabilities. Attempts at reforming and improving reserve service conditions over the previous few years did not appear to have any significant effect in the context of the Second Lebanon War. Clearly the experiences of reservists during the conflict seemed to augment the disaffection that many combat reservists have felt over the last decade or so. One reservist stated, for example:

> I still have faith in my company commander, my platoon commander, my brigade commander and even the division commander, but above them, the brigadier generals and up – I've lost my faith in them. If they can't understand the importance of taking care of the simple reserve soldier who drops everything to go wherever the army tells him, to risk his life, then I can't have faith in them anymore.[10]

Statements such as the one above are quite disquieting given that the IDF still has to rely heavily on the reserves. As it discovered the hard way during the war, without proper provision of training and equipping, reserves at best operate ineffectively and at worst suffer unnecessary casualties and deaths.

Third, a dearth of intelligence on *Hizbullah*'s tactical methods and precise positions within South Lebanon meant that most units operated very cautiously in order to avoid their own casualties.[11] When tactical intelligence became available during battles it could not be taken advantage of by higher-echelon commanders due to the fact that they were ordering operations from rear-based command headquarters. According to an internal IDF committee, led by Maj. Gen. (res.) Yoram Yair, seven out of the eight brigade commanders from Division 91, which played a crucial role during the conflict, gave orders from command centres behind enemy lines instead of leading their brigades from the front as has been customary in the IDF. Confusion on the ground was compounded by the fact that brigade commanders 'did not properly understand their missions ... [and that] they did not know [what] their objectives were and how long they had to fulfil their missions.... Since the orders were not clear they were changed in some cases on an hourly basis.'[12]

Various factors are attributed to why ground commanders issued confusing and sometimes contradictory orders during the conflict. The political echelon, unable to comprehend fully what could be achieved politically through the use of the IDF in Lebanon and often overdependent and susceptible to Halutz's optimistic views on the potential for the air campaign to 'defeat' *Hizbullah*, was not able to provide the appropriate civilian and political oversight over as well as direction to the IDF's strategic mission during the war. Such hesitancy and lack of clarity affected various levels of the chain of command and even led to the replacement of Maj. Gen. Udi Adam, then head of the Northern Command, by the COS' 'personal representative', Deputy COS Maj. Gen. Moshe Kaplinsky.[13]

Confusing orders from the General Staff and down the chain of command can also be attributed, according to Avi Kober, to 'the infiltration of postmodern approaches into the officer corps training processes at the expense of classic military theory'.[14] Indeed, in order to develop the IDF's technological capabilities in keeping with its RMA transformation efforts, the IDF created 'often incomprehensible command jargon'.[15] According to another IDF committee of inquiry, headed by former IDF COS Dan Shomron, 'the ... battle doctrine and ... vague command language were so deeply embedded in the IDF's new culture that even if it had wanted to change things in the middle of the war, it wouldn't have been able to do so'.[16]

In any case, one cannot discount the level of preparedness that *Hizbullah* had achieved since 2000 with the help of both Iran and Syria. The resistance carried out by the highly professional and well-equipped guerrilla fighters proved a major challenge to IDF units. The IDF had to deal with an intricately camouflaged and reinforced foxhole and tunnel system through which *Hizbullah* fighters carried out deadly ambush attacks. *Hizbullah* preparations for war were attested by the fact that it had carved up South Lebanon into over 170 combat quadrants managed from *c.* 50 scattered command bunkers. This bunker network, situated in what many call the 'Triangle of Death' given its dense vegetation and deep crevices that allow for deadly ambushes, incorporated war rooms equipped with the best hi-tech instruments such as computers, (C3) electronics and night-vision equipment. Many IDF units found it difficult to operate amongst this bunker network as they had not received appropriate training for combat against camouflaged bunkers.

Many of the casualties that IDF units suffered were also due to the lack of knowledge on and preparation against *Hizbullah*'s anti-tank missile techniques. Several units complained that they lacked the appropriate training relevant to the combat conditions in South Lebanon. The IDF, as seen previously, has over the last 20 years struggled to maintain a thorough training regime given the extensive use of ground forces units in the Territories. As seen earlier on in the book, until very recently division-level manoeuvres have not really taken place and brigade-level manoeuvres have been rare. Most training within the IDF has been carried out at battalion level, but company-level training had become the norm since the outbreak of the *Al-Aqsa Intifada* in September 2000. This lack of relevant training led the outgoing IDF Chief Infantry and Paratroopers Officer, Brig. Gen. Yossi Hyman, to admit recently that, 'we [IDF forces] were guilty of the sin of arrogance.... I failed to prepare the infantry better for war.'[17]

Many of the infantry units fought, in fact, by using methods they had learnt and adopted whilst serving in the Territories, but which were not pertinent to the combat experienced in Lebanon.[18] For example, when dealing with the enormous number of anti-tank missiles being fired by *Hizbullah*, many soldiers instinctively took cover in the closest house. Whereas such methods worked against small weapons or machine-gun fire in the Territories, in Lebanon many soldiers were killed by *Hizbullah* anti-tank rockets that easily breached walls behind which IDF soldiers had taken cover.

The enemy the IDF was pursuing is not, in fact, a regular military that moves large divisions around. It is a small terrorist-guerrilla militia of 3,000+ highly equipped, trained and motivated *jihadist* guerrillas. And yet, the IDF was sufficiently able to learn and adapt again on a tactical level in order to inflict enough damage on *Hizbullah* strongholds and casualties so that *Hizbullah* had to change appreciably its tactics during the conflict. Following initial close-quarter combat skirmishes with the IDF, *Hizbullah* fighters were ordered to pull out from most urban areas and conduct guerrilla-style operations from the dense woods, forests and crevices within the surrounding mountainous areas.

Nonetheless, despite the IDF's last-minute large ground invasion and the IAF's continuous massive retaliatory strikes, the conflict ended only when both Israel and *Hizbullah* accepted to abide by the UN-brokered ceasefire resolution. The IDF was neither able to impose a battlefield decision in Lebanon, nor was it able, in effect, to reduce the number of *Hizbullah* rocket attacks. Whilst PM Olmert ultimately declared that Israel had achieved its goals through the creation of a reinforced UNIFIL mandate in Southern Lebanon, the fact that *Hizbullah* survived the IDF onslaught and is rearming in any case does not bode well for Israel's deterrent image within the greater Middle East.

Such a deterrent image will be hard to restore unless widespread reforms are put into action within the IDF on a: (1) doctrinal, (2) organisational and (3) cultural level. Such reforms, moreover, cannot be effective unless the nature of civilian oversight over the IDF is strengthened and more clearly delineated. As the Winograd Commission interim report stated, amongst other things, on 30 April 2007, that:

> On the political–security strategic level, the lack of preparedness was also caused by *the failure to update and fully articulate Israel's security strategy doctrine*, in the fullest sense of that term, so that it could not serve as a basis for coping comprehensively with all the challenges facing Israel [emphasis mine].[19]

Even though the IDF, under the leadership of newly appointed COS Lt. Gen. Gabi Ashkenazi, has begun implementing within the IDF organisational changes on the basis of the various committees of inquiry set up after the war,[20] until there is a full revision of Israel's national security doctrine that reflects realistically the new geo-strategic realities of the Middle East, then such organisational changes will not be fit-for-purpose, but mere short-term solutions, which if tested under taxing warfare conditions might prove again to be wanting.

Such doctrinal reform cannot occur, likewise, without the clear direction and input of the civilian leadership, which in order to do this will need to have similar strategic research and planning capabilities to those which the IDF has had until now. Hence, one of the Winograd Commission's key implementation recommendations has been that of bolstering the National Security Council in the Prime Minister's Office.[21] By providing clear leadership and strategic goals, the IDF will be able to train and plan for future conflict contingencies without having to second-guess them. With clear civilian leadership and acknowledged strategic objectives, the IDF will also avoid falling into the trap of having to seek constantly short-term tactical solutions at the expense of its long-term force preparedness.

Finally, due to its *bitsuist* ethos, the IDF has very often had a laid-back attitude towards developing long-term detailed planning, training and education programmes for the next war to come. Although this has been encouraged by the nature of civil–military relations in Israel, if the IDF is to really undergo major doctrinal and organisational changes, its organisational culture will have to go through a similar transformation process. How this complex process will be carried out goes beyond the scope of this study. Nevertheless, it will be all the more necessary if the IDF is to adapt to the increasingly unforgiving geo-strategic environment of the Middle East.

Notes

Acknowledgements

1 'Motivating soldiers: the example of the Israeli Defence Forces', *Parameters* (US Army War College Quarterly), vol. 34, no. 3 (Autumn 2004), pp. 108–21; 'The security imperative in counterterror operations: the Israeli fight against suicidal terror', *Terrorism and political violence*, vol. 17, no. 1–2 (Spring–Summer 2005), pp. 245–64 (available online at www.informaworld.com); 'The strategic impasse in low-intensity conflicts: the gap between Israeli Counter-Insurgency strategy and tactics during the *Al-Aqsa Intifada*', *Journal of Strategic Studies*, vol. 28, no. 1 (February 2005), pp. 57–75; 'Israel Defence Forces organizational changes in an era of budgetary cutbacks', *The Royal United Services Institute Journal*, vol. 149, no. 5 (October 2004), pp. 72–6; 'The Israeli-*Hezbollah* rocket war: a preliminary assessment', September 2006, *Global Strategy Forum*, www.globalstrategyforum.org/upload/upload26.pdf; 'The Israel Defence Forces' strategic and tactical adaptation to "intercommunal warfare" and its effect on troop morale', in Christopher R. Bullock and Jean-Pierre Marchant (eds), *Perspectives on war: new views on historical and contemporary security issues* (Calgary, AT: Society for Military and Strategic Studies, 2003), pp. 39–57; 'Leadership in low-intensity conflicts', in Allister MacIntyre and Karen Davis (eds), *Dimensions of military leadership* (Kingston, ON: Canadian Defence Academy Press, 2007), pp. 157–82.

1 Introduction

1 Although the IDF comprises of the naval, air and ground forces, the focus of this book will be mainly on the conduct of the IDF's ground forces, which were the most heavily involved during the two *Intifadas*.
2 Henceforth, the Occupied/Disputed Territories of the West Bank and Gaza Strip will be designated as 'the Territories'.
3 Yoram Peri, 'Israel: conscientious objection in a democracy under siege', in Charles Moskos and J.W. Chambers (eds), *The new conscientious objection: from sacred to secular resistance* (Oxford: Oxford University Press, 1993), p. 146.
4 See: Ronit Chacham, *Breaking ranks: refusing to serve in the West Bank and Gaza Strip* (New York: Other Press, 2003) and Peretz Kidron, *Refusenik! Israel's soldiers of conscience* (London: Zed Books, 2004).
5 Avi Kober, 'Low-intensity conflicts: why the gap between theory and practice?', *Defence and Security Analysis*, vol. 18, no. 1 (March 2002), p. 22.
6 Although John Mackinlay argues that the 'consequence of globalisation is that insurgencies now manifest themselves in several distinct forms, not as variations of the same form', this book maintains that the dilemmas and problems

that Western *conventional* militaries face during counter-insurgency campaigns are similar enough to reach some general conclusions regarding the complex nature of conducting missions against hostile insurgents that use a mix of terror and guerrilla tactics in order to oust what they perceive as foreign occupying forces. See: John Mackinlay, *Globalisation and insurgency*, Adelphi Paper 352 (Oxford: Oxford University Press, 2002), p. 99.

7 Notwithstanding the ongoing polemical debate on the definition of what constitutes a low-intensity conflict/war, see: Alan Stephens, 'The Transformation of "Low-intensity" Conflict', *Small Wars and Insurgencies*, vol. 5, no. 1 (Spring 1994), pp. 143–61.

8 See: Jonathan Shimshoni, *Israel and conventional deterrence: border warfare from 1953 to 1970* (Ithaca, NY: Cornell University Press, 1988).

9 Brig. Gen. Aviv Kohavi, 'Learning in a changing reality' (PowerPoint Presentation), *First International Low-Intensity Conflict Warfare Conference*, 22–25 March 2004, Tel Aviv, Israel [CD-ROM].

10 Boas Shamir and Eyal Ben-Ari, 'Leadership in an open army?, Civilian connections, interorganizational frameworks and changes in military leadership', in J.G. Hunt *et al.* (eds), *Out-of-the-box leadership: transforming the twenty-first-century army and other top-performing organisations* (Stamford, CT: JAI Press, 1999), p. 43.

11 See: Alan Baker, 'Legal and tactical dilemmas inherent in fighting terror: experience of the Israeli army in Jenin and Bethlehem' (April–May 2002), in Yoram Dinstein and Fania Domb (eds), *Israel Yearbook on Human Rights 34* (Leiden: Martinus Nijhoff Publishers, 2004), pp. 179–91; Asa Kasher and Amos Yadlin, 'Military ethics of fighting terror: an Israeli perspective', *Journal of Military Ethics*, vol. 4, no. 2 (April 2005), pp. 3–32.

12 See: Amos Yadlin, 'Ethical dilemmas in fighting terrorism', *Jerusalem Issue Brief*, vol. 4, no. 8 (25 November 2004), *Jerusalem Centre for Public Affairs*, www.jcpa.org/brief/brief004-8.htm (accessed 20 January 2005).

13 Boas Shamir and Eyal Ben-Ari, 'Leadership', p. 22.

14 Kenneth A. Romaine, 'Developing lieutenants in a transforming army', *Military Review*, vol. 84, no. 4 (July–August 2004), p. 74.

15 Col. Roi Elcabets, Head of Doctrine and Training, IDF Ground Forces Command. Interview with author, 26 August 2004, Tel Aviv, Israel.

16 In June 2000, for example, then Coordinator of Operations in the Territories, Maj. Gen Amos Gilad, declared that 'the purpose of the IDF's campaign was to reduce the level of terror, which in the scope and depth of its damage has become a strategic threat, with the first signs of threatening our existence in terms of our quality of life'. Cited in: Yehuda Wegman, 'Israel's security doctrine and the trap of "limited conflict"', *Jerusalem Viewpoints*, no. 514 (1 March 2004), *Jerusalem Centre for Public Affairs*, www.jcpa.org/jl/vp514.htm (accessed 18 March 2004).

17 Baruch Nevo and Yael Shur, *Morality, ethics and law in wartime* (Jerusalem: The Israel Democracy Institute, 2003), p. 20.

18 See: 'Dr Condoleezza Rice discusses President's national security strategy', *Presidential News and Speeches*, *The White House*, 1 October 2002, www.whitehouse.gov/news/releases/2002/10/20021001-6.html (accessed 5 August 2005).

19 See: 'Blair terror speech in full', *BBC Online*, 5 March 2004, *BBC*, http://news.bbc.co.uk/1/hi/uk_politics/3536131.stm (accessed 5 August 2005).

20 Dan Horowitz, 'A civilianized military in a partially militarized society', in Roman Kolkowitz and Andrzej Korbonski (eds), *Soldiers, Peasants and Bureaucrats* (London: George Allen and Unwin, 1982), p. 96.

Notes 197

21 See for example: 'British Army Chief condemns Abuse', *BBC News*, 19 January 2005, http://news.bbc.co.uk/go/pr/fr/-/1/hi/uk/4184279.stm (accessed 10 September 2006); Michael Evans and Anthony Loyd, 'Soldiers held for questioning over Iraq tape', *The Times*, 14 February 2006, www.timesonline.co.uk/article/0,,7374-2039266,00.html (accessed 10 September 2006); 'Iraq: one year on the human rights situation remains dire', *MDE 14/006/2004*, 18 March 2004, *Amnesty International*, 10 September 2006.
22 Former British Defence Minister stated, in February 2006 during a keynote address at King's College London, that 'Al-Qaeda has become adept at using the media to spread its messages, and to exploit any isolated transgressions by our Forces, who do act legally. There is an "asymmetry of scrutiny" in play today thanks to modern media. Our forces operate under a microscope which turns many once-tactical decisions into strategic ones.' Cited in: John Reid, 'We must be "slower to condemn, quicker to understand" the Forces', *Defence News*, 20 February 2006, www.mod.uk/DefenceInternet/Defencenews/DefencePolicyAndBusiness/WeMustBeslowerToCondemnQuickerToUnderstand TheForcesJohnReid.htm (accessed 10 September 2006).
23 See for example: Charles W. Hoge *et al.*, 'Combat duty in Iraq and Afghanistan, mental health problems, and barriers to care', *New England Journal of Medicine*, vol. 351, no. 1 (July 2004), pp. 13–22; Hamza Hendawi, 'U.S. troops in Iraq to get ethics training', *CBS News*, www.cbsnews.com/stories/2006/06/01/ap/world/mainD8HVL8EO3.shtml (accessed 1 June 2006).
24 Yoram Peri, 'Coexistence or hegemony? Shifts in the Israeli security concept', in D. Caspi *et al.* (eds), *The roots of Begin's success: the 1981 Israeli elections* (London: Croom Helm, 1984), p. 191.
25 Edward Luttwak and Dan Horowitz, *The Israeli army* (London: Allen Lane, 1975).
26 Dan Horowitz, 'The Israeli concept of national security', in Avner Yaniv (ed.), *National security and democracy in Israel* (London: Lynne Rienner, 1993), p. 30.
27 Ariel Levite, *Offence and defence in Israeli military doctrine* (Boulder, CO: Westview Press, 1989).
28 Ibid. pp. 157–62.
29 Israel Tal, *National security: the Israeli experience* (London: Praeger, 2000).
30 Ibid. pp. 223 and 227.
31 Ibid. p. 227.
32 Mark A. Heller, *Continuity and change in Israeli security policy*, Adelphi Paper 335 (Oxford: Oxford University Press, July 2000), p. 7.
33 Mark A. Heller, *Continuity and change*, p. 52.
34 Heller defines this struggle as the 'internationalist – backlash' (i.e. ethnonationalist) contest. See: Mark A. Heller, *Continuity and change*, pp. 57–69.
35 Yaakov Hasdai, '"Doers" and "Thinkers" in the IDF', *The Jerusalem Quarterly*, no. 24 (Summer 1982), p. 19.
36 As tackled by, for example: Gabriel Ben-Dor *et al.*, 'Israel's national security doctrine under strain: the crisis of the reserve army', *Armed Forces and Society*, vol. 28. no. 2 (Winter 2002), pp. 233–55; Stuart A. Cohen, 'The Israel Defense Forces (IDF): From a "people's army" to a "professional military" – causes and implications', *Armed Forces and Society*, vol. 21, no. 2 (Winter 1995), pp. 237–54; Stuart A. Cohen, 'Military service in Israel: no longer a cohesive force?' *The Jewish Journal of Sociology*, vol. 39, no. 1–2 (1997), pp. 5–23.
37 According to Chris Demchak, 'if the widespread presumption is that some kind of threat is always imminent in unpredictable ways, then improvisation as a

cultural norm is also consistent with a widespread military need to provide novel responses unpredictable in advance'. Cited in: Chris Demchak, 'Technology's knowledge burden, the RMA, and the IDF: organizing the hypertext organization for future "wars of disruption"?', *Journal of Strategic Studies*, vol. 24, no. 2 (June 2001), p. 105.
38 Emanuel Wald, *The Wald report: the decline of Israeli national security since 1967* (Boulder, CO: Westview Press, 1992), p. 187.
39 See: Allan D. English, *Understanding military culture: a Canadian perspective* (London: McGill-Queen's University Press, 2004), pp. 10–38.
40 See: Terry Terriff and Theo Farrell, *The sources of military change: norms, politics, technology* (Boulder, CO: Lynne Rienner, 2002); Peter J. Katzenstein (ed.) in *The culture of national security: norms and identity in world politics* (NY: Columbia UP, 1996), pp. 33–74.
41 Robert M. Cassidy, 'Back to the street without joy: counterinsurgency lessons from Vietnam and other small wars', *Parameters*, vol. 34, no. 2 (Summer 2004), pp. 73–83.
42 Elizabeth Kier, 'Culture and military doctrine: France between the wars', *International Security*, vol. 19, no. 4 (Spring 1995), pp. 67–71.
43 Clive Jones, 'A reach greater than the grasp': Israeli intelligence and the conflict in South Lebanon 1990–2000, *Intelligence and National Security*, vol. 16, no. 3 (Autumn 2001), pp. 1–26.
44 Ann Swidler, 'Culture in action: symbols and strategies', *American Sociological Review*, vol. 51, no. 2 (April 1986), p. 273.
45 Terry Terriff, ' "Innovate or Die": organizational culture and the origins of maneuver warfare in the United States Marine Corps', *Journal of Strategic Studies*, vol. 29, no. 3 (June 2006), pp. 475–503.
46 Yaacov Hasdai, ' "Doers" and "Thinkers" ', pp. 13–25.
47 Eliot Cohen *et al.*, '*Knives, tanks, and missiles': Israel's security revolution* (Washington, DC: Washington Institute for Near East Policy, 1998), p. 69. Shimon Naveh argues that even on the operational level the IDF has never had an operational doctrine. See: Shimon Naveh, 'The cult of offensive preemption and future challenges for Israeli operational thought', in Efraim Karsh (ed.), *Between war and peace: dilemmas of Israeli security* (London: Frank Cass, 1996), pp. 168–87.
48 Eliot Cohen *et al.*, '*Knives*', p. 68.
49 Ze'ev Drory, *Israel's reprisal policy 1953–1956: the dynamics of military retaliation* (London: Frank Cass, 2005), pp. 4, 32.
50 John A. Nagl, *Counter-insurgency lessons from Malaya and Vietnam: learning to eat soup with a knife* (London: Praeger, 2002), p. 29.
51 Amos Perlmutter, 'The dynamic of Israeli national security decision making', in Robert J. Art *et al.* (eds), *Reorganising America's defence: leadership in war and peace* (Washington, DC: Pergamon-Brassey's, 1985), p. 131.
52 See: Gabriel Sheffer, 'Has Israel been a garrison democracy? Sources of change in Israel's democracy', *Israel Affairs*, vol. 3, no. 1 (Autumn 1996), pp. 13–38.
53 See: Robin A. Luckham, 'A comparative typology of civil–military relations', *Government and Opposition*, vol. 6, no. 1 (1971), pp. 5–35.
54 See: Moshe Lissak, 'The permeable boundaries between civilians and soldiers in Israeli society', in Daniella Ashkenazy (ed.), *The military in the service of society and democracy* (London: Greenwood Press), pp. 56–68.
55 Dan Horowitz, 'A Civilianized Military', pp. 77–106.
56 See also: Ranan D. Kuperman, 'Who should authorize the IDF to initiate a military operation? A brief history of an unresolved debate', *Israel Affairs*, vol. 11, no. 4 (October 2005), pp. 672–94.

57 Ze'ev Schiff and Ehud Ya'ari, *Intifada*: the Palestinian uprising – Israel's third front (London: Simon and Schuster, 1990).
58 Efraim Inbar, 'Israel's small war: the military response to the *Intifada*', *Armed Forces and Society*, vol. 18, no. 1 (Fall 1991), pp. 29–50; Aryeh Shalev, *The Intifada: causes and effects*, Jaffee Centre for Strategic Studies Study no. 16 (Oxford: Westview Press, 1991).
59 See: Martin Van Creveld, *The sword and the olive: a critical history of the Israeli Defence Forces* (New York: Public Affairs, 1998) and Stuart A. Cohen, 'How did the *Intifada* affect the IDF?' *Conflict Quarterly*, vol. 14 (Summer 1994), pp. 7–22.
60 Yaacov Bar-Siman-Tov *et al.*, *The Israeli–Palestinian violent confrontation 2000–2004: from conflict resolution to conflict management* (Jerusalem: Jerusalem Institute for Israel Studies, 2005), p. 60.
61 Yoram Peri, *Between battles and bullets: Israeli military in politics* (Cambridge: Cambridge University Press, 1983), p. 1.
62 For the rationale of selecting a qualitative research approach see: Simeon J. Yates, *Doing social science research* (London: Sage, 2004), pp. 135–6; Catherine Marshal and Gretchen B. Robertson, *Designing qualitative research* (London: Sage, 1989), p. 46.
63 Some concepts were expressed in Hebrew, which were translated verbatim during transcription.
64 Certain events and statistics, particularly those regarding deaths and casualties, which have often been inflated by Palestinian or overlooked by Israeli sources, were normally cross-referenced with other sources of such information in order to ensure their validity. When significant disparity existed between various sources, this was highlighted in the book.
65 Although I will use the concept of 'intercommunal warfare', which has been used previously by Gad Barzilai and Anthony Horowitz, to define the nature of the Israeli–Palestinian conflict (see below), Clive Jones has pointed out how difficult it is to define the Israeli–Palestinian conflict without limiting one's full understanding of the dynamics of the conflict itself. See: Clive Jones, 'A framework for analysis', in Clive Jones and Ami Pedahzur (eds), *Between terrorism and civil war: the Al-Aqsa Intifada* (London: Routledge, 2005), pp. 1–8.

2 Combat motivation

1 Reuven Gal, *A portrait of the Israeli soldier* (London: Greenwood, 1986), p. 151.
2 Nora K. Stewart, 'Military cohesion', in Lawrence Freedman (ed.), *War* (Oxford: Oxford University Press, 1994), p. 148.
3 Daniel E. Liddell, 'Operational art and the influence of will', *Marine Corps Gazette* (February 1998), vol. 82, no. 2, p. 52.
4 Carl Von Clausewitz, Michael Howard and Peter Paret (eds), *On war* (Princeton, NJ: Princeton University Press, 1976), p. 75.
5 On the nature of the revolution in military affairs and the debate relating to its potential to change the modern battlefield see: Thierry Gongora and Harald von Riekhoff (eds), *Toward a revolution in military affairs?: defence and security at the dawn of the twenty-first century* (London: Greenwood Press, 2000); Eliot A. Cohen, 'Change and transformation in military affairs', *Journal of Strategic Studies*, vol. 27, no. 3 (Sep 2004), pp. 395–407.
6 Brian R. Reinwald, 'Retaining the moral element of war', *Military Review*, vol. 78, no. 1 (January–February 1998), p. 69.
7 William J. Harkins, 'Honing all marines' psychological edge for combat', *Marine Corps Gazette*, vol. 83, no. 10 (October 1999), p. 27.

8 Frederick J. Manning, 'Morale, cohesion and *esprit de corps*', in Reuven Gal and David A. Mangelsdorff (eds), *Handbook of military psychology* (Chichester: John Wiley & Sons, 1991), p. 455.
9 Reuven Gal, 'Unit morale: from a theoretical puzzle to an empirical illustration – an Israeli example', *Journal of Applied Social Psychology*, vol. 6, no. 6 (1986), p. 550.
10 Frederick J. Manning, 'Morale', p. 454.
11 William D. Henderson, *Cohesion: the human element in combat* (Washington, DC: National Defence University Press, 1985), p. 4.
12 Reuven Gal, *A portrait*, p. 235.
13 See: 'Doctrine', *IDF Spokesperson's Office*, <www.idf.il/english/doctrine/doctrine.stm (accessed on 15 December 2003).
14 Reuven Gal, *A portrait*, p. 235.
15 William L. Hauser, 'The will to fight', in Sam C. Sarkesian (ed.), *Combat effectiveness: cohesion, stress, and the volunteer military* (London: Sage, 1980), p. 190.
16 See: Roy F. Baumeister and Mark R. Leary, 'The need to belong: desire for interpersonal attachments as a fundamental human motivation', *Psychology Bulletin*, vol. 117, no. 3 (1985), pp. 497–529.
17 Eyal Ben-Ari, 'Masks and soldiering: the Israeli army and the Palestinian uprising', in Edna Lomsky-Feder and Eyal Ben-Ari (eds), *The military and militarism in Israeli society* (Albany: State University of New York Press, 1999), p. 172.
18 Anthony Kellett, *Combat motivation: the behaviour of soldiers in battle* (London: Kluwer Publishing, 1984), p. 250.
19 'The human being's human doctrine', *Soldiers' Rights Commissioner*, www.idf.il/english/organization/nakhal/kavod.stm (accessed 17 December 2003).
20 Reuven Gal, 'Unit morale', p. 558.
21 Capt. (Res.) Shahar Amit, Platoon Commander, IDF Paratroopers Brigade. Interview with author, 20 August 2004, Tel Aviv, Israel.
22 Donald M. Bradshaw, 'Combat stress casualties: a commander's influence', *Military Review*, vol. 75, no. 4 (July–August 1995), p. 20.
23 Avigdor Kahalani, *A warrior's way* (Bnei Brak: Steimatzky, 1999), p. 141.
24 See: Reuven Gal, 'Unit morale', p. 560.
25 Eric Ouellet, 'Low-intensity conflicts and military leadership: the Canadian experience', *Low Intensity Conflict and Law Enforcement*, vol. 10, no. 3 (Autumn 2001), p. 80.
26 See: Victor E. Frankl, *Man's search for meaning* (New York, NY: Pocket Books, 1963).
27 Micha Popper, 'Leadership in military combat units and business organisations: a comparative psychological analysis', *Journal of Managerial Psychology*, vol. 11, no. 1 (February 1996), p. 17.
28 Leonard Wong *et al.*, *Why they fight: combat motivation in the Iraq war* (Carlisle, PA: Strategic Studies Institute, July 2003), pp. 24 and 28.
29 Leonard Wong *et al.*, *Why they fight*, p. 24. For an analysis of the effects that downsizing has on those left behind in the US Army, see: Leonard Wong and Jeffrey McNally, 'Downsizing the army: some policy implications affecting the survivors', *Armed Forces and Society*, vol. 20 (Winter 1994), pp. 199–216.
30 See: Frederick J. Manning *et al.*, 'An investigation into the value of unit cohesion in peacetime', in Gregory Belenky (ed.), *Contemporary studies in combat psychiatry* (London: Greenwood Press, 1987), p. 49.
31 Nora K. Stewart, 'Military cohesion', p. 147.
32 Clark Brown, 'Cohesion', *Infantry Magazine* (March–April 1982), p. 10.

33 Daniel F. Sullivan, 'The platoon leader: keys to success', *Infantry Magazine* (May–June 1989), p. 14.
34 'Combat stress reaction is a condition in which soldiers are unable to perform their duty because of extreme situational psychological disturbance.' Cited in: Zahava Solomon *et al.*, 'Effects of social support and battle intensity on loneliness and breakdown during combat', *Journal of Personality and Social Psychology*, vol. 51, no. 6 (December 1986), pp. 1269 and 1273.
35 Reuven Gal, *A portrait*, p. 154. For an account of battle stress and combat reactions see also: Reuven Gal, *A portrait*, pp. 207–30.
36 Gregory Belenky *et al.*, 'Battle stress, morale, cohesion, combat effectiveness, heroism and psychiatric casualties: the Israeli experience', in Gregory Belenky (ed.), *Contemporary studies in combat psychiatry* (London: Greenwood Press, 1987), p. 15.
37 Eyal Ben-Ari, *Mastering soldiers: conflict, emotions, and the enemy in an Israeli military unit* (Oxford: Berghahn Books, 1998), p. 98.
38 Ibid.
39 Willam D. Henderson, *Cohesion*, p. 17.
40 Robert J. Rielly, 'Confronting the tiger: small unit cohesion in battle', *Military Review*, vol. 80, no. 6 (November–December 2000), p. 63.
41 Mark H. Gerner, 'Leadership at the operational level', *Military Review*, vol. 67, no. 6 (June 1987), p. 30.
42 Samuel L.A. Marshall, *Men against fire* (New York: William Morrow and Company, 1947), p. 161.
43 On the transformation of Israeli society and the effect that it had on its national security consensus and Zionist ethos see, for example: Judith Elizur, 'The fracturing of the Jewish self-image: the end of "we are one"?', vol. 8, no. 1–2 (Autumn/Winter 2002), pp. 14–30; Lilly Weissbrod, 'Israeli Identity in Transition', *Israel Affairs*, vol. 3, no. 1 (Autumn 1996), pp. 47–65.
44 Israel Tal, 'National security', *Israel Defense Forces Journal*, vol. 1, no. 3 (August 1983), p. 40.
45 Since the Lebanon War, the Arab–Israeli conflict has reverted to an extent from a purely interstate conflict to an intercommunal one involving Israel and the Palestinians, similar to the conflict that existed between Jews and Arabs prior to the 1948 establishment of the state of Israel. According to Horowitz, 'an intercommunal conception of the conflict implies the lack of a territorial demarcation line separating the two communities which could prevent the friction resulting from daily, direct interaction between members of the two groups'. Dan Horowitz and Moshe Lissak, *Trouble in utopia: the overburdened polity of Israel* (New York: Suny Press, 1989), p. 199. See also: Shmuel Sandler and Hillel Frisch, *Israel, the Palestinians and the West Bank: a study in intercommunal conflict* (Toronto: Lexington Books, 1984), pp. 3–12.
46 Frederick J. Manning, "Morale, cohesion and *esprit de corps*', in Reuven Gal and David A. Mangelsdorff (eds), *Handbook of military psychology* (Chichester: John Wiley & Sons, 1991), p. 460.
47 Thomas W. Britt, 'Responsibility, commitment and morale', *Military Review*, vol. 78, no. 1 (January–February 1998), p. 79.
48 Baruch Nevo and Yael Shur, *The IDF and the press during hostilities* (Jerusalem: The Israel Democracy Institute, 2003), p. 74.
49 John Keegan and Richard Holmes, *Soldiers: a history of men in battle* (London: Sphere Books, 1985), p. 52.
50 See: Eyal Ben-Ari, 'Masks and soldiering: the Israeli army and the Palestinian uprising', *Cultural Anthropology*, vol. 4, no. 4 (November 1989), pp. 372–89.

3 Political–military relations

1. Moshe Lissak, 'Civilian components in the national security doctrine', in Avner Yaniv (ed.), *National security and democracy in Israel* (London: Lynne Rienner, 1993), p. 58.
2. Amos Perlmutter, 'Israel: the routinized revolutionary army', in Amos Perlmutter (ed.), *The military and politics in modern times: on professionals, praetorians and revolutionary soldiers* (London: Yale University Press, 1977), p. 253.
3. For a detailed account of the pre-state Israeli militias and of civil–military relations during the *Yishuv* era, see: Amir Bar-Or, 'The Evolution of the Army's Role in Israeli Strategic Planning: a documentary record', *Israel Studies*, vol. 1, no. 2 (Fall 1996), pp. 98–121; Yoav Gelber, 'Ben-Gurion and the formation of the Israel Defence Forces, 1947–1948', in Ronald W. Zweig (ed.), *David Ben-Gurion: politics and leadership in Israel* (London: Frank Cass, 1991), pp. 193–215.
4. Natanel Lorch, *Major Knesset debates 1948–1981*, vol. 1 (Lanham, MD: University Press of America, 1993), p. 135.
5. Yoram Peri, 'Civilian control during a protracted war', in Ernest Krausz (ed.), *Politics and society in Israel: studies in Israeli society*, vol. 3 (Oxford: Transaction Books, 1985), p. 363.
6. Amos Perlmutter, *Military and politics in Israel: nation building and role expansion* (London: Frank Cass, 1969), p. 55.
7. Victor Azarya and Baruch Kimmerling, 'New immigrants in the Israeli armed forces', *Armed Forces and Society*, vol. 6, no. 3 (Spring 1980), pp. 455–6.
8. Avraham Avi-hai, *Ben-Gurion state-builder: principles and pragmatism* (New York: John Wiley and Sons, 1974), p. 142.
9. On immigration statistics, see: Victor Azarya and Baruch Kimmerling, 'New immigrants', p. 458.
10. For an overview of the IDF's educational activities see: Daniella Ashkenazy, 'Mainstreaming marginal populations through military service', in Daniella Ashkenazy (ed.), *The military in the service of society and democracy: the challenge of a dual-role military* (London: Greenwood Press, 1992), pp. 157–64.
11. Ehud Gross, 'Military, democracy and education', in Daniella Ashkenazy (ed.), *The military in the service of society and democracy: the challenge of the dual-role military* (London: Greenwood Press, 1994), p. 61.
12. Mordechai Bar-On, 'Small wars, big wars: security debates during Israel's first decade', *Israel Studies*, vol. 5, no. 2 (Fall 2000), p. 113.
13. See: 'The *Nahal* brigade', *IDF Spokesperson's Office*, www.idf.il/english/organization/nahal/nahal.stm (accessed 19 November 2002).
14. Peter Y. Medding, *The founding of Israeli democracy 1948–1967* (Oxford: Oxford University Press, 1990), p. 135.
15. Avraham Avi-hai, *Ben-Gurion state-builder*, p. 144.
16. Yaron Ezrahi, *Rubber bullets: power and conscience in modern Israel* (New York: Farrar, Straus and Giroux, 1997), p. 157.
17. Dan Horowitz and Baruch Kimmerling, 'Some social implications of military service and the reserves system in Israel', *European Journal of Sociology*, vol. 15, no. 1 (1974), p. 265.
18. Sara Helman, 'Militarism and the construction of the life-world of Israeli males', in Edna Lomsky-Feder and Eyal Ben-Ari (eds), *The military and militarism in Israeli society* (Albany, NY: State University of New York Press, 2000), pp. 197–8.
19. Daniel Shimshoni, *Israeli democracy: the middle of the journey* (New York: Free Press, 1982), p. 186.
20. The promotion of military personnel to the rank of colonel or above as well as

appointments to important IDF posts require the approval of the prime minister and defence minister.
21 See: Yoram Peri, 'The first and second careers of Israel army officers', *Public Administration in Israel and Abroad*, vol. 14 (1974), pp. 106–22.
22 Daniel Maman and Moshe Lissak, 'Military–civilian élite networks in Israel: a case study of boundary structure', in Benjamin Frankel (ed.), *A restless mind: essays in honor of Amos Perlmutter* (London: Frank Cass, 1996), pp. 67–8.
23 Daniel Maman and Moshe Lissak, 'Military–civilian élite networks', pp. 71–2.
24 See: Maier Asher, 'Mrs Meir enlists generals', *Daily Telegraph*, 11 January 1972, p. 9.
25 Yossi Beilin, *Israel: a concise political history* (London: Weidenfeld and Nicolson, 1992), p. 208.
26 'Mofaz sworn in as defence minister, Sharon survives no-confidence', *Jerusalem Post*, 4 November 2002.
27 Ilan Marciano, 'Civil–military reform bill OK'd', *Yediot Ahronot*, 10 July 2005.
28 Since the start of the 1970s around 10 per cent of *Knesset* members and 20 per cent of government ministers have been retired senior military officers. See: Yoram Peri, *The Israeli military and Israel's Palestinian policy: from Oslo to the Al-Aqsa Intifada*, Peaceworks no. 47 (Washington, DC: United States Institute for Peace, November 2002), note 2, p. 58.
29 Jacob C. Hurewitz, *Middle East politics: the military dimension* (Boulder, CO: Westview Press, 1982), pp. 372–3.
30 Baruch Kimmerling, 'The code of security: the Israeli military–cultural complex', in Baruch Kimmerling (ed.), *The invention and decline of Israeliness: state, society and the military* (London: University of California Press, 2001), p. 217.
31 Yoram Peri, *Between battles and bullets: Israeli military in politics* (Cambridge: Cambridge University Press, 1983), pp. 42–3.
32 Cited in: Yoram Peri, *Generals in the cabinet room: how the military shapes Israeli policy* (Washington, DC: United States Institute of Peace Press, 2006), pp. 21–2.
33 Uri Ben-Eliezer, *The making of Israeli militarism* (Bloomington, IN: Indiana University Press, 1998), pp. 10–15.
34 Yoram Peri, 'The political–military complex: the IDF's influence over policy towards the Palestinians since 1987', *Israel Affairs*, vol. 11, no. 2 (April 2005), p. 331.
35 See: Yoram Peri, 'The political–military complex', pp. 332–3.
36 Ian Murray, 'Kimche attacks defence ministry influence on Israel foreign policy', *Times*, 16 October 1986.
37 Yoram Peri, 'Civilian control', p. 370.
38 Yehuda Ben-Meir, *Political–military relations in Israel* (New York: Columbia University Press, 1995), p. 144.
39 An initial crisis between the upper military and civilian echelons actually occurred during Ben-Gurion's short break from Israeli politics in 1954 when an IDF intelligence unit carried out an unsuccessful sabotage mission in Egypt, which had not been officially sanctioned by then Defence Minister Pinhas Lavon. For a full analysis of the 'Lavon Affair' see: Uri Bar-Joseph, *Intelligence intervention in the politics of democratic states: the United States, Israel, and Britain* (University Park, Pennsylvania: Pennsylvania State University Press, 1995), pp. 149–254.
40 For a compelling account of the waiting period see: Michael Oren, *Six days of war: June 1967 and the making of the modern Middle East* (London: Penguin Books, 2003).

41 See: Yoram Peri, *Between battles*, p. 245.
42 See: Ariel Sharon, *Warrior: an autobiography* (London: Simon and Schuster, 2001), pp. 218–27.
43 Eric Silver, 'General Sharon can remain a candidate in Israeli elections', *Guardian*, 28 December 1973.
44 Yoram Peri, *Between battles*, p. 118.
45 See: Ephraim Kahana, 'Early warning versus concept: the case of the Yom Kippur war 1973', *Intelligence and National Security*, vol. 17, no. 2 (June 2002), pp. 81–104 and Uri Bar-Joseph, *The watchman fell asleep* (New York: State University of New York Press, 2005).
46 Andrew H. Dank, 'Israel's surprise in 1973 (should it have happened?)', 1 April 1984, *Global Security*, www.globalsecurity.org/military/library/report/1984/DAH.htm (accessed 6 December 2002).
47 Charles Holley, 'Israel after Agranat', *Middle East* (September 1977), pp. 26–7.
48 Yoram Peri, 'Civilian control', p. 371.
49 The Basic Law in essence set down the institutional relationship between the civilian and military leadership echelons, reiterated the subordination of the IDF to the civil authority. 'Basic law: the army', *The Jewish Virtual Library*, www.us-israel.org/jsource/Politics/Basic_Law_Army.html (accessed 6 December 2002).
50 Yehuda Ben-Meir, *Political–military relations*, p. 148.
51 See: Avner Yaniv, *Dilemmas of security: politics, strategy and the Israeli experience in Lebanon* (Oxford: Oxford University Press, 1987), pp. 134–5.
52 'Sharon vs. The army', *Times*, 11 October 1982, p. 20.
53 Michal Yudelman, 'Berman: Sharon misled all of us', *Jerusalem Post*, 6 November 1997.
54 Cited in: Richard A. Gabriel, *Operation 'Peace for Galilee': The Israeli–PLO war in Lebanon* (New York: Free Press, 1982), p. 158.
55 Yehuda Ben-Meir, *Political–military relations*, p. 156.
56 Dan Horowitz, 'A civilianized military in a partially militarized society', in Roman Kolkowitz and Andrzej Korbonski (eds), *Soldiers, peasants and bureaucrats* (London: George Allen and Unwin, 1982), p. 79.

4 National security doctrine

1 Michael Howard, 'The forgotten dimensions of strategy', *Foreign Affairs*, vol. 57, no. 5 (Summer 1979), p. 975.
2 Basil H. Liddell-Hart, *Strategy: the indirect approach* (London: Faber, 1967), p. 334.
3 Ariel Levite, *Offence and defence in Israeli Military Doctrine* (Boulder, CO: Westview Press, 1989), pp. 9–10.
4 Carl Von Clausewitz, Michael Howard and Peter Paret (eds), *On War* (Princeton, NJ: Princeton University Press, 1976), p. 87.
5 See: Robert E. Osgood, *NATO: the entangling alliance* (Chicago: University of Chicago Press, 1962), p. 5.
6 Yoram Peri, 'Coexistence or hegemony? Shifts in the Israeli security concept', in D. Caspi *et al.* (eds), *The roots of Begin's success: the 1981 Israeli elections* (London: Croom Helm, 1984), p. 191.
7 Israel Tal, *National security: the Israeli experience* (London: Praeger, 2000), p. viii.
8 Moshe Lissak, 'Civilian components in the national security doctrine', in Avner Yaniv (ed.), *National security and democracy in Israel* (London: Lynne Rienner, 1993), p. 64.

9 Michael Handel, *Israel's political–military doctrine*, Occasional Papers in International Affairs no. 30 (Harvard, MA: Harvard University Press, 1973), p. 69.
10 Reuven Pedatzur, 'Ben-Gurion's enduring legacy', in Daniel Bar-Tal *et al.* (eds), *Security concerns: insights from the Israeli experience* (London: JAI Press, 1998), p. 139.
11 John A. Nagl, *Counter-insurgency lessons from Malaya and Vietnam: learning to eat soup with a knife* (London: Praeger, 2002), p. 35.
12 Reuven Pedatzur, 'Ben-Gurion's enduring legacy', p. 140.
13 Ze'ev Drory, *Israel's reprisal policy 1953–1956: the dynamics of military retaliation* (London: Frank Cass, 2005), p. 41.
14 Moshe Lissak, 'Civilian components', p. 57.
15 See: Yagil Levy, 'Military doctrine and political participation: toward a sociology of strategy', January 1996, www.ciaonet.org/wps/ley02/index.html (accessed 28 December 2004).
16 Yigal Allon, *The making of Israel's army* (London: Vallentine, Mitchell, 1970), p. 101.
17 Zvi Lanir, 'Political aims and military objectives – some observations on the Israeli experience', in Zvi Lanir (ed.), *Israeli security planning in the 1980s: its politics and economics* (Eastbourne: Praeger, 1984), p. 17.
18 David Ben-Gurion, *Recollections* (London: Macdonald Unit 75, 1970), p. 66.
19 Zvi Lanir, 'Political aims', p. 24.
20 See: Gil Merom, 'Israel's national security and the myth of exceptionalism', *Political Science Quarterly*, vol. 114, no. 3 (Autumn 1999), pp. 409–34.
21 Dan Horowitz, 'Is Israel a garrison state?', *The Jerusalem Quarterly*, no. 4 (Summer 1977), p. 68.
22 David Rodman, 'Israel's national security doctrine: an appraisal of the past and a vision of the future', *Israel Affairs*, vol. 9, no. 4 (June 2003), p. 117.
23 That is, after 1967.
24 Gunther E. Rothenberg, 'Israeli Defence Forces and Low-Intensity operations', in David A. Charters and Maurice Tugwell (eds), *Armies in Low-Intensity Conflict: a comparative analysis* (London: Brassey's Defence Publishers, 1989), p. 56.
25 Michael Walzer, *Just and unjust wars* (New York: Basic Books, 1977), p. 216.
26 Gunther E. Rothenberg, 'Israeli defence', p. 56.
27 Foreign Broadcast Information Service, 'Rabin Addresses Knesset on Terrorism', *Tel Aviv IDF Radio*, 1404 GMT, 21 October 1985, p. 16.
28 For a detailed account of Israel's strategy of deterrence and its centrality to its strategic thinking, see: Uri Bar-Joseph, 'Variations on a theme: the conceptualisation of deterrence in Israeli strategic thinking', *Security Studies*, vol. 7, no. 3 (Spring 1998), pp. 145–81.
29 See, for example: Stuart A. Cohen and Efraim Inbar, 'Varieties of counter-insurgency activities: Israel's military operations against the Palestinians, 1948–1990', *Small Wars and Insurgencies*, vol. 2, no. 1 (April 1991), pp. 41–60.
30 David Rodman, 'Combined arms warfare in the Israel Defence Forces: an historical overview', *Defence Studies*, vol. 2, no. 1 (Spring 2002), p. 123.
31 David Ben-Gurion, *Recollections*, pp. 70 and 73.
32 Aaron Wolf, *A purity of arms: an American in the Israeli army* (New York: Doubleday, 1989), p. 72.
33 Yigal Allon, *The making of Israel's army*, p. 50.
34 Moshe Dayan, *Story of my life* (London: Weidenfeld and Nicolson, 1976), p. 369.

35 Ariel Levite, *Offence and defence*, p. 28.
36 Efraim Inbar, 'The "no choice war" debate in Israel', *Journal of Strategic Studies*, vol. 12, no. 1 (March 1989), p. 24.
37 Cited in: Emanuel Wald, *The Wald report: the decline of Israeli national security since 1967* (Boulder, CO: Westview Press, 1992), pp. 217–18.
38 John. A. Nagl, *Counter-insurgency*, p. 27.
39 Ze'ev Drory, *Israel's reprisal policy*, p. 4.
40 According to Gen. Israel Tal, 'staying power expresses the total human and material resources of a nation, the size of its territory, its geopolitical situation, its spiritual, technological and political values and assets, and above all, the degree of motivation'.... Strike [i.e. assault] power means "national military strength".' Cited in: Moshe Lissak, 'Civilian components', p. 55.
41 Samuel Rolbant, *The Israeli soldier: profile of an army* (London: South Brunswick, 1970), p. 69.
42 Ariel Levite, *Offence and defence*, p. 36.
43 See: Arye Naor, 'The security argument in the territorial debate in Israel: rhetoric and policy', *Israel Studies*, vol. 4, no. 2 (Fall 1999), pp. 150–77.
44 Arye Naor, 'The security argument', p. 151.
45 David Newman, 'The geographical and territorial imprint on the security discourse', in David Bar-Tal *et al.* (eds), *Security concerns: insights from the Israeli experience* (London: JAI Press, 1998), p. 75.
46 See: Gal Luft, 'All quiet on the eastern front? Israel's national security doctrine after the fall of Saddam', *Analysis Paper no. 2* (Washington, DC: Saban Center for Middle East Policy, March 2004).
47 Dan Horowitz, 'The Israeli concept of national security', in Avner Yaniv (ed.), *National security and democracy in Israel* (London: Lynne Rienner, 1993), pp. 14 and 15.
48 Yitzhak Rabin, *The Rabin memoirs* (London: Weidenfeld and Nicolson, 1979), p. 79.
49 David Ben-Gurion, *Recollections*, p. 73.
50 Moshe Dayan, *Story of my life*, p. 141.
51 Shimon Naveh, 'The cult of the offensive preemption and future challenges for Israeli operational thought', in Efraim Karsh (ed.), *Between war and peace: dilemmas of Israeli security* (London: Frank Cass, 1996), p. 177.
52 Zvi Lanir, 'Political aims', p. 23.
53 'Former Egyptian President, Gamal Abdel Nasser, is attributed with the quip that a state whose newspapers publish on their front pages the photograph and biography of each of its fallen soldiers is unlikely to be able to cope with a war of attrition.' Cited in: Avi Kober, 'A paradigm in crisis? Israel's doctrine of military decision', in Efraim Karsh (ed.), *Between war and peace: dilemmas of Israeli security* (London: Frank Cass, 1996), p. 193. Such sensitivity has increased over the years.
54 See: Avi Kober, 'From *blitzkrieg* to attrition: Israel's attrition strategy and staying power', *Small Wars and Insurgencies*, vol. 16, no. 2 (June 2005), p. 220.
55 Yigal Allon, *The making of Israel's army*, p. 99. See also: Yigal Allon, 'Israel: the case for defensible borders', *Foreign Affairs*, vol. 55, no. 1 (October 1976), pp. 38–53.
56 Cited in: Jonathan Shimshoni, *Israel and conventional deterrence*, p. 195.
57 See: Robert S. Bolia, 'Israel and the War of Attrition', *Military Review*, vol. 84, no. 2 (March–April 2004), pp. 47–51 and Israel Tal, *National security*, pp. 150–4.
58 Zvi Lanir, 'Political aims', p. 29.

59 Anthony H. Cordesman and Abraham R. Wagner, *The lessons of modern war: the Arab–Israeli conflicts, 1973–1989* (London: Mansell Publishing, 1990), p. 42.
60 David Ben-Gurion and Moshe Pearlman, *Ben-Gurion looks back in talks with Moshe Pearlman* (London: Weidenfeld and Nicolson, 1965), p. 136.
61 Stuart A. Cohen, *Towards a new portrait of the (new) Israeli soldier, security and policy studies 35* (Ramat Gan: Bar-Ilan University Press, 1997), p. 83.
62 Anthony H. Cordesman, *Perilous prospects: the peace process and the Arab–Israeli military balance* (Oxford: Westview Press, 1996), p. 76.
63 These were mainly new immigrants until the early 1960s. Between 15 May 1948 and the end of 1960, 968,700 Jews immigrated to Israel. Thus, by 1960 new immigrants comprised 50.7 per cent of the total Israeli Jewish population in Israel (1,911,200). See: *Statistical abstract of Israel 2004, no. 55* (Jerusalem: Central Bureau of Statistics, 2004), pp. 2–11.
64 Ephraim Halevy, National Security Advisor. Interview with author, Jerusalem, Israel, 19 August 2003.
65 Ultra-Orthodox (*Haredi*) Jewish *Yeshiva* students and Ultra-Orthodox religious women are exempted from compulsory military service.
66 Reuven Gal, 'The IDF structural model', in Daniella Ashkenazy (ed.), *The military in the service of society and democracy: the challenge of the dual-role military* (London: Greenwood Press, 1994), p. 20.
67 See: Avner Yaniv, 'A question of survival: the military and politics under siege', in Avner Yaniv (ed.), *National security and democracy in Israel* (London: Lynne Rienner, 1993), p. 95.
68 Dan Horowitz, 'Strategic limitations of "a nation in arms"', *Armed Forces and Society*, vol. 13, no. 2 (Winter 1987), p. 290.
69 Yoav Ben-Horin and Barry Posen, 'Israel's strategic doctrine', *Rand Report R-2845-NA* (Santa Monica, CA: Rand, 1981), p. 42.
70 Jim Storr, 'A command philosophy for the information age: the continuing relevance of mission command', *Defence Studies*, vol. 3, no. 3 (Autumn 2003), p. 119.
71 Brig. Gen. Aviv Kohavi, 'Learning in a changing reality' (PowerPoint presentation), *First International Low-Intensity Conflict Warfare Conference*, 22–25 March 2004, Tel Aviv, Israel [CD-ROM].
72 Michael Handel, *Israel's political–military doctrine*, p. 67.
73 Douglas. L. Bland, 'A unified theory of civil–military relations', *Armed Forces and Society*, vol. 26, no. 1 (Fall 1999), p. 6.
74 The definition and explanation of *bitsuism* is based on a working paper authored by Eitan Shamir and Sergio Catignani, 'Mission Command and *Bitsuism* in the Israeli Defence Forces: are they complementary or contradictory in today's counter-insurgency campaign?' (IUS Armed Forces and Society Conference Paper, September 2005).
75 See: Yaakov Hasdai, ' "Doers" and "Thinkers" in the IDF', *The Jerusalem Quarterly*, no. 24 (Summer 1982), pp. 16–18.
76 This concept has Biblical origins. The famous medieval Jewish rabbi, Maimonides, distinguished between an obligatory war, *milkhemet mitzvah*, and discretionary war, *milkhemet reshut*. See: Stuart Cohen, *The scroll or the sword? Dilemmas of religion and military service in Israel* (Amsterdam: Harwood Academic Publishers, 1997), pp. 10–12.
77 Reuven Gal, *A portrait of the Israeli soldier* (London: Greenwood, 1986), p. 147.
78 Ze'ev Drory, *Israel's reprisal policy*, p. 49.

5 Land and the rise of the LIC struggle

1. Yigal Allon, *The Making of Israel's Army* (London: Vallentine, Mitchell, 1970), p. 50.
2. For an historical and analytical overview of Israeli positions on the future of the West Bank and Gaza Strip since the Six Day War see: Jonathan Rynhold, 'Re-conceptualizing Israeli approaches to "land for peace" and the Palestinian question since 1967', *Israel Studies*, vol. 6, no. 2 (Fall 2001), pp. 33–52.
3. Dan Horowitz, 'The Israeli concept of national security', in Avner Yaniv (ed.), *National security and democracy in Israel* (London: Lynne Rienner, 1993), p. 30.
4. Avner Yaniv, *Deterrence without the Bomb: the politics of Israeli strategy* (Lexington, MA: Lexington Books, 1987), p. 234.
5. Yoram Peri, 'Coexistence or hegemony? Shifts in the Israeli security concept', in D. Caspi *et al.* (eds), *The roots of Begin's success: the 1981 Israeli elections* (London: Croom Helm, 1984), p. 203.
6. Ariel Sharon, *Warrior: an autobiography* (London: Simon and Schuster, 2001) p. 456.
7. Yoram Peri, 'Coexistence or hegemony?' pp. 210–11.
8. Avner Yaniv, *Dilemmas of security: politics, strategy and the Israeli experience in Lebanon* (Oxford: Oxford University Press, 1987), p. 103.
9. See: Dan Horowitz, 'The Israeli concept', pp. 41–2.
10. Zvi Lanir, 'Political aims and military objectives – some observations on the Israeli experience', in Zvi Lanir (ed.), *Israeli security planning in the 1980s: its politics and economics* (Eastbourne: Praeger, 1984), p. 42.
11. See: Dan Horowitz, 'Israel and occupation', *The Jerusalem Quarterly*, no. 43 (Summer 1987), pp. 25–7.
12. Yitzhak Rabin and Efraim Inbar, *Yitzhak Rabin and Israeli national security, security and policy studies 25* (Ramat Gan: Bar-Ilan University, 1996), p. 2.
13. With the exception, thus, of the Begin period of government, ' "current security" in the past [...] referred to border clashes with Arab armies [and today] relates to Palestinian terrorist incursions aimed at targets in Israel [...] and to fundamentalist Islamic terrorism and the *Intifada*'. Cited in: Yitzhak Rabin and Efraim Inbar, *Yitzhak Rabin and Israeli national security*, p. 2.
14. Caroline Glick, 'Sharon: no military solution to the war with the Palestinians', *Jerusalem Post*, 26 September 2002.
15. Clive Jones, ' "One size fits all": Israel, intelligence, and the *Al-Aqsa Intifada*', *Studies in Conflict and Terrorism*, vol. 26, no. 4 (July–August 2003), p. 284.
16. Reuven Gal, *A portrait of the Israeli soldier* (London: Greenwood, 1986), p. 143.
17. Dan Horowitz, 'The Israeli concept', p. 43.
18. Ibid.
19. Reuven Pedatzur, 'Ben-Gurion's enduring legacy', in Daniel Bar-Tal *et al.* (eds), *Security concerns: insights from the Israeli experience* (London: JAI Press, 1998), p. 153.
20. Gad Barzilai, 'National security crises and voting behavior: the *Intifada* and the 1988 elections', in Asher Arian and Michal Shamir (eds), *The elections in Israel – 1988* (Oxford: Westview Press, 1990), p. 65.
21. Avi Kober, 'Israeli war objectives into an era of negativism', *Journal of Strategic Studies*, vol. 24, no. 2 (2001), p. 193.
22. In the Israeli–Palestinian communal conflict this entails the operational destruction of terrorist groups.
23. This entails the complete destruction and eradication of the Palestinian terrorist infrastructure.

24 Richard A. Gabriel, *Operation peace for Galilee: the Israeli–PLO war in Lebanon* (New York: Free Press, 1982), p. 191.
25 Clive Jones, 'Israeli counter-insurgency strategy and the war in South Lebanon 1985–97', *Small Wars and Insurgencies*, vol. 8, no. 3 (Winter 1997), p. 83.
26 For more on the South Lebanese Army see: Al J. Venter, 'Independence on the border: the South Lebanese army today', *International Defence Review*, vol. 22, no. 7 (July 1989), pp. 915–17.
27 On Hizbullah's combat tactics, see: Nicholas Blanford, '*Hizbullah* attacks force Israel to take a hard look at Lebanon', *Jane's Intelligence Review*, vol. 11, no. 4 (April 1999), pp. 32–7.
28 The following section, which will focus on the first three core elements of Israel's counter-guerrilla strategy and operational doctrine in the South Lebanon Security Zone, is based on: Shmuel Gordon, *The vulture and the snake. Counter-guerrilla air warfare: the war in Southern Lebanon*, Security policy studies 39 (Ramat Gan: Begin–Sadat Centre for Strategic Studies, July 1998), pp. 20–2.
29 Clive Jones, 'Israeli counter-insurgency', p. 94.
30 Ibid. p. 95.
31 Figures taken from: 'Israel/Lebanon: "Operation Grapes of Wrath"', *Human Rights Watch Report*, vol. 9, no. 8 (September 1997), Human Rights Watch, http://hrw.org/reports/1997/isrleb/Isrleb.htm (accessed 20 March 2003).
32 *Katyusha* rocket attack statistics cited in: 'Israel/Lebanon: "Operation Grapes of Wrath"'.
33 See: Yigal Levy, 'Military Doctrine and Political Participation: toward a sociology of strategy', January 1996, www.ciaonet.org/wps/ley02/index.html (accessed 28 December 2004).
34 Gabriel Ben-Dor, 'Responding to the threat: the dynamics of the Arab–Israeli conflict', in Daniel Bar-Tal *et al.* (eds), *Security concerns: insights from the Israeli experience* (London: JAI Press, 1998), p. 127.

6 The *Intifada*

1 Mark Tessler, 'The impact of the *Intifada* on Israeli political thinking', in Rex Brynen and Neil Caplan (eds), *Echoes of the Intifada on Israeli political thinking: regional repercussions of the Palestinian–Israeli conflict* (Oxford: Westview Press, 1991), p. 65.
2 Yaacov Bar-Siman-Tov, *Israel and the Intifada: adaptation and learning*, Davis occasional papers no. 78 (Jerusalem: The Leonard Davis Institute, Hebrew University of Jerusalem, 2000), p. 4.
3 Even though the Lebanon War was legally an inter-state war, the two major parties involved in it were the Israelis and the Palestinians. Following the defeat and departure of the PLO in Lebanon and the re-deployment of the IDF to the South Lebanon Security Zone, the conflict involved for the most part the IDF and Lebanon's Maronite Christians against the Shi'ites.
4 Martin Gilbert, *Israel: a history* (London: Black Swan, 1999), p. 398.
5 Yoram Peri, 'The impact of occupation on the military: the case of the IDF, 1967–1987', in Ilan Peleg and Ofira Seliktar (eds), *The emergence of a binational Israel: the second republic in the making* (London: Westview Press, 1989), p. 144.
6 Yizhar Be'er and Saleh Abdel-Jawad, *Collaborators in the occupied territories: human rights abuses and violations* (Jerusalem: B'Tselem, January 1994), p. 25.
7 Ibid. p. 26.

8 Ruth M. Beitler, 'The *Intifada*: Palestinian adaptation to Israeli counter-insurgency tactics', *Terrorism and Political Violence*, vol. 7, no. 2 (Summer 1995), p. 55.
9 Meron Benvenisti, *1987 Report: demographic, legal, social and political developments in the West Bank* (Jerusalem: Jerusalem Post, 1987), p. 11.
10 Joost R. Hilterman, *Behind the Intifada: labor and women's movements in the occupied territories* (Princeton: Princeton University Press, 1991), p. 20.
11 Meron, Benvenisti, *1987 Report*, p. 32.
12 Ruth M. Beitler, 'The *Intifada*', p. 52.
13 Robert F. Hunter, *The Palestinian uprising: a war by other means* (Berkeley, CA: University of California Press, 1993), p. 93.
14 Rex Brynen and Neil Caplan, 'Israel and Palestine: implications of the *Intifada*', in Rex Brynen and Neil Caplan (eds), *Echoes of the Intifada on Israeli political thinking: regional repercussions of the Palestinian–Israeli conflict* (Oxford: Westview Press, 1991), p. 7.
15 Yoram Peri, 'The impact', p. 158.
16 Ibid. p. 154.
17 Ibid.
18 Giora Goldberg *et al.*, *The Impact of Intercommunal Conflict: the Intifada and Israeli public opinion*, Davis Occasional Papers no. 43 (Jerusalem: The Leonard Davis Institute, Hebrew University of Jerusalem, 1991), p. 11.
19 Samih K. Farsoun, *Palestine and the Palestinians* (Oxford: Westview Press, 1997), p. 228.
20 Ahron Bregman, *Israel's wars, 1947–93* (London: Routledge, 2000), p. 118.
21 Ruth M. Beitler, 'The *Intifada*', p. 55.
22 Joost R. Hilterman, *Behind the Intifada*, p. 33.
23 Ahron Bregman, *Israel's wars*, p. 121.
24 Ze'ev Schiff and Ehud Ya'ari, *Intifada: the Palestinian uprising – Israel's third front* (London: Simon and Schuster, 1990), p. 17.
25 Al Haq/Law in the Service of Man, *Twenty years of Israel occupation of the West Bank and Gaza* (Ramallah: Al Haq, 1987), p. 26.
26 Andrew Bigby, *Living the Intifada* (London: Zed Books, 1991), p. 54.
27 Ibid. p. 55.
28 Figures taken from: Meron Benvenisti, *1987 Report*, p. 40.
29 Serg. Maj. (Res.) Eitan Shamir, Squad Leader, Paratroop Brigade. Interview with author, Shrivenham, England, 23 June 2004.
30 Meron Benvenisti, *1987 Report*, p. 41.
31 Uri Davis, *Israel: an apartheid state* (London: Zed Books, 1987), p. 70.
32 Ibid. p. 71.
33 For a detailed account of such an amendment see: Ibid. p. 72.
34 For a detailed account of the UNLU's underground communiqués see: Shaul Mishal and Reuben Aharoni, *Speaking stones: communiques from the Intifada underground* (Syracuse, NY: Syracuse University Press, 1994).
35 Rex Brynen and Neil Caplan, 'Israel and Palestine', p. 8.
36 Kenneth Kaplan, 'The IDF's political war', *Israel yearbook 1989* (Tel Aviv: Israel Yearbook Publications, 1989), pp. 88–9.
37 Edgar O'Balance, *The Palestinian Intifada* (London: Macmillan Press, 1998), p. 47.
38 Martin Van Creveld, *The sword and the olive: a critical history of the Israeli Defence Forces* (New York: Public Affairs, 1998), p. 344.
39 Yaacov Bar-Siman-Tov, *Israel*, p. 3.
40 Ibid. p. 4.

Notes 211

41 Aryeh Shalev, *The Intifada: causes and effects*, Jaffee Centre for Strategic Studies Study no. 16 (Oxford: Westview Press, 1991), p. 101.
42 Yitzhak Rabin, 'Moving in the right direction', *Israel yearbook 1989* (Tel Aviv: Israel Yearbook Publications, 1989), p. 71.
43 Yehoshua Porath, 'Human rights in Judea-Samaria and the Gaza District', *Israel yearbook 1989* (Tel Aviv: Israel Yearbook Publications, 1989), p. 238.
44 *Israel yearbook 1988*, 'Israeli Arabs and the situation in the territories', *Israel yearbook 1988* (Tel Aviv: Israel Yearbook Publications, 1988), p. 190.
45 The IDF Chief-of-Staff (COS), Dan Shomron, acknowledged that by early January 1988 'there were more troops in Gaza alone than had been used to occupy all the Territories in 1967'. Cited in: Don Peretz, *Intifada: Palestinian uprising* (London: Westview Press, 1990), p. 45.
46 Mark Tessler, 'The impact', p. 46.
47 Aryeh Shalev, *The Intifada*, p. 109.
48 Andrew Bigby, *Living the Intifada*, p. 61.
49 Aryeh Shalev, *The Intifada*, p. 111.
50 Ibid. p. 114.
51 Joe Stork, 'The significance of stones: notes from the seventh month', *Middle East Report*, no. 154, vol. 18/5 (September–October 1988), p. 8.
52 Ibid. p. 6.
53 See also: Salim Tamari, 'Limited rebellion and civil society: the uprising's dilemma', *Middle East Report*, no. 164/165, vol. 20/3–4 (May–August 1990), pp. 4–8.
54 Aryeh Shalev, *The Intifada*, p. 110.
55 Uzi Amit-Kohn, *Israel, the Intifada and the rule of law* (Israel: Israel Ministry of Defence Publications, 1993), p. 242.
56 Aryeh Shalev, 'The uprising in Judea, Samaria and the Gaza Strip', *Israel Yearbook 1989* (Tel Aviv: Israel Yearbook Publications, 1988), p. 150.
57 Serg. Maj. (Res.) Yaron Hachmov, Infantry Reserve Brigade 5, Squad Leader. Interview with author, Herzliya, Israel, 11 August 2004.
58 Robert F. Hunter, *The Palestinian uprising*, p. 106.
59 Andrew Bigby, *Living the Intifada*, pp. 59–60.
60 Serg. Maj. (Res.) Aviram Shemer, Armoured Corps. Interview with author, Tel Aviv, Israel, 28 August 2003.
61 Uzi Amit-Kohn, *Israel*, pp. 244–5.
62 Ruth Linn, *Conscience at war: the Israeli soldier as a moral critic* (Albany: State University of New York Press, 1996), p. 114.
63 Martin Van Creveld, *The sword*, p. 362.
64 Serg. Maj. (Res.) Aviram Shemer. Interview with author.
65 Amos Elon, *A blood-dimmed tide: dispatches from the Middle East* (London: Penguin Books, 2000), p. 147. Such behaviour was particularly rife within the Border Police as noted in various interviews conducted during 2003 and 2004.
66 Serg. Maj. (Res.) 'Downtown' Dave, *Givati* Brigade. Interview with author, Tel Aviv, Israel, 19 August 2004.
67 Don Peretz, *Intifada*, p. 49.
68 Mark Tessler, *The impact*, p. 49.
69 Don Peretz, *Intifada*, p. 130.
70 On the activities of peace organisations in Israel see: Michael Feige, 'Peace now and the legitimation crisis of "civil militarism"', *Israel Studies*, vol. 3, no. 1 (Spring 1998), pp. 85–111.
71 On the growing vigilantism of the national religious settler movement see: Ami Pedahzur, 'The transformation of Israel's extreme right', *Studies in Conflict and Terrorism*, vol. 24, no. 1 (January 2001), pp. 25–42.

72 Reuven Gal, *A portrait of the Israeli soldier* (London: Greenwood, 1986), p. 250.
73 Quoted in Glenn Frankel, 'In Israel, army comes under fire over unrest', *International Herald Tribune*, 4 March 1988.
74 James Paul, 'Israel and the *Intifada*: points of stress', *Middle East Report*, no. 154, vol. 18, no. 5, September–October 1988, p. 14.
75 James Paul, 'Israel', pp. 14–15.
76 Don Peretz, *Intifada*, p. 133.
77 Reuven Gal, *A portrait*, p. 239.
78 Ruth Linn, *Conscience*, pp. 144–5.
79 Eyal Ben-Ari, *Mastering soldiers: conflict, emotions, and the enemy in an Israeli military unit* (Oxford: Berghahn Books, 1998), p. 75.
80 Ruth Linn, *Conscience*, pp. 144–7.
81 Ian Murray, 'West Bank general admits to excessive force by the Israelis', *Times*, 29 January 1989.
82 Jerusalem Post Staff, 'War by other means', *Jerusalem Post*, 17 September 1988.
83 Richard Beeston, 'Scornful Israelis rub salt into army's latest wounds', *Times*, 17 February 1992.
84 Lt. Col. Ilan Malka, Head of Training, *Givati* Brigade. Interview with author, Qiryat Gat, Israel, 9 August 2004.
85 Stuart A. Cohen, 'How did the *Intifada* affect the IDF?' *Conflict Quarterly*, vol. 14 (Summer 1994), p. 12.
86 Andrew Bigby, *Living the Intifada*, p. 74.
87 Maj. Gen. (Ret.) Danny Yatom, former Head of IDF Central Command (March 1991–March 1993). Interview with author, Tel Aviv, Israel, 5 August 2004.
88 Ruth Linn, *Conscience*, p. 72.
89 Yechezkel Dar *et al.*, 'The imprint of the *Intifada*: response of kibbutz-born soldiers to military service in the West Bank and Gaza', *Armed Forces and Society*, vol. 26, no. 2, Winter 2000, p. 299.
90 On the socio-economic transformation of Israel and the fragmentation of the national security consensus see: Eliot A. Cohen *et al.*, 'Israel's revolution in security affairs', *Survival*, vol. 40, no. 1 (Spring 1998), pp. 48–67 and Mark A. Heller, *Continuity and change in Israeli security policy*, Adelphi paper 335 (Oxford: Oxford University Press, July 2000), pp. 40–7.
91 Bart Horeman and Marc Stolwijk, *Refusing to bear arms: a world survey of conscription and conscientious objection* (London: War Resisters International, 1998), p. 158.
92 Tamar Liebes and Shoshana Blum-Kulka, 'Managing the moral dilemma: Israeli soldiers in the *Intifada*', *Armed Forces and Society*, vol. 21, no. 1 (Fall 1994), p. 50.
93 Tamar Liebes and Shoshana Blum-Kulka, 'Managing', p. 54.
94 Stuart A. Cohen, 'How did the *Intifada*', p. 13.
95 Maj. Gen. (Ret.) Danny Yatom. Interview with author.
96 Tamar Liebes and Shoshana Blum-Kulka, 'Managing', p. 61.
97 Hugh Sebag-Montefiore, 'We won't fight in West Bank', *Observer*, 16 October 1988. All of the conscientious objectors interviewed stated, in fact, how their immediate superiors would try to accommodate them in order to avoid making their decision to refuse final and consequently subject to official military disciplining.
98 Mordechai Bar-On, *In pursuit of peace: a history of the Israeli peace movement* (Washington, DC: US Institute of Peace Press, 1996), p. 229.
99 See: Ruth Linn, 'Soldiers with conscience never die – they are just ignored by their society. Moral disobedience in the Israel Defence Forces', *Journal of Military Ethics*, vol. 1, no. 2 (July 2002), pp. 57–76.

100 For an account of other conscientious objectors during the first *Intifada* see: Peretz Kidron, *Refusenik! Israel's soldiers of conscience* (London: Zed Books, 2004), pp. 23–54.
101 Colin Shindler, 'The people's army', in Colin Shindler (ed.), *Ploughshares into swords? Israelis and Jews in the shadow of the Intifada* (London: I.B. Tauris, 1991), p. 202.
102 Capt. (Res.) Ely Peretz, Company Commander, *Nahal* Brigade. Interview with author, Hadera, Israel, 12 August 2003.
103 Serg. Maj. (Res.) Yaron Hachmov. Interview with author.
104 See: Glenn Frankel, 'Israeli aide sets limits on soldiers' use of force', *International Herald Tribune*, 25 February 1988.
105 Eyal Ben-Ari, 'Masks and soldiering: the Israeli army and the Palestinian uprising', *Cultural anthropology*, vol. 4, no. 4 (November 1989), p. 381.
106 Ibid.
107 Lt. Col. Hadass Ben-Eliyahu, Head of Research, IDF Behavioural Sciences Department (*MAMDA*). Interview with author, Tel Aviv, Israel, 10 August 2004.
108 Stuart A. Cohen, 'How did the *Intifada*', p. 8.
109 Yechezkel Dar *et al.*, *The imprint*, p. 303.
110 Ibid. p. 301.
111 Ayala M. Pines, 'The Palestinian *Intifada* and Israelis' burnout', *Journal of Cross-Cultural Psychology*, vol. 25, no. 4 (December 1994), p. 447.
112 Yechezkel Dar *et al.*, *The imprint*, p. 154.
113 Ruth Linn, *Conscience*, pp. 88–9. For a detailed profile of Israeli conscientious objectors during the *Intifada* see also: Ruth Linn, 'When the individual soldier says "no" to war: a look at selective refusal during the *Intifada*', *Journal of Peace Research*, vol. 33, no. 4 (November 1996), pp. 421–31.
114 Ruth Linn, *Conscience*, p. 91.
115 PLO headquarters were, furthermore, pounded by IAF F-15s in 1985 resulting in over 60 deaths.
116 On the events leading up to the Madrid peace conference as well as what it had achieved see: William B. Quandt, *Peace process: American diplomacy and the Arab–Israeli conflict since 1967* (Los Angeles: University of California Press, 2001), pp. 301–18.
117 The collapse of the Soviet Union, which until then had supported states and terrorist organisations belonging to the 'rejectionist' faction (i.e. those contrary to any compromise with the state of Israel) led to their weakening.
118 Ilan G. Gewurz, 'Transition from conflict: the importance of pre-negotiations in the Oslo Peace Process', *Israel Affairs*, vol. 6, no. 3–4 (Spring/Summer 2000), p. 185.
119 On the events leading up to and during the Madrid peace conference as well as what impact it had on the Middle East peace process see: William B. Quandt, *Peace Process*, pp. 303–18.
120 For more detailed accounts and analyses of the Oslo Peace Process see: Yossi Beilin, *Touching peace: from the Oslo Accord to a final agreement* (North Pomfret: Trafalgar Square, 2000); William B. Quandt, *Peace process*, pp. 321–76.
121 Nadav Morag, 'Unambiguous ambiguity: the opacity of the Oslo Peace Process', *Israel Affairs*, vol. 6, no. 3–4 (Spring/Summer 2000), p. 200.
122 'Declaration of Principles on interim self-government arrangements', Article III (1), 13 September 1993, *Jerusalem Media and Communication Centre*, www.jmcc.org/research/series/dop.html#declare (accessed 1 July 2004).
123 'Declaration of principles on interim self-government arrangements', Article

IV (3), 13 September 1993, *Jerusalem Media and Communication Centre*, www.jmcc.org/research/series/dop.html#declare (accessed 1 July 2004).
124 Nadav Morag, 'Unambiguous ambiguity', p. 202.
125 See: 'Judea and Samaria showing Palestinian Authority Areas A and B', *Israeli Ministry of Foreign Affairs*, www.mfa.gov.il/mfa/facts%20about%20israel/israel%20in%20maps/judea%20and%20samaria%20showing%20palestinian%20authority%20ar (accessed 3 September 2005).
126 See: '1993–2000: Major terror attacks', 26 September 2000, *Israel Ministry of Foreign Affairs*, www.mfa.gov.il/MFA/Facts+About+Israel/Israel+in+Maps/1993-2000-+Major+Terror+Attacks.htm (accessed 21 August 2005).
127 The most notable example of Israeli settler vigilantism occurred when Dr Baruch Goldstein, an Ultra Orthodox physician and resident of the Kiryat Arba settlement near Hebron, killed on 25 February 1994 (i.e. *Purim* day according to the Jewish calendar) 29 Muslims during their Friday prayers in the Cave of the Patriarchs of Hebron, which is the burial site of Biblical figures Abraham, Sarah, Isaac, Jabob, Rebecca and Leah.

7 The *Al-Aqsa Intifada*

1 According to PA Communications Minister Imad Falouji, Arafat had planned another violent uprising since his return from Camp David in July 2000. See: '*Al-Aqsa Intifada* reportedly planned in July', *Intelligence briefs: Israel/Palestinians*, vol. 3, no. 3 (March 2001), *Middle East Intelligence Bulletin*, www.meib.org/articles/0103_ipb.htm (accessed 12 March 2003).
2 The main points at Taba were: (1) a Palestinian state in 96 per cent of the West Bank and Gaza; (2) Jerusalem under joint sovereignty; and (3) the absorption of 150,000–200,000 Palestinian refugees into Israel.
3 Daniel Sobelman, '*Hizbullah* lends its services to the Palestinian *Intifada*', *Jane's Intelligence Review*, vol. 13, no. 11 (November 2001), p. 12.
4 David Eshel, 'The *Al-Aqsa Intifada*: tactics and strategies', *Jane's Intelligence Review*, vol. 13, no. 5 (May 2001), p. 37.
5 Yaacov Bar-Siman-Tov *et al.*, *The Israeli–Palestinian violent confrontation 2000–2004: from conflict resolution to conflict management* (Jerusalem: The Jerusalem Institute for Israel Studies, 2005), p. 25.
6 See: Akiva Eldar, 'Popular misconceptions', *Ha'aretz*, 11 June 2004; and Reuven Pedatzur, 'More than a million bullets', *Ha'aretz*, 29 June 2004.
7 See: Ephraim Yaar and Tamar Hermann, 'Peace index' (January 2000–January 2001), *The Tami Steinmetz Centre for Peace Research*, http://spirit.tau.ac.il/socant/peace (accessed 16 January 2005).
8 Amos Harel, *Shin Bet*: 145 suicide bombers since the start of the *Intifada*', *Ha'aretz*, 1 October 2002.
9 Hillel Frisch, 'Debating Palestinian strategy in the *Al-Aqsa Intifada*', *Terrorism and Political Violence*, vol. 15, no. 2 (Summer 2003), p. 64.
10 Joshua Sinai, '*Intifada* drives both sides to radical arms', *Jane's Intelligence Review*, vol. 13, no. 5 (May 2001), p. 33.
11 See also: Alan Baker, 'Legal and tactical dilemmas inherent in fighting terror: experience of the Israeli army in Jenin and Bethlehem (April–May 2002)', in Yoram Dinstein and Fania Domb (eds), *Israel yearbook on human rights 34* (Leiden: Martinus Nijhoff, 2004), pp. 179–91.
12 Lt. Joshua, Deputy Company Commander, 7th Armoured Brigade. Interview with author, Nebi Musa, Israel, 24 August 2004.
13 Steve Rodan, 'Interview: Lt. Gen. Shaul Mofaz', *Jane's Defence Weekly*, vol. 36, no. 16 (17 October 2001), p. 32.

Notes 215

14 Leslie Susser, 'We are saving many lives', *The Jerusalem Report* (December 2000), www.jrep.com/Israel/Article-36.html (accessed 1 March 2003).
15 'Total daily numbers of deaths and injuries – West Bank and Gaza', *Palestinian Red Crescent Society*, http://palestinercs.org/crisistables/table_of_figures.htm (accessed 17 April 2005). Statistics on Palestinian deaths and injuries were approximately similar to those provided by the International Policy Institute for Counter-Terrorism. See next footnote.
16 Figures for the period 27 September 2000–31 October 2000 were compiled from: 'Incidents and casualties database', *International Policy Institute for Counter-Terrorism*, www.ict.org.il (accessed 10 April 2005).
17 David Eshel, 'The *Al-Aqsa Intifada*', p. 37.
18 See: Reuven Paz, 'From Tehran to Beirut to Jerusalem: Iran and *Hizbullah* in the Palestinian uprising', *PeaceWatch 313*, 26 March 2001, *The Washington Institute for Near East Policy*, www.washingtoninstitute.org/templateC05.php?CID=2004 (accessed 2 June 2004).
19 See: Matthew Levitt, '*Hamas*: toward a Lebanese-style war of attrition?', *PeaceWatch 367*, 26 February 2002, *The Washington Institute for Near East Policy*, www.washingtoninstitute.org/templateC05.php?CID=2058 (accessed 2 June 2004).
20 *Hizbullah* activists were by 2004 operating on the ground side-by-side with local Palestinians in the Occupied Territories. IDF military intelligence Col. Yossi Kupperwasser stated, in fact, in February 2005 that *Hizbullah* had more than 50 terror cells operating in the Occupied Territories. See: 'IDF say *Hizbullah* has 50 terror cells in territories', *Yediot Ahronot*, 14 February 2005.
21 See: 'Seizing of the Palestinian weapons ship *Karine A*', 4 January 2002, *Israeli Ministry of Foreign Affairs*, www.mfa.gov.il/mfa/government/communiques/2002/ (accessed 10 January 2002).
22 'Sharon Equates *Intifada* and Terror', *The Middle East Reporter*, vol. 101, no. 1171 (15 December 2001), p. 10.
23 Brig. Gen. Gershon HaCohen, Head of Doctrine and Training Division. Interview with author, Tel Aviv, Israel, 31 August 2003.
24 Capt. (Res.) Ely Peretz, Company Commander, *Nahal* Brigade. Interview with author, Hadera, Israel, 12 August 2003.
25 Asher Arian, *Israeli national public opinion on national security 2002*, memorandum no. 61 (Tel Aviv: Jaffee Centre for Strategic Studies, July 2002), pp. 13 and 35.
26 See: Steve Rodan, 'Interview: Maj. Gen. Dan Halutz, Commander-in-Chief of the Israel Air Force', *Jane's Defence Weekly*, vol. 37, no. 3 (16 January 2002), p. 32.
27 Steve Rodan, 'Israel wants to replenish West Bank weapons', *Jane's Defence Weekly*, vol. 38, no. 2 (10 July 2002), p. 18.
28 Steve Rodan, 'IDF debates main battle tank role in *Intifada*, *Jane's Defence Weekly*, vol. 36, no. 8 (22 August 2001), p. 16.
29 Amos Harel, 'Top IDF officer admits "exaggerated" force in Rafah shelling incident', *Ha'aretz*, 30 October 2002.
30 Gal Luft, 'Fighting a "terror-supporting entity": what next for the Israel Defence Forces?', *Peacewatch 354* (6 December 2001), *The Washington Institute for Near East Policy*, www.washingtoninstitute.org/watch/Peacewatch/peacewatch2001/354.htm (accessed 6 October 2002).
31 Binyamin Ben-Eliezer, 'Israeli defense policy: responding to challenges near and far', *Peacewatch 364* (12 February 2002), *The Washington Institute for Near East Policy*, www.washingtoninstitute.org/watch/Peacewatch/peacewatch2002/364.htm (accessed 6 October 2002).

32 Colonel Gal Hirsh, Head of the IDF Officer Candidate School. Interview with author, Tel Aviv, Israel, 6 August 2003.
33 Capt. (Res.) Shahar Amit, Platoon Commander, IDF Paratroopers Brigade. Interview with author, 20 August 2004, Tel Aviv, Israel.
34 Capt. (Res.) Noam Wiener, Infantry brigade reservist *Ometz le-Sarev Refusenik*. Interview with author, Tel Aviv, Israel, 24 August 2003.
35 That is, the Jewish Passover celebration conducted at the Hotel Park in Netanya whereby 29 Israelis were killed and another 150 were injured by a *Hamas* suicide bomber.
36 Mark A. Heller, 'Operation "Defensive Wall": a change in Israeli strategy?', *Tel Aviv Notes 34* (Tel Aviv: Jaffee Centre for Strategic Studies, 4 April 2002), p. 1.
37 Shaul Mofaz, 'The Israeli–Palestinian Conflict: what next?', *Peacewatch 400* (8 October 2002), *The Washington Institute for Near East Policy*, www.washingtoninstitute.org/pubs/speakers/mofaz.htm (accessed 13 October 2002).
38 Moshe Yaalon, 'Press release of the third Herzliya conference on the balance of Israel's national security', 3 December 2002, *The Institute of Policy and Strategy*, www.1.idc.ac.il/ips/content/2002PressAyalon.asp (accessed 7 January 2003).
39 Brig. Gen. Gershon HaCohen. Interview with author.
40 Shlomo Brom, 'Operation "Defensive Shield": an interim assessment', *Tel Aviv Notes 35* (Tel Aviv: Jaffee Centre for Strategic Studies, 11 April 2002), p. 1.
41 Yagil Henkin, 'Urban Warfare and the Lessons of Jenin', *Azure*, vol. 15 (Summer 2003), www.shalem.org.il/azure/15-henkin.htm (accessed 23 May 2003).
42 'Briefing by the IDF Chief of The General Staff', International Conference on Low-intensity Conflict, *IDF Spokesperson's Office*, 23 March 2004, www.idf.il/newsite/English/032304-4.stm (accessed 23 March 2004).
43 See: 'IDF Steps up intelligence war against Palestinians', *Jane's Defence Weekly* (5 January 2001), *Jane's Information Group*, http:jdw.janes.com (accessed 23 June 2004).
44 David A. Fulghum and Robert Wall, 'Israel's future includes armed, long-range UAVs', *Aviation Week and Space Technology*, 25 June 2002, www.aviationnow.com (accessed 14 July 2002).
45 David Eshel, 'Israel hones intelligence operations to counter *Intifada*', *Jane's Intelligence Review* (1 October 2002), *Jane's Information Group*, http://jir.janes.com (accessed 23 June 2004).
46 According to various estimates the GSS and Military Intelligence 'ran about 7,000 informers throughout the West Bank and Gaza during the first *Intifada*'. See: 'Israel uses *Intifada* informers to abet assassination campaign', *Jane's Intelligence Review* (1 December 2001), *Jane's Information Group*, http://jir.janes.com (accessed 23 June 2004).
47 Lt. X, Classified Unit within the Paratroopers Brigade. Interview with author, Herzliya, Israel, 25 August 2004.
48 Capt. E., *Sayeret Matkal* (General Staff Élite Commando Unit). Interview with author, Tel Aviv, Israel, 18 August 2003. See also: Barbara Opall-Rome, 'Israeli gunships, troops team for pinpoint strikes', *Defense News*, 21 April 2003, www.defensenews.com (accessed on 20 May 2003).
49 Jeremy Gwinn, 'Jenin and the fundamentals of urban operations', *Infantry Online*, 15 March 2003, http://www.benning.army.mil/OLP/InfantryOnline/issue_21/art_125.htm (accessed 28 June 2003).

Notes 217

50 Ibid.
51 Colonel Gal Hirsh. Interview with the author, 6 August 2003.
52 Barbara Opall-Rome, 'Israel redefines tactics', *Defense News*, 16 June 2002.
53 On the IDF's attempts at trying to grapple with media exposure during the Al-Aqsa Intifada, see: Baruch Nevo and Yael Shur, *The IDF and the press during hostilities* (Jerusalem: The Israel Democracy Institute, 2003).
54 Barbara Opall-Rome, 'Israeli leaders to move to combat negative perceptions', *Defense News*, 22 July 2001.
55 Barbara Opall-Rome, 'Tanks fill wider role in Israel's anti-terror war', *Defense News*, 17 March 2003.
56 Serg. Maj. (Res.) Sean Sachs, Squad Leader, IDF *Nahal* Brigade. Interview with author, 11 August 2003, Tel Aviv, Israel.
57 See: Barbara Opall-Rome, 'Objective: re-create the fog of war', *Defense News*, 24 June 2002.
58 Barbara Opall-Rome, 'Israel test anti-sniper system in combat', *Defense News*, 15 July 2002.
59 See: Dror Marom, 'Corner shot invests $2m in weapons systems', *Globes Online*, 15 December 2003, www.globes.co.il/DocsEn/did=751435.htm (accessed 7 April 2004).
60 See: Alon Ben-David, 'Israel unveils *Refa'im* rifle grenade system', *Jane's Defence Weekly*, vol. 40, no. 11 (September 17, 2003), p. 15.
61 See: Amir Buhbut, 'On target', *Ma'ariv*, 19 March 2004.
62 IDF infantry brigades usually rotate among the three Territorial Commands (North, South and Central).
63 Amos Harel, 'Infantry boosted in leaner army', *Ha'aretz*, 29 July 2003.
64 For a detailed account of the IDF Code of Conduct see: Amos Guiora, 'Balancing IDF checkpoints and international law: teaching the IDF code of conduct', *Jerusalem Issue Brief*, vol. 3, no. 8 (19 November 2003), *Jerusalem Centre for Public Affairs*, www.jcpa.org/brief/brief3-8.htm (accessed 11 November 2004).
65 Col. Roi Elcabets, Head of Doctrine and Training, IDF Ground Forces Command. Interview with author, 26 August 2004, Tel Aviv, Israel.
66 Soldiers often find themselves guarding checkpoints from around 8 to 12 hours a day and dealing with up to 5,000 frustrated and hostile Palestinians. See: Eitan Rabin, 'Army cameras catch soldiers' abuse', *Ma'ariv*, 11 July 2004.
67 Capt. (Res.) Noam Wiener. Interview with author.
68 See: 'IDF readjusts to the needs of the Palestinian population', *IDF Spokesperson's Office*, 8 July 2004, www.1.idf.il/DOVER/site/mainpage.asp?sl=ENandid=7anddocid=32567.EN (accessed 11 July 2004).
69 See: 'Security crossing improvements in Judea and Samaria', 9 June 2005, *IDF Spokesperson's Office*, http://www1.idf.il/DOVER/site/mainpage.asp?sl=ENandid=Docid=41216.ENandunit=13869 (accessed 15 June 2005).
70 Ibid.
71 Lt. Col. Timna Shmueli, Head of IDF School of Leadership Development. Interview with author, 19 August 2004, Netanya, Israel.
72 Maj. (Res.) Danny Gal, Field Psychologist, *MAMDA* (Department of Behavioural Sciences). Interview with author, 12 August 2004, Herzliya, Israel.
73 Peter Kilner, 'Military leaders' obligation to justify killing in war', *Military Review*, vol. 82, no. 2 (March–April 2002), p. 29.
74 Capt. (Res.) Shahar Amit. Interview with author.
75 Jonathan Lis and Baruch Kra, 'Officers defend "human shield" practice', *Ha'aretz*, 16 August 2002.

218 Notes

76 Serg. Maj. (Res.) Mike Outmezgin, Infantry Brigade Reservist. Interview with author, Tel Aviv, Israel, 24 August 2003.
77 See: Amos Harel, 'MI: Arafat steps up actions against terrorist organizations', *Ha'aretz*, 1 January 2002 and Danny Rubinstein, 'The liquidation as a boomerang', *Ha'aretz*, 21 January 2002.
78 Ami Ayalon, 'Front lines', in Robert B. Satloff (ed.), *War on terror: the Middle East dimension* (Washington, DC: The Washington Institute for Near East Policy, 2002), p. 4.
79 See: Ze'ev Schiff, 'Thwarting suicide missions is not enough', *Ha'aretz*, 6 March 2003.
80 Gideon Alon, '150 would-be bombers nabbed during *Intifada*', *Ha'aretz*, 30 April 2003.
81 See also: Associated Press, 'Terror report: fewer Palestinian successes, but not for lack of trying', *Israelinsider*, 7 January 2005, www.israelinsider.com (accessed 11 January 2005).
82 See: Amos Harel, 'Analysis: beware the Gaza quagmire', *Ha'aretz*, 24 February 2003.
83 According to one estimation, income tax revenue from Palestinians working in Israel comprises two-thirds of the Palestinian Authority's budget. As a result of curfews, closures and the withholding of income tax revenue, the PA endured a sizeable loss of revenue since the start of the *Al-Aqsa Intifada*. See: Joshua Sinai, '*Intifada* drives', p. 34.
84 Akiva Eldar, '65 manned roadblocks, 58 trenches, 95 concrete barriers, 464 mounds of earth', *Ha'aretz*, 23 December 2003.
85 Ari Shavit, 'The enemy within', *Ha'aretz*, 29 August 2002.
86 Ibid.
87 Barbara Opall-Rome, 'Interview Maj. Gen. Doron Almog: Southern Commander, Israel Defence Forces', *Defense News*, 1 December 2002.
88 Yoram, Peri, *The Israeli Military and Israel's Palestinian Policy: from Oslo to the Al-Aqsa Intifada*, Peaceworks no. 47 (Washington, DC: United States Institute for Peace, November 2002), p. 35.
89 Rami Hazut, 'The Palestinians are an existential threat: Iraq is not', *Yediot Ahronot*, 23 August 2002, *Israel Resource Review*, http://israelvisit.co.il/cgi-bin/friendly.pl?url=Aug-23–02!IDF (accessed 14 March 2003).
90 Matthew Levitt and Seth Wikas, 'Defensive shield counter-terrorism accomplishments', *Peacewatch 377* (17 April 2002), *The Washington Institute for Near East Policy*, www.washingtoninstitute.org/watch/Peacewatch/peacewatch2002/377.htm (accessed 6 October 2002).
91 Lt. Col. Avi Peled, Head of the *Sayeret Egoz* Battalion. Interview with author, Shrivenham, England, 23 June 2004.
92 Caroline B. Glick, 'Sharon: no military solution to the war with the Palestinians', *Jerusalem Post*, 26 September 2002.
93 See: 'A performance-based roadmap to a permanent two-state solution to the Israeli–Palestinian conflict', 30 April 2003, *Office of the spokesman, US Department of State*, www.state.gov/r/pa/prs/ps/2003/20062.htm (accessed 5 July 2004).
94 See: John Ward Anderson, 'Israel approves construction of more homes at settlements', *Washington Post*, 3 December 2003, p. A16.
95 Ellis Shuman, 'Sharon hints at "unilateral" evacuation of isolated settlements', 23 November 2003, *Israelinsider*, http://web.israelinsider.com/Articles/Diplomacy/3003.htm (accessed 25 November 2003).
96 See: 'Map of security fence project', *Israeli Ministry of Defence*, www.securityfence.mod.gov.il/Pages/ENG/route.htm (accessed 20 May 2005).

Notes 219

97 Ariel Sharon, 'Prime Minister's speech at the Herzliya conference' (Transcript), 18 December 2003, *Isracast*, www.isracast.com/PMherzelia03_transcript.htm (accessed 20 January 2004).
98 David Makovsky, 'A defensible fence', *The Review*, vol. 29, no. 8 (August 2004), *Australia/Israel and Jewish Affairs Council*, www.aijac.org.au/review/2004/298/essay298.htm (accessed 20 May 2005).
99 Anthony Cordesman, 'From peace to war: land for peace or settlements for war' (DC: *Centre for Strategic and International Studies*, August 2003), www.csis.org/features/EscalatingToNoWhere/Ch02.pdf (accessed 19 May 2005), pp. 12–13.
100 David Makovsky, 'How to build a fence', *Foreign Affairs*, vol. 83, no. 2 (March/April 2004), p. 54.
101 See: 'Judgment of the High Court of Justice regarding Beit Sourik', 26 February 2004, *B'Tselem*, www.btselem.org/English/Separation_Barrier/Beit_Surik_Ruling.asp (accessed 28 January 2005).
102 See: 'Statute of the International Court of Justice', *International Court of Justice*, www.icj-cij.org/icjwww/ibasicdocuments/ibasictext/ibasicstatute.htm#CHAPTER_II (accessed 20 February 2005).
103 See: 'IDF soldier convicted of six charges for the killing of Mr Tom Hurndall', 27 June 2005, *IDF Spokesperson's Office*, http://www1.idf.il/DOVER/site/mainpage.asp?clr=1andsl=ENandid=7anddocid=41713 (accessed 8 July 2005).
104 Ephraim Yaar and Tamar Hermann, 'Peace index: October 2003', *The Tami Steinmetz Centre for Peace Research*, http://spirit.tau.ac.il/socant/peace (accessed 25 January 2005).
105 Ed Blanche, 'Israel faces war of attrition as *Intifada* reaches critical mass', *Jane's Intelligence Review*, vol. 14, no. 4 (April 2002), p. 45.
106 Matthew Gutman, 'Background: Nablus attack likely to lead to change in IDF doctrine', *Jerusalem Post*, 7 February 2003.
107 See: JPost Staff, 'Tactic was designed to destroy tanks', *Jerusalem Post*, 11 May 2004.
108 See: Ellis Shuman, 'Operations in Gaza will continue until soldiers' body parts recovered', *Israelinsider*, 12 May 2004, www.israelinsider.com (accessed 12 May 2004).
109 Ha'aretz Staff, 'IDF pulls troops out of Rafah', *Ha'aretz*, 25 May 2004.
110 Arieh O'Sullivan, 'IDF: 44% fall in terror victims', *Jerusalem Post*, 30 December 2004.
111 See: Amir Buhbut and Marwan Athamna, 'IDF targets Gaza following attack on outpost', *Ma'ariv*, 28 June 2004.
112 Amos Harel, 'Going quietly', *Ha'aretz*, 8 October 2004.
113 See: Amos Harel, 'IAF role grew in Days of Penitence operation', *Ha'aretz*, 19 October 2004.
114 See: 'UNRWA Gaza field assessment of IDF operation Days of Penitence', 20 October 2004, *United Nations Relief and Works Agency*, www.un.org/unrwa/news/incursion_oct04.pdf (accessed 3 August 2005).
115 B'Tselem, *Lethal curfew: the use of live ammunition to enforce curfew* (Jerusalem: B'Tselem, October 2002), p. 8.
116 Amos Harel, 'IDF quietly pulls out of Jenin, surrounds city with trench', *Ha'aretz*, 18 October 2002.
117 Gideon Levy, 'The IDF's "permissiveness" in the territories', *Ha'aretz*, 9 February 2003.
118 Serg. Maj. (Res.), Amit Almog. Interview with author.
119 'Petition for an order nisi and a temporary injunction, Lt. (Res.) David Zoneshine *et al.* versus The Military Advocate General, Israel High Court of

Justice Petition 5062/02', *Courage to refuse*, www.seruv.org.il/Bagatz/BagatzAppealEng_2.pdf (accessed 28 April 2003), p. 31.
120 Ibid. p. 32.
121 Ibid.
122 Lt. X, classified unit within the Paratroopers Brigade. Interview with author, Herzliya, Israel, 25 August 2004.
123 'The battle in Jenin – The Israel Defence Force's response to the report by Amnesty International', *IDF Spokesperson's Office*, www.idf.il/newsite/english/amnesty0407–2.htm (accessed 30 April 2003).
124 Maj. Gen. Amos Gilad, 'Inside the maelstrom', *The Review*, vol. 27, no. 12 (December 2002), p. 13.
125 Amos Harel, 'Razing terrorists' houses is effective deterrent, Army Says', *Ha'aretz*, 9 December 2002.
126 'B'Tselem Report: 80% of Palestinians killed in curfew violations are children', *Jerusalem Post*, 16 October 2002.
127 Matthew Gutman, 'Destruction, constructively speaking', *Jerusalem Post*, 9 January 2003.
128 The total number of *refuseniks* was compiled from the following *refusenik* organisations on 11 July 2004: *Yesh Gvul*, Courage to Refuse, *Shministim* (High school *refuseniks*), New Profile and The Pilots (Air Force pilot *refuseniks*). See: http://oznik.com/web_masters.html.
129 'The combatant's letter', *Courage to refuse*, 25 January 2003, www.seruv.org.il/english/combatants_letter.asp (accessed 28 April 2003).
130 Capt. (Res.) Noam Wiener. Interview with author.
131 Noam Livne, 'A moment before the abyss', *Courage to refuse*, www.seruv.org.il/Signers/34_1_Eng.htm (accessed 2 September 2002).
132 'Frequently asked questions', *Courage to refuse*, www.seruv.org (accessed 1 February 2003).
133 Avner Kokhavi, 'Black commands', *Courage to refuse*, www.seruv.org.il/signers/AvnerKokhaviEng.asp (accessed 3 September 2003).
134 Michael Ben-Yair, 'The war's seventh day', *Courage to refuse*, www.seruv.org.il/MoreArticles/English/MichaelBenYairEng_1.htm (accessed 3 September 2003).
135 Barbara Plett, 'Reservists' rebellion highlights cracks', *BBC News*, 2 February 2002, http://news.bbc.co.uk/2/hi/middle_east/1797637.stm (accessed 5 December 2002).
136 See for example: 'Israeli Settlements in the West Bank', *BBC*, http://news.bbc.co.uk/1/shared/spl/hi/middle_east/03/v3_israel_palestinians/maps/html/settlements_checkpoints.stm (accessed 20 May 2005).
137 Baruch Kimmerling, 'Conscientious objection and the democratization of Israel', *Courage to refuse*, www.seruv.org.il/MoreArticles/English/BaruchKimmerlingEng_1.htm (accessed 3 September 2003).
138 Maj. (Res.) Rami Kaplan, Deputy Reserve Battalion Commander, Armoured Corps. Former leading *refusenik* of the *Ometz le-Sarev* ('Courage to Refuse') movement. Interview with author, Tel Aviv, Israel, 25 August 2003.
139 'From army officer to conscientious objector', *Hardtalk, BBC News*, 6 November 2002, http://news.bbc.co.uk/1/hi/programmes/hardtalk/2412343.stm (accessed 5 December 2002).
140 Amit Mashiah, '*Refuseniks* speak out', *60 Minutes*, 2 May 2002, *CBS News*, www.cbsnews.com/stories/2002/05/02/60minutes/printable507886.shtml (accessed 5 December 2002). For other accounts of conscientious objectors during the *Al-Aqsa Intifada* see: Ronit Chacham, *Breaking ranks: refusing to serve in the West Bank and Gaza Strip* (New York: Other Press, 2003).

141 'Conscientious objection to military service in Israel: an unrecognized human right', *War Resisters' International*, 3 February 2003, www.wri-irg.org/pdf/-co-isr-03.pdf (accessed 28 April 2003), p. 8.
142 According to Avi Dichter, 'terror attacks have destroyed the lives of people who were sitting in restaurants or shopping malls; suddenly we were experiencing something we had not experienced since the Holocaust'. Cited in: Shmulik Hadad, 'Terror reminiscent of Holocaust', *Yediot Ahronot*, 7 May 2005.
143 Col. (Res). Dr Efraim Kam, Deputy Head of the Jaffee Center for Strategic Studies. Interview with author, Tel Aviv, Israel, 28 June 2003.
144 Colonel Gal Hirsh, Head of the IDF Officer Candidate School. Interview with author, Tel Aviv, Israel, 6 August 2003.
145 Capt. Dan Goldfus, Company Commander, *Sayeret Nahal*. Interview with author, undisclosed place, Israel, 5 August 2003.
146 Professor Eyal Ben-Ari, Professor of Sociology, Hebrew University of Jerusalem. Interview with author, Jerusalem, Israel, 15 August 2004.
147 Maj. Gen. (Res.) Danny Yatom, Member of the *Knesset* (Labour Party). Interview with author, Tel Aviv, Israel, 5 August 2005.
148 Asher Arian, *Israeli national public opinion on national security 2003*, Memorandum no. 67 (Tel Aviv: Jaffee Center for Strategic Studies, October 2003), pp. 37–8.
149 'IDF notes rising motivation to serve in combat units', *IDF Spokesperson's Office*, 2 April 2003, www.idf.il/newsnite/english/0402-1.stm (accessed 30 April 2003).
150 'Gung-ho draft', *Yediot Ahronot*, 25 November 2004.
151 See: Reuven Gal, 'The motivation for serving in the IDF: in the mirror of time', *Strategic Assessment*, vol. 2, no. 3 (December 1999), www.tau.ac.il/jcss/sa/v2n3p2.html (accessed 6 September 2002).
152 Editorial, '25 per cent of IDF recruits refer to army's mental health officer', *Ma'ariv*, 27 July 2004.
153 Amos Harel, 'The army now listens when recruits don't fit in', *Ha'aretz*, 7 November 2002.
154 Kathryn Westcott, 'Israel's culture of reservists', *BBC News*, 1 February 2002, http://news.bbc.co.uk/1/hi/world/middle_east/1796102.stm (accessed 1 February 2002).

8 Strategic impasse

1 Mandy Turner, *Arming the occupation: Israel and the arms trade* (London: Campaign Against Arms Trade, October 2002), p. 5.
2 See also: Moti Bassok, 'Intifada so far has cost economy NIS35 billion', *Ha'aretz*, 1 October 2002.
3 Margot Dudkevitch, '60% more apply for regular army', *Jerusalem Post*, 19 February 2003.
4 Uri Dan, 'Where's Ariel Sharon's Sharon?', *Jerusalem Post*, 7 June 2001.
5 Steve Rodan, 'Israeli MoD may lose budget authority', *Jane's Defence Weekly*, vol. 38, no. 4 (24 July 2002), p. 31.
6 Nina Gilbert, 'Mofaz: defence cuts threaten IDF's ability to protect Israel', *Jerusalem Post*, 4 November 2003.
7 See: Margot Dudkevitch, 'Budget cuts force IDF to halt all training for reservists', *Jerusalem Post*, 5 February 2003.
8 Amos Harel, 'Economy drive forces IDF to cut classes for career soldiers', *Ha'aretz*, 3 March 2003.

9 Amos Harel, 'Intifada continues to disrupt IDF training', Ha'aretz, 22 October 2002.
10 Amos Harel, 'IDF cuts infantry basic training from 14 to 10 months', Ha'aretz, 30 October 2002.
11 See: Margot Dudkevitch, 'Budget cuts'.
12 Serg. Maj. (Res.) Jonathan Javor, Squad Leader, Barak Armoured Brigade. Interview with author, London, England, 26 May 2004.
13 Tal Belo, 'Go figure why you are alive', Courage to refuse, www.seruv.org.il/signers/TalBeloeng.asp (accessed 2 September 2002).
14 Bar Dadon, 'The need for an economic model for the IDF reserves', Policy Studies 40 (May–June 1999), Institute for Advanced Strategic and Political Studies, www.israeleconomy.org/policystudies/ps40.pdf (accessed 28 April 2003), p. 20.
15 See: Amos Harel, 'Faith of a dead soldier's mother in the IDF is shaken', Ha'aretz, 15 October 2002.
16 Amos Harel, 'IDF cites poor plans in Jenin battle where 13 reservists died', Ha'aretz, 2 October 2002.
17 Captain (Res.) Khaim, Company Commander, Infantry Reserve Brigade 5. Interview with author, Jaffa, Israel, 12 August 2004. See also: Amos Harel, 'Jenin battle hero echoes criticisms against operation', Ha'aretz, 9 May 2003.
18 See: Amir Buhbut, 'IDF troops going into battle improperly equipped', Ma'ariv, 1 October 2004.
19 'The budget towards defence equipment for combat soldiers will increase by 400%', IDF Spokesperson's Office, 28 November 2004, www.idf.il/dover/site/mainpage.asp?sl=ENandid=7anddocid=35654andPos=8andlast=1andbScope=True (accessed 1 December 2004).
20 Serg. Maj. (Res.) Mike Dacks, Squad Leader, Reserve Armoured Reconnaissance Unit (Paratroopers Brigade whilst serving as a conscript). Interview with author, 2 August 2004, Tel Aviv, Israel.
21 See: Arieh O'Sullivan and Tal Muscal, 'On the defensive', Jerusalem Post, 11 September 2003.
22 Absolute numbers were not disclosed by the IDF. Amos Harel, 'IDF worried by steep rise in desertion', Ha'aretz, 18 November 2002.
23 Aaron Lightner, 'Conscientious objector groups have new life as Intifada drags on', Jewish Telegraph Agency, 15 January 2003, www.jta.org/page_print_story.asp?Intarticleid=10779 (accessed 20 June 2004).
24 Yinon Cohen, 'War and social integration: the effects of the Israeli–Arab conflict on Jewish emigration from Israel', American Sociological Review, vol. 53, no. 6 (December 1988), p. 916.
25 See: Nehemia, Strasler, 'Minimum wage for every soldier', Ha'aretz, 13 February 2003.
26 Arieh Sullivan, 'Fewer serving in IDF, but their motivation is higher', Jerusalem Post, 9 July 2001.
27 For example, former Israeli State Comptroller, Miriam Ben-Porath, warned in February 1996 that 'the army has avoided tackling the problem of sinking morale by simply calling up more reservists to fill the gaps, in some cases by as much as 500 per cent'. Cited from: Ed Blanche, 'Is the myth fading for the Israeli army? – Part one', Jane's Intelligence Review, vol. 8, no. 12 (December 1996), p. 548.
28 Absolute numbers were not disclosed. Erik Schechter, 'reservist groups express outrage over latest service extension bill', Jerusalem Post, 14 March 2003.
29 An organisation made up of reservists, which fights for better reserve duty conditions.

Notes 223

30 Gideon Alon, 'Reserve duty emergency orders extended until May', *Ha'aretz*, 13 November 2002.
31 Moshe Reinfeld, 'Nearly half of draft-age Israelis avoid army service', *Ha'aretz*, 1 November 2002.
32 See: Matthew Guttman, 'Reservists threaten to stay home in protest of Tal Law', *Jerusalem Post*, 2 August 2002 and 'Only 31 haredim drafted in 3.5 years', *Jerusalem Post*, 10 July 2005.
33 Col. (Res.) Itay Landsberg, Reserve Infantry Battalion Commander. Interview with author, Tel Aviv, Israel, 18 August 2004.
34 Col. (Res.) Ofer Ofir, 'Leadership of reserve battalion commanders', *Ma'arachot*, vol. 394 (May 2004), p. 72 [in Hebrew].
35 Matthew Gutman, 'Israel's minutemen', *Jerusalem Post*, 19 September 2002.
36 Amos Harel, 'Soldier dies in accidental shooting', *Ha'aretz*, 27 April 2003.
37 Matthew Gutman, 'Israel's minutemen'.
38 *Shovrim Shtika* (i.e. 'Breaking the silence') is a supposedly apolitical organisation set up by recently discharged conscripts that attempt to recount the abuses they have witnessed or carried out against Palestinian civilians in the Territories during the *Al-Aqsa Intifada*. By doing so, *Shovrim Shtika* hopes to raise greater awareness within Israel on the negative moral and psychological effects that military service in the Territories has on conscript and regular soldiers without, however, explicitly advocating the end of the occupation itself.
39 Serg. Maj. (Res.) Yehuda Shaul, Squad Leader, *Nahal* Brigade. Interview with author, Jerusalem, Israel, 15 August 2004.
40 'Standard routine: beating and abuse of Palestinians by Israeli security forces during the *Al-Aqsa Intifada*', *B'Tselem*, May 2001, www.btselem.org/Download/Standard_Routine_Eng.doc (accessed 1 March 2003).
41 Serg. Maj. (Res.) Amit Almog, *Nahal* Brigade Squad Leader. Interview with author, Jerusalem, Israel, 23 August 2004.
42 Gideon Alon, '58 per cent of soldiers' gripes found justified', *Ha'aretz*, 26 March 2003.
43 Ze'ev Schiff, 'Operational revolution in the IDF', *Ha'aretz*, 7 September 2004.
44 See for example: David A. Deptula, 'Effects-Based Operations: change in the nature of warfare', *Defense and Airpower Series* (Arlington, VA: Aerospace Education Foundation, 2001).
45 During the first 30 months of the *Al-Aqsa Intifada*, direct and indirect defence costs of the conflict amounted to around $3.66 billion. See: Zeev Klein, '*Intifada* Costs Israel NIS 16.5b in 30 months', *Globes Online*, 4 June 2003, www.globes.co.il (accessed 20 June 2004).
46 In 2002 the defence budget was $8.79 billion, in 2003 it was $8.12 billion and in 2004 it was $7.21 billion. See: Nina Gilbert, 'Mofaz: budget cut would cripple IDF', *Jerusalem Post*, 5 November 2003 and Mati Wagner, 'Treasury advocates defence budget cut', *Jerusalem Post*, 6 June 2004.
47 Alon Ben-David, 'Extensive cuts to hit Israeli ground forces the most', *Jane's Defence Weekly*, vol. 40, no. 2 (16 July 2003), p. 17.
48 Eliot A. Cohen *et al.*, 'Israel's revolution in security affairs', *Survival*, vol. 40, no. 1 (Spring 1998), p. 58.
49 Ibid.
50 Amnon Barzilai, 'IDF prepares for changed warfare, shrinking budgets', *Ha'aretz*, 7 January 2004.
51 See: Hanan Greenberg, 'IDF reservists' training problematic', *Yediot Ahronot*, 15 March 2005.

224 Notes

52 See: Bar Dadon, 'The need for an economic model for the reserves', *Policy Study no. 40* (May–June 1999), *Institute for Advanced Strategic and Political Studies*, www.iasps.org/policystudies/ps40.pdf (accessed 23 February 2000).
53 Alon Ben-David, 'Israel reviews duties of reserves', *Jane's Defence Weekly*, vol. 41, no. 14 (7 April 2004), p. 39.
54 For a description of the holiday see: 'The counting of Omer', *Judaism 101*, www.jewfaq.org/holidayb.htm (accessed 10 September 2004).
55 For an inside view of the social life that reservists experience during their reserve duty see: Eyal Ben-Ari and Liora Sion, 'Hungry, weary and horny: joking and jesting among Israel's combat reserves', *Israel Affairs*, vol. 11, no. 4 (October 2005), pp. 655–71.
56 Staff Sergeant (Res.) Amos Harel, Defence Correspondent, *Ha'aretz*. Interview with the author, Tel Aviv, Israel, 22 June 2003.
57 Col. (Res.) Itay Landsberg. Interview with author.
58 Gabriel Ben-Dor *et al.*, 'Israel's national security doctrine under strain: the crisis of the reserve army', *Armed Forces and Society*, vol. 28. no. 2 (Winter 2002), p. 234.
59 On the implications of such a transformation see: Stuart A. Cohen, 'The Israel Defense Forces (IDF): from a "people's army" to a "professional military" – causes and implications', *Armed Forces and Society*, vol. 21, no. 2 (Winter 1995), pp. 237–54.
60 Professor Eyal Ben-Ari, Professor of Sociology, Hebrew University of Jerusalem. Interview with author, Jerusalem, Israel, 15 August 2004.
61 Alon Ben-David, 'Interview: Maj. Gen. Yiftah Ron-Tal, Commander, IDF Ground Forces Command', *Jane's Defence Weekly*, vol. 41, no. 2 (24 March 2004), p. 34.
62 Alon Ben-David, 'Inner conflict: Israel's Low-Intensity Conflict doctrine briefing', *Jane's Defence Weekly*, vol. 41, no. 35 (1 September 2004), p. 27.
63 See: Amir Buhbut, 'IDF purchases advanced mobile shooting simulators', *Ma'ariv*, 9 June 2004.
64 See: Amir Buhbut, 'IDF to set up "Simulator City"', *Ma'ariv*, 1 July 2004.
65 See: 'Good news for soldiers', *Yediot Ahronot*, 10 May 2005.
66 See: Amir Rapaport, 'IDF considering revolutionary changes', *Ma'ariv*, 27 June 2004.
67 See: Amir Buhbut, 'IDF to form new infantry division', *Ma'ariv*, 16 November 2004.
68 Alon Ben-David, 'All quiet on the eastern front, so Israel will revise IDF organisation and doctrine', *Jane's International Defense Review*, vol. 37 (March 2004), p. 52.
69 Professor Eyal Ben-Ari. Interview with author.
70 See: Amir Rapaport, 'IDF signs NIS 3.5 billion mega-deal with Elbit', *Ma'ariv*, 16 July 2004.
71 Amnon Barzilai, 'General staff okays $2.5 billion budget for IDF work-plan', *Ha'aretz*, 30 June 2004.
72 Alon Ben-David, 'Israel set to restructure ground forces', *Jane's Defence Weekly*, vol. 41, no. 10 (10 March 2004), p. 20.
73 Amnon Barzilai, 'Hacking away at the IDF's layers of fat', *Ha'aretz*, 7 July 2004.
74 Reuven Gal, 'The Israeli Defense Forces (IDF): a conservative or an adaptive organization?', in Daniel Maman *et al.* (eds), *Military, state and society in Israel: theoretical and comparative perspectives* (New Brunswick, NJ: Transaction Publishers, 2001), p. 367.
75 See: *The military balance 2005/2006*, The International Institute for Strategic Studies (London: Routledge, 2005), pp. 192–4.

76 See: Shimon Naveh, 'The cult of offensive preemption and future challenges for Israeli operational thought', in Efraim Karsh (ed.), *Between war and peace: dilemmas of Israeli security* (London: Frank Cass, 1996), pp. 168–87.
77 See: Gal Luft, 'All quiet on the eastern front? Israel's national security doctrine after the fall of Saddam', *Analysis Paper no. 2* (Washington, DC: Saban Centre for Middle East Policy, March 2004).
78 Alon Ben-David, 'All quiet'.
79 Eliot A. Cohen et al., *'Knives, tanks, and missiles': Israel's security revolution* (Washington, DC: Washington Institute for Near East Policy, 1998), p. 68.
80 Beatrice Heuser and Lawrence Freedman, 'Strategy', in Lawrence Freedman (ed.), *War* (Oxford: Oxford University Press, 1994), p. 192.
81 Martin Van Creveld, *On future war* (London: Brassey's, 1991), p. 208.
82 Maj. Gen. (Res.) Giora Eiland, National Security Advisor. Interview with author, Ramat HaSharon, Israel, 6 August 2004.
83 Eliot A. Cohen et al., *'Knives'*, p. 71.
84 Avi Kober, 'Israeli war objectives into an era of negativism', *Journal of Strategic Studies*, vol. 24, no. 2 (June 2001), p. 187.
85 Efraim Inbar, 'Israel national security, 1973–1996', *Annals of the American Academy of Political and Social Science*, no. 555 (January 1998), p. 71.
86 See: Chaim Herzog, *The war of atonement: the inside story of the Yom Kippur war* (London: Greenhill Books, 2003), pp. 270–91.
87 Uri Bar-Joseph, 'Variations on a theme: the conceptualization of deterrence in Israeli strategic thinking', *Security Studies*, vol. 7, no. 3 (Spring 1998), p. 153.
88 '"Public order and security" September 13, 1993, declaration of principles on interim self-government arrangements', Article VIII, *Jerusalem Media and Communication Centre*, www.jmcc.org/research/series/dop.html#declare (accessed 1 July 2004).
89 Capt. (Res.) Shahar Amit, Platoon Commander, IDF Paratroopers Brigade. Interview with author, 20 August 2004, Tel Aviv, Israel.
90 See: Raviv Droker and Ofer Shelach, *Boomerang: the failure of Israeli leadership in the second Intifada* (Jerusalem: Keter Press, 2005), pp. 404–5 [in Hebrew].
91 See: Giora Goldberg et al., *The impact of intercommunal conflict: the Intifada and Israeli public opinion*, Davis Occasional Papers no. 43 (Jerusalem: The Leonard Davis Institute, Hebrew University of Jerusalem, 1991), pp. 11–14.
92 Moti Bassok and Eynav Ben Yehuda, 'Survey: 46 per cent of households cannot meet monthly outlays', *Ha'aretz*, 10 August 2004.
93 Reuven Gal, 'The Israeli Defence Forces', pp. 364–5.
94 Eliot A. Cohen et al., *'Knives'*, p. 50.
95 Major (Res.) Danny Gal, Field Psychologist, MAMDA (Department of Behavioural Sciences). Interview with author, 12 August 2004, Herzliya, Israel.
96 Yaakov Hasdai, '"Doers" and "Thinkers" in the IDF', *The Jerusalem Quarterly*, no. 24 (Summer 1982), pp. 16–18.
97 Lt. Col. Avi Peled, Head of the *Sayeret Egoz* Battalion. Interview with author, Shrivenham, England, 23 June 2004.
98 Arieh O'Sullivan, 'Soldiers to undergo "disengagement training"', *Jerusalem Post*, 14 September 2004.
99 Lt. X, Classified Unit within the Paratroopers Brigade. Interview with author, Herzliya, Israel, 25 August 2004.
100 Lt. Col. Avi Peled, Head of the *Sayeret Egoz* Battalion. Interview with author.
101 Even though IDF ground forces are built around divisions, they very often train as battalions. During the *Al-Aqsa Intifada*, even such training has suffered serious cutbacks.

226 *Notes*

102 See: Arieh O'Sullivan, 'IDF: 44% fall in terror victims', *Jerusalem Post*, 30 December 2004.
103 As mentioned in Chapter 2, the IDF's anti-intellectual and highly pragmatic tradition created a system within the IDF by which officers with greater combat experience were promoted often at the expense of officers who, although considered strategically or operationally creative, had less combat experience or were deemed too intrepid.
104 Chris Demchak, 'Technology's knowledge burden, the RMA, and the IDF: organizing the hypertext organization for future "wars of disruption"?', *Journal of Strategic Studies*, vol. 24, no. 2 (June 2001), p. 105.
105 Emanuel Wald, *The Wald report: the decline of Israeli national security since 1967* (Boulder, CO: Westview Press, 1992), p. 187.
106 Avi Kober, 'The intellectual and modern focus in Israeli military thinking as reflected in *Ma'arachot* articles, 1948–2000', *Armed Forces and Society*, vol. 30, no. 1 (Fall 2003), pp. 141–60.
107 Yoram Peri, *The Israeli military and Israel's Palestinian policy: from Oslo to the Al-Aqsa Intifada*, Peaceworks no. 47 (Washington, DC: United States Institute for Peace, November 2002), p. 39.
108 See: Pierre Klochendler, 'Israeli general apologizes for civilian deaths', 23 July 2002, *CNN*, www.cnn.com/2002/WORLD/meast/07/23/hamas.assassination (accessed 10 August 2003).
109 Quoted in: 'Israel needs Yaalon', *Foreign Report, Jane's Information Group*, 6 November 2003, http://frp.janes.com (accessed 23 June 2004).
110 See: 'Report of the Secretary-General prepared pursuant to General Assembly resolution ES-10/10 (Report on Jenin)', *United Nations General Secretariat*, 30 July 2002, www.un.org/peace/jenin/ (accessed 22 August 2006).
111 David A. Fulghum and Robert Wall, 'Israel refocuses on urban warfare', *Aviation Week and Space Technology*, vol. 156, no. 19 (13 May 2002), p. 25.
112 See: Margot Dudkevitch, '50% fewer terror victims in 2003', *Jerusalem Post*, 9 January 2004.
113 See: Arieh O'Sullivan, 'Mofaz terror in decline, pressure to continue', *Jerusalem Post*, 22 June 2004.
114 See: Ephraim Yaar and Tamar Hermann, 'Peace index: June 2004', *The Tami Steinmetz Centre for Peace Research*, http://spirit.tau.ac.il/socant/peace (accessed 25 January 2005).
115 See: Edward H. Kaplan *et al.*, 'What happened to suicide bombings in Israel? Insights from a terror stock model', *Studies in Conflict and Terrorism*, vol. 28, no. 3 (May–June 2005), pp. 225–35.
116 Brig. Gen. (Ret.) Shlomo Brom, former IDF Head of the Strategic Planning Division. Interview with author, Tel Aviv, Israel, 13 June 2003.
117 Statistics quoted in: Avi Kober, 'Has battlefield decision become obsolete? The commitment to the achievement of battlefield decision revisited', *Contemporary Security Policy*, vol. 22, no. 2 (August 2001), p. 111.
118 See: Gil Merom, *How Democracies Lose Small Wars* (Cambridge: Cambridge University Press, 2003).

9 Unilateral disengagement

1 The belief that there was no one to negotiate with on the Palestinian side was slightly mitigated following Yasser Arafat's death, on 11 November 2004. However, as we shall see further on, it was reinforced once *Hamas* won the Palestinian legislative elections in January 2006.
2 From the Office of the Chief of Staff, Diary, 17 September 1956. Cited in:

Mordechai Bar-On, 'Small wars, big wars: security debates during Israel's first decade', *Israel Studies*, vol. 5, no. 2 (Fall 2000), p. 111.
3 Maj. Gen. (Res.) Danny Yatom, Member of the *Knesset* (Labour Party). Interview with author, Tel Aviv, Israel, 5 August 2004.
4 The Gaza Strip settlements comprised of the Gush Katif settlement bloc, Netzarim, Morag, Kfar Darom, whilst the West Bank comprised of four small and fairly isolated settlements of Homesh, Ganim, Kadim and Sa-Nur in northern Samaria.
5 For an overview of the *Gush Emunim* movement and activities see: David Newman (ed.), *The impact of Gush Emunim: politics and settlement in the West Bank* (London: Croom Helm, 1985).
6 See: Ronny Shaked, 'Hamas plans victory parades', *Yediot Ahronot*, 8 July 2005.
7 Ilan Marciano, 'Hamas building popular army', *Yediot Ahronot*, 16 May 2005.
8 Gideon Alon, 'IDF official: pullout to expose 46 Negev towns to rocket fire', *Ha'aretz*, 11 January 2005.
9 'The *Likud* referendum', *Ha'aretz*, 3 May 2004.
10 See: Mazal Mualem, '3 key *Likud* ministers refuse to actively support Gaza plan', *Ha'aretz*, 26 April 2004. Benjamin Netanyahu finally did resign from his cabinet position on 8 August 2005 a week prior to the actual start of the unilateral disengagement from the Gaza Strip.
11 See: Uri Glickman, 'Sharon vows to continue disengagement', *Ma'ariv*, 26 July 2004.
12 Figures taken from: 'Disengagement and its discontents: what will the Israeli settlers do?', *Middle East Report no. 43* (7 July 2005), International Crisis Group, www.crisisgroup.org/home/index.cfm?id=3550andl=1 (accessed 15 July 2005), p. 2.
13 Ibid.
14 See: Hanan Greenberg, '6 security rings planned for pullout', *Yediot Ahronot*, 5 April 2005.
15 See: Shlomo Gazit, *Trapped fools: thirty years of Israeli policy in the Territories* (London: Frank Cass, 2003), pp. 241–88.
16 Many national religious Israelis over the last 40 years had been joining the IDF through the *Yeshivat Hesder* (combined *yeshiva* study and military service) programme and the *Mechinot* (pre-military academies) in order to improve their chances of becoming officers and of entering combat and elite units. For an account of the growing phenomenon and the potential effects on the IDF see: Stuart A. Cohen, *The scroll or the sword? Dilemmas of religion and military service in Israel* (Amsterdam: Harwood Academic Publishers, 1997).
17 See: Avi Shavit and Yair Sheleg, 'Nobody is listening', *Ha'aretz*, 24 July 2005.
18 See: Arieh O'Sullivan, 'IDF prepares "evacuation kits"', *Yediot Ahronot*, 10 February 2005.
19 Hanan Greenberg, 'IDF distributes "disobedience guide"', *Yediot Ahronot*, 14 March 2005.
20 'IDF Chief of Staff: take the army out of political dispute', *Yediot Ahronot*, 7 July 2005.
21 See: Mark Lavie, 'Israeli parliament rejects Gaza referendum', *Associated Press*, http://abcnews.go.com/International/wireStory?id=620397 (accessed 28 March 2005).
22 'A dangerous game', *Jerusalem Post*, 5 January 2005.
23 See: 'IDF dismisses 34 reserve officers for implying refusal', *Arutz Sheva*, 10 January 2005, *Israel National News*, www.israelnn.com/news.php3?id=75049 (accessed 11 January 2005).

228 *Notes*

24 Yaacov Katz, 'Noam Livnat presents 10,000 refuser signatures', *Jerusalem Post*, 9 February 2005.
25 Nadav Shragai, 'Religious anti-refusal supporters go public', *Ha'aretz*, 27 January 2005.
26 See: Nadav Shragai, 'Anti-pullout IDF reservists announce refusal to serve', *Ha'aretz*, 11 May 2005.
27 See: Amos Harel, 'Golani commander leaves military over pullout qualms', *Ha'aretz*, 16 May 2005.
28 See: Hanan Greenberg, 'IDF tries 12 objectors', *Yediot Ahronot*, 27 June 2005.
29 See: Efrat Weiss and Hanan Greenberg, 'Refusal phenomenon growing in IDF', *Yediot Ahronot*, 17 July 2005.
30 See: 'Insubordinate *yeshiva* soldiers warned', *Yediot Ahronot*, 18 July 2005.
31 Stuart A. Cohen, *The scroll or the sword?*, p. 110.
32 See: Nadav Shragai, 'Army reservist rabbis say they will refuse to uproot settlements', *Ha'aretz*, 3 January 2005.
33 See: Hanan Greenberg and Ilan Marciano, 'We won't close down *hesder yeshivas*', *Yediot Ahronot*, 18 July 2005.
34 See: 'Police: 320 soldiers, police officers hurt during pullout', *Yediot Ahronot*, 30 August 2005.
35 Attila Somfalvi, 'Dan Harel: unity begins now', *Yediot Ahronot*, 22 August 2005.
36 Hanan Greenberg, 'Mofaz: no tolerance for *Qassams*', *Yediot Ahronot*, 12 September 2005.
37 Efrat Weiss, '5,000 will refuse draft', *Yediot Ahronot*, 5 September 2005.

10 Conclusion

1 Lt. Yonatan, Barak Armoured Brigade Platoon Commander. Interview with author, Tel Aviv, Israel, 4 August 2004.
2 Raviv Droker and Ofer Shelach, *Boomerang: the failure of Israeli leadership in the second Intifada* (Jerusalem: Keter Press, 2005), p. 220 [in Hebrew].
3 See: Amos Harel and Avi Yissacharoff, *The seventh war: how we won and why we lost the war with the Palestinians* (Jerusalem: Gefen Publishing, 2004), p. 328 [in Hebrew].
4 See: Baruch Kimmerling, *The interrupted system* (New Brunswick, NJ: Transaction, 1986).
5 Moshe Yaalon *et al.*, 'Lessons from the fight against terrorism', *PeaceWatch* 533, 29 December 2005, *Washington Institute for Near East Policy*, www.washingtoninstitute.org/templateC05.php?CID=2427 (accessed 30 December 2005).
6 Ariel Dloomy, 'The Israeli *Refuseniks*: 1982–2003', *Israel Affairs*, vol. 11, no. 4 (October 2005), p. 707.
7 See: Samuel Huntington, *The clash of civilizations and remaking of world order* (New York: Simon and Schuster, 1997).
8 Former Defence Minister John Reid again compared the West's values with its Islamist enemies' ones in the following manner: 'Where we intrinsically value life, they do not. And worse of all – these are not isolated aberrations [i.e. their methods of violence], condemned or punished when discovered by their superiors. They are the systematic tools of terror.' Cited in: John Reid, 'We must be "slower to condemn, quicker to understand" the Forces', *Defence News*, 20 February 2006 www.mod.uk/DefenceInternet/Defencenews/DefencePolicyAnd Business/WeMustBeslowerToCondemnQuickerToUnderstandTheForcesJohn Reid.htm (accessed 10 September 2006). President George W. Bush recently

Notes 229

commemorated the fifth anniversary since 9/11 by stating that, 'This struggle has been called a clash of civilizations. In truth, it is a struggle for civilization.' Cited in: George W. Bush, 'Text of President Bush's address to the nation', *Washington Post*, www.washingtonpost.com/wp-dyn/content/article/2006/09/11/AR 2006091100775.html (accessed 11 September 2006).

9 See, for example: Julian Borger, 'Bush warns Syria and Iran over terror', *Guardian*, 3 February 2005, www.guardian.co.uk/usa/story/0,12271, 1404776, 00.html (accessed 10 September 2006).

11 Postscript: The Lebanon Summer War

1 The main Israeli goal was that of delivering an irrecoverable blow to *Hizbullah*, but as it became apparent throughout the campaign that this goal would be unachievable through the pure use of military force and as diplomatic initiatives gained ground, the Israeli government opted for the downgrading/ removal of *Hizbullah* military capability from southern Lebanon. This would be achieved through the reinforcement and activities of both the UNIFIL and Lebanese military within Southern Lebanon. See, for example: David Makovsky and Jeffrey White, *Lessons and implications of the Israel–Hizballah war: a preliminary assessment*, Policy Focus No. 60 (Washington, DC: Washington Institute for Near East Policy, October 2006).

2 During the month-long conflict, *Hizbullah* was not only able to fire around 125–150 rockets per day, but was able to augment the number of rockets fired against Israeli targets in northern Israel to 200 rockets on the last day of the conflict. For an analysis of *Hizbullah*'s rocket campaign and the IDF's attempt at negating it, see: Uzi Rubin, *The rocket campaign against Israel during the 2006 Lebanon war*, Mideast Security and Policy Studies No. 71 (Ramat Gan: Bar-Ilan University Press, 2007).

3 Ari Shavit, 'No way to go to war' (interview with Moshe Yaalon), *Ha'aretz Magazine*, 15 September 2006, p. 10.

4 The 33-day naval blockade permitted in any case over 200 vessels through in order to conduct evacuation and humanitarian aid missions. See: '7,000 Targets in Lebanon', *IDF Spokesperson's Office*, www.idf.il/DOVER/site/main page.asp?sl=EN&id=7&docid=56765.EN (accessed on 15 August 2006).

5 Ofer Shelah, 'Anti-war', *Strategic Assessment*, vol. 9, no. 3 (November 2006), www.tau.ac.il/jcss/sa/v9n3p2Shelah.html (accessed on 3 January 2007).

6 See: Larry Derfner, 'Lambs to the slaughter?', *Jerusalem Post*, 24 August 2006.

7 Hanan Greenberg, 'Why did armoured corps fail in Lebanon?', *Yediot Ahronot*, 30 August 2006. The IDF, overall, lost 118 soldiers during the conflict.

8 Yaacov Katz, 'IDF report card', *Jerusalem Post*, 24 August 2006.

9 Larry Derfner, 'Lambs to the slaughter?'.

10 Ibid.

11 Aerial intelligence maps of the terrain given to ground units operating in Southern Lebanon were from 2000; only towards the end of the conflict did such units get up-to-date ones.

12 Yaakov Katz, 'IDF panel slams Division 91 commanders for severe failures in Lebanon war', *Jerusalem Post*, 16 October 2006.

13 'In controversial move, head of IDF Northern Command is pushed aside mid-war', *IsraelInsider*, 8 August 2006, http://web.israelinsider.com/Articles/ Security/9103.htm (accessed on 10 September 2006).

14 Cited in: B.C. Kessner, 'IDF did not recognize war, slow to transition, report says', *Defense Daily International*, 10 November 2006, www.lexisnexis.com

(accessed on 10 January 2007). For an account of this process see: Kobi Michael, 'The Israel Defense Forces as an epistemic authority: an intellectual challenge in the reality of the Israeli–Palestinian conflict', *Journal of Strategic Studies*, vol. 30, no. 3 (June 2007), pp. 421–46.
15 Leslie Susser, 'IDF's new commander: back to the basics', *The Jerusalem Report*, 5 March 2007, p. 17.
16 Ibid.
17 Amos Harel, 'Outgoing infantry chief says military "guilty of arrogance"', *Ha'aretz*, 21 August 2006.
18 This is the classic example of a military fighting on the basis of its previous conflict experiences rather than on the basis of prospective warfare scenarios.
19 *Ha'aretz* Staff, 'The main findings of the Winograd partial report on the Second Lebanon War', *Ha'aretz*, 1 May 2007.
20 Zeev Schiff, 'Ashkenazi to annul Halutz's organizational changes to IDF', *Ha'aretz*, 27 February 2007.
21 Aluf Benn, 'Winograd task force: bolster PMO National Security Council', *Ha'aretz*, 28 June 2007.

Bibliography

Interviews

The status of interviewees corresponded to their current position at the time of interview as well as to previously held positions that were relevant to the interview questions asked.

1. Serg. Maj. (Res.) Almog, Amit, 23 August 2004, Jerusalem, Infantry Corps reservist. Served in *Nahal* Brigade as a reservist (1994–97).
2. Capt. (Res.) Amit, Shahar, 20 August 2004, Tel Aviv, Platoon Commander, Paratroopers Brigade.
3. Professor Ben-Ari, Eyal, 15 August 2004, Jerusalem, Professor of Sociology, Hebrew University of Jerusalem.
4. Lt. Col. Ben-Eliyahu, Hadas, 10 August 2004, Tel Aviv, Head of Research, *MAMDA* (IDF Behavioural Sciences Unit).
5. Maj. Ben-Shalom, Uzi, 22 August 2004, Netanya, Head of Research Section, Military Psychology Centre, *MASI* (Ground Forces Command).
6. Maj. Ben-Yehuda, Yoram, 31 August 2003, Tel Aviv, Head of the Combat Reaction Unit.
7. Brig. Gen. Brom, Shlomo, 19 June 2003, Tel Aviv, Senior Research Associate, Jaffee Centre for Strategic Studies. Former IDF Head of the Strategic Planning Division (1993–98).
8. Cassuto, David, 17 August 2003, Jerusalem, Former Deputy Mayor of Jerusalem.
9. Serg. Maj. (Res.) Dacks, Mike, 2 August 2004, Tel Aviv, Reserve armoured corps reconnaissance unit. Paratrooper Brigade Squad Leader 2000–03.
10. Serg. Maj. (Res.) Dardic, Lionel, 19 August 2003, Tel Aviv, *Kharuv* Battalion conscript (1996–98). Injured during Hasmonean tunnel riots in Nablus (Sept. 1996).
11. Serg. Maj. (Res.) 'Downtown' Dave, 19 August 2004, Tel Aviv. Served in the *Givati* Infantry Brigade (1989–92).
12. Maj. Gen. (Res.) Eiland, Giora, 6 August 2004, Ramat HaSharon, National Security Advisor. Former IDF Head of Planning and Policy (2001–04).
13. Col. Elcabets, Roi, 26 August 2004, Tel Aviv, Head of Doctrine and Planning, IDF Ground Forces Command (*MASI*).
14. Brig. Gen. (Res.) Eldad, Arieh, 16 August 2005, Jerusalem, *Moledet* Party Member of the *Knesset*. Former IDF Chief Medical Officer (1997–2000).
15. Capt. (Res.) E., 18 August 2004, Tel Aviv, *Sayeret Matkal* commander.

16 Maj. (Res.) Gal, Danny, 12 August 2004, Herzliya, *MAMDA* Field Psychologist.
17 Serg. Maj. Gal, 25 August 2004, Tel Aviv, *Sayeret Egoz* Squad Leader.
18 Capt. Goldfus, Dan, 5 August 2003, Undisclosed place, *Sayeret Nahal* Company Commander.
19 Serg. Goodriche, Sam, 31 August 2003, Tel Aviv, Paratroopers Brigade.
20 Serg. Maj. (Res.) Hachmov, Yaron, 11 August 2004, Herzliya, Infantry Reserve Brigade 5, Squad Leader.
21 Brig. Gen. HaCohen, Gershon, 31 August 2003, Tel Aviv, IDF Head of Doctrine and Training.
22 Serg. Hagai, 25 August 2004, Tel Aviv, *Sayeret Egoz* soldier.
23 Brig. Gen. (Res.) Haiman, Ariel, 23 August 2004, Tel Aviv, IDF Chief Reserve Officer.
24 Halevy, Ephraim, 19 August 2003, Jerusalem, National Security Advisor. Former *MOSSAD* Director (1998–2003).
25 Serg. Maj. (Res.) Harel, Amos, 22 June 2003, Tel Aviv, *Ha'aretz* defence correspondent. Infantry Brigade reservist.
26 Col. Hirsh, Gal, 6 August 2003, Tel Aviv, Head of the IDF Officer Candidate School. Former Head of Operations, IDF Central Command.
27 Hoffstater, Noam, 19 August 2003, Jerusalem, Spokesperson for *BT'Selem* (Israeli human rights group).
28 Serg. Maj. (Res.) Javor, Jonathan, 26 May 2004, London, Armoured Corps reservist. *Barak* Armoured Brigade (2000–03).
29 Lt. Joshua, 24 August 2004, Nebi Musa, Deputy Company Commander, 7th Armoured Brigade.
30 Col. (Res.) Kam, Ephraim, 19 June 2003, Tel Aviv, Deputy Head of the Jaffee Centre for Strategic Studies. Former Assistant Director of IDF Military Intelligence Research Division.
31 Maj. (Res.) Kaplan, Rami, 25 August 2003, Tel Aviv, Deputy Reserve Battalion Commander, Armoured Corps. Leading *Refusenik* of the *Ometz le-Sarev* ('Courage to Refuse') movement.
32 Professor Kasher, Asa, 24 August 2003, Tel Aviv, Professor in Professional Ethics and Philosophy of Practice. Co-author of the IDF's code of ethics.
33 Keller, Adam, 7 August 2003, Tel Aviv, Spokesperson for *Gush Shalom* (Israeli Peace Bloc).
34 Cap. (Res.) Khaim, 12 August 2004, Jaffa, Infantry Reserve Brigade 5 Company Commander.
35 Dr Kober, Avi, 11 August 2003, Tel Aviv, Senior Research Associate, The Begin–Sadat Centre for Strategic Studies.
36 Col. (Res.) Landsberg, Itay, 18 August 2004, Tel Aviv, Brigade 408 infantry reserve battalion commander. Co-Coordinator for the Battalion Officers' Reserve Forum.
37 Lt. Col. Malka, Ilan, 9 August 2004, Qiryat Gat, Head of Training *Givati* Brigade. Served as conscript and platoon commander in *Intifada*.
38 Lt. Col. (Res.) Naiger, Arieh, 14 August 2003, Tel Aviv, Reserve Paratroopers Battalion Commander. Co-Coordinator for the Battalion Officers' Reserve Forum.
39 Cap. Oken, Danny, 26 August 2003, Gush Katif, *Givati* Brigade Company Commander.

40 O'Sullivan, Arieh, 12 August 2004, Tel Aviv, The *Jerusalem Post* defence correspondent.
41 Serg. Maj. (Res.) Outmezgin, Mike, 24 August 2003, Tel Aviv, Infantry Brigade reservist. Former *Kharuv* Battalion Squad Leader.
42 Lt. Col. Peled, Avi, 23 June 2004, Shrivenham, Head of *Sayeret Egoz* Battalion.
43 Capt. (Res.) Peretz, Ely, 12 August 2003, Hadera, *Nahal* Brigade Company Commander.
44 Maj. Gen. (Ret.) Rotem, Avraham, 18 June 2003, Tel Aviv, Senior Research Associate, The Begin–Sadat Centre for Strategic Studies.
45 Capt. (Res.) Roye, Ron, 10 August 2004, Kfar Saba, Spokesperson for *BALTAM*, a reservists' advocacy group.
46 Serg. Maj. (Res.) Sachs, Sean, 11 August 2003, Tel Aviv, Infantry Brigade reservist. *Nahal* 50 Brigade Squad Leader (2000–02).
47 Dr Schleifer, Ron, 28 August 2003, Tel Aviv, Research Associate, The Begin–Sadat Centre for Strategic Studies.
48 Serg. Maj. (Res.) Shamir, Eitan, 23 June 2004, Shrivenham, *MAMDA* Reserve Organizational Psychology Unit. Served in the *Nahal* 50 Paratroopers Brigade Squad Leader (1983–86) and in the Infantry Reserve Brigade 5 (1986–94).
49 Serg. Maj. (Res.) Shaul, Yehuda, 15 August 2004, Jerusalem, Spokesperson for *Shovrim Shtika*. Former *Nahal* Battalion 50 Squad Leader (2001–4).
50 Serg. Maj. (Res.) Shemer, Aviram, 28 August 2003, Tel Aviv, Armoured Corps Brigade reservist. Conscript during first *Intifada*.
51 Serg. (Res.) Smooha, Shahar, 18 August 2003, Tel Aviv, Armoured Corps Reservist. *Ometz le-Sarev Refusenik*.
52 Lt. Col. Shmueli, Timna, 19 August 2004, Netanya, Head of IDF School of Leadership.
53 Maj. Gen. (Res.) Vilnai, Matan, 17 June 2003, Jerusalem, Labour Party Member of the *Knesset*. Member of the Foreign Affairs and Defence Committee. Former IDF Deputy Chief of Staff (late 1990s).
54 Capt. (Res.) Wiener, Noam, 24 August 2003, Tel Aviv, Infantry Brigade reservist. *Ometz le-Sarev Refusenik*. Paratroopers Brigade (1993–97).
55 Lt. X, 25 August 2004, Herzliya, Classified Unit within the Paratroopers Brigade.
56 Col. Yaar, Itamar, 16 August 2004, Ramat HaSharon, Deputy National Security Advisor.
57 Maj. Gen. Yatom, Danny, 5 August 2004, Tel Aviv, Labour Party Member of the *Knesset*. Member of the Foreign Affairs and Defence Committee. Former IDF Head of Central Command (1991–93).
58 Lt. Col. Yehudai, Avner, 22 August 2003, Tel Aviv, Reserve Paratroopers Battalion Commander. Co-Coordinator for the Battalion Officers' Reserve Forum.
59 Lt. (Res.) Yonatan, 4 August 2004, Tel Aviv, Platoon Commander, Barak Armoured Brigade.
60 Serg. Maj. (Res.) Yossi, 5 August 2004, Tel Aviv, Infantry Brigade reservist. Paratroopers Brigade (2000–03).
61 Group Interviev: Lt. Guy, Lt. Eli and Serg. Maj. Omer, 24 August 2004, Shovrei Shomron, *Kharuv* Battalion Platoon Commander, Deputy Commander and NCO.

Select bibliography of books and edited chapters

Allon, Yigal, *The making of Israel's army* (London: Vallentine, Mitchell, 1970).

Ashkenazy, Daniella, 'Mainstreaming marginal populations through military service', in Daniella Ashkenazy (ed.), *The military in the service of society and democracy: the challenge of a dual-role military* (London: Greenwood Press, 1992), pp. 157–64.

Avi-hai, Avraham, *Ben-Gurion state-builder: principles and pragmatism* (New York: John Wiley and Sons, 1974).

Ayalon, Ami, 'Front lines', in Robert B. Satloff (ed.), *War on terror: the Middle East dimension* (Washington, DC: The Washington Institute for Near East Policy, 2002), pp. 3–7.

Baker, Alan, 'Legal and tactical dilemmas inherent in fighting terror: experience of the Israeli army in Jenin and Bethlehem (April–May 2002)', in Yoram Dinstein and Fania Domb (eds), *Israel yearbook on human rights 34* (Leiden: Martinus Nijhoff Publishers, 2004), pp. 179–91.

Bar-Joseph, Uri, *Intelligence intervention in the politics of democratic states: the United States, Israel, and Britain* (University Park, Pennsylvania: Pennsylvania State University Press, 1995).

—— *The watchman fell asleep* (New York: State University of New York Press, 2005).

Bar-On, Mordechai, *In pursuit of peace: a history of the Israeli peace movement* (Washington, DC: US Institute of Peace Press, 1996).

Bar-Siman-Tov, Yaacov et al., *The Israeli–Palestinian violent confrontation 2000–2004: from conflict resolution to conflict management* (Jerusalem: Jerusalem Institute for Israel Studies, 2005).

Barzilai, Gad, 'National security crises and voting behavior: the *Intifada* and the 1988 elections', in Asher Arian and Michal Shamir (eds), *The elections in Israel – 1988* (Oxford: Westview Press, 1990), pp. 65–76.

Beilin, Yossi, *Israel: a concise political history* (London: Weidenfeld and Nicolson, 1992).

—— *Touching peace: from the Oslo Accord to a final agreement* (North Pomfret: Trafalgar Square, 2000).

Belenky, Gregory et al., 'Battle stress, morale, cohesion, combat effectiveness, heroism and psychiatric casualties: the Israeli experience', in Gregory Belenky (ed.), *Contemporary studies in combat psychiatry* (London: Greenwood Press, 1987), pp. 11–20.

Ben-Ari, Eyal, *Mastering soldiers: conflict, emotions, and the enemy in an Israeli military unit* (Oxford: Berghahn Books, 1998).

Ben-Dor, Gabriel, 'Responding to the threat: the dynamics of the Arab–Israeli conflict', in Daniel Bar-Tal et al. (eds), *Security concerns: insights from the Israeli experience* (London: JAI Press, 1998), pp. 113–39.

Ben-Eliezer, Uri, *The making of Israeli militarism* (Bloomington, IN: Indiana University Press, 1998).

Ben-Gurion, David, *Recollections* (London: Macdonald Unit 75, 1970).

Ben-Gurion, David and Pearlman, Moshe, *Ben-Gurion looks back in talks with Moshe Pearlman* (London: Weidenfeld and Nicolson, 1965).

Ben-Meir, Yehuda, *Political–military relations in Israel* (New York: Columbia University Press, 1995).

Benvenisti, Meron, *1987 Report: demographic, legal, social and political developments in the West Bank* (Jerusalem: Jerusalem Post, 1987).
Bigby, Andrew, *Living the Intifada* (London: Zed Books, 1991).
Bregman, Ahron, *Israel's wars, 1947–93* (London: Routledge, 2000).
Brynen, Rex and Caplan, Neil, 'Israel and Palestine: implications of the *Intifada*', in Rex Brynen and Neil Caplan (eds), *Echoes of the Intifada on Israeli political thinking* (Oxford: Westview Press, 1991), pp. 5–12.
Chacham, Ronit, *Breaking ranks: refusing to serve in the West Bank and Gaza Strip* (New York: Other Press, 2003).
Cohen, Eliot A. et al., *'Knives, tanks, and missiles': Israel's security revolution* (Washington, DC: Washington Institute for Near East Policy, 1998).
Cohen, Stuart A., *The scroll or the sword? Dilemmas of religion and military service in Israel* (Amsterdam: Harwood Academic Publishers, 1997).
Cordesman, Anthony H., *Perilous prospects: the peace process and the Arab–Israeli military balance* (Oxford: Westview Press, 1996).
Cordesman, Anthony H. and Wagner, Abraham R., *The lessons of modern war: the Arab–Israeli conflicts, 1973–1989* (London: Mansell Publishing, 1990).
Davis, Uri, *Israel: an apartheid state* (London: Zed Books, 1987).
Dayan, Moshe, *Story of my life* (London: Weidenfeld and Nicolson, 1976).
Droker, Raviv and Shelach, Ofer, *Boomerang: the failure of Israeli leadership in the second Intifada* (Jerusalem: Keter Press, 2005) [in Hebrew].
Drory, Ze'ev, *The Israel defence force and the foundation of Israel* (London: Frank Cass, 2004).
—— *Israel's reprisal policy 1953–1956: the dynamics of military retaliation* (London: Frank Cass, 2005).
Elon, Amos, *A blood-dimmed tide: dispatches from the Middle East* (London: Penguin Books, 2000).
English, Allan D., *Understanding military culture: a Canadian perspective* (London: McGill-Queen's University Press, 2004).
Ezrahi, Yaron, *Rubber Bullets: power and conscience in modern Israel* (New York: Farrar, Straus and Giroux, 1997).
Farsoun, Samih K., *Palestine and the Palestinians* (Oxford: Westview Press, 1997).
Frankl, Victor E., *Man's search for meaning* (New York, NY: Pocket Books, 1963).
Gabriel, Richard A., *Operation 'Peace for Galilee': the Israeli–PLO war in Lebanon* (New York: Free Press, 1982).
Gal, Reuven, *A portrait of the Israeli soldier* (London: Greenwood, 1986).
—— 'The IDF Structural Model', in Daniella Ashkenazy (ed.), *The military in the service of society and democracy: the challenge of the dual-role military* (London: Greenwood Press, 1994), pp. 20–6.
—— 'The Israeli Defense Forces (IDF): a conservative or an adaptive organization?', in Daniel Maman et al. (eds), *Military, state and society in Israel: theoretical and comparative perspectives* (New Brunswick, NJ: Transaction Publishers, 2001), pp. 361–70.
Gazit, Shlomo, *Trapped fools: thirty years of Israeli policy in the Territories* (London: Frank Cass, 2003).
Gelber, Yoav, 'Ben-Gurion and the formation of the Israel Defence Forces, 1947–1948', in Ronald W. Zweig (ed.), *David Ben-Gurion: politics and leadership in Israel* (London: Frank Cass, 1991), pp. 193–215.

Gilbert, Martin, *Israel: a history* (London: Black Swan, 1999).
Gongora, Thierry and von Riekhoff, Harald, *Toward a revolution in military affairs?: defence and security at the dawn of the twenty-first century* (London: Greenwood Press, 2000).
Gross, Ehud, 'Military, Democracy and education', in Daniella Ashkenazy (ed.), *The military in the service of society and democracy: the challenge of the dual-role military* (London: Greenwood Press, 1994), pp. 55–68.
Harel, Amos and Yissacharoff, Avi, *The seventh war: how we won and why we lost the war with the Palestinians* (Jerusalem: Gefen Publishing, 2004) [in Hebrew].
Hauser, William L., 'The will to fight', in Sam C. Sarkesian (ed.), *Combat Effectiveness: cohesion, stress, and the volunteer military* (London: Sage, 1980), pp. 186–211.
Helman, Sara, 'Militarism and the construction of the life-world of Israeli males', in Edna Lomsky-Feder and Eyal Ben-Ari (eds), *The military and militarism in Israeli society* (Albany, NY: State University of New York Press, 2000), pp. 197–8.
Henderson, William D., *Cohesion: the human element in combat* (Washington, DC: National Defence University Press, 1985).
Herzog, Chaim, *The war of atonement: the inside story of the Yom Kippur war* (London: Greenhill Books, 2003).
Heuser, Beatrice and Freedman, Lawrence, 'Strategy', in Lawrence Freedman (ed.), *War* (Oxford: Oxford University Press, 1994), pp. 191–4.
Hilterman, Joost R., *Behind the Intifada: labor and women's movements in the Occupied Territories* (Princeton: Princeton University Press, 1991).
Horeman, Bart and Stolwijk, Marc, *Refusing to bear arms: a world survey of conscription and conscientious objection* (London: War Resisters International, 1998).
Horowitz, Dan, 'A civilianized military in a partially militarized society', in Roman Kolkowitz and Andrzej Korbonski (eds), *Soldiers, peasants and bureaucrats* (London: George Allen and Unwin, 1982), pp. 77–106.
—— 'The Israeli concept of national security', in Avner Yaniv (ed.), *National security and democracy in Israel* (London: Lynne Rienner, 1993), pp. 11–53.
Horowitz, Dan and Lissak, Moshe, *Trouble in utopia: the overburdened polity of Israel* (New York: Suny Press, 1989).
Hunter, Robert F., *The Palestinian uprising: a war by other means* (Berkeley, CA: University of California Press, 1993).
Huntington, Samuel, *The clash of civilizations and remaking of world order* (New York: Simon and Schuster, 1997).
Hurewitz, Jacob C., *Middle East politics: the military dimension* (Boulder, CO: Westview Press, 1982).
Jones, Clive, 'A framework for analysis', in Clive Jones and Ami Pedahzur (eds), *Between terrorism and civil war: the Al-Aqsa Intifada* (London: Routledge, 2005), pp. 1–8.
Kahalani, Avigdor, *A warrior's way* (Bnei Brak: Steimatzky, 1999).
Katzenstein, Peter J., *The culture of national security: norms and identity in world politics* (NY: Columbia UP, 1996), pp. 33–74.
Keegan, John and Holmes, Richard, *Soldiers: a history of men in battle* (London: Sphere Books, 1985).

Kellett, Anthony, *Combat Motivation: the behaviour of soldiers in battle* (London: Kluwer Publishing, 1984).
Kidron, Peretz, *Refusenik! Israel's soldiers of conscience* (London: Zed Books, 2004).
Kimmerling, Baruch, *The interrupted system* (New Brunswick, NJ: Transaction, 1986).
—— 'The code of security: the Israeli military–cultural complex', in Baruch Kimmerling (ed.), *The invention and decline of Israeliness: state, society and the military* (London: University of California Press, 2001), pp. 208–28.
Kober, Avi, 'A paradigm in crisis? Israel's doctrine of military decision', in Efraim Karsh (ed.), *Between war and peace: dilemmas of Israeli security* (London: Frank Cass, 1996), pp. 188–211.
Lanir, Zvi, 'Political aims and military objectives – some observations on the Israeli experience', in Zvi Lanir (ed.), *Israeli Security Planning in the 1980s: its politics and economics* (Eastbourne: Praeger, 1984), pp. 14–49.
Levite, Ariel, *Offence and defence in Israeli Military Doctrine* (Boulder, CO: Westview Press, 1989).
Liddell-Hart, Basil H., *Strategy: the indirect approach* (London: Faber, 1967).
Linn, Ruth, *Conscience at war: the Israeli soldier as a moral critic* (Albany: State University of New York Press, 1996).
Lissak, Moshe, 'Civilian components in the national security doctrine', in Avner Yaniv (ed.), *National security and democracy in Israel* (London: Lynne Rienner, 1993), pp. 55–80.
—— 'The permeable boundaries between civilians and soldiers in Israeli society', in Daniella Ashkenazy (ed.), *The military in the service of society and democracy* (London: Greenwood Press), pp. 56–68.
Lorch, Natanel, *Major Knesset debates 1948–1981*, vol. 1 (Lanham, MD: University Press of America, 1993).
Luttwak, Edward and Horowitz, Dan, *The Israeli army* (London: Allen Lane, 1975).
Maman, Daniel and Lissak, Moshe, 'Military–civilian élite networks in Israel: a case study of boundary structure', in Benjamin Frankel (ed.), *A Restless Mind: essays in honor of Amos Perlmutter* (London: Frank Cass, 1996), pp. 49–76.
Manning, Frederick J., 'Morale, cohesion and *esprit de corps*', in Reuven Gal and David A. Mangelsdorff (eds), *Handbook of military psychology* (Chichester: John Wiley & Sons, 1991), pp. 453–71.
Manning, Frederick J. et al., 'An investigation into the value of unit cohesion in peacetime', in Gregory Belenky (ed.), *Contemporary studies in combat psychiatry* (London: Greenwood Press, 1987), pp. 47–67.
Marshal, Catherine and Robertson, Gretchen B., *Designing qualitative research* (London: Sage, 1989).
Marshall, Samuel L.A., *Men against fire* (New York: William Morrow and Company, 1947).
Medding, Peter Y., *The founding of Israeli democracy 1948–1967* (Oxford: Oxford University Press, 1990).
Merom, Gil, *How democracies lose small wars* (Cambridge: Cambridge University Press, 2003).
Mishal, Shaul and Aharoni, Reuven, *Speaking stones: communiques from the Intifada underground* (Syracuse, NY: Syracuse University Press, 1994).

Nagl, John A., *Counter-insurgency lessons from Malaya and Vietnam: learning to eat soup with a knife* (London: Praeger, 2002).

Naveh, Shimon, 'The cult of offensive preemption and future challenges for Israeli operational thought', in Efraim Karsh (ed.), *Between war and peace: dilemmas of Israeli security* (London: Frank Cass, 1996), pp. 168–87.

Nevo, Baruch and Shur, Yael, *The IDF and the press during hostilities* (Jerusalem: The Israel Democracy Institute, 2003).

—— *Morality, ethics and law in wartime* (Jerusalem: The Israel Democracy Institute, 2003).

Newman, David (ed.), *The impact of Gush Emunim: politics and settlement in the West Bank* (London: Croom Helm, 1985).

—— 'The geographical and territorial imprint on the security discourse', in David Bar-Tal *et al.* (eds), *Security concerns: insights from the Israeli experience* (London: JAI Press, 1998), pp. 73–94.

Novack, Dorit, 'The cultural branch of the IDF education corps', in Daniella Ashkenazy (ed.), *The military in the service of society and democracy* (London: Greenwood Press, 1994), pp. 76–9.

O'Balance, Edgar, *The Palestinian Intifada* (London: Macmillan Press, 1998).

Oren, Michael, *Six days of war: June 1967 and the making of the modern Middle East* (London: Penguin Books, 2003).

Osgood, Robert E., *NATO: the entangling alliance* (Chicago: University of Chicago Press, 1962).

Pedatzur, Reuven, 'Ben-Gurion's enduring legacy', in Daniel Bar-Tal *et al.* (eds), *Security concerns: insights from the Israeli experience* (London: JAI Press, 1998), pp. 139–64.

Peretz, Don, *Intifada: Palestinian uprising* (London: Westview Press, 1990).

Peri, Yoram, *Between battles and bullets: Israeli military in politics* (Cambridge: Cambridge University Press, 1983).

—— 'Coexistence or hegemony? Shifts in the Israeli Security Concept', in Dan Caspi *et al.* (eds), *The roots of Begin's success: the 1981 Israeli elections* (London: Croom Helm, 1984), pp. 191–215.

—— 'Civilian control during a protracted war', in Ernest Krausz (ed.), *Politics and society in Israel: studies in Israeli society*, vol. 3 (Oxford: Transaction Books, 1985), pp. 362–84.

—— 'The impact of occupation on the military: the case of the IDF, 1967–1987', in Ilan Peleg and Ofira Seliktar (eds), *The emergence of a binational Israel: the second republic in the making* (London: Westview Press, 1989), pp. 143–68.

—— 'Israel: conscientious objection in a democracy under siege', in Charles Moskos and J.W. Chambers (eds), *The new conscientious objection: from sacred to secular resistance* (Oxford: Oxford University Press, 1993), pp. 146–57.

—— *Generals in the cabinet room: how the military shapes Israeli policy* (Washington, DC: United States Institute of Peace Press, 2006).

Perlmutter, Amos, *Military and politics in Israel: nation-building and role expansion* (London: Frank Cass, 1969).

—— 'Israel: the routinized revolutionary army', in Amos Perlmutter (ed.), *The military and politics in modern times: on professionals, praetorians and revolutionary soldiers* (London: Yale University Press, 1977), pp. 251–80.

—— 'The dynamic of Israeli national security decision making', in Robert J. Art *et*

al. (eds), *Reorganising America's defence: leadership in war and peace* (Washington, DC: Pergamon-Brassey's, 1985), pp. 130–5.
Quandt, William B., *Peace process: American diplomacy and the Arab–Israeli conflict since 1967* (Los Angeles: University of California Press, 2001).
Rabin, Yitzhak, *The Rabin memoirs* (London: Weidenfeld and Nicolson, 1979).
Rolbant, Samuel, *The Israeli soldier: profile of an army* (London: South Brunswick, 1970).
Rothenberg, Gunther E., 'Israeli defence forces and Low-Intensity operations', in David A. Charters and Maurice Tugwell (eds), *Armies in Low-Intensity Conflict: a comparative analysis* (London: Brassey's Defence Publishers, 1989), pp. 49–76.
Sandler, Shmuel and Frisch, Hillel, *Israel, the Palestinians and the West Bank: a study in intercommunal conflict* (Toronto: Lexington Books, 1984).
Schiff, Ze'ev and Ya'ari, Ehud, *Intifada: the Palestinian uprising – Israel's third front* (London: Simon and Schuster, 1990).
Shamir, Boas and Ben-Ari, Eyal, 'Leadership in an open army?, Civilian connections, interorganizational frameworks and changes in military leadership', in J.G. Hunt *et al.* (eds), *Out-of-the-box leadership: transforming the twenty-first-century army and other top-performing organisations* (Stamford, CT: JAI Press, 1999), pp. 15–42.
Sharon, Ariel, *Warrior: an autobiography* (London: Simon and Schuster, 2001).
Shimshoni, Daniel, *Israeli democracy: the middle of the journey* (New York: Free Press, 1982).
Shindler, Colin, 'The people's army', in Colin Shindler (ed.), *Ploughshares into swords? Israelis and Jews in the shadow of the Intifada* (London: I.B. Tauris, 1991), pp. 187–204.
Stewart, Nora K., 'Military cohesion', in Lawrence Freedman (ed.), *War* (Oxford: Oxford University Press, 1994), pp. 144–9.
Tal, Israel, *National security: the Israeli experience* (London: Praeger, 2000).
Terriff, Terry and Farrell, Theo, *The sources of military change: norms, politics, technology* (Boulder, CO: Lynne Rienner, 2002).
Tessler, Mark, 'The Impact of the *Intifada* on Israeli Political Thinking', in Rex Brynen and Neil Caplan (eds), *Echoes of the Intifada: regional repercussions of the Palestinian–Israeli conflict* (Oxford: Westview Press, 1991), pp. 43–96.
Van Creveld, Martin, *On future war* (London: Brassey's, 1991).
—— *The sword and the olive: a critical history of the Israeli Defence Forces* (New York: Public Affairs, 1998).
Von Clausewitz, Carl, Michael Howard and Peter Paret (eds), *On war* (Princeton, NJ: Princeton University Press, 1976).
Wald, Emanuel, *The Wald report: the decline of Israeli national security since 1967* (Boulder, CO: Westview Press, 1992).
Walzer, Michael, *Just and unjust wars* (New York: Basic Books, 1977).
Williams, Louis, *Israel Defence Forces: a people's army* (New York: Authors Choice Press, 2000).
Wilson, James Q., *Bureaucracy* (New York: Basic Books, 1989).
Wolf, Aaron, *A purity of arms: an American in the Israeli army* (New York: Doubleday, 1989).
Wong, Leonard *et al.*, *Why they fight: combat motivation in the Iraq war* (Carlisle, PA: Strategic Studies Institute, July 2003).

Yaniv, Avner, *Dilemmas of security: politics, strategy and the Israeli experience in Lebanon* (Oxford: Oxford University Press, 1987).
—— *Deterrence without the bomb: the politics of Israeli strategy* (Lexington, MA: Lexington Books, 1987).
—— 'A question of survival: the military and politics under siege', in Avner Yaniv (ed.), *National security and democracy in Israel* (London: Lynne Rienner, 1993), pp. 81–103.
Yates, Simeon J., *Doing social science research* (London: Sage, 2004), pp. 135–6.

Index

Abbas, Mahmoud 125, 172
absenteeism 23
abuse 85–7, 96–7, 131–5
'active defence' 68
Adam, Maj. Gen. Udi 187, 192
Agranat report (1974) 40–1
Al-Aqsa Intifada: casualties 115–16; circumvention and 'swarm' tactics 113–15; combat motivation 138–40; conscientious objection 135–8; construction of security fence 125–7; costs of 142–3; counter-terrorism 119–24; ethical dilemmas 116–19; grey refusal 140–1; intelligence 112–13; Israeli response 107–10; ongoing violence 128–31; Operation 'Defensive Shield' 110–12; overview 64–5, 102–7; reserve burden 146–50; rules of engagement 131–5; tactics 104, 105, 106, 113–14, 190; training capabilities 115–16; unilateral disengagement 124–6, 170–9; weapons and training programmes 143–6
Ala, Abu 99, 125
Allon, Yigal 34, 39, 49
Almog, Maj. Gen. Doron 123
Almog, Serg. Maj. (Res.) Amit 150
Alsop, Joseph 73
Amal (Lebanese Resistance Brigades) 66, 70–1
Amidror, Maj. Gen. (Res.) Yaacov 176
Amit, Capt. (Res.) Shahar 110, 161
Amit, Maj. Gen. Meir 34
appointments, IDF 32, 35
Arab–Israeli War (1948) 28–9
Arafat, Yasser: ceasefire declaration 119–20; death of 159, 170; and Oslo Accord 99; strategic objectives 102–4; weapons imports 106
Arian, Asher *108*, 140
arrest raids 119
Ashkenazi, Lt. Gen. Gabi 194
asymmetry of forces 50–1, 53–5
Ayalon, Ami 120

Baldwin, Hanson W. 45
Bar-Lev, Haim 34, 39–40
Bar-Lev Line 55–6
Barak, Col. Gil 164–5
Barak, Ehud 35, 103–4, 126, 157
Barel, Col. Mikki 132
Barghouti, Marwan 102
Barzani, Brig. Gen. Avner 152
'Basic Law: The Army' (1976) 41
battlefield decisions, speed of 51, 54–5
Baynes, John 18
Begin, Menachem 25, 34–5, 42, 51, 64–5, 79, 171; and strategic doctrine 62–3
Beilin, Yossi 99, 119
Belo, Tal 145
Ben-Ari, Eyal 22, 26, 95–6, 139, 154, 156
Ben-Eliezer, Binyamin 103, 143
Ben-Eliezer, Uri 36
Ben-Eliyahu, Lt. Col. Hadass 96
Ben-Gurion, David: and civil–military relations 38; *Mapai* 32–5; security doctrine 34, 50, 53, 60; security imperative 35–8; setting up of IDF 12, 15, 23, 28–33, 148
Ben-Nun, Maj. Gen. Avihu 91
Benvenisti, Meron 79
Berman, Yitzhak 42
bitchonism 31, 36, 42–3, 45
bitsuism 9, 10–11, 13, 26–7, 57–9, 95, 164–7, 181, 183, 185, 194
Bland, Douglas 58
borders, defensible 55–6
British Defence (Emergency) Regulations (1945) 77–8
Brom, Brig. Gen. (Rtd) Shlomo 168–9
Buchbinder, Col. Uzi 172
Bush, George W. 124

Camp David Accords (1978) 99
career benefits 144
career officers 33–5, 142
career soldiers 151–2
Carmel, Moshe 34

Index

Cassidy, Robert 10
casualties 114; avoidance of 115–16; civilian 47, 69, 70–1, 81–2, 84, 104–6, 128–31, 168–9; IDF 67, 114, 145, 190, 193
Chacham, Ronit 2
Checkpoint Unit 117–18
checkpoints 121, 128, 138, 145, 161
circumvention tactics 113–14
civil–military relations 12, 175
civil–military tensions 12, 42–3
civilian control of the military 38–9, 41–2
Cohen, Eliot 11
Cohen, Stuart 13, 142
Cohen, Yinon 147
collaborators 84, 113
collateral damage 48, 68–70, 165–8
combat motivation 3–4, 185; *Al-Aqsa Intifada* 138–40; defining 18–20
Combat Readiness Questionnaire survey 19
Command and Staff College 92
Compulsory Conscript Service (*Sherut Hova*) 57, 155
conscientious objection: conscription 23, 92–3, 94, 97, 135–8, 139–41, 145, 181; evacuation of settlers 174–7, 178–9
conscription: acceptance of 31; establishment of 24
conservative organisation, IDF as 2, 11, 157–9, 182–3
coping mechanisms 92–7
counter-guerrilla strategy, Lebanon 67–8
counter-insurgency (COIN) operations 3, 6–7, 12, 24–5, 47–9, 65, 80, 91, 180–1
counter-terrorism 47–9, 119–24
Courage to Refuse (*Ometz Le'sarev*) 135–7
cross-border terror raids 47–9
curfews 84, 121–2, 133
current security (*bitachon shotef*) operations 4, 9, 95, 152, 155, 160, 161; threats 47, 64, 160

Dagan, Brig. Gen. Nehemia 88–9
Dayan, Lt. Gen. Moshe: appointment of Bar-Lev 39–40; and COIN 47–8; election to *Knesset* 34; and minimal contact principle 74; and Occupied Territories 73; and 'purge system' 32–3; and retirement system 152
Dayan, Maj. Gen. (Rtd) Uzi 37, 142
defence funding 142–6
Defence Ministry 37
Defence Service Law (1949) 31
defensible borders strategy 55–6
defensive strategy 49
dehumanisation 96–7, 181–2
delegation 58
Demchak, Chris 165–6
Democratic Movement for Change 34
demographic issues 126, 170–1
demoralisation 87–90; coping with 92–7
Department of Behavioural Sciences, IDF 19
depoliticisation, IDF 31, 32
deportation 77–8, 83
desensitisation 149–50
desertion 147
detention measures 77–8
Dichter, Avi 138–9
'Digital Ground Forces' (DGF) project 156
diplomacy 46, 47
disengagement: accomplishment of 177–9; operational and ethical preparation 174–6
Disengagement Plan 125–6, 172–3
domestic opposition, unilateral disengagement 172–3, 176–7
Dromi, Uri 91
Drori, Maj. Gen. Amir 41–2
Drory, Ze'ev 11, 51

Eban, Abba 55
economic dependency, Palestine 74
Edelstein, Col. Mickey 176
Education Branch 174
Eiland, Maj. Gen. Giora 114, 159–60
Ein-Ariq checkpoint 145
Eisenstadt, Michael 67
Eitam, Effi 172
Eitan, Gen. Yitzhak 109–10
Eitan, Lt. Gen. Rafael 41–2, 63
Elcabets, Col. Roi 5, 116–17
elite networking 33
Elon, Benyamin 172
emigration 147
equipment, lack of 145–6, 191
Eshkol, Levi 39
esprit de corps 18–19, 22
ethical dilemmas 116–19, 145, 185
ethical preparation for disengagement 174–6
Evacuation and Compensation Bill 173
evacuation operation 173–6
evacuation orders, refusal to obey 176–7
exemptions 140–1, 148
existential threats 5, 6, 23–5, 26, 27, 45–7, 52–3, 64, 107, 122–3, 139, 162, 185, 186

Farrell, Theo 9
Fatah 104, 106, 120
Fatah Tanzim paramilitary organisation 102, 105–6
Field Intelligence Corps 113
financial costs of conflict 142–3
financial reimbursement, settlers 173
force, excessive 109, 131–5
forces, asymmetry of 53–5
Foreign Affairs and Defence Committee 38, 162
Foreign Ministry 37

fundamental security (*bitachon yisodi*) threats 47, 160

Gabriel, Richard 66
Gal, Reuven 20
Gavish, Brig. Gen. Yeshiyahu 39
Gazit, Maj. Gen. (Rtd) Shlomo 75
Gedaliah, Lt. Col. David 41
General Staff, control of 38
generals: battle of 39–40; in government and politics 33–5
Gilad, Maj. Gen. Amos 103, 133
global war on terrorism 6–7, 185–6
goals, attainment of 25–6
Golan Heights War (1973) 22, 52, 55–6
Goldfus, Capt. Dan 139
Goldwasser, Ehud 187
Gonen, Maj. Gen. Shmuel 40
Gordon, Shmuel 67
government, 'parachuting' of generals into 33–5
Gozansky, Tamar 35
Gray, Jesse 23, 24
'Greater Israel' concept 52, 98
Green Line 72, 106, 117–18, 126
grey refusal 94, 140–1
Gulf War (1991) 98
Gush Emunim (Bloc of the Faithful) religious movement 88, 171, 172–3
Gush Shalom (Peace Bloc) 88

Hachmov, Serg. Maj. (Res.) 95
HaCohen, Brig. Gen. Gershon 107, 111, 178
Hagana (Defence) militia 28–9
Halevy, Ephraim 56
Halutz, Lt. Gen. Dan 175, 177, 187, 188, 189
Hamas (Islamic Resistance Movement): challenge to PLO 98–9; cooperation with *Fatah* 120; electoral victory 184–5; formation of 87–8; targeted killings 129–31; and unilateral disengagement 171
Harel, Maj. Gen. Dan 166, 178
Harel, Staff Serg. (Res.) Amos 153
Hariri, Rafiq 70
Hasdai, Yaacov 11
'hearts and mind' strategy 66, 184
Heller, Mark 8–9
Hendel, Zvi 172
high-intensity conflicts (HICs) 4, 166
Hirschfeild, Yair 99
Hirsh, Col. Gal 109–10, 114, 139
Hizbullah (Party of God): in Lebanon 66–8; 187–8, 191–2, 193; and Operation 'Accountability' 68–9; and Operation 'Grapes of Wrath' 70–1; operational links 106
Holocaust 59–60, 89, 138

Horowitz, Dan 6, 7–8, 43, 53, 63–4, 123, 142
house demolitions 133–5
Huntington, Samuel 186
Hurndall, Tom 127
Hussein, Saddam 98
Hyman, Brig. Gen. Yossi 193

immigration 30
Inbar, Efraim 13, 50
induction motivation 140
intelligence 112–13, 184, 191–2
intercommunal warfare 43, 63–6, 144, 186
International Court of Justice (ICJ) 126–7
interstate warfare 63–6
interviews 13–14
Intifada (first): break-out of 76–81; mission definition 90–2; morale of IDF 85–90, 92–7; Oslo Peace Accord 97–101; tactical reactions to 81–4; *see also Al-Aqsa Intifada*
Iran 106, 192
Iranian Revolutionary Guards Corps (IRGC) 67
Israel Air Force (IAF) 68, 70, 78, 113, 131, 146, 188, 189, 193
Israel Defence Forces (IDF): birth of 28–9; criticism of 88–90
Israeli Defence Forces Order (1948) 29
Israeli–Egyptian peace treaty (1979) 61–2
Israeli High Court of Justice 118–19, 126, 127
Israeli Secret Service 80–1
Israeli Supreme Court 136

Jabalya refugee camp 76–7, 131
Jabril, Ahmad 68
Javor, Serg. Maj. (Res.) Jonathan 144
Jenin refugee camp 112, 146
Jihad, Abu 81
Jones, Clive 10

Kam, Col. (Res.) Dr Efraim 138–9
Kaplan, Maj. (Res.) Rami 137–8
Kaplinsky, Maj. Gen. Moshe 176, 192
Karmi, Raed 120
Katzenstein, Peter 9, 10
'*Kela 2008*' programme 116, 150, 151, 156, 158, 183
Kellett, Anthony 19
Kibbutz HaArtzi movement 89
Kidron, Peretz 2
Kimche, David 37
Kimmerling, Baruch 36, 137
Kitri, Brig. Gen. Ron 105
Klein, Brig. Gen. Avigdor 114–15
Knesset 30, 31, 33–5, 79–80, 103–4, 172, 175
Knesset Elections Bill (1951) 32
Kober, Avi 160, 166, 192
Kochavi, Maj. Gen. Aviv 178
Kohavi, Brig. Gen. Aviv 4

244 *Index*

Kokhavi, Serg. Maj. Avner 136
Kremnitzer, Mordechai 82
Kupperwaser, Col. Yossi 103
Kurdi, Zuhair 134

Labour government 99
Land of Israel Worker's Party *see Mapai*
Landau, Uzi 175–6
Landsberg, Col. (Res.) Itay 148, 154
Larsen, Terje 99
Law of Associations 79
leadership: professional competency of 20; as protector 21–2; as source of information 20–1
Lebanon: counter-guerrilla strategy in 67–8; Shi'ite challenge in 66–7
Lebanon War (1982) 41–2, 62–5, 66, 72–3, 88, 98, 160
Lebanon War (2006) 187–94
legal system, Occupied Territories 78
legitimacy 4–6
Levite, Ariel 8
Levy, Yitzak 172
Lieberman, Avigdor 172
Likud 34–5, 52, 65, 98, 172, 175
Linn, Ruth 97
Lipkin-Shahak, Lt. Gen. Amnon 35, 37, 109–10, 157
Lissak, Moshe 28, 33
'Litani Operation' (1978) 62
literature review 6–13
Livnat, Limor 172, 176
Livnat, Noam 176
Livne, Noam 136
logistics 190–1
low-intensity conflicts (LICs) 1–2, 3–6, 11, 20, 58, 86, 159–60, 162, 166, 183–4
Luft, Lt. Col. Gal 109
Luttwak, Edward 7

Madrid peace process 98–9
Malka, Lt. Col. Ilan 91
Maman, Daniel 33
Manning. Frederick J. 18
Mapai 32, 33–4
Mardawi, Tabaat 114
Marshall, Samuel L.A. 23, 26
Mashiah, Amit 138
media 5, 7, 114–15
Meir, Golda 34
Menahem, Col. David 155
Mendelbiet, Brig. Gen. Avi 162
Menuchin, Ishai 94, 141
Meridor, Dan 164
methodology 13–14
military aid 106
military–civilian tensions 42–3
Military Government (MG), Occupied Territories 73–6, 77–9, 80, 84

Military Intelligence Division, IDF 37, 157
military–political relations 32–3
military transformation 150–1
minimal contact principle 74
Ministry of Defence (MOD) 29
mission accomplishment 25–6, 91
'mission command' principles 53–4, 57–9
mission definition 90–2
Mitzna, Maj. Gen. Amram 89, 90
Mofaz, Lieut. Gen. Shaul 35, 103, 104–5, 108–10, 122, 143, 162
moral dilemmas 87–90
morale, IDF troops 85–90, 92–7

Nagl, John 12, 50
Nasrallah, Sheikh Hassan 139
nation-builder, IDF as 30–2
National Defence Service Law (1986) 93
national survival, 45–7
National Unity government 65, 88, 91
nationalisation 30–2
nationalist organisations, regulation of 79–80
Nationality Law (1952) 79–80
'neighbour practice' 118–19
Netanyahu, Benjamin 126, 144, 171, 172
non-combatant: casualties 115–16
Northern Command 42, 187, 192
Nufal, Mamduh 104

'occupation tax' 74
Occupied Territories: control of 52–3; military government in 73–6
'offensive operations' 68
Olmert, Ehud 187–8, 189, 193
Operation 'Accountability' 68–9, 71
Operation 'Days of Penitence' 129, 131, 146, 171
Operation 'Defensive Shield' 108, 110–12, 114, 115, 120, 121, 145–6, 167–8
Operation 'Determined Path' 121–2
Operation 'Early Dawn' 102
Operation 'Grapes of Wrath' 70–1
Operation 'Iraqi Freedom' 155, 158
Operation 'Peace for Galilee' 62–3; *see also* Lebanon War (1982)
Operation 'Rainbow' 128–9, 171
operational preparation for disengagement 174–6
operational–tactical offensive 4, 183
Order Eight (*Tsav-Shmone*) orders 146–7
organisational changes 43, 194
organisational culture 9–10, 11, 45, 58, 164, 183
organisational ethos 57–9
Oslo Peace Accord 37, 97–101
Oslo Peace Process (1993–2000) 102–4, 109–10

Ottoman Associations Law (1909) 79

Palestine Liberation Organisation (PLO): COIN operations against 48–9; developments within 97–9; exile to Tunis 78; and Operation 'Peace for Galilee' 62–3; and UNLU 80–1; *see also* Fatah Tanzim
Palestine Security Service (PSS) 104, 182
Palestinian Authority (PA): 'A' areas 121–2, 168; call for violence 102–3; complicity in terror attacks 119–20; government/security buildings 109; handing of control to 100–1; and Operation 'Defensive Shield' 111–12, 121; power struggles 124–6; and unilateral disengagement 178
Palestinian National Charter (1968) 99
'passive defence' 55, 67–8
Peace Now 88
peace, 'road map' for 124–6
Peled, Lt. Col. Avi 124, 165
'people's army', IDF as 23, 33, 47, 56, 57, 154
Peres, Shimon 37, 51
Peretz, Amir 187, 188
performance, emphasis on 9, 11–12
Peri, Ya'acov 113
Peri, Yoram 2, 7, 13, 73
perimeter defence system 49
Perlmutter, Amos 12
Permanent Service Corps (*Sherut Keva*) 57
personnel issues, IDF 151–2
plastic bullets 82
political–military relations 12, 28, 32–3, 41, 42–3
political–strategic status quo 50–1, 54, 76, 81, 90
politics, 'parachuting' of generals into 33–5
Popular Front for the Liberation of Palestine – General Council Command (PFLP–GC) 68–9
poverty levels, Israel 163
power struggles, PA 124–6
preparedness, IDF 91–2, 109–10, 145, 190–1, 194
Prevention of Terrorism Ordinance (1948) 80
professional competency 20, 94–5
profile '21'/'24' exemptions 140–1
properties, demolition/sealing of 83, 134–5, 162
psychological burnout 97, 149–50
psychological exemptions 141
public opinion: on IDF 108, 140; on unilateral disengagement 172–3
'purge' system 32–3
purity of arms concept 49

qualitative edge, IDF 56
Qurei, Ahmed 125

Rabbinical academies (*Yeshivot*) 31
Rabin, Yitzhak: and *Intifada* 81–2, 85, 90, 93, 97, 99; 'iron fist' policy 78, 87; and Oslo Accord 100; security doctrine 48, 53, 125–6
Rantisi, Abdel Aziz 124–5, 129
Regev, Eldad 187
reprisal raids 47, 49, 51, 65, 111
retaliatory operations 68, 70, 71, 84, 103, 131, 179
reserve battalion commanders 148–9
reserve corps reforms 152–4
Reserve Service (*Sherut Miluim*) 57
reservist system 46–7; acceptance of 31
reservists: burden on 146–9; burnout of 97, 149–50
retirement, career officers 33–5
'Return Brigades' 106
Revolution of Military Affairs (RMA) 150–1, 189
right-wing parties 52
right-wing refusal, evacuation orders 176–7, 178–9
risk, acceptance of 58
road closures 133–4
'road map' for peace 124–6, 170, 179
Ron, Ro'i 147–8
Ron-Tal, Maj. Gen. Yiftah 11, 144, 154, 158
rules of conduct 116–17
rules of engagement (ROE) 82–3, 90, 131–5; violations of 85–7

Sapir, Col. Pinhas 34
Sarid, Yossi 35
Schiff, Zeev 12
Schneller, Otniel 176
School of Leadership 117–18
School of Military Law 116
security consensus 7–8, 12, 24, 25, 35, 52–3, 57, 61, 63, 64, 75, 162–3, 174, 178–9, 181
security doctrine assumptions 45
security fence 125–7, 167–8
security imperatives 35–8
Security Service Law (1949) 32
security strategy 160–4
Segal, Col. Ofer 155
'SELA' (Assistance to Settlers in Gaza and Northern West Bank Administration) 173
self-confidence 26–7, 58, 91–2
settlements/settlers 30, 61, 76, 101, 124, 125, 136–8, 170–1, 172–8
Shalev, Brig. Gen. Aryeh 13, 41, 83
Shalom, Silvan 172

Shamir, Yitzhak 171
Shani, Brig. Gen. Udi 109, 161–2
Sharett, Moshe 34, 37
Sharon, Ariel: and Al-Aqsa Intifada 102, 107–8, 120, 122–3, 124, 125–6; and Lebanon War (1982) 41–2; and Oslo Accord 103–4; reaction to terrorism 64; resignation 65; rivalry with Bar-Lev 40; and strategic doctrine 62–3; and unilateral disengagement 175–6, 179
Shaul, Serg. Maj. Yehuda 149
Shehade, Salah 166
Shelah, Ofer 190
Shi'ite challenge, Lebanon 66–7
Shin Bet (GSS) 73, 74–5, 104, 122, 129
Shlein, Brig. Gen Eyal 145
Shmueli, Lt. Col. Timna 118
Shomron, Lt. Gen. Dan 85, 157, 192
short wars, necessity for 53–5
Six Day War 34, 38, 39–40, 54, 55, 73
'small head' (*rosh katan*) 93
societal crystallisation (*gibush*) 22–3
Solomon, Col. Nir 146
South Lebanese Security Zone 66–7, 68
South Lebanon: counter-guerrilla strategy in 67–8; occupation of 62–3
Southern Command 39–40, 41
statism (*mamlachtiut*) 30–2
status quo 50–1, 54, 62, 160, 162–3, 181
Steinitz, Yuval 35
Stork, Joe 84
strategic aims, national consensus 52–3
strategic depth: dilemmas 53–5; versus land for peace 61–2
strategic doctrine, Begin/Sharon era 62–3
strategic impasse 168–9
Strategic Planning Division, IDF 37
strategic–political status quo 50–1
strategy 159–64
structural changes, IDF 155–7
structural separation 65
Suez War (1956) 37, 54, 136, 170
suicide bombings 106–7, 110, 114, 120–1, 125, 127, 168
'swarm' tactics 113–15
Syria 157–8

Taba peace negotiations (2000) 102, 103
tactical errors 5
tactical reactions 81–4, 183
Tal, Maj. Gen. (Rtd) Israel 8, 39, 44, 50
Tel Hashomer Induction Centre 140
Terriff, Terry 9, 10
terror network, destruction of 184–5
threat perception 23–5
threats 45–7, 72, 92
training: capabilities 115–16; curtailment of programmes 143–6; cuts in 154–5; focus on 110; lack of 191, 193; officers 192; self-confidence effects of 26

'training through fighting' concept 155
Tzadka, Brig. Gen. Dov 166
Tze'elim National Training Centre 115–16

Ultra-Orthodox Jews (*Haredim*) 31, 148
unemployment 77, 142, 143
Unified National Leadership of the Uprising (UNLU) 80, 84
unilateral disengagement 124–6; domestic opposition to 172–3
unit cohesion 18, 22–3
unit leaders 21
United Nations (UN): ceasefire resolution 193; Charter 127; Officer for the Coordination of Humanitarian Affairs (OCHA) 121–2; Resolution 1701 189; Resolutions 181 242
United Nations Interim Forces in Lebanon (UNIFIL) 70, 193
Unity of Labour (*Achdut Haavoda*) Party 34

Valtam (Committee for Coordination of Release from Reserve Service) 94
Van Creveld, Martin 13, 86–7, 92, 149
violations, rules of engagement 85–7
Von Clausewitz, Carl 17

Waltzer, Michael 47
War of Attrition (1969–70) 34, 54
wars of no choice (*milkhemet ein briera*) 18, 59–60, 160
weapons 82, 106, 108–9, 111–12, 116, 129–31, 132, 143–6
Weizman, Brig. Gen. Ezer 34, 39
Wiener, Capt. (Res.) Noam 110
Winograd Commission 187, 194
World War II 23

Yaalon, Lt. Gen. Moshe: and Al-Aqsa Intifada 122–3, 162, 166–7; and Lebanon Summer War 188–9; on LIC 113, 183–4; and Operation 'Defensive Shield' 111; and unilateral disengagement 172
Ya'ari, Ehud 12
Yadin, Lt. Gen. Yigal 34, 57
Yadlin, Maj. Gen. Amos 183–4
Yaffe, Avraham 39
Yair, Maj. Gen. Yoram 191–2
Yassin, Sheikh Ahmed 106, 129, 130
Yatom, Maj. Gen. Danny 37, 92, 93, 170–1
Yedidya, Col. (Res.) Didi 145
Yesh Gvul 89, 136–7, 141
Yesha Council of Jewish Settlements 88
yeshiva movement 177
Yom Kippur War 39–41, 158, 161, 190

Zakkai, Brig. Gen. Shmuel 129, 131
Zeira, Maj. Gen. 41
Ziv, Brig. Gen. Yisrael 109